AFRICAN AMERICAN WOMEN
CONFRONT THE WEST
1600–2000

African American Women
Confront the West
1600–2000

Edited by

QUINTARD TAYLOR

SHIRLEY ANN WILSON MOORE

UNIVERSITY OF OKLAHOMA PRESS : NORMAN

For Rosa Mae Lewis Wilson and Viola Vivian Washington Moore, two African American women who confronted the West.

ALSO BY QUINTARD TAYLOR
The Making of the Modern World: A History of the Twentieth Century (Dubuque, Iowa, 1990)
The Forging of a Black Community: Seattle's Central District, from 1870 through the Civil Rights Era (Seattle, 1994)
In Search of the Racial Frontier: African Americans in the American West, 1528–1990 (New York City, 1998)
(ed. with Lawrence B. de Graaf and Kevin Mulroy) *Seeking El Dorado: African Americans in California, 1769–1997* (Seattle, 2001)

ALSO BY SHIRLEY ANN WILSON MOORE
To Place Our Deeds: The African American Community in Richmond, California, 1910–1963 (Berkeley, 2000)

Publication of this book is made possible through the generosity of Edith Kinney Gaylord.

LIBRARY OF CONGRESS CATALOGING-IN-PUBLICATION DATA

African American women confront the West : 1600–2000 / edited by Quintard Taylor, Shirley Ann Wilson Moore.
    p. cm.
   Includes bibliographical references and index.
   ISBN 0–8061–3524–7 (hc. : alk. paper)
    1. African American women—West (U.S.)—History.   2. African American women—West (U.S.)—Social conditions.   3. West (U.S.)—History.   4. West (U.S.)—Social conditions.   5. West (U.S.)—Race relations.   I. Taylor, Quintard.   II. Moore, Shirley Ann Wilson, 1947–

E185.925 .A45 2003
978'.00496073'0082—dc21

             2002032479

Contents

Introduction

The Spanish-Mexican Period

The Antebellum West

The Post–Civil War Era

The Early Twentieth Century

World War II

The Civil Rights Era

Illustrations

Acknowledgments

This book represents the culmination of the efforts of many people over the past four years. We would like to thank all of the individuals who contributed their scholarship, expertise, advice, and good humor to this work. We are particularly grateful to Charles Rankin, Susan A. Garrett, Julie Shilling, Angelika Tietz, and the staff at the University of Oklahoma Press. We are especially indebted to OU Press's Jean Hurtado, whose editorial guidance, ceaseless encouragement, and abundant patience supported us during every stage of this work. The tireless efforts of research assistants Susan Bragg and Turkiya Lowe were indispensable to this project from its inception. Without their efforts and advice this anthology would not exist. We also acknowledge the invaluable assistance provided by Sandra Chin, W. W. Norton; Teresa Hamann, University of Montana; Vincent Hayes, Seattle; James E. Henley and Patricia Johnson, Sacramento Archives and Museum Collection; Nancy Trystad Koupal, South Dakota State Historical Society; Esther Hall Mumford, Ananse Press; Carla Rickerson, Karyl Winn, and Sandra Kroupa, University of Washington Archives, Manuscripts, and Special Collections; Galen Schroeder, Fargo; Susan Snyder, the Bancroft Library; Irene Webster, Association for the Study of Afro-American Life and History; and Patricia Zline, Madison Books.

Thanks are also due to William Robbins and the Editors at the Oregon State University Press for allowing us to reprint Quintard Taylor's article on Susie Revels Cayton and Beatrice Morrow Cannady, as well as to Karla Kelling, University of Washington, for granting permission to use her research on Pacific Northwest clubwoman Nettie Asberry. We also wish to thank the staffs of the following organizations for helping us collect vignettes and photographs: Clarity Productions, Manhattan Beach, California; Direct Cinema Ltd., Santa Monica, California; International Creative Management, New York City, New York; and the Sod House Society, Holdrege, Nebraska.

Although a number of historians guided our writing and inspired our work, the following deserve special recognition: Anne Butler, Utah State University; Darlene Clark Hine, Michigan State University; Elizabeth Jameson, University of Calgary; Joan Jensen, New Mexico State University; Patricia Limerick, University of Colorado; Peggy Pascoe, University of Oregon; Vicki Ruiz, University of California, Irvine; and Virginia Scharff, University of New Mexico.

We reserve our deepest gratitude for the contributors of this volume. Their articles have brought to life the stories of remarkable and heretofore unheralded African American women whose experiences in the West have shaped and enriched western, African American, and American history. While we are profoundly indebted to so many for the successful completion of this anthology, any errors contained herein are ours alone.

Introduction

CHAPTER 1

The West of African American Women, 1600–2000

Shirley Ann Wilson Moore and Quintard Taylor

The history of the American West has undergone a profound transformation in the past two decades. The saga of inevitable expansion and "conquest" of the region by indomitable white settlers, primarily males, has given way to a more complex discussion of environmental change, economic manipulation, social inequality, labor conflict, and urban expansion. Discussions of gender and ethnicity are now central to the understanding of an inclusive western history. As Elizabeth Jameson and Susan Armitage have so aptly written, "[A]ll people are historical actors, and half these actors are women." Indeed, Glenda Riley notes these changes in chapter 2. Historians have begun to incorporate the voices of women and people of color precisely because they complete the mosaic of experience formed through encounters of diverse peoples and cultures in this region over the past five centuries. *African American Women Confront the West* adds to this array of voices by addressing the history of African American women in the West.[1]

The historian Elsa Barkely Brown reminds us that "we have still to recognize that being a woman is, in fact, not extractable from the context in which one is a woman—that is race, class, time, and place."[2] The contributors to this volume have pursued this theme by providing specialized studies of western black women from the era of Spanish colonial settlement to postwar urban

America. As these essays demonstrate, black women's lives have been shaped not only by historically specific experiences of race and gender; they also have been influenced by class, sexuality, and culture.

Women of African ancestry have been present in western history since the period of initial Spanish contact with the indigenous people of northern New Spain. In 1598 the Juan de Oñate expedition that colonized New Mexico included Francisco de Sosa Penalosa, who brought to the area "three female negro slaves, one mulatto slave, and other men and women servants." Two years later the Juan Guerra de Resa expedition, which arrived in New Mexico to strengthen Oñate's New Mexico colony, included several soldiers and their mulatto women and children.[3] In the second essay in this volume, Dedra McDonald introduces us to Isabel de Olvera, a servant with the Guerra de Resa party who enters history with her predeparture affidavit to Don Pedro Lorenzo de Castilla, the *alcalde* (mayor) of Querétaro, in which she described her status as a freeborn woman concerned that her race and gender might prompt discrimination. De Olvera concluded her statement with the words, "I demand justice."[4] Her affidavit appears as the first vignette in this volume.

For the next two centuries Spanish-speaking women of African ancestry moved north from central Mexico to the frontier of New Spain. These women were among the founders and first inhabitants of San Antonio, Laredo, El Paso, Albuquerque, Tucson, San Diego, and San Francisco. In 1781 they were also among the first settlers of the largest metropolis in the West, Los Angeles. When Spanish colonial officials chose to locate a settlement between Mission San Gabriel and the Presidio of Santa Barbara, they recruited settlers from the province of Sinaloa. Twelve families, mainly from Rosario, two-thirds of whose inhabitants were mulatto, left Sinaloa in February 1781, under military escort for their five-hundred-mile, seven-month journey to the site that would become Nuestra Señora la Reina de Los Angeles de Porciuncula. Colonial records detail the race and place of birth of most of these settlers. Among those women of African ancestry were nineteen-year-old María Guadalupe, twenty-seven-year-old Gertrudis Perez, and forty-year-old María Petra Rubio.[5]

The presence of women of African ancestry among the first colonial settlers of northern New Spain reflects the long history of Africans in Mexico, dating to the arrival of the first conquistadors. Although Isabel de Olvera's affidavit suggested an awareness both of racial discrimination and of her agency in confronting it, racial consciousness and categorization developed differently on the northern frontier of New Spain than in British North America. Women of African ancestry, or for that matter Native American or Asian ancestry, were deemed *gente de razón* (people of reason) by virtue of their embrace of Spanish culture and, crucially, Catholicism, as opposed to indigenous peoples who challenged the Spanish presence. Over time, their African ancestry was submerged into Spanish and, after 1821, Mexican identity, as in the case of Jacinta de la Cruz Pico, grandmother of Pío Pico, governor of Mexican California. The Anglo introduction of large-scale slavery and its corollary, racial subordination, for even nominally free English-speaking blacks transformed the racial dynamics of the region and significantly reduced but did not completely eliminate the likelihood of interaction between these groups of women of African ancestry.[6]

After Mexico gained its independence from Spain in 1821, the first English-speaking black women settlers arrived in Texas, the new nation's northern province. Some of these women were fugitive slaves seeking refuge from the United States. However, others were freeborn women, among them Harriet Newell Sands, a Michigan emigrant. Zelina Husk of Georgia and Diana Leonard, listed only as "from the states," also arrived in Texas by 1835. Husk and Leonard were employed as laundresses near San Jacinto, and Sands found work as a housekeeper. Fanny McFarland of Harris County also arrived during the period of Mexican rule in Texas and "by industry, prudence, and economy" bought and sold small plots of real estate.[7]

Yet by the 1830s free black women in Texas lived in an environment increasingly dominated by slaveholders. The first black slaves arrived from the United States in the early 1820s, and by 1835 one-tenth of the thirty-five thousand English-speaking Texans were black slaves. Because slavery was theoretically illegal in Mexico, in 1828 slaveholders devised the contract labor system as an insidious subterfuge for human bondage. Under this system, a U.S.-born slaveholder could free his slave in Mexico but then recoup his monetary loss by appropriating the labor of the former slave through lifetime indentured servitude. The contract between Clarissa, "a girl of color," and Marmaduke D. Sandifer before the alcalde at San Felipe de Austin on Christmas Day 1833 was typical. Clarissa agreed to "conduct & demean herself as an honest & faithful servant, renouncing and disclaiming all her right and claim to personal liberty for & during the term of ninety-nine years." In return Sandifer promised to furnish her "food, lodging, and medical care and, should she be disabled, to support her in a decent and comfortable manner."[8]

The Texas War of Independence in 1836 established the legality of slavery in the new republic and subsequent state of Texas. Consequently, the black bond servant population increased from 3,000 at the time of independence to 250,000 by the end of the Civil War. Before that conflict the vast majority of black women in the West resided in Texas—91,551 in 1860, only 174 of whom were free. Black female slaves resided in virtually all of the state's 105 counties in 1860. Some of these individuals worked as cooks, maids, or vegetable vendors in San Antonio, Houston, or Galveston. A few black slave women were taken to the frontier, where they worked with Anglo women and men in agriculture and, like Anglo and Latina women, often faced the possibility of capture and incorporation into Comanche communities. The greatest concentrations of black slave women were in rice, sugarcane, and cotton plantations along the Gulf Coast and the Brazos and Colorado Rivers. By 1860 thirteen counties in the state, mainly in this region, had black majorities.[9]

Slavery provided a powerful framework for constructions of race, gender, and class in the antebellum West, sanctioning the exploitation of black women's physical labor as well as their familial interests and sexual autonomy. Women, men, and children alike harvested the crops, either picking cotton, pulling corn, or cutting sugarcane, and performed the numerous chores associated with nineteenth-century farming. Women planted corn and cotton, drove horses that cultivated the crops, and hoed cotton, corn, and vegetables. Some slave women specialized as cooks, laundresses, maids, seamstresses, and spinners.[10]

Plantation life for Texas slaves demanded the harshest, least remitting toil under the most oppressive social conditions, but it also afforded the greatest opportunity for the development of family life. Familial ties provided love, individual identity, and a sense of personal worth for black bond servants, a validation often denied by dominant perspectives of black women as "mammies" or sexualized "Jezebels." The second vignette presents an alternative portrait of African American women, featuring an 1862 letter from a black Harrison County slave known only as Fannie to her husband, Norfleet, who was away with his owner, a Confederate officer. "I haven't forgot you nor I never will forget you as long as the world stands, even if you forget me," she wrote. "If I never see you again, I hope to meet you in Heaven."[11]

Approximately four thousand black women were held in bondage by Native Americans in Indian Territory in 1860. The work of these women differed little from their Texas counterparts. In this context, however, many African American women acquired the language and assimilated much of the culture of their owners. Those who successfully embraced Native American culture while retaining a command of English often became tribal interpreters. Washington Irving, who visited the home of a Cherokee farmer in 1832, remembered an unnamed African American woman who served as a translator. One commentator, writing of another black female interpreter for the Cherokees, reported,

"[T]he spectacle seems strange[,] . . . the coal black girl speaking both English and Cherokee and keeping the old woman informed as to what was being said."12

African American slave women resided in other western states and territories. Amanda Johnson, a former slave living in Oregon, left a narrative of her life in bondage beginning with her forced migration from Missouri to the Pacific Northwest in 1853. Polly Holmes and her husband, Robin, were also former Missouri slaves who were brought to Oregon in 1844. The Holmeses were granted their freedom in 1849 and obtained the freedom of their three children through a lawsuit decided by the Territorial Supreme Court. Three years later a California court freed Bridget "Biddy" Mason and her extended family of thirteen women and children in one of the most celebrated trials of the era.13

Mason, the slave of a Mississippi Mormon named Robert Marion Smith, migrated to San Bernardino, California, from Utah in 1851. Elizabeth and Charles Rowan, free blacks who were also members of the one-hundred-fifty-wagon caravan from Utah to southern California, encouraged her to contest her servile status, as did former Texas slaves Minnie and Robert Owens whom she met in California. When Robert Owens and Elizabeth Rowan informed local officials that Smith was illegally holding black slaves, the Los Angeles County sheriff placed Mason and her family in protective custody. Mason seized this opportunity to petition for freedom for herself and her family. After three days of hearings in January 1856, Los Angeles District Court Judge Benjamin Hayes handed down his decision. Citing California law that prohibited both slavery and involuntary servitude, Hayes ruled that "all of the said persons of color are entitled to their freedom and are free forever."14

On the eve of the Civil War, the approximately fifteen hundred black women of California comprised the vast majority of the free African American women in the West. Many of these women crossed half a continent to reach California, enduring great hardship as they made their way overland. One overland traveler wrote in her journal, "[A] white woman and a colored one died yesterday of cholera." Margaret Frink described a lone black woman she encountered in 1850 near the Humboldt Sink, the desert just east of the Sierra Nevada. Frink recalled the woman "trampling along through the heat and dust, carrying a cast iron bake stove on her head with her provisions and a blanket piled on top—all she possessed in the world—bravely pushing on for California."15

Although most black women and men traveled overland to California, some fortunates, such as Anne Fuller, reached the state by ship. Fuller paid for her passage by working as a stewardess on a passenger ship that sailed around Cape

Horn to San Francisco. An oceangoing vessel was also the mode of arrival for Mary Ellen Pleasant, the woman destined to become the most prominent African American in nineteenth-century California. Pleasant's reputation as a cook preceded her arrival in San Francisco in 1852, and she found herself besieged at the wharf by men anxious to employ her. She ultimately selected an employer who promised $500 a month, a gold miner's average income.[16] In chapter 4 Lynn Hudson profiles Pleasant's life in San Francisco.

Despite the work opportunities in California's gold rush economy, many African American women were ambivalent about the prospects of a better life there. They were keenly aware of the numerous restrictions on access to public schools and accommodations, public transportation, homesteading, and court testimony, as well as other forms of discrimination. When news of the Fraser River gold strike reached the Golden State, many African American women and men followed the stream of migrants north to British Columbia. The vignette "A Voice from the Oppressed to the Friends of Humanity," a poem by San Francisco resident Priscilla Stewart, chronicles this exodus.

By the Civil War, black Californians mounted increasing attacks on racial discrimination in the state. In particular, African American women entered the nineteenth-century civil rights movement by challenging their exclusion from public transportation. Three of the four lawsuits of that era were initiated by San Franciscans Charlotte Brown, Emma Jane Turner, and Mary Ellen Pleasant, black women who insisted that race did not negate their standing as respectable "ladies." In chapter 5 Barbara Welke describes that remarkable campaign and its consequences for California and the nation.[17] Black protest during these years often found institutional sustenance through churches, civic organizations, and other community groups, which frequently depended on black women's participation. The crucial support that black women provided the *Mirror of the Times*, the first African American newspaper in California, through its fund-raising vehicle, the Mirror Association, even prompted the all-male California Colored Convention to vote a special tribute at its meeting in Sacramento in 1856. In chapter 6 Susan Bragg describes the efforts of African American women to attain educational equity for their children in California's public school system.

Fifteen hundred miles to the east, in Kansas, another group of African American women found new homes. These women represented approximately half of the Civil War–era migration of former slaves from neighboring states. This migration increased the black population of Kansas from 627 in 1860 to approximately 12,000 in 1865. Using the meager skills acquired in bondage, the freedwomen eagerly sought all available employment in their new home. Most became agricultural workers, often helping white farm wives harvest wheat and corn while their husbands were serving in the Union Army. Black women in cities such as Leavenworth, Lawrence, Wyandotte (Kansas City), and Atchison worked as domestics, washerwomen, housekeepers, servants, and cooks.[18]

Despite their humble occupations and meager incomes, these early black women in Kansas helped to establish the first churches in the state and offered aid and comfort to former slaves who came later. African American women in Lawrence organized the Ladies Refugee Aid Society to collect food, clothing, and money to assist destitute freedpeople. The society foreshadowed the Kansas Federation of Colored Women's Clubs, providing a model for self-help activities that extended well into the twentieth century.[19]

The influx of former slaves into Kansas during the Civil War era presaged a much larger postwar migration of African American women and men into the West. On a thousand-mile frontier from the northern plains of Dakota south to Oklahoma, African American migrants moved west propelled by the twin desire for land and freedom from racial discrimination. Although the conquest of the plains has been cast as a male-centered story, historians are now examining the role of women as homesteaders, as farm wives, and as settlers in dozens of small towns, including predominantly African American municipalities such as Nicodemus, Kansas, and Langston, Oklahoma, to get a richer, more complex narrative of life there.

Willianna Hickman's saga illustrates that complexity. Traveling in 1878 from her native Kentucky to western Kansas, Hickman was a member of a one-hundred-fifty-person homesteading party destined for Nicodemus, soon to become the most famous of the predominantly black High Plains farming communities. Hickman wrote excitedly of navigating across the plains by compass. Finally, she heard fellow travelers exclaim, "There is Nicodemus!" Expecting to find buildings on the horizon, she said, "I looked with all the eyes I had. 'Where is Nicodemus? I don't see it.'" Her husband responded to her query by pointing to the plumes of smoke coming out of the ground. "The families lived in dugouts," she dejectedly recalled. "We landed and struck tents. The scenery was not at all inviting and I began to cry."[20] Hickman's Nicodemus saga appears as the fourth vignette in this volume.

Hickman's response suggests that women did not always share their husbands' dream of a new life and viewed the region far differently. They saw far less economic opportunity and far greater danger, and they often expressed concern about the constraints on family life. The stark, treeless countryside, the summer and winter temperature extremes, and the isolation of High Plains life all tested their physical and psychological resolve. "The Negro pioneers worked hard," Ava Speese Day recalled of her childhood among a group of 185 settlers who homesteaded forty thousand acres in the Sand Hills of Nebraska just before World War I. "It was too sandy for grain so the answer was cattle." Yet in a pattern much like Oklahoma and Kansas, by the early 1920s black farm families began to abandon their lands for Denver, Omaha, or Lincoln. "Looking back, it seems that getting our [land] was the beginning of the end for us in Nebraska," Day remembered. "There was one thing after another.... In March 1925, we left the Sand Hills for Pierre, South Dakota."[21] Speese's recollections are presented in the fifth vignette.

With the exception of the women of Texas and Oklahoma, most nineteenth-century African American women in the West resided in the region's small towns such as Topeka, Kansas, and Helena, Montana, or rapidly growing cities such as Denver and Los Angeles. These women migrated to the towns and cities in search of the employment opportunities they offered. In the process they laid the foundation for most of the African American urban communities in the contemporary West. The sixth vignette describes Kate D. Chapman's Dakota Territory memories, and the next describes the life of Sarah G. Bickford, owner of the municipal water works of Virginia City, Montana.

Whether in small town or rapidly expanding metropolis, African American women were disproportionately active in creating and maintaining churches, literary societies, women's clubs, and civil rights organizations such as the Colored Ladies Legal Rights Association, which challenged racial discrimination in Denver in the early 1870s. In chapter 7 Peggy Riley describes the efforts of a group of women to build and maintain a church in one small urban community.[22] Yet all-black churches were never the exclusive mode of worship for African American women westerners. In chapter 8 Ronald Coleman provides a portrait of Jane Elizabeth Manning James, a black woman who remained a devout Mormon throughout her life despite restrictions on African American membership in the Church of Latter-day Saints.

Regardless of geographic location, nineteenth-century western black urban women performed similar work: most were personal servants for wealthy households. Discriminatory racial ideologies confined most black women to such menial labor, reinforcing existing social hierarchies by promoting visions of black women's subservience and poverty. Yet some black women managed to transcend economic and social obstacles. Notable examples are Justina Ford, a Denver physician; Lutie Lytle, a Topeka policeman's daughter who in the mid-1890s became the second black female lawyer in the nation; and mining stock investors Mary Ellen Pleasant in San Francisco and Mary E. Phelps in Denver who was also president of the Bonita Silver and Gold Mining Company.[23]

By the early twentieth century a significant number of middle-class black women had emerged in the West. Indeed, black women's efforts in church and community organizations demonstrate that many exhibited a particular racial-ized class consciousness, promoting uplift in the face of adversity through a variety of means.[24] Some women such as Dr. Ruth Flowers of Boulder, Colorado, challenged existing conventions through education. Susan Armitage's interview with Flowers, presented in chapter 9, profiles her personal history. And in chapter 10 Quintard Taylor examines the lives of two Pacific Northwest polit-ical activists, Susie Revels Cayton and Beatrice Morrow Cannady. In the vignette that follows, Seattle resident Juanita Warfield Proctor recalls another activist who influenced the black women and men of the region, Universal Negro Improvement Association founder Marcus Garvey, who visited the city in the early 1920s.

Other middle-class black western women, like their counterparts elsewhere in the nation, created women's clubs to promote education, respectability, and reform. Club women eagerly sought cultural and intellectual improvement, self-help, and mutual support. The clubs also engaged in "racial uplift," which usually meant encouraging education and moral rectitude among lower-class black women. Invoking the geographic symbol of the region, the president of the Colorado Association of Colored Women's Clubs, in her address at the sixth annual convention in 1909, called on the state's black club women "[to lift] . . . a down trodden race above the rockies of prejudice." For all of their outwardly directed activity, these clubs also offered black women the opportunity for self-expression and informal education while linking them to an emerging national network of black women's organizations. Moreover, these women took charge of their collective lives and fates and avoided victimization by the world around them. As the Kansas Federation of Women's Clubs stated in its motto, they were "rowing, not drifting."[25]

Black women's clubs sprang up in virtually every western community that had a concentration of black women. These clubs established day care centers, nurseries, and industrial schools or led campaigns to close pool halls and gambling dens. Their history is long and illustrious. The Ladies' Refugee Aid Society of Lawrence, Kansas, the first black women's club in the West, was organized to assist fugitive slaves entering the area from Missouri, Arkansas, and Indian Territory. The Heart's Ease Circle of King's Daughters, organized in Austin, Texas, in 1894, established a home for the elderly that served the community for nearly a century. The Fanny Jackson Coppin Club, the "mother club" of the black women's club movement in California, was founded in Oakland in 1899 to provide accommodations to blacks visiting the East Bay. In 1904 black women in Cheyenne, Wyoming, formed the Searchlight Club in response to the lynching of an African American male. An alliance of Denver clubs supported the Colored Orphanage and Old Folks Home in Pueblo, Colorado, through the first decade of the twentieth century, and the Dorcas Charity Club was founded in Seattle 1906 to care for abandoned babies.[26] The work of Pacific Northwest club woman Nettie Asberry, described in the eighth vignette, suggests the range of activities of these women.

Black women in Los Angeles, the city with the largest African American population west of Dallas, maintained a number of uplift organizations. In 1904 they formed the Sojourner Truth Industrial Club to "establish a . . . safe refuge" for the hundreds of young working women streaming into the city. Black Angeleno club women also created the Women's Day Nursery. Building on Bridget Mason's earlier efforts to assist impoverished families, the nursery provided day care facilities for children of working parents. Although they did not yet have the right to vote, black female Angelenos were heard prominently in the Women's Civic League, which sponsored candidate debates and held rallies for office seekers they endorsed.[27]

Western African American women quickly realized that affiliation of the individual clubs would strengthen their standing and influence both locally and regionally. To that end, the various clubs formed statewide federations. Kansas women's clubs came together in 1900; Colorado followed in 1903, Texas and Nebraska in 1905, and California in 1906. The clubs in Oklahoma formed a statewide federation in 1910. Over the next fifteen years state federations were created in Oregon (1912), Arizona (1915), Washington (1917), Montana (1921), New Mexico (1923), and Wyoming (1925).[28]

The first decades of the twentieth century represent continuity rather than change in the lives of most western black urban women. African American women continued to migrate to the region's cities and towns, and by 1900 they formed the majority of black residents in Los Angeles, Denver, and Kansas City and in small towns such as Topeka, Pasadena, and Berkeley. As workers they remained concentrated in "domestic service." As late as 1930 the proportion of black women in that occupational category ranged from a low of 83 percent in Seattle to a high of 93 percent in Dallas. In 1937 Kathryn Bogle discovered one consequence of that concentration—the reluctance of white employers to consider even high school graduates for any other work. She wrote, "I visited large and small stores. . . . I visited the telephone company; both power and light companies. I tried to become an elevator operator in an office building. I answered ads for inexperienced office help. In all of these places I was told there was nothing about me in my disfavor except my skin color." Bogle then described how several employers who refused to hire her downtown nonetheless offered her work "as a domestic . . . where her color would not be an embarrassment."[29] In chapter 11 Moya Hansen illuminates the evolving challenges faced by black women in one western city.

Occasionally African American women found work in the most glamorous western industry, motion pictures. By the second decade of the twentieth century, the motion picture industry was centered in Hollywood, California. African American film actors who often had had sensitive, nonstereotypical roles in the pre-California period of the industry now found their opportunities for work and control over the type of images they portrayed severely restricted. The vignette "Hattie McDaniels Wins an Oscar" illustrates both the difficulties and achievements of McDaniels, who won an Academy Award for her Mammy character in the popular film *Gone With the Wind*. Restrictions on acting roles would last, with minor exceptions, through much of the remainder of the twentieth century. In chapter 12 Alicia I. Rodríquez-Estrada describes the fate of two of Hollywood's most famous pre-1960 black actors, Fredi Washington and Dorothy Dandridge.

World War II transformed the lives of black western women. That transformation was seen in the explosive growth of the black population, particularly in Pacific Coast cities, where the majority of newcomers were women. It was seen in the growing militancy of longtime residents and migrants alike, as they united their voices to demand the opportunity to share in the wartime prosperity. One example occurred in 1942 in Los Angeles as several hundred black women protesters vowed to make the local office of the U.S. Employment Service look like "little Africa" until the agency opened production jobs to them. It was also seen in the creation of unparalleled employment opportunities in the military and defense industries. Fanny Christina Hill, a Los Angeles aviation worker, captured this change when she recalled, "The war made me live better. Hitler was the one that got us out of the white folks' kitchen."[30]

By 1942 numerous barriers fell as black women entered the industrial workplace in unprecedented numbers. Black women from throughout the nation flocked to Pacific Coast shipyard and aircraft jobs. The Kaiser Corporation, the largest World War II–era shipbuilder, hired its first female employees in July 1942, heralding them as the "vanguard of American Women gone to work." Female shipyard employment peaked at 24,500 of the nearly 100,000-person Kaiser workforce. Blacks represented nearly 10 percent of women shipyard workers. Although Kaiser boasted that women workers earned "precisely the same wages as men doing comparable work," black women were frequently denied membership in the International Brotherhood of Boilermakers and confined to entry-level occupations once hired. Frances Mary Albrier, a welder in the Kaiser shipyards in Richmond, California, challenged the Boilermakers' color and gender bars by becoming the first black woman welder to be admitted to work there. Even so, her union membership was transferred to an auxiliary union in Oakland until the Richmond yards could establish a segregated division for its African American employees. Nonetheless, shipyard employment for most black women represented a substantial improvement in their economic status.[31]

African American women encountered less resistance from employers and union officials as they joined the wartime aircraft construction industry. Boeing Aircraft in Seattle hired its first African American production worker, Dorothy West Williams, a sheet metal worker, in May 1942. By July 1943, 329 blacks, mostly women, worked at Boeing. That number peaked at 1,600 by 1945. In June 1942 Consolidated Aircraft in San Diego and Lockheed-Vega in Los Angeles began placing black women workers. By August 1942 Lockheed-Vega employed 400 blacks, including 50 women, among their 41,000 workers. One year later nearly half of the company's 2,500 black workers were women.[32]

Wartime labor demands guaranteed black women would work; they did not guarantee equitable treatment. "They did everything they could to keep you separated," declared Fanny Christina Hill. "They just did not like for a Negro and a white person to get together to talk." Black women in the shipyards were relegated to auxiliary unions, and their counterparts in aircraft plants in Texas and Oklahoma worked in segregated buildings or lunched in separate cafeterias. Moreover, advertisements in Texas and Oklahoma openly labeled positions "white" and "colored."[33]

Throughout the war black women workers made the workplace contested terrain as they engaged shipyard managers and union officials in a struggle for equitable working conditions. Ruby Black, for example, filed suit in Seattle Superior Court against the Boeing Aircraft Company and Local 751 asking for a restraint against the automatic deduction of $3.50 from black female employees for a work permit while white women were charged $1.50. Black noted in her suit that when she complained about the higher dues for black women, she was fired.[34]

In May 1943 twenty-nine black employees, most of them women, at Pacific Foundry in Renton, Washington, near Seattle, led by Marjorie Pitter, engaged in a protest against signs designating segregated restrooms. Pitter explained the incident to a reporter for the *Northwest Enterprise*, a Seattle African American newspaper: "We protested to the superintendent of the foundry. He told us the signs were ordered by higher officials and would remain." Then Pitter said tersely, "We declined to work." Ultimately these women won their protest, and the naval official who introduced the segregation policy was transferred. Doris Mae Williams, originally a Kaiser Vancouver shipyard welder, took a job as a laborer rather than suffer continued abuse from her supervisor and coworkers who refused to accept her credentials. "I am now scaling. [It is] hard labor," Williams wrote to the Fair Employment Practices Committee. "Our crew is mixed, we are all treated alike. Why couldn't the same be said for skilled workers?"[35] San Francisco shipyard worker Lyn Childs describes racism on the job site in the vignette "Lyn Childs Confronts a Racist Act." The letter that another Bay Area woman, Etta Germany, wrote to President Franklin Roosevelt protesting racial discrimination appears in the next vignette.

Despite the difficulties may black women faced during World War II, African American migration westward to San Francisco, Los Angeles, Seattle, and Las Vegas transformed the region, as Gretchen Lemke-Santangelo points out in chapter 13. Similarly, Claytee White, in chapter 14, describes African American women's agency in refashioning the urban environment in the western city that received, in terms of percent, the largest influx of black newcomers.

Thousands of African American women came west in uniform. Fort Huachuca in the Arizona desert had the largest concentration of black soldiers in the nation after the army decided in 1942 to create the U.S. 93rd Infantry Division. By December 1942 the 32nd and 33rd Companies of the Women's Army Auxiliary Corps (WAACs) joined the men of the 93rd in the Arizona desert. These women were postal clerks, stenographers, switchboard operators, motor truck drivers, and typists, fulfilling jobs that released the men for combat. Muriel Fawcett, a former West Virginia State College professor, exuded the confidence of the women on the post when she said, "Each WAAC is bursting with pride that she made the grade. If the men doubt that we can to the job efficiently, they will soon change their minds.[36]

Post–World War II African American western women continued to shape the course of cultural and regional history. Some black women became recognized leaders in the continuing campaign for racial and social justice, including at least two women profiled in this volume. Lulu White, an important figure in the postwar racial politics of the Lone Star State who championed equal opportunity in higher education, is the subject of Merlene Pitre's chapter. In the vignette that follows, Ada Lois Sipuel Fisher recounts her experience petitioning the Supreme Court for entrance into the University of Oklahoma Law School. While White and Sipuel Fisher, among other African American female activists, emerged as important public figures in the civil rights movement, other women worked behind the scenes to promote racial justice. Black Kansas women, for example, led a seven-decade legal campaign against school segregation that began with an 1881 lawsuit, *Tinnon v. Ottawa School Board*, the first of eleven desegregation cases to reach the Kansas supreme court between 1881 and 1949. These lawsuits culminated in the 1954 U.S. Supreme Court decision in *Brown v. Board of Education of Topeka, Kansas*, one of the most influential court rulings of the twentieth century. In chapter 16 Cheryl Brown Henderson describes the remarkably dedicated women who brought *Brown* forward.[37] In 1958 Oklahoma City African Americans initiated the longest direct action campaign in the West, a six-year effort to desegregate public accommodations in the state's capital city. The leader of that campaign, Clara Luper, is profiled by Linda Williams Reese in chapter 17.

By the late 1960s the Black Power movement was supported and occasionally led by young black women despite the masculinized rhetoric of black nationalism. The fourteenth vignette describes Elaine Brown's leadership of the Black Panthers. In chapter 18 Jane Rhodes describes the impact of gender politics on this organization that symbolized the post–civil rights revolutionary movement. Women such as Lulu White, Clara Luper, Elaine Brown, Lucinda Todd, and eighteen-old Tracy Simms, a Berkeley High School student who in 1964 led a fifteen-hundred-person demonstration against the Sheraton Palace Hotel's hiring practices in what was to that date California's single largest civil rights protest, clearly illustrated the leadership capabilities of African American women in the western protest movement.[38]

As the chapters in this volume demonstrate, African American women in the West have played critical and varied roles in the region's development, from the earliest days of Spanish exploration and settlement to the social and political battlefields of the twentieth-century civil rights movement. Whether they resided in populous urban areas or in small, agrarian communities, African American women in the West immersed themselves in the political and social currents affecting all black people and, by the twentieth century, all westerners.

Indeed, black western women often stood at the forefront of change. Whether individually or collectively, they turned to their work of building communities, caring for families, founding and maintaining institutions, and attaining social and economic justice with a profound conviction in their own abilities to move beyond the limitations racism and sexism had placed on them. In doing so, western women of African ancestry constructed solid platforms for black female agency that spanned time and space and continue to inspire generations of women and men.

NOTES

1. The Jameson and Armitage quotation appears in Elizabeth Jameson and Susan Armitage, eds., *Writing the Range: Race, Class, and Culture in the Women's West* (Norman: University of Oklahoma Press, 1997), 5. This combination of new voices and new modes of analysis has created a discourse that has incorporated African American history into the region's saga. The appearance of a number of volumes, including John W. Ravage, *Black Pioneers: Images of the Black Experience on the North American Frontier* (Salt Lake City: University of Utah Press, 1997); Monroe Lee Billington and Roger D. Hardaway, eds., *African Americans on the Western Frontier* (Niwot: University Press of Colorado, 1998); and Quintard Taylor, *In Search of the Racial Frontier: African Americans in the American West, 1528–1990* (New York: W. W. Norton, 1998), indicate that African American history in the West has evolved into a recognizable subfield in both western regional history and African American history.

2. Elsa Barkely Brown, "'What Has Happened Here': The Politics of Difference in Women's History and Feminist Politics," *Feminist Studies* 18 (Summer 1992): 300. See also Evelyn Brooks Higginbotham's powerful essay, "African American Women's History and the Metalanguage of Race," *Signs* 17 (Winter 1992): 251–74; and Jameson and Armitage, eds., *Writing the Range*, 8–9.

3. The de Sosa quotation appears in Ramón Gutiérrez, *When Jesus Came, the Corn Mothers Went Away: Marriage, Sexuality and Power in New Mexico, 1500-1846* (Stanford: Stanford University Press, 1991), 104. See also Caroll L. Riley, "Blacks in the Early Southwest," *Ethnohistory* 19 (Summer 1972): 252–57; Jack D. Forbes, "Black Pioneers: The Spanish-speaking Afroamericans of the Southwest," *Phylon* 27 (Fall 1966): 233–34; and Oakah L. Jones Jr., *Los Paisanos: Spanish Settlers on the Northern Frontier of New Spain* (Norman: University of Oklahoma Press, 1979), 40–41.

4. The de Olvera statement and account appear in George P. Hammond, ed., and Agapito Rey, trans., *Don Juan de Oñate: Colonizer of New Mexico, 1595–1628* (Albuquerque: University of New Mexico Press, 1953), 560–62.

5. Twenty-six of the forty-six original settlers of Los Angeles were of African or part African ancestry. For a rich discussion of the role of blacks in the settlement of Los Angeles, see Antonio Rios-Bustamante, "Los Angeles, Pueblo and Region, 1781-1850:

Continuity and Adaptation on the North Mexican Periphery" (Ph.D. dissertation, University of California, Los Angeles, 1985), 56–59, 71–72; and Lonnie Bunch III, *Black Angelenos: The Afro-American in Los Angeles, 1850–1950* (Los Angeles: California Afro-American Museum, 1988), 10–12. Rios-Bustamante describes the settlers' background in Sinaloa, including the reasons for the heavy concentration of mulattoes in the province. The list of original settlers can be found in David Weber, "Mestizaje: The First Census of Los Angeles, 1781," in *Foreigners in Their Native Land: Historical Roots of the Mexican Americans*, ed. David Weber (Albuquerque: University of New Mexico Press, 1973), 34–35.

6. See Jack D. Forbes, "The Early African Heritage of California," in *Seeking El Dorado: African Americans in California*, ed. Lawrence B. De Graaf, Kevin Mulroy, and Quintard Taylor (Seattle: University of Washington Press, 2001), 73–97; and Gloria E. Miranda, "Racial and Cultural Dimensions of Gente de Razón Status in Spanish and Mexican California," *Southern California Quarterly* 70 (Fall 1988): 265–78. Ironically, Spanish-speaking women were increasingly marginalized regardless of the degree of their African ancestry. See Tomas Almaguer, *Racial Fault Lines: The Historical Origins of White Supremacy in California* (Berkeley: University of California Press, 1994), chap. 2; and Neil Foley, *The White Scourge: Mexicans, Blacks, and Poor Whites in Texas Cotton Culture* (Berkeley: University of California Press, 1997), 24–63.

7. These black women are described in Harold Schoen, "The Free Negro in the Republic of Texas: Origin of the Free Negro in the Republic," *Southwestern Historical Quarterly* 39 (April 1936): 301–2; and Ruthe Winegarten, *Black Texas Women: 150 Years of Trial and Triumph* (Austin: University of Texas Press, 1995), 8–9.

8. Quoted in Randolph B. Campbell, *An Empire for Slavery: The Peculiar Institution in Texas, 1821–1865* (Baton Rouge: Louisiana State University Press, 1989), 24; see also pp. 18-23.

9. Ibid., 56–58.

10. Ibid., 118–23; Higginbotham, "The Metalanguage of Race," 187–89.

11. The statement appears in Randolph B. Campbell and Donald Pickens, "'My Dear Husband': A Texas Slave's Love Letter, 1862," *Journal of Negro History* 65 (Fall 1980): 363.

12. Quoted in Theda Perdue, *Slavery and the Evolution of Cherokee Society, 1540–1866* (Knoxville: University of Tennessee Press, 1979), 107. The Washington Irving visit is described on pp. 106–107.

13. The Johnson narrative is found in Fred Lockley, "Some Documentary Records of Slavery in Oregon," *Oregon Historical Quarterly* 17 (June 1916): 107–15. See also George P. Rawick, ed., *The American Slave: A Composite Autobiography,* supplement series 1, *Arkansas, Colorado, Minnesota, Missouri, Oregon and Washington Narratives* (Westport, Conn.: Greenwood Press, 1977), vol. 2, 273–78. For a detailed account of the Mason case, see Dolores Hayden, "Biddy Mason's Los Angeles, 1851-1891," *California History* 68 (Fall 1989): 89–91. On the Holmeses' legal campaign to free their children, see Fred Lockley, "The Case of Robin Holmes vs. Nathaniel Ford," *Oregon Historical Quarterly* 23 (June 1922): 111–37; and Quintard Taylor, "Slaves and Free Men: Blacks in the Oregon Country, 1840–1860," *Oregon Historical Quarterly* 83 (Summer 1982): 153–70.

14. The quotation appears in Hayden, "Biddy Mason," 91; see also pp. 89–91.

15. The Margaret Frink quotation appears in her *Adventures of a Party of California Gold Seekers* (Oakland: Privately printed, 1897), 92. See also Rudolph Lapp, *Blacks in Gold Rush California* (New Haven: Yale University Press, 1977), 25–29.

16. On Pleasant's arrival in San Francisco, see Lynn Hudson, "A New Look, or 'I'm Not Mammy to Everybody in California': Mary Ellen Pleasant, a Black Entrepreneur," *Journal of the West* 32 (July 1993): 36. On Fuller, see Albert Broussard, "The New Racial Frontier: San Francisco's Black Community, 1900–1940" (Ph.D. dissertation, Duke University, 1977), 3.

17. For the *Mirror of the Times* tribute, see *Proceedings of the Second Annual Convention of the Colored Citizens of the State of California* (San Francisco: J. H. Udel and W. Handall, Printers, 1856), 60.

18. See Kathe Schick, "The Lawrence Black Community, 1860–1866," unpublished manuscript, Watkins Community Museum, Lawrence, Kan., n.d., 13–17.

19. See Marilyn Dell Brady, "Kansas Federation of Colored Women's Clubs, 1900–1930," *Kansas History* 9 (Spring 1986): 21; Richard B. Sheridan, "From Slavery in Missouri to Freedom in Kansas: The Influx of Black Fugitives and Contrabands into Kansas, 1854–1864," *Kansas History* 12 (Spring 1989): 39–40; and Schick, "The Lawrence Black Community," 12–13.

20. The Hickman quotation appears in Glen Schwendemann, "Nicodemus: Negro Haven on the Solomon," *Kansas Historical Quarterly* 34 (Spring 1968): 14.

21. The quotations are from Ava Speese Day, "The Ava Speese Day Story," in *Sod House Memories*, ed. Frances Jacobs Alberts (Hastings, Neb.: Sod House Society, 1972), 263–64, 275. On women's attitudes toward High Plains settlement, see Anne F. Hyde, "Cultural Filters: The Significance of Perception in the History of the American West," *Western Historical Quarterly* 24 (August 1993): 360–61.

22. On the Colored Ladies Legal Rights Association, see William M. King, *Going to Meet a Man: Denver's Last Legal Public Execution, 27 July 1886* (Niwot: University Press of Colorado, 1990), 2, 4–5, 71; Lynda Faye Dickson, "The Early Club Movement Among Black Women in Denver: 1890–1925" (Ph.D. dissertation, University of Colorado, 1982), 72–84; and Brian R. Werner, "Colorado's Pioneer Blacks: Migration, Occupations and Race Relations in the Centennial State" (M.A. thesis, University of Northern Colorado, 1979), 12–15.

23. See Thomas C. Cox, *Blacks in Topeka, Kansas, 1865–1915: A Social History* (Baton Rouge: Louisiana State University Press, 1982), 97, 98, 129, 140, 152. On Phelps, see Dickson, "The Early Club Movement"; and Werner, "Colorado's Black Pioneers," 9–10, 27, 52.

24. Dickson, "The Early Club Movement," 129. Regarding uplift ideologies, see Higginbotham, "Metalanguage of Race," 199–200; and Elsa Barkely Brown, "Womanist Consciousness: Maggie Lena Walker and the Independent Order of Saint Luke," *Signs* 14 (Spring 1989): 610–33.

25. Brady, "Kansas Federation of Colored Women's Clubs," 19. For background on the national women's club movement, see Paula Giddings, *When and Where I Enter: The Impact of Black Women on Race and Sex in America* (New York: William Morrow, 1984), chaps. 5, 6.

26. See Brady, "The Kansas Federation," 21; Winegarten, *Black Texas Women*, 189; Lawrence P. Crouchett, Lonnie G. Bunch III, and Martha Kendall Winnacker, *Visions toward Tomorrow: The History of the East Bay Afro-American Community, 1852–1977* (Oakland: Northern California Center for Afro-American History and Life, 1989), 14; Stacey Shorter, "Forgotten Pioneers: African American Women's Community Formation in Cheyenne, Wyoming, 1867–1904," unpublished paper in author's possession, 6; Dickson, "The Early Club Movement," 145; and Quintard Taylor, *The Forging of a Black Community: Seattle's Central District from 1870 through the Civil Rights Era* (Seattle: University of Washington Press, 1994), 140.

27. The Sojourner Truth Industrial Club quotation appears in Lonnie G. Bunch, "A Past Not Necessarily Prologue: The African American in Los Angeles," in *20th Century Los Angeles: Power, Promotion, and Social Conflict*, ed. Norman M. Klein and Martin J. Schiesl (Claremont, Calif.: Regina Books, 1990), 108. The Women's Day Nursery Association, founded in January 1907 at the Wesley Chapel AME Church, was profiled in the *Los Angeles Times*, February 12, 1909, sec. 3, p. 4. On the role of black women in politics in the first two decades of the twentieth century, see Douglas Flamming, "African Americans and the Politics of Race in Progressive-Era Los Angeles," in *California Progressivism Revisited*, ed. William Deverall and Tom Sitton (Berkeley: University of California Press, 1994), 203–28.

28. See Charles H. Wesley, *The History of the National Association of Colored Women's Clubs, Inc.: A Legacy of Service* (Washington, D.C.: Associated Publishers, 1984), 406–519.

29. The Bogle quotations are from E. Kimbark MacColl, *The Growth of a City: Power and Politics in Portland, Oregon, 1915 to 1950* (Portland: Georgian Press, 1980), 536. On 1930 employment statistics, see Taylor, *In Search of the Racial Frontier*, 224.

30. The quotations appear in Taylor, *In Search of the Racial Frontier*, 260, 261, respectively.

31. All quotations regarding Kaiser shipyard employment are found in Shirley Ann Wilson Moore, *To Place Our Deeds: The African American Community in Richmond, California, 1910–1963* (Berkeley: University of California Press, 2000), 57–59.

32. On the demonstration by black women, see *California Eagle*, July 16, 1942, pp. 1A, 8B. For a general discussion of the transition to black labor among the companies, see Taylor, *In Search of the Racial Frontier*, 257–61.

33. The Hill quotation appears in Taylor, *In Search of the Racial Frontier*, 261.

34. *Northwest Enterprise*, June 2, 1943, p. 1. The discriminatory practices of the Aero-Mechanics' Union lasted throughout most of the war. See Calvin F. Schmid, *Social Trends in Seattle* (Seattle: University of Washington Press, 1944), 320; and John McCann, *Blood in the Water: A History of District Lodge 751, International Association of Machinists and Aerospace Workers* (Seattle: District Lodge 751, IAMAW, 1989), 49, 87–88.

35. The Williams quote appears in Amy Kesselman, *Fleeting Opportunities: Women Shipyard Workers in Portland and Vancouver during World War II and Reconversion* (Albany: State University of New York Press, 1990), 43. The Pitter quotation appears in the Seattle *Northwest Enterprise*, May 19, 1943, p. 1. See also Taylor, *Forging*, 165–66. Karen Tucker Anderson suggests differing origins of discrimination against black male and

female workers. Black men were feared because they would be rivals for promotion; black women, however, were the objects of social discrimination such as objection over sharing bathroom facilities as seen in the Pacific Foundry incident. See Anderson, "Last Hired, First Fired: Black Women Workers during World War II," *Journal of American History* 69 (June 1982): 86.

36. Quoted in Robert Franklin Jefferson, "Making the Men of the 93rd: African American Servicemen in the Years of the Great Depression and the Second World War, 1935–1947" (Ph.D. dissertation, University of Michigan, 1995), 242.

37. For background on the campaign to end school segregation in Kansas, see Taylor, *In Search of the Racial Frontier*, 216–18.

38. On Tracy Simms, see David Lance Goines, *The Free Speech Movement: Coming of Age in the 1960s* (Berkeley: Ten Speed Press, 1993), 93. See also James Richardson, *Willie Brown: A Biography* (Berkeley: University of California Press, 1996), 86–87; and Taylor *In Search of the Racial Frontier*, 290–91.

CHAPTER 2

African American Women in Western History

PAST AND PROSPECT

Glenda Riley

In a 1988 article, "American Daughters: Black Women in the American West," I argued that black women in the Trans-Mississippi West deserved far more notice from scholars than they had received thus far. I lamented the dearth of research and writing and offered suggestions for research topics, including black women's clubs and the intersections between black and white women.[1]

Because women in general and African Americans in particular fell near the bottom of the status ladder, western African American women suffered near-invisibility in western history. Most archivists had neglected to collect these women's source materials, and most historians disregarded their stories. Of course, a similar circumstance surrounded African American men's history in the West, but at least African American soldiers and cowboys had received some scholarly attention by the 1960s.[2]

Only a few writers with foresight viewed black women in the West as a topic deserving further investigation. As early as 1919 African American club woman Delilah Beasley placed women prominently in her history, *The Negro Trail Blazers of California*.[3] Over the next four decades, no other major works followed Beasley's volume. One might expect a plethora of articles and books concerning various aspects of black women's history during and immediately following the civil rights movement of the 1960s. Yet western black women received little attention.

By the post–civil rights era, African American women in the West were slowly and unevenly included in a growing discourse on race and gender in the region. During the 1970s, the research of Sue Armitage, Theresa Banfield, and Sarah Jacobus revealed the wealth of information that existed concerning black women in the Pacific Northwest and in Colorado.[4] Although few historians focused explicitly on black women's history, many important social histories of western black communities were published during these years, studies that included important discussions about the role of black women in the American West. Nell Irvin Painter's *Exodusters*, Rudolph M. Lapp's *Blacks in Gold Rush California*, Elmer F. Rusco's *"Good Time Coming?"* Douglas Henry Daniel's *Pioneer Urbanites*, Thomas Cox's *Blacks in Topeka, Kansas, 1865–1915*, Jimmie L. Franklin's *Journey toward Hope*, and other works provided a strong foundation for analysis of black women's history.[5]

The year 1980 seemed a turning point. An article by the historian Lawrence B. De Graaf demonstrated the many ways in which census data and other records could be used to illuminate the lives of black women in the American West between 1850 and 1920. De Graaf's creative approach should have provoked numerous scholars to follow his lead, although the reality of elusive source materials remained a stumbling block.[6]

During the mid-1980s, a few historians demonstrated what might be done with the topic. These included Marilyn Dell Brady, who pointed out that black women in Kansas had established a strong and effective network of women's clubs, and Lynda F. Dickson, who wrote of a similar pattern for black women's clubs in Denver. Ann Patton Malone turned to black women in Texas during the West's frontier years, Anne M. Butler published a breakthrough article on black women in western prisons in the late nineteenth century, and Julia Kirk Blackwelder included black women in her important comparative study, *Women of the Depression*.[7] In fact, this scholarship demonstrated the increasing attention paid to race in western women's history as the historians Susan Armitage, Joan Jensen, Darlis Miller, and Elizabeth Jameson, among many others, repeatedly called for diverse approaches to the field.[8]

The 1990s not only promised to be better for western black women's history, but it has fulfilled that promise. Such movements as affirmative action and multiculturalism finally bore fruit. Numerous archivists collected black women's source materials, regional historians incorporated black women in their surveys of the West, and a handful of black historians had entered the history profession, declaring western black women's history one of their major interests. As a result of these changes, individual black women such as "Aunt" Clara Brown, Mary Ellen Pleasant, Biddy Mason, Carlotta Stewart Lai, Susie Revels Cayton, and Beatrice Morrow Cannady became subjects for study; Anne Butler enlarged on her earlier research on prisons; and Ruthe Winegarten and Gretchen Lemke Santangelo published significant monographs on black women's western migration experiences in the twentieth century.[9]

Also in 1997, the historian Roger D. Hardaway published an essay on black women in the *Negro History Bulletin* as well as a bibliography of blacks on the frontier. One year later Hardaway and Monroe Lee Billington put together an anthology of writings about western African Americans, which appeared as *African Americans on the Western Frontier,* as did Quintard Taylor's *In Search of the Racial Frontier.* The Hardaway and Billington anthology and Taylor's survey history acknowledge the growing interest in western African Americans, including women. The Hardaway and Billington collection also resurrected my 1988 article, "American Daughters," which concluded with the plea to write women into the history of the American West.[10]

A year or so after "American Daughters" first appeared, Quintard Taylor congratulated me and told me that he was using the essay in his classes. I knew that he would eventually answer my challenge to restore to black women in the West their historical identity and heritage. In this book, Quintard Taylor and Shirley Ann Wilson Moore bring together writings by historians of black women in the West, which clearly demonstrate that black western women can no longer be ignored, overlooked, or neglected. This anthology also includes "vignettes," which prove not only that African American women were present in the West but also that they constituted an integral part of the western tradition.

At the same time, this volume demonstrates that black women experienced the West differently from their white counterparts or even from other women of color. For instance, to be an African American woman on Spain's frontier, El Norte, which later became the American Southwest, was at times a nerve-shattering experience. Or imagine trying to exist as a black Mormon woman in a church that ranked blacks lower than whites. This volume does not stop, however, with the West's early years. The twentieth-century West is examined as well. Here the reader learns about Hollywood's portrayal of black women, about African American women in the campaign to integrate the University of Texas, and black women's employment in the Las Vegas gaming industry.

The volume concludes with essays on black women in the civil rights movement in Oklahoma and in the Black Panther Party.

Taylor and Moore have taken the story of black western women farther than I ever imagined possible. *African American Women Confront the West* covers the period from 1600 to 2000, incorporates black women's writings, and includes the work of some of the best younger scholars of our day. In achieving so much, Taylor and Moore suggest numerous possibilities for the future. Black women in the Roman Catholic Church, western black women's experiences of desertion and divorce, and black women who marry men of other races are a few of many topics that beg for investigation.

The turning point in western black women's history that I had hoped for in 1980 will begin instead in the twenty-first century. *African American Women Confront the West* will stand as a model for those aspiring to research and write the history of black women in the West. As a result, western history will become more inclusive, more exciting, and more just, great accomplishments for which the editors, as well as the individual authors, can take much of the credit.

NOTES

1. Glenda Riley, "American Daughters: Black Women in the West," *Montana: The Magazine of Western History* 38 (Spring 1988): 14–27.

2. See, for example, the essays in Monroe Lee Billington and Roger D. Hardaway, eds., *African Americans on the Western Frontier* (Niwot: University Press of Colorado, 1998).

3. Elsa Barkely Brown provides a review of Beasley's work in Delilah L. Beasley, *The Negro Trail Blazers of California* (Los Angeles, 1919; rept. New York: G. K. Hall, 1998). See also Lorraine J. Crouchett, *Delilah Leontium Beasley: Oakland's Crusading Journalist* (El Cerrito, Calif.: Downey Place Publishing House, 1990).

4. Susan Armitage, Theresa Banfield, and Sarah Jacobus, "Black Women and Their Communities in Colorado," *Frontiers* 2 (Summer 1977): 45–51; and Susan Armitage and Deborah Gallacci Wilbert, "Black Women in the Pacific Northwest: A Survey and Research Prospectus," in *Women in Pacific Northwest History: An Anthology*, ed. Karen J. Blair (Seattle: University of Washington Press, 1988), 45–51.

5. Nell Irvin Painter, *Exodusters: Black Migration to Kansas after Reconstruction* (New York: Alfred A. Knopf, 1977); Rudolph M. Lapp, *Blacks in Gold Rush California* (New Haven: Yale University Press, 1977); Elmer F. Rusco, *"Good Time Coming?" Black Nevadans in the Nineteenth Century* (Westport, Conn.: Greenwood Press, 1975); Douglas Henry Daniels, *Pioneer Urbanites: A Social and Cultural History of Black San Francisco*

(Philadelphia: Temple University Press, 1980); Thomas Cox, *Blacks in Topeka, Kansas, 1865–1915: A Social History* (Baton Rouge: Louisiana State University Press, 1982); and Jimmie L. Franklin, *Journey toward Hope: A History of Blacks in Oklahoma* (Norman: University of Oklahoma Press, 1982). For additional examples of social histories from this era, see Esther Hall Mumford, *Seattle's Black Victorians, 1852–1901* (Seattle: Ananse Press, 1980); Elizabeth McLagan, *A Peculiar Paradise: A History of Blacks in Oregon* (Portland: Georgian Press, 1980); Emory J. Tolbert, *The UNIA and Black Los Angeles* (Berkeley: University of California Press, 1980); and Lonnie Bunche III, *Black Angelenos: The Afro-American in Los Angeles, 1850–1950* (Los Angeles: California Afro-American Museum, 1988). During the 1990s, other significant works were Amy Kesselman, *Fleeting Opportunities: Women Shipyard Workers in Portland and Vancouver during World War II and Reconversion* (Albany: State University of New York Press, 1990); Albert S. Broussard, *Black San Francisco: The Struggle for Racial Equality in the West, 1900–1954* (Lawrence: University Press of Kansas, 1993); Quintard Taylor, *The Forging of a Black Community: Seattle's Central District from 1870 through the Civil Rights Era* (Seattle: University of Washington Press, 1994); and Bradford Luckingham, *Minorities in Phoenix: A Profile of Mexican American, Chinese American, and African American Communities, 1860–1992* (Tucson: University of Arizona Press, 1994).

6. Lawrence B. De Graaf, "Race, Sex, and Region: Black Women in the American West, 1850–1920," *Pacific Historical Review* 49 (May 1980): 285–313.

7. Marilyn Dell Brady, "Kansas Federation of Colored Women's Clubs, 1900–1930," *Kansas History* 9 (1986): 19–30; Anne M. Butler, "'Still in Chains': Black Women in Western Prisons, 1865–1910," *Western Historical Quarterly* 20 (February 1989): 19–36; Lynda Fae Dickson, "Toward a Broader Angle of Vision in Uncovering Women's History: Black Women's Clubs Revisited," *Frontiers* 9 (1987): 62–68; Ann Patton Malone, *Women on the Texas Frontier: A Cross-Cultural Perspective* (El Paso: Texas Western Press, 1983); and Julia Kirk Blackwelder, *Women of the Depression: Caste and Culture in San Antonio, 1929–1939* (College Station: Texas A&M University Press, 1984).

8. See this interest in multiculturalism in Joan Jensen and Darlis Miller, "The Gentle Tamers Revisited: New Approaches to the History of Women in the American West," *Pacific Historical Review* 49 (1980): 173–213; and *New Mexico Women: Intercultural Perspectives* (Albuquerque: University of New Mexico Press, 1986); Elizabeth Jameson, "Toward a Multicultural History of Women in the Western United States," *Signs* 13 (1988): 761–91; Lillian Schlissel, Vicki L. Ruiz, and Janice Monk, eds., *Western Women: Their Land, Their Lives* (Albuquerque: University of New Mexico Press, 1988); and Elizabeth Jameson and Susan Armitage, eds., *Writing the Range: Race, Class, and Culture in the Women's West* (Norman: University of Oklahoma Press, 1997). See also Antonia I. Castaneda's powerful historiographical essay, "Women of Color and the Rewriting of Western History: The Discourse, Politics, and Decolonization of History," *Pacific Historical Review* 61 (1992): 501–33.

9. Dolores Hayden, "Biddy Mason's Los Angeles, 1856–1891," *California History* 68 (Fall 1989): 86–99; Lynn M. Hudson, "A New Look, or 'I'm Not Mammy to Everybody in California': Mary Ellen Pleasant, a Black Entrepreneur," *Journal of the West* 32 (July 1993): 35–40; Quintard Taylor, "Mary Ellen Pleasant," in *By Grit and Grace: Women Who*

Shaped the Pioneer West, ed. Glenda Riley and Richard Etulain (Golden, Colo.: Fulcrum, 1997), 115–34; Albert S. Broussard, "Carlotta Stewart Lai: A Black Teacher in the Territory of Hawaii," *Hawaiian Journal of History* 24 (1990): 129–54; Quintard Taylor, "Susie Revels Cayton, Beatrice Morrow Cannady, and the Campaign for Social Justice in the Pacific Northwest," in *The Great Northwest: The Search for Regional Identity*, ed. William G. Robbins (Corvallis: Oregon State University Press, 2001), 32–46; Anne M. Butler, *Gendered Justice in the American West: Women Prisoners in Men's Penitentiaries* (Urbana: University of Illinois Press, 1997); Ruthe Winegarten, *Black Texas Women: 150 Years of Trial and Triumph* (Austin: University of Texas Press, 1995); Gretchen Lemke-Santangelo, *Abiding Courage: African American Migrant Women and the East Bay Community* (Chapel Hill: University of North Carolina Press, 1996); and Shirley Ann Wilson Moore, "'Not in Somebody's Kitchen': African American Women Workers in Richmond, California, and the Impact of World War II," in Jameson and Armitage, eds., *Writing the Range,* 517–32; Shirley Ann Wilson Moore, *To Place Our Deeds: The African American Community in Richmond, California, 1910–1963* (Berkeley: University of California Press, 2000); Shirley Ann Wilson Moore, "Your Life Is Really Not Just Your Own: African American Women in Twentieth Century California," in Lawrence B. De Graaf, Kevin Mulroy, and Quintard Taylor, eds., *Seeking El Dorado: African Americans in California* (Los Angeles: Autry Museum of Western Heritage in association with University of Washington Press, 2001), 210–46.

10. Roger D. Hardaway, "African-American Women on the Western Frontier," *Negro History Bulletin* 60 (January–March 1997): 8–14; Billington and Hardaway, eds., *African Americans on the Western Frontier*; and Quintard Taylor, *In Search of the Racial Frontier: African Americans in the American West, 1528–1990* (New York: W. W. Norton, 1998).

The Spanish-Mexican Period

Isabel de Olvera Arrives in New Mexico

The sixteenth- and seventeenth-century historical records of the U.S. Southwest are replete with examples of persons of African ancestry who accompanied Spanish explorers and colonizers. The Juan de Oñate party, which established a colony along the upper Rio Grande near Santa Fe in 1598, included at least five blacks and mulattoes, two of whom were soldiers. Most of those explorers and settlers were men. However, in 1600 one black woman, Isabel de Olvera of Querétaro, daughter of a black father and Indian mother, accompanied the Juan Guerra de Resa expedition to Santa Fe, sent to strengthen the Spanish claim on the region. Her arrival predates by nineteen years the landing at Jamestown, Virginia, of twenty persons of African ancestry in British North America. De Olvera, who was a servant for one of the Spanish women, was concerned about her safety and status in the frontier region and gave the following deposition to the *alcalde mayor* (mayor) of Querétaro. To buttress her claim, Olvera presented three witnesses, Mateo Laines, a free black man living in Querétaro, Anna Verdugo, a mestiza who lived near the city, and Santa Maria, a black slave of the alcalde mayor.

In the town of Querétaro in New Spain, January 8, 1600, there appeared before don Pedro Lorenzo de Castilla, his majesty's alcalde mayor in this town, a mulatto woman named Isabel, who presented herself before his grace in the appropriate legal manner and declared:

> As I am going on the expedition to New Mexico and have reason to fear that I may be annoyed by some individual since I am a mulatto, and as it is proper to protect my rights in such an eventuality by an affidavit showing that I am a free women, unmarried, and the legitimate daughter of Hernando, a negro, and an Indian named Magdalena, I therefore request your grace to accept this affidavit, which shows that I am free and not bound by marriage or slavery. I request that a properly certified and signed copy be given to me in order to protect my rights, and that it carry full legal authority. I demand justice.

The alcalde mayor instructed her to present the affidavits which she thought could be used and ordered that they be examined in accordance with this petition and that she be given the original. He so ordered and signed. Don Pedro Lorenzo de Castillo. Before me, Baltasar Martinez, royal notary.

Source: George P. Hammond, ed., and Agapito Rey, trans., *Don Juan de Oñate: Colonizer of New Mexico, 1595–1628* (Albuquerque: University of New Mexico Press, 1953), 560–62.

CHAPTER 3

To Be Black and Female
in the Spanish Southwest

TOWARD A HISTORY OF AFRICAN WOMEN
ON NEW SPAIN'S FAR NORTHERN FRONTIER

Dedra S. McDonald

In 1600 Isabel Isabel de Olvera, a free mulatta of Querétaro, Mexico, joined the Juan Guerra de Resa relief expedition to New Spain as a servant to a Spanish woman. To protect her status as a free woman of color on the unfamiliar northern frontier, Olvera filed a deposition with the Querétaro *alcalde* (mayor), don Pedro Lorenzo de Castilla:

> I am going on the expedition to New Mexico and have some reason to fear that I may be annoyed by some individual since I am a mulatta, and it is proper to protect my rights in such an eventuality by an affidavit showing that I am a free woman, unmarried and the legitimate daughter of Hernando, a negro and an Indian named Magdalena. . . . I therefore request your grace to accept this affidavit, which shows that I am free and not bound by marriage or slavery. I request that a properly certified and signed copy be given to me in order to protect my rights, and that it carry full legal authority. I demand justice.

Three witnesses, free black Mateo Laines, mestiza Anna Verdugo, and black slave Santa María, signed Isabel de Olvera's deposition in support of her bid for official protection.[1] Her words reveal an acute consciousness of the ever-changing constructions of race and freedom. Perhaps this consciousness arose as a reaction to someone's attempts to deny her status as a free woman. Whatever the case, through appealing to a colonial official for protection from possible perils, Olvera made a preemptive strike against whatever exploitation awaited her in the north. She also realized the need to record her racial heritage in an official document; because her mother was an Indian, Olvera could not be enslaved, even if her father had been a slave. In 1542 Spain decreed that Spanish America's indigenous population could not be formally enslaved. This ruling ensured the freedom of women like Magdalena, Isabel de Olvera's mother. In addition, Olvera's deposition twice noted her status as unmarried, emphasizing her independence from the bonds of matrimony as well as from the bonds of involuntary servitude. Through this deposition, Olvera ensured that no one in New Mexico could deny her freedom. She revealed an awareness of the potential conflicts precipitated by the unequal distribution of power in the Spanish colonies. As a female of African descent, Olvera saw little if any of the power held by Spanish colonial society. Thus she had to take precautions to protect her legal standing in society.

Many discussions of the Spanish colonial period in today's American Southwest begin with the story of the explorer and black slave Esteban de Dorantes and his demise at Zuni Pueblo in 1539. Esteban's story illustrates the significance of people of color, especially Africans, to borderlands history. But it is a masculine-centered story, full of his aggression and womanizing—characteristics that allegedly led to his downfall. Questions concerning the indigenous women "given" to him and the children he might have left in his wake—the gendered implications of the European-African encounter with Native America—never arise. I propose a new introductory story, one that features the mulatta servant Isabel de Olvera, who arrived in New Mexico in 1600. Her experience as a servant and her social position as a casta, or person of mixed blood, make her life quite similar to that of many other women living in the far northern provinces of New Spain and her Native American neighbors in New Mexico. Also like her indigenous neighbors, Olvera possessed confidence and a spirit of defiance that her condition of servitude would not erase.

Extant records reveal a substantial mulatto and black population in New Spain's far northern provinces. Hence Isabel de Olvera's experience is not unique. In addition, Olvera's deposition provides scholars with extraordinary insight into individual constructions of racial identity and freedom. Like the scholarly treatises that use Esteban as a protagonist, this chapter seeks to make a point about the presence and importance of people of color, as exemplified by Isabel de Olvera. Unlike them, this chapter claims significance for women of African descent who lived on the far northern frontier of colonial New Spain.

Although other women of African descent joined Olvera, few left such compelling clues to their thoughts on race and freedom. Even basic information about Afrohispanas must be gleaned from civil and ecclesiastical records. Recent interest in the history of the African diaspora has encouraged historians to examine Spanish documents for evidence regarding Africans in the Americas. Similarly, women's historians have begun to examine women's lives in the northern provinces of colonial New Spain. Scholarly treatments published over the past decade have repeopled the northern provinces of California, New Mexico, and Texas with women. Whereas earlier works, such as Hubert Howe Bancroft's volumes on Spanish California and New Mexico, virtually ignored women, more recent examinations of the borderlands' colonial past have revealed the presence and importance of women to colonial endeavors.[2]

To date, however, only one book, Ruthe Winegarten's *Black Texas Women*, offers a substantive discussion of African women in a Spanish colonial context. Winegarten describes free and enslaved black women living in Spanish and Mexican Texas. "Since Spain [and later Mexico] recognized free people of color," she writes, "Mexican Texas became a haven for runaway and freed slaves from the nearby United States South. This kind of immigration was fueled by word of mouth and continued even after Texas independence."[3] Her examination of black Texas women in the Spanish and Mexican periods is among the first secondary accounts of female African descendants in the borderlands. It provides a basic framework for the history of Afrohispanas in Texas and paves the way for future historical investigations.

Although somewhat scattered, primary documentation for such investigations exists. Extant records from colonial New Mexico, Texas, and California contain numerous references to mulattas and black women. Inquisition records in the Archivo General de la Nación in Mexico document mulattas' involvement in witchcraft, herbal medicine, and bigamy cases. The Spanish Archives of New Mexico include, for instance, a petition from mulatta Simona Hernández de Bejar describing Juan Páez Hurtado's recruitment of colonists from Zacatecas for the reconquest of New Mexico. The Archives of the Archdiocese of Santa Fe document marriages, baptisms, and burials of mulatta and black women. Eighteenth-century Spanish colonial censuses show a substantial number of mulatta residents, particularly in Albuquerque but also in Los Angeles. Pieced together, these documents reveal an African presence heretofore unrecognized in historical literature.

Afrohispanas were more than fixtures on the high desert landscape. They fully participated in Spanish frontier society as wives, sisters, daughters, mothers, *curanderas* (healers), settlers, servants, and petitioners. Conscious of their identity, Afrohispanas constructed Spanish colonial civil and criminal legal systems into sites of recourse and protection. Afrohispanas in northern New Spain employed available multicultural models—Spanish, Indian, and African—to exercise a measure of control over the precarious frontier world in which they lived. Elements of their African heritage remained, although Hispanicization modified those elements to some extent. When traditional strategies for survival and control failed, Afrohispanas adapted new strategies from indigenous, mestizo, and Spanish neighbors. These strategies encompassed acts of resistance ranging from witchcraft to godparentage alliances to court petitions. Although the prevailing system of power distribution on the Spanish, and later Mexican, northern frontiers favored European over indigenous or African, male over female, Afrohispanas forged alternative means to gain access to that power and to secure their status as freewomen or as enslaved women who were entitled to humane treatment.

AFRICANS IN THE AMERICAS

Free and enslaved Africans (mostly men) accompanied Spanish conquistadors to the Americas as early as 1493. Largely Hispanicized, they parlayed their roles in the conquest of the Caribbean and Mesoamerica into economic and social mobility. Initial Spanish settlements on Caribbean islands between 1493 and 1530 included free African men and women. In addition, from 1501 to 1503 large numbers of African slaves entered the Americas, many of them Christians from Seville. When silver and gold mines could no longer be worked by an indigenous population decimated by European diseases and harsh working conditions, wealthy Spaniards imported enslaved men and women directly from Africa. By 1550 at least 18,500 Africans and their descendants lived in New Spain (Mexico).[4]

Africans in the Americas frequently initiated intimate unions with indigenous peoples—so frequently that sixteenth-century Spanish authorities issued numerous laws and decrees in an often futile attempt to control Indian-African alliances and offspring. For example, a 1527 law required that blacks only marry other blacks. African descendants also formed unions with mestizos and Spaniards, as well as with free and enslaved Afrohispanos. The status of New Mexico, Texas, and California as provinces of New Spain meant that the above laws applied to Indians and Africans living there as well. To that end, the Spanish Archives of New Mexico include copies of decrees and declarations issued by kings and viceroys that clarified or changed earlier rulings. For example, a 1706 order compelled African descendants to attend church. Furthermore, in 1785 New Mexico governor Joseph Antonio Rengel received a letter advising him that the custom of branding Africans on the cheek and shoulder had been abolished. A 1790 viceregal order granted freedom to slaves escaping into Spanish territory. In the interests of agriculture, in 1804 King Carlos IV renewed the privilege held by Spaniards and foreigners of importing African slaves into specified Spanish American ports. A related 1804 *cédula* (royal decree) renewed the privilege of tax-free importation of African slaves. Finally, in 1817 King Fernando VII abolished the African slave trade. Hence documents in New Mexico archives trace the gradual abolition of African slavery.[5]

Decrees and laws also focused on revolts and communities of runaway slaves. A 1540 decree allowed for *cimarrones*, or runaway African slaves, to be pardoned once. Another decree issued the same year stated that male cimarrones should not be castrated as punishment for having run away. Two years later laws appeared that placed limitations on black mobility. As of 1542 blacks were not permitted to wander through the streets at night. In 1551 Africans could no longer serve Indians and neither free nor enslaved blacks or *lobos* (offspring of Indians and mulattoes) could carry weapons. In a further limitation of African freedom, a 1571 law forbade free and enslaved black women and mulattas from wearing gold, pearls, and silk. An exception could be made, however, for free mulattas married to Spaniards, who had the right to wear gold earrings and pearl necklaces. Another curtailment of liberties came in 1577 with a decree that free blacks and mulattoes should live with known employers, which would facilitate the payment of tribute. In addition, a census would be taken in each district, and free people of color were obligated to advise local justice officials when they absented themselves from their employer's household. Finally, a report in 1585 noted that mestizos and mulattoes frequently played leading roles among Chichimeca rebels in the Zacatecas-Coahuila region.[6] Such armed resistance made the earlier restrictions on African and Indian movements and public behavior all the more necessary in the eyes of Spanish authorities. Whether these laws had any impact on the two groups remains unknown, but their very existence suggests that Africans frequently participated in all the activities forbidden to them.

AFRICANS IN FAR NORTHERN NEW SPAIN

Sixteenth-century silver strikes in northern New Spain, notably in Zacatecas and Parral, brought Afrohispanos to that area in large numbers as slaves and as free wage laborers. Exploration and settlement expeditions heading north from the Zacatecas region also included Afrohispanos. For example, Esteban de Dorantes, an enslaved black Moor from Azamor who had wandered today's American Southwest with Alvar Nuñez Cabeza de Vaca, accompanied fray Marcos de Niza's 1539 expedition to the unexplored north. Also, a mulatto woman journeyed into present-day Kansas with the 1594 Leyva y Bonilla expedition, where she was severely but not fatally burned in a Wichita attack. Furthermore, don Juan de Oñate's 1598 settlement of New Mexico included several African slaves, who may have lived in Zacatecas as servants of the wealthy Oñate family.

Oñate's slaves and other New Mexicans of African descent found themselves in a dry, mountainous land of few trees and even less water. Indigenous peoples, called Pueblos by the Spanish, populated the best lands along the Rio Grande, where they practiced irrigated agriculture. Seminomadic Athapascan and Shoshonean peoples also called the high desert plateau home. Africans arriving in eastern and central Texas and along the California coast found a more humid and green landscape, also inhabited by indigenous groups who fished, hunted, gathered, and cultivated the land and waters. Spanish ventures into these lands featured military and missionary components as well as highly organized migrations of settlers. New Mexico spent its first decade as a proprietary colony, but Oñate's efforts to forge a new colony faltered. To maintain its commitments to converted Indians, the crown took over the colony in 1607.[7]

Intense church and state rivalry for jurisdiction over the Pueblos, among other things, split the less than two hundred New Mexico *vecinos* (citizens, including Spaniards, mestizos, and African descendants) into two vitriolic factions. In 1643 Governor Alonso de Pacheco de Herédia executed eight leading citizens of Santa Fe. Incensed Franciscan friars claimed he could not have done so without the support of strangers, a Portuguese man, mestizos, *sambahigos* (sons of Indian men and African women), and mulattoes. This charge suggests the existence of a "racial cleavage in New Mexico, with the persons of non-Spanish ancestry supporting the secular side of the dispute."[8] The importance of these alliances to Pueblo resistance remains unknown, but Spaniards forced to abandon New Mexico in 1680 viewed casta cooperation with Indians as a disloyal and threatening act. Although scholarship and extant documents on the 1680 Pueblo Revolt do not reveal whether the Indian-casta alliance continued after 1682, allied mestizos and mulattoes no doubt interacted and even intermarried with Pueblos during the Revolt years (through 1696). Native Americans and castas shared a marginal status in Spanish New Mexican society, in which pretensions to power required at least the illusion of *limpieza de sangre* (clean bloodlines). Both groups stood to gain from rebellion against Spanish authority. By joining Pueblo rebels, New Mexico castas constructed a group identity as "not-Spanish," which meant they would no longer acquiesce, at least for the Revolt years, in Spanish domination over Pueblos or over castas.

Enslaved Afrohispanos, however, had less opportunity to exercise power against Spanish slaveholders. Both before and after the Pueblo Revolt, enslaved blacks and mulattoes accompanied their masters to New Mexico, assisting in both the seventeenth-century colonization and eighteenth-century recolonization of the region. High prices and a shortage of slaves on the far northern frontier made slave ownership prohibitive for all but the wealthiest landowners, government officials, and merchants.[9] In eighteenth-century El Paso del Norte, slaveholders included the landowning Valverde y Cossío family. Merchant José de Colarte and his wife, Manuela García de Noriega, owned six mulatto slaves, ages ten to forty-six, during the years 1760 to 1785. Colarte's slaves ranged in value from 120 pesos for twelve-year-old Rafael and ten-year-old Juana to 150 pesos for forty-six-year-old María Antonia. Even El Paso clergyman Rafael Telles Girón owned a mulatta and her child. The youth of several of these slaves suggests that natural increase, along with outright purchase, added to the slave population in northern New Spain.[10]

Colonists residing to the north of El Paso also owned slaves. Francisco Javier's mulatta slave, María Madrid, known as "la Mozonga" (robust maidservant), was captured by Picurís Pueblo when the Pueblo Revolt broke out in 1680. Diego de Vargas's forces "liberated" her in 1692. According to some sources, María Madrid had three small daughters, in addition to a son born prior to the Revolt, when rescued in 1692. Given the existence of three children likely fathered by a Pueblo man and the twelve years she lived at Picurís, she may not have desired liberation.[11] Finally, some slaves accompanied high-ranking government officials such as Diego de Vargas as they moved from one post to the next. While not all New Mexicans could afford to own slaves, enough colonists acquired bond servants to make the institution of slavery and interactions with African descendants a part of everyday life in New Mexico.

The 1750 Albuquerque census reveals the extent to which such interaction occurred. A substantial population of African descendants resided in Albuquerque. Out of some two hundred families, fifty-seven had at least one mulatto or mulatta spouse. Some households included mulatta servants, although most servants were Indian women. For example, fifty-year-old mulatta Juana Carrillo and her husband, sixty-year-old mulatto Bartholomé Lobato, had two daughters, Bisenta, age seventeen, and Rita, age fifteen. Their household also included two mulatta orphans, fifteen-year-old Bárbara and six-year-old Anna María. Some mulattas appeared in the census as widowed or single female heads of household. For instance, thirty-five-year-old mulatta Juliana García ran a household consisting of five children ranging in age from two to fifteen, an Indian servant, an Indian girl, and an orphan.[12] Thus northern frontier areas served as a "cultural merging ground and a marrying ground." As the historian Gary Nash explains, "Nobody left the frontier cultural encounters unchanged."[13]

Some mulattas, such as Pasquala Candelaria, married Spaniards, mestizos, or *coyotes* (a racial or caste designation for the offspring of mestizo and Indian parents) rather than other African descendants, reflecting racial fluidity. These exogamous marriages allowed mulattas to redefine their ethnicities. For instance, in Cochiti (de los Españoles), the mulatto family of Manuel Aragón and María Francisca Gutiérrez and four daughters reclassified themselves as "español" in church marriage records over the course of sixteen years. In 1779 daughter Ana María de Aragón, mulatta, married Joseph Manuel Maese, español. Sixteen years later María Casilda Dionisia Aragón (same parents), española, married Francisco Sales Crespin. Another daughter, Antonia Rosa Aragón, española, married Antonio José Apodaca, español, in 1799. Finally, in 1802 daughter María Bárbara Antonia Aragón married Juan Cristobal Lobato. Their ethnicities were not recorded.[14] An individual's racial and ethnic status in New Spain shifted in accordance with economic mobility. Perhaps the Aragón family experienced economic mobility to such an extent that they were able to whitewash their African heritage. As the historian Jack Forbes states, "[R]ace . . . was not definite by the late eighteenth century and many people were of such a mixed character that they were simply *de color quebrado*, that is to say, 'all mixed up.'"[15]

Similarly, Texas census records reveal a substantial African presence. According to a 1792 census, out of a total Hispanic population of 2,510, 167 mulattas and 19 black women, both free and enslaved, resided in Spanish Texas.[16] The same census showed that at least 11 out of 22 female slaves and servants in San Antonio de Bexar were of African descent.[17] In 1836 an estimated 150 free blacks lived in the newly formed Republic of Texas. Rough population estimates from that year include 30,000 Anglos, 5,000 African Americans, 3,470 Mexicans, and 14,500 Indians.[18]

Enslaved and free African descendants called Spanish California home as well. Male African descendants accompanied the earliest Spanish military expeditions to Alta California and comprised 21.7 percent of the population of Baja California in 1790. Some of Baja California's Afrohispanos migrated to Alta California, where Afrohispanos from northern Sinaloa and Sonora joined them.[19] In September 1781 twelve families consisting of forty-six people founded the Pueblo de la Reina de los Angeles de Porciuncula(present-day Los Angeles). The 1781 Los Angeles *Padron* (census) delineates the racial heritage of the original settlers, or *pobladores*. Twenty-six of the pobladores were of African descent. Six of the adult women in the group were listed in the census as mulattas. Among them were María Regina Gloria de Soto, mulatta from Rosario, Sinaloa, married to mestizo José Antonio Navarro; María Manuela Calistra, mulatta spouse of Basilio Rosas, Indian; María Guadalupe Gertrudis Perez, mulatta from Rosario and wife of mulatto José Cesario Moreno; María Ana Gertrudis López, mulatta from Alamos, Sonora, married to Antonio Mesa, black; María Tomasa García, mulatta from Acaponeta, Nayarit, wife of mulatto Manuel Camero; and María Petra Rubio, mulatta from Alamos, Sonora, married to Luis Manuel Quintero, black.[20]

The 1790 Los Angeles census revealed a population increase from 46 to 141, with 22 persons listed as mulattoes. As Jack Forbes has noted, many of the original families of African descent "whitened up" in the 1790 census: "everyone acquired some fictitious Caucasian ancestry and shed Negro backgrounds— becoming, in effect, lighter as they moved up the social scale."[21] Some pobladores, however, continued to claim their African heritage. For instance, María Tomasa García, wife of Manuel Camero, gained mention as a thirty-two-year-old mulatta, and Maria Manuela Calistra, spouse of Basilio Rosas, Indian, maintained her racial identity as a mulatta between 1781 and 1790. Some newcomers arriving in Los Angeles after 1781 also appeared on the 1790 census as mulattas. For instance, Anna María Carasca, mulatta, her mestizo husband, José Ontiveros, and their seven-year-old daughter, María Encarnación, mulatta, originally from Rosario, Sonora, now lived in Los Angeles. Two additional mulattas and their families resided in Los Angeles by 1790.[22]

Santa Barbara's 1785 census also revealed an Afrohispano population. Forbes found that 37 of the 191 persons whose racial identity was given were of African descent. Six of these were mulattas. San José's 1790 census also listed Afrohispanos, including one mulatta and two *pardas* (offspring of a mulatto and a mestiza). African descendants constituted 24.3 percent of the population of that settlement's population. Similar to Los Angeles, later censuses for both Santa Barbara and San José reflected a reclassification of Afrohispanos as Spaniards. Finally, a 1790 San Francisco census listed two mulattas and two mulattoes. The census of 1782 had listed only males, six of whom were mulattoes. Some reclassification as Spaniards occurred between the two censuses. It may have served as a manifestation of the upward social mobility available to non-Spaniards living on the sparsely populated far northern frontier. By becoming mulattoes, mestizos, or even españoles, African descendants could ensure better marriages as well as enhanced social and economic opportunities for themselves and their children.[23]

INTERSECTIONS WITH SPANISH INSTITUTIONS

Much of the available information on Afrohispanas' lives must be gleaned from documents recording their participation in colonial institutions, such as Catholic sacraments of baptism, marriage, and burial. Notations from these occasions provide glimpses into women's lives, delineating life-changing events and simultaneously revealing networks of kin and fictive kin. For example, enslaved black women and mulattas expanded their connections with free men and women of color through the daily relations of work, religion, and family. Networks linking slaves to free persons were frequently noted through the testimonies given by witnesses in prenuptial investigations. For example, on July 25, 1718, in Santa Fe, Nicolás de Los Angeles, age twenty-nine, native of Guadalajara and slave of Governor don Antonio de Valverde y Cossío, married María Francisca Enríquez, age twenty-four, freed slave of Valverde. In Chihuahua, Los Angeles had run away from his former master Lucas de Quiñones, whom he had served at San Juan del Río. After the runaway slave had lived in Santa Fe for more than a year, Valverde purchased him.[24] One can only assume that Los Angeles's whereabouts or identity were discovered despite the chaos and anonymity of the New Mexico frontier. A more intriguing point of inquiry in this story concerns María Francisca Enríquez's motivations for marrying a slave. Her freedom ensured the free status of any children they might produce, but their marriage did not release Los Angeles from the bonds of slavery. Perhaps this selection of marriage partners reflects the small number of available blacks and mulattoes in the Santa Fe area, or simply suggests the power of love. Interestingly, Valverde y Cossío's will provided Enríquez, whom the former New Mexico governor had reared, with the unimpeded use of an *apachuela* (young female Apache servant) that he had given her and also thirty goats for her support if she did not wish to remain in the house.[25]

Baptisms also provided occasions for blacks and mulattas to form social networks. Afrohispano families living in Albuquerque during the eighteenth century selected *padrinos* (godparents) for their children from among all ethnic groups residing in the *villa*. Baptismal records for San Felipe de Albuquerque parish record the baptisms and christenings of twenty-one mulattoes (nine females, twelve males) and one *morisca*(the offspring of a Spaniard and a mulatto) between 1730 and 1752. In 1744 the town boasted a population of one hundred families, and in 1752 it had 476 *gentes de razón* (people of reason).[26] When compared to the numbers of mulatto baptisms, these low population figures suggest that mulattoes constituted a significant percentage of eighteenth-century Albuquerqueans.

In addition, marriage records exist for ten couples in which at least one spouse was listed as an Afrohispano for the years 1738 to 1763. Three of these marriages produced children who are included in the church's baptismal records. Manuel Carrillo and María Barela married on November 30, 1727. Although their ethnicity does not appear in the record, their daughter, Anastasia Carrillo, baptized on May 6, 1730, is listed as a *morisca*. The second marriage occurred on May 30, 1728, when Juan Antonio de la Candelaria wed Manuela Barela. Likewise, neither spouse's ethnicity appears in the church record, but their daughter, Francisca Juliana de la Candelaria, baptized on March 24, 1745, is listed as a *mulatta*. The third marriage record does mention the ethnicity of both spouses. On March 19, 1742, Juan Zamora, a single mulatto, married Ynes de la Candelaria, a mulatta maiden, and on March 31, 1745, the couple baptized their mulatto son, Juan Vicente Zamora.[27]

Although the ethnicities of the various witnesses and godparents remain unknown, these sacramental records indicate that mulatto families formed substantive social links with the fledgling Albuquerque community, founded in 1706 by thirty-five families.[28] Of the ten mulatto marriages recorded for eighteenth-century Albuquerque, seven were interethnic unions. Through participation in marriages and baptisms as the nuptial couple, the baptized child, or witnesses, women of African descent established connections with people within their ethnic group as well as with people outside their group. The rate at which black women and mulattas formed these linkages suggests that their lives in colonial New Mexico featured fluidity in social relations and both physical and social mobility.

Documents connected with the institution of slavery also provide glimpses into Afrohispanas' lives. In what must have been a life-changing event, enslaved black and mulatta women sometimes achieved status as freedwomen. Doña Manuela García de Noriega's will illustrates one method of gaining freedom—manumission by her owner. Overcome by illness and believed to be on her deathbed, the Spanish doña Manuela dictated a will on December 19, 1783. In the will she expressed her desire that the mulatta slave María Antonia be freed "later when God takes me from this life to the next." María Antonia's enslaved daughter, Juana, was to be rewarded with her freedom as well but only after serving doña Manuela's niece, doña Rafaela Villa Cevallos, until the latter's death. The remainder of the slaves were to serve the mistress's husband, don José Colarte, until his death, after which they were all to be freed. Doña Manuela hoped that her slaves would note "the good that she had served some, and the love and care that she had for the others."[29] Doña Manuela's willingness to free all of her slaves may indicate deep personal relationships with the entire group, or perhaps she possessed religious convictions that profoundly influenced her final hours. Granting freedom to all of her slaves may have been a last-minute effort to ensure her entry into heaven. Whatever her motivations, doña Manuela's conditional manumissions gave her slaves the promise of freedom in the future, with the exception of María Antonia, whose freedom went into effect almost immediately. In general, manumission was commonly practiced by Spanish American slaveholders, who freed their slaves "for a variety of reasons ranging from old age, guilt and gratitude to hard times."[30]

BEING BLACK AND FEMALE

By filing lawsuits and petitioning governors, Afrohispanas laid claim to justice and human dignity. Details of their daily lives also emerge from civil and ecclesiastical court depositions and from petitions similar to the one filed by Isabel de Olvera. Their participation in court cases and petitions represents their attempts to establish control and assert power in situations of mistreatment, violence, and betrayal. For example, witchcraft provided a means for New Mexico women to work together to regain control over their lives and to impose their wills on others. The anthropologist Ruth Behar suggests that the "aim of women in these cases, according both to the women themselves and to the men who accused them, was to reverse their subordination to men and gain some degree of control over their husbands or lovers." Witchcraft enabled women to turn the patriarchal world inside out by making husbands subordinate to their wives.[31]

In one seventeenth-century New Mexico witchcraft case, mulatta Juana Sanches, wife of Captain Juan Gomes, testified that she obtained herbs from a Tewa Indian women living at San Juan Pueblo. Juana Sanches wanted to make her husband stop treating her badly. She claimed that he beat her and that he was engaged in a sexual relationship (*mala amistad*) with a concubine. The Indian woman gave Sanches two yellow roots and two grains of blue corn with white hearts inside. She chewed the corn and anointed the chest and heart of her husband and repeated the exercise with the herbs. Sanches added to her 1631 testimony before New Mexico's agent of the Inquisition that ten or twelve years earlier, *ladino* (Hispanicized) Mexican Indian Beatris de los Angeles, wife of the *alférez* (field-grade officer) Juan de la Cruz, visited her. Finding Juana Sanches sad because her husband mistreated her, Beatris de los Angeles counseled her to take a few worms that live in excrement and toast them, then put them in her husband's food. With this, he would love her very much and stop beating her. Sanches did this, but the potion did not alleviate her situation. Women engaged in witchcraft frequently mixed special powders and potions in food, taking advantage of their roles as food providers and nurturers. According to Behar, "The belief that food could be used to harm rather than to nurture gave women a very specific and real power that could serve as an important defense against abusive male dominance."[32]

Sanches also implicated her sister, mulatta Juana de los Reyes, in similar activities. As her references to other women's involvement in witchcraft suggests, women formed cross-class and cross-caste networks in which they passed along knowledge of potions and remedies. Hence Sanches declared that five or six years before, Juana de los Reyes claimed to know something about herbs and roots, which she had given to her husband, mulatto Alvaro García, so that he would stop visiting concubines. An Indian woman supplied Reyes with the herbs and roots to anoint her husband's chest. Reyes gave her own declaration, stating that she had been very sad because her husband was sleeping around and not staying in their house with her. So she asked her sister,

Juana Sanches, for help. Sanches said that she had an herb, given to her by an Indian woman, that was good for such occasions. Sanches gave Reyes three or four grains of corn, and Reyes gave this potion to her husband in his food twice and also made an ointment for his chest. Thereafter her husband loved her very much and forgot his vices. She gave him the potion another time in his food and anointed his chest once more, with the result that he woke up, threw off her hand, and left her. Because the potion now had no effect, she left the situation in God's hands. Juana de los Reyes also described another remedy told to her by the Indian woman: suck on your two big fingers and give the saliva from the sucked fingers to your spouse in his food and he will love you well and stop seeing concubines. Reyes declared that she tried this once but did not want to try it again because it made her nauseous and it had no effect on her husband. Finally, at the same time that the above testimonies were made, Beatris de la Pedraza also made a declaration. She claimed that one day when visiting Juana Sanches, her hostess noticed that she was sad. Pedraza's husband had gone to Mexico and left her behind. Sanches informed her guest of a remedy for this sadness. If Pedraza so desired, Sanches would give her an herb to chew and then use as an ointment for her husband's chest when he went to sleep at night. While he slept, she should keep a grain of maize in her mouth all night, then chew it in the morning and use it as an ointment. She should repeat this exercise for three nights, and then her husband would remember nothing and would desire her and treat her well. Beatris de la Pedraza did not indicate whether she had tried this remedy, but the Inquisitor characterized her as a woman of dishonest opinion.[33]

The New Mexico Inquisitor chose not to pursue the case. In New Mexico during the 1630s, the Inquisition pursued cases of heresy more often than those of witchcraft. Moreover, the New Mexico Inquisitor did not have the power to try cases. He could only make arrests and send those under suspicion to Mexico City to be tried. Thus it is likely that nothing came of Juana Sanches's and Juana de los Reyes's experiments in herbal remedies. A far more interesting question surrounds the two mulattas' close working relationship with Indian curanderas. How they made connections with Indian women and why they did not implicate medicine women by name in their depositions remain unanswerable questions. Perhaps gendered concerns—the bonds of womanhood—brought Native American and African women together. Or perhaps Reyes and Sanches served alongside Pueblo women in Spanish households. Or, because the Inquisition did not have jurisdiction over Pueblo Indians, the notary may have omitted the names of Pueblo women involved in the case.

As Forbes argues, in early Spanish colonial usage, "mulatto" frequently referred to a person of Indian and African heritage rather than to the offspring of an African-European union, as it was later used.[34] Given this definition, it is possible that Juana Sanches and her sister, Juana de los Reyes, had African and Indian parentage. If so, they may have long held knowledge of Indian and African curanderas and the types of situations that could be remedied with herbal potions. In addition, Sanches and Reyes used their connections with Indian medicine women in desperate attempts to control their husbands' abusive behavior. To gain control, these two mulattas relied on female knowledge and cross-cultural community. Whatever the case, the mulattas' involvement with the Hispanicized Indian Beatris de los Angeles and with Beatris de Pedraza underscores the existence of an interethnic, interclass network of women, a New Mexico version of the female world of love and ritual, advising one another about solutions to marital and sexual problems.[35]

Sanches's and Reyes's confessions offered a discourse firmly anchored on the body. These women sought control not just of own bodies but of their husbands' bodies as well. Though they may not have been witches, they were not innocent bystanders either. The mulatta sisters may not have been accused of murder, or even of witchcraft, but they nonetheless put into play the knowledge of herbal remedies that Indian women had passed along to them. By dabbling in witchcraft, they refused to become victims of unfaithful, abusive husbands. Yet the sisters did not win in the end. Both confessed to have met with little success in their attempts to control their husbands' behavior. Furthermore, both regretted their forays into the underworld of sorcery and superstition. Hence practitioners of witchcraft simultaneously could be victims and victimizers. Whatever the case, it is clear that Juana Sanches and Juana de los Reyes refused to accept continued mistreatment from their husbands. They turned to Native American curanderas for assistance, thereby seeking cross-cultural solutions to their problems.

Civil and ecclesiastical courts offered another avenue through which Afrohispanas could assert control over their own lives. Fair-minded governors, who issued rulings in civil cases, could serve as advocates for women in situations requiring legal recourse. In one such case, two mulatto slaves in San Antonio de Bexar petitioned the province's governor for a change in ownership. Citing mistreatment, slaves Maria Simona de Jesus Moraza and Santiago Phelipe del Fierro left their owners, Doña Juana de Oconitrillo and Don Marcario Sambrano, in 1791. The owner's daughter and daughter-in-law, Maria Astasia and Concepción de la Santa, had whipped Maria Moraza without cause, precipitating her departure. Because Moraza's owner, Juana de Oconitrillo, demanded that her slave return, the governor ordered the alcalde, Francisco de Arocha, to investigate the situation. When Arocha entered the home with Maria Moraza in tow, Oconitrillo was not present. Instead they found Oconitrillo's daughter and daughter-in-law, who proceeded to threaten and insult Moraza, calling her "mal criada" (poorly raised). Moraza now refused to return to that household.

Next, Santiago Phelipe del Fierro declared that had abandoned his owners' home because of the mistreatment his wife, Maria Moraza, received at the hands of Maria Astasia, who beat her with small sticks and kicked her without provocation. Having witnessed the threats made by Maria Astasia and Concepción de la Santa against the two slaves, the alcalde decided that Fierro and Moraza should be allowed to seek another work situation. This change of venue proved difficult. In 1792 Maria Moraza asked the governor to intervene in her sale price. She had reached the age of forty, was somewhat sick, and was weary from twenty-eight years of servitude in the home of Don Marcario Sambrano and Doña Juana de Oconitrillo.

Hence, despite their marginalized and seemingly powerless status as slaves, Moraza and Fierro mobilized the justice system in their favor. To do this required a strong sense of self and consciousness of one's own humanity and worth, despite the chains of involuntary servitude. Two years later, however, the commandant general of the Internal Provinces, don Felipe de Nava, overturned that decision. He ordered that the two slaves not be sold to another slaveholder, even though they had located a potential buyer (Juan Barrera of the Presidio of La Bahia del Espiritu Santo), because their motives were groundless and insufficient. Their principal owner, don Marcario Sambrano, had passed away in 1792, and his son begged the courts to reconsider their initial decision in the case. His mother, don Pedro Sambrano pleaded, needed the assistance of her slaves and should not be punished for the thoughtless mistreatment her slaves had suffered at the hands of her misguided daughter.[36] Hence shifting notions of justice kept enslaved persons such as Maria Moraza and Santiago Phelipe del Fierro in constant flux. As this case illustrates, justice could be meted out, but it could also be easily taken away. The stigma of perpetual enslavement made such ambiguous legal structures simultaneously precarious and promising.

Free women of African descent also turned to the courts for protection and for recourse. Despite their legal freedom, nonenslaved persons also faced an arbitrary justice system that depended on the character and priorities of governors. In one such case, free mulatta Antonia Lusgardia Hernández, resident of

Spanish colonial Texas, filed a petition with the governor of San Antonio de Bexar. In this document, Hernández explained that she and her child had lived in don Miguel Nuñez's household. While there, she bore another child, whom Nuñez's wife had baptized. She suffered great mistreatment in that household and left it for Alberto Lopez's household, taking the two children with her. Nuñez absconded with her second child, a son, who she described as "the only man I have and the one who I hope will eventually support me." Hernández pleaded with the governor, appealing to him as a powerful patriarch.

> I being but a poor, helpless woman whose only protection is a good administration and a good judicial system[,] Your Lordship will please demand that the said don Miguel Nuñez, without the least delay, shall proceed to deliver my son to me without making any excuses. I wish to make use of all the laws in my favor, and of our Lordship, as a father and protector of the poor and helpless, as well as anything else which might be in my favor.[37]

Hernández's appeal to the governor worked. The child was returned to her on the condition that she provide a proper home for him. Case notes indicated that Nuñez had fathered the boy. Nuñez claimed that Hernández had given the child to his wife. In petitioning the governor to take action against don Miguel Nuñez, Antonia Lusgardia Hernández participated in a strategy the historian Steve Stern has termed "pluralizing patriarchs." Stern contends that "in effect, this strategy set up male-male rivalries and hierarchies as a check on the power of the patriarch with the most immediate claim of authority."[38] Hence Hernández sabotaged Nuñez's power over her by calling on a more powerful patriarch, the governor. She was able to solicit this assistance despite her position as a marginalized woman of color and single mother dependent on household servitude for survival.

· · ·

Census, civil, and church records depict a landscape peopled by significant numbers of women and men of African descent. Women of African descent formed families and social networks, took part in daily economic interactions, and in all likelihood passed along bits of African cultural heritage to their children. These women participated in the fluid racial and ethnic interrelations that characterized colonial New Mexico, Texas, and California. They obtained potions from Native American curanderas to keep their husbands in line, filed petitions to ensure their rights, gained freedom from slavery, witnessed baptisms and marriages, married both African descendants and non-Africans, and baptized their children. These case studies exemplify the documentary evidence available for studies of black women in Spanish colonial New Mexico, Texas, and California and demonstrate the significance of these women to the trajectory of borderlands history.

New Spain's far northern frontier served as a cross-cultural meeting ground, playing host to a diverse group of women who competed for scarce resources as often as they shared strategies for surviving without those same resources.[39] Strategies for survival and control also hinged on civil and ecclesiastical judicial systems. Through depositions and petitions, Afrohispanas and their non-African neighbors invoked powerful patriarchs to protect individual freedom. Control over ill-tempered and untrustworthy husbands could be achieved through church and state as well but more often, and perhaps more successfully, through localized practices of witchcraft and herbal medicine. Furthermore, Afrohispanas expressed racial consciousness through these same strategies. Witchcraft, which likely had its basis in African traditions, and petitions safeguarded personal and legal freedom. Racial reclassification also worked to protect legal freedom. Afrohispanas and their families may well have recognized race as an arbitrary social construction and decided to redefine their racial heritage in order to enhance their social and economic mobility. After all, as españolas, African descendants would be far less likely to lose their legal freedoms.

Perhaps even more important than the strategies Afrohispanas employed is the sheer fact of their presence in Spanish colonial Texas, California, and New Mexico. In the mid-nineteenth century, these provinces and their Afrohispana residents became part of the American West. Hence women of African descent are anything but newcomers to the region. Esteban may have arrived sooner than Isabel de Olvera, but she inhabited today's West years before most nonindigenous westerners. Her story, I would argue, is every bit as compelling as Esteban's. Moreover, Isabel de Olvera's story shows that the area that became the American West after 1848 was a potentially dangerous but also promising crossroads. To be black and female in the Spanish and Mexican northern frontier required racial and gender consciousness, wariness, and a willingness to indulge in a wide variety of cross-cultural strategies, both formal and informal, for survival.

NOTES

1. From George P. Hammond, ed., and Agapito Rey, trans., *Don Juan de Oñate: Colonizer of New Mexico, 1595–1628* (Albuquerque: University of New Mexico Press, 1953), 560–62, quoted in Quintard Taylor, *In Search of the Racial Frontier: A History of African Americans in the American West* (New York: W. W. Norton, 1998), 30.

2. See Hubert Howe Bancroft, *Works,* 39 vols. (San Francisco: A. L. Bancroft, 1882–90). Several articles and dissertations have filled in blanks left by traditional historians. These include Salomé Hernández, "The U.S. Southwest: Female Participation in Official Spanish Settlement Expeditions: Specific Case Studies in the Sixteenth, Seventeenth, and Eighteenth Centuries" (Ph.D. dissertation, University of New Mexico, 1987). See also her article on women during the Pueblo Revolt in *New Mexico Women: Intercultural Perspectives,* ed. Joan Jensen and Darlis Miller (Albuquerque: University of New Mexico Press, 1987), 41–69. Another key dissertation and forthcoming book is Antonia I. Castañeda, "Presidiarias y Pobladoras: Spanish-Mexican Women in Frontier Monterey, Alta California, 1770–1821" (Ph.D. dissertation, Stanford University, 1990). See also Rosalind Rock, "'Pido y Suplico': Women and the Law in Spanish New Mexico, 1697–1763," *New Mexico Historical Review* 65 (April 1990): 145–59; Rosalind Rock, "Mujeres de Substancia: Case Studies of Women of Property in Northern New Spain," *Colonial Latin American Historical Review* 2 (Fall 1993): 425–40; and Yolanda Chávez Leyva, "'A Poor Widow Burdened with Children': Widows and Land in Colonial New Mexico"; James F. Brooks, "'This Evil Extends Especially to the Feminine Sex': Captivity and Identity in New Mexico, 1700–1846"; and Albert L. Hurtado, "When Strangers Met: Sex and Gender on Three Frontiers," all in *Writing the Range: Race, Class, and Culture in the Women's West,* ed. Elizabeth Jameson and Susan Armitage (Norman: University of Oklahoma Press, 1997), 85–96, 97–121, 122–42, respectively. Several books and articles have highlighted the black presence in the Southwest. Yet they have given only cursory attention to women of African descent. The historians George R. Woolfolk, Jack D. Forbes, and Quintard Taylor have discussed the African diaspora in New Spain's northern provinces. Woolfolk studies African American interactions with Native Americans, Mexicans, Germans, and Anglo-Americans in the Texas borderlands before the American Civil War. See Woolfolk, *The Free Negro in Texas, 1800–1860: A Study in Cultural Compromise* (Ann Arbor: University Microfilms International, 1976). Forbes traces census records in Spanish colonial California in his article, "Black Pioneers: The Spanish-speaking Afroamericans of the Southwest," *Phylon* 27 (Fall 1966): 233–46. Finally, Taylor's synthesis, *In Search of the Racial Frontier,* pulls together scholarship on Afrohispanos in northern New Spain, an area that would later be incorporated into the American West.

3. Ruthe Winegarten, *Black Texas Women: 150 Years of Trial and Triumph* (Austin: University of Texas Press, 1995).

4. Thomas C. Patterson, "Early Colonial Encounters and Identities in the Caribbean: A Review of Some Recent Works and Their Implications," *Dialectical Anthropology* 16 (1991): 7; Jack D. Forbes, *Black Africans and Native Americans: Color, Race, and Caste in the Evolution of Red-Black Peoples* (New York: Basil Blackwell, 1988), 61; and Nicolás

Leon, "Las castas del México colonial o Nueva España," from the series *Noticias etno-antropológicas* (Museo Nacional de Arqueología, Historia, y Etnografía: Publicaciones del Departamento de Antropología Anatómica, no. 1, 1924), 7.

5. Spanish Archives of New Mexico, Twitchell nos. 914, 1094, 1684, 1723, 1761, 2437, 2704, microfilm, Center for Southwest Research (CSWR), Zimmerman Library, University of New Mexico, Albuquerque.

6. Jack D. Forbes, *Apache, Navaho, and Spaniard* (Norman: University of Oklahoma Press, 1960), 135, 138–39.

7. Marc Simmons, *New Mexico: An Interpretive History*, 2d ed. (Albuquerque: University of New Mexico Press, 1988), 84.

8. Forbes, *Apache*, 135.

9. Vincent Mayer, *The Black on New Spain's Northern Frontier: San José de Parral, 1631 to 1641* (Durango, Colo.: Center of Southwest Studies, 1974), 5.

10. Rebeca A. Gudiño Quiroz, *Don Antonio Valverde y Cossío, Gobernador de Nuevo México: Una aproximación a su vida pública y privada*, Working Papers Series (Ciudad Juárez: Universidad Autónoma de Ciudad Juárez, Unidad de Estudios Regionales, 1994), 21. Juárez Municipal Archives microfilm; Valverde reel 10; Telles Jiron reel 11, frames 116–41; Colarte reel 12, frames 181–285, Special Collections, University of Texas at El Paso.

11. Fray Angelico Chavez, "Addenda to New Mexico Families," *El Palacio* 64, nos. 3–4 (March–April 1957): 123–26.

12. Virginia Langham Olmsted, comp., *Spanish and Mexican Censuses of New Mexico, 1750–1830* (Albuquerque: New Mexico Genealogical Society, 1981), 75–87; from Biblioteca Nacional, Legajo 8, Parte 4, CSWR.

13. Gary B. Nash, "The Hidden History of Mestizo America," *Journal of American History* 82 (December 1995): 947.

14. Archives of the Archdiocese of Santa Fe (AAASF), Marriages, microfilm reel 27, frames 84–129, CSWR.

15. Forbes, "Black Pioneers," 235.

16. The Hispanic (non-Indian) population numbered 2,510 in 1790. David J. Weber, *The Spanish Frontier in North America* (New Haven: Yale University Press, 1992), 195.

17. 1792 Census, San Antonio de Bexar, Nacogdoches Archives, from photostat copies at the Center for American History, University of Texas at Austin.

18. Winegarten, *Black Texas Women*, 5; overall population figures from Randolph B. Campbell, *An Empire for Slavery: The Peculiar Institution in Texas, 1821–1836* (Baton Rouge: Louisiana State University Press, 1989), 54.

19. Forbes, "Black Pioneers," 235–36.

20. Hubert Howe Bancroft, *History of California*, vol. 2 (*Works*, vol. 19); Marie E. Northrup, *Spanish-Mexican Families of Early California: 1769–1850*, 2 vols. (Burbank, Calif.: Southern California Genealogical Society, 1984); Forbes, "Black Pioneers," 236–37.

21. Forbes, "Black Pioneers," 237.

22. Bancroft Archives of California, vol. 5, 158–64, Bancroft Library, University of California, Berkeley.

23. Forbes, "Black Pioneers," 239–42. Forbes does not include overall population figures for California settlements.

24. Chavez, New Mexico Roots, Diligencias Matrimoniales 1718, June 5 (no. 25).

25. Gudiño Quiroz, *Don Antonio Valverde y Cossío*, 23. "Apachuela" is an unusual term that does not appear in Spanish-language dictionaries. I have arrived at this translation through consultation with Robert Himmerich y Valencia and Joseph Sánchez.

26. Oakah L. Jones Jr., *Los Paisanos: Spanish Settlers on the Northern Frontier of New Spain* (Norman: University of Oklahoma Press, 1979), 123–24.

27. Baptisms from Books of Baptism, B-2 Alburquerque, microforms, reel 1, AASF; and marriages from Books of Marriage, M-3 Alburquerque, microforms reel 26, frames 143–87, AASF. A significant portion of the AASF microfilms are unreadable, making it possible that additional records of mulatto baptisms and marriages do exist.

28. Simmons, *New Mexico*, 84.

29. José Colarte, Execution of power to make a will, El Paso del Norte, February 28, 1783, Juárez Municipal Archives, microfilm reel 11, book 1, 1783, frames 124–30.

30. Murdo J. MacLeod, "Aspects of the Internal Economy," in *Colonial Spanish America*, ed. Leslie Bethell (New York: Cambridge University Press, 1987), 332.

31. Ruth Behar, "Sexual Witchcraft, Colonialism, and Women's Powers: Views from the Mexican Inquisition," in *Sexuality and Marriage in Colonial Latin America*, ed. Asunción Lavrin (Lincoln: University of Nebraska Press, 1989), 179.

32. Behar, "Sexual Witchcraft," 180.

33. Declaration of Beatris de Pedraza, June 21, 1632, AGN-Inquisición, Legajo 372, Expediente 16. From transcription by Scholes, "First Decade," 231. Perea's characterizations are listed in Scholes, "First Decade," 224n41.

34. Forbes, *Black Africans and Native Americans*, 165.

35. AGN-Inquisición, Legajo 372, phototstat copies, CSWR. From transcription in Scholes, "First Decade," Appendix, 230–32.

36. Saltillo Archives, Vol. 5, 79–146, photostat copies located at CFAH.

37. "Child Custody, Mulatto Woman," Bexar Archives Inventory, Center for American History, University of Texas, Austin, quoted in Susan Armitage, Helen Bannan, Katherine G. Morrissey, and Vicki L. Ruiz, *Women in the West: A Guide to Manuscript Sources* (New York: Garland, 1991), xix–xx.

38. Steve J. Stern, *The Secret History of Gender: Women, Men, and Power in Late Colonial Mexico* (Chapel Hill: University of North Carolina Press, 1995), 99.

39. Peggy Pascoe, "Western Women at the Cultural Crossroads," in *Trails: Toward a New Western History*, ed. Patricia Nelson Limerick, Clyde A. Milner II, and Charles Rankin (Lawrence: University Press of Kansas, 1991), 40–58.

The Antebellum West

A Texas Slave's Letter to Her Husband, 1862

Because most slaves could not read and write, only rarely do we have the opportunity to read the thoughts expressed by someone in bondage. Fanny Perry, a Harrison County, Texas, slave woman has provided one such opportunity with the letter she wrote to her husband, Norfleet Perry, personal servant of Theophilus Perry, who at the time was serving with the 28th Texas Cavalry in Arkansas. Here is Fanny's letter of December 28, 1862. We do not know if she and Norfleet were reunited during or after the Civil War.

Spring Hill, Dec. 28th 1862

My Dear Husband,

I would be mighty glad to see you and I wish you would write back here and let me know how you are getting on. I am doing tolerable well and have enjoyed very good health since you left. I haven't forgot you nor I never will forget you as long as the world stands, even if you forget me. My love is just as great as it was the first night I married you, and I hope it will be so with you. My heart and love is pinned to your breast, and I hope yours is to mine. If I never see you again, I hope to meet you in Heaven. There is not time night or day but what I am studying about you. I haven't had a letter from you in some time. I am very anxious to hear from you. I heard once that you were sick but I heard afterwards that you had got well. I hope your health will be good hereafter. Master gave us three days Christmas. I wish you could have been here to enjoy it with me for I did not enjoy myself much because you were not here. I went up to Miss Ock's to a candy stew last Friday night, I wish you could have been here to have gone with me. I know I would have enjoyed myself so much better. Mother, Father, Grandmama, Brothers & Sisters say Howdy and they hope you will do well. Be sure to answer this soon for I am always glad to hear from you. I hope it will not be long before you can come home.

Your Loving Wife
Fanny

Source: Randolph B. Campbell and Donald K. Pickens, "'My Dear Husband,' a Texas Slave's Love Letter, 1862," *Journal of Negro History* 65 (Fall 1980): 361–64.

CHAPTER 4

Mining a Mythic Past

THE HISTORY OF MARY ELLEN PLEASANT

Lynn M. Hudson

More than any other African American woman who lived in the nineteenth-century West, San Francisco entrepreneur Mary Ellen Pleasant (1814–1904) left a tangled legacy. She was called a mammy, madam, voodoo queen, and sorceress during her life, and after her death she was celebrated as the "mother of civil rights in California."[1] Weeding fact from fiction in the life of this remarkable California pioneer proves nearly impossible. Virtually every detail of Pleasant's history has been contested: her birthplace, her parents, her name, her occupation, and her wealth. The latter especially has been the subject of intense speculation on the part of journalists, novelists, folklorists, and historians. Although she figures at critical junctures in U.S. history—the gold rush, John Brown's raid on Harper's Ferry, the Civil War, and the urbanization of the West—she is largely absent from its annals.

Historians have traditionally looked to churches, families, slave quarters, and female societies and clubs to trace nineteenth-century black women's history.[2] But these are not the spaces and institutions where Pleasant is most visible. As an abolitionist and businesswoman, much of Pleasant's work remained hidden. Pleasant chose to mask many of her endeavors and in so doing obscured her allegiances and her wealth.[3]

In an era when wealthy African American women were anomalies, Pleasant's fortune and her interaction with San Francisco's financial elite inspired controversy throughout her life. Her San Francisco business activities ranged from so-called women's work such as operating boardinghouses to male-centered endeavors such as investing in quicksilver mines and real estate. She helped to finance major enterprises that shaped the western economy in the second half of the nineteenth century, often employing tactics common to the robber barons of this era: stock speculation and insider trading. But while using the tactics normally associated with the Rockefellers and Carnegies, Pleasant also adopted strategies that fell outside the realm of traditional business practices—strategies most often practiced by those on the margins of the economy.[4] Parlaying businessmen's secrets revealed in her boardinghouses into capital became one of her most successful techniques.

Pleasant published her autobiography in 1901 in the short-lived journal, the *Pandex of the Press*. In this brief narrative, she carefully revealed selected details of her past:

> I was born on the nineteenth day of August, 1814. Some people have reported that I was born in slavery, but as a matter of fact I was born in Philadelphia, at number 9 Barley Street. My parents, as nearly as I know, must have been a strange mixture. My father was a native Kanaka and my mother a full-blooded Louisiana negress. Both were of large frame, but I think I must have got my physical strength from my father, who was, like most of his race, a giant in frame.[5]

Pleasant's focus on race and physical characteristics and her vagueness about her youth sparked tremendous speculation. Some biographers claim she masked her slave status, while others believe that she was freeborn. It was not unusual for African Americans to conceal their slave past. Fugitive slaves in particular had to hide, steal, and conceal themselves and their identities after the passage of the Fugitive Slave Act in 1850.[6] Pleasant's relationship to slavery remains a strong if uncertain part of her legacy: she is purported by some to have been born a slave, to have alerted slaves to John Brown's raid, and to have hidden escaped slaves in California. Although we can be fairly sure of the last two points, there is no evidence available that confirms Pleasant's status at birth.[7] Given the multiplicity of tales that have surfaced regarding Pleasant's birthplace and slave status, it seems safe to assume that Pleasant did not want the details revealed or did not know the details herself.

As a young girl, Pleasant worked on the island of Nantucket for a woman named Mary Hussey. In her autobiography, Pleasant invested these years with tremendous significance in terms of shaping her future in business:

I was a girl full of smartness and quick at coming back at people when they tried to have a little fun talking with me. I suppose I got in the habit of talking too much, for when young people find they can raise a laugh they are liable to talk too much. . . . All this brought customers to the shop, and I would call people in and get them to buy things of me. I was always on the watch, and few people ever got by that shop without buying something of me.[8]

Although Pleasant highlighted her skills and business acumen, it is also the case that she, like many free and enslaved African Americans, struggled to educate herself.

Pleasant bemoaned the fact that she was refused a formal education. "When my father sent me to live with the Husseys, he also gave them . . . plenty of money to have me educated, but they did not use it for that purpose," she explained, "and that's how I came to have no education."[9] Although there were schools for girls on Nantucket in the 1820s and 1830s, they were not open to African Americans.[10]

Pleasant married in the late 1830s or early 1840s.[11] In an 1895 interview she described her first husband, James Smith, as "a foreman, carpenter and contractor, who had a good business and possessed considerable means."[12] There is little agreement about James Smith's identity and background; some described him as European, others as Cuban.[13] One characteristic of the first husband, about which all the sources agree, however, is his penchant for abolitionist work. Whatever his background, Smith committed himself to the fight against slavery. When he died in 1844, he was a wealthy man whose will left at least $15,000 to his wife, Mary Ellen, for the purpose of continuing their abolitionist endeavors.[14]

Between the death of her first husband and her arrival in San Francisco during the gold rush, Mary Ellen met and married John James Pleasants. Stories about his background are as murky as those about the first husband. Mary Ellen testified in court in the 1860s that she had married John in 1847 in Nantucket.[15] Census records reveal that John was born in Virginia and that he was a waiter in New Bedford, Massachusetts, in 1850. It is possible that Mary Ellen and John met in New Bedford, a hotbed of abolitionist activity where others, including Frederick Douglass, took refuge.[16]

With the discovery of gold in California in 1848, the possibilities for African Americans seemed limitless. Like thousands of other migrants, the Pleasants were tempted by stories of riches that could be had in the new territory of the

United States. The dangers of the Fugitive Slave Act of 1850 also propelled them West. Stories of free blacks being harassed or enslaved were common after the bill became law. Certainly the fact that California became a free rather than slave state in 1850 made it more attractive to abolitionists like the Pleasants who were leaving the East. The combination of economic opportunities and sweeping social changes may have encouraged the Pleasants to seek a new home in the Far West.[17]

Mary Ellen and John may not have always lived together during their marriage. She set up household with John Pleasants—later the *s* was dropped— in California. By 1865 John was listed in the San Francisco directory as a resident and cook on the steamship *Orizaba*. Whatever their precise arrangement, Mary Ellen and John Pleasant would set up household together intermittently for more than twenty years, work together as abolitionists in Canada, and launch a legal battle against discrimination in California in the 1860s.

In 1866 Mary Ellen and John Pleasant initiated a lawsuit against the North Beach & Mission Railroad Company (NBMRR). They accused the NBMRR of refusing to allow people of African descent to board their streetcars. By initiating this lawsuit, Mary Ellen Pleasant also joined the concerted efforts of black San Franciscans to end discrimination and harassment on the city's streetcars. Pleasant's litigation against the NBMRR lasted for nearly two years. The first hearing resulted in a victory; the Twelfth District Court determined that Pleasant was "willfully and purposefully deprived by the defendant of the exercise of a plain legal right" and awarded Pleasant $500 in damages. The company appealed and the case was heard before the California supreme court, which reversed the lower court's decision and ruled in favor of the streetcar company. The court found that the damages that had been awarded were excessive. Although Pleasant argued that she had suffered damages to mind and body, the court was not convinced. In the post–Civil War era, harms inflicted on African Americans by Jim Crow and white supremacy were immense, and Pleasant's effort to draw attention to these was successful if not legally sanctioned.[18]

Pleasant's insistence on equal treatment on public transportation in the 1860s politicized public space during Reconstruction. Throughout the next three decades, Pleasant would fight several battles in San Francisco's public arenas—especially the courtrooms. Demanding her rights as a citizen remained a constant focus of Pleasant's life. Her public appearances in court made headlines throughout the century. This is the place, paradoxically, where her power and status were most visible; it is also the place where she would be stripped of both.

The year the state supreme court overturned Pleasant's streetcar case, 1868, was also the first year she listed herself as a boardinghouse keeper in the city directory. In previous years, she described her occupation as a "domestic." This indicates an important shift in Pleasant's occupation but also in her self-perception and in the way she presented herself to the public. Pleasant transformed herself from a worker into an entrepreneur—a transition very few black women of her day experienced. Most San Franciscans knew Mary Ellen Pleasant as a boardinghouse keeper, a role not unusual for African American women of the era.[19] This occupation was the one most San Franciscans recognized as the role that best described Mary Ellen Pleasant. It also meshed nicely for some with the stereotype of a mammy—the other role with which she is most often associated.

In 1869 Pleasant moved to 920 Washington Street, near the city's central plaza, where she established a boardinghouse that would be her most successful and most elaborate business enterprise.[20] The plaza, officially called Portsmouth Square, bordered Washington, Kearny, Clay, and Dupont (now Grant) Streets; Pleasant's establishment was on the corner of Washington and Dupont. Her property was strategically placed near the city hall, the opera, and the largest gambling house and attracted businessmen, politicians, and investors.[21] Pleasant's forays to the markets, banks, shops, and courts could easily be observed from the city center, as could the galas and meetings that took place at 920 Washington.

Although operating boardinghouses was a common occupation for women in San Francisco, Pleasant, more than any other female innkeeper or boardinghouse operator, maintained high visibility among the city's elite. According to one source, 920 Washington Street was known for its "fine food and wines and its mysterious, lavishly furnished upstairs rooms."[22] This house, temporarily the home of several of the state's leading politicians, brought Pleasant political as well as financial capital. When Newton Booth, one of Pleasant's admirers and a boarder at Washington Street, was elected the new governor of California in 1871, Pleasant threw a party and boasted, "This is Governor Booth who has been elected from my house."[23]

According to the 1870 census, Pleasant owned at least $15,000 worth of real estate and $15,000 in personal assets. While she invested in both gold and silver mines, she also profited by providing a private venue for the most successful investors of the day: the Bonanza Kings and their compatriots who demanded exclusive establishments in which to conduct their business transactions.[24] These men frequented her boardinghouses and revealed information—financial and social—that Pleasant used to further her own enterprise. Pleasant's use of private space for furthering her business played on the naive assumptions of her clientele—that "domestics" would not understand financial affairs.[25] The ways in which Pleasant exploited gendered and racialized codes of behavior constituted one of her most profitable strategies.

Pleasant entered into a new phase of her life in the 1870s. She continued to buy property and appear at philanthropic functions associated with the city's African American institutions but moved her home and headquarters to a hill above the city center.[26] At a time when many African Americans in the United States experienced a retreat from civil rights and the promise of citizenship, Pleasant reached her financial zenith. Pleasant's experience, and that of other black women entrepreneurs such as banker Maggie Lena Walker, shifts the traditional periodization that interprets the post-Reconstruction period as an era associated solely with African American defeat.[27]

Pleasant benefited directly and indirectly from the huge profits made during the Comstock mining boom in the 1860s and 1870s. The San Francisco Stock Exchange opened in 1862 in response to Nevada's emerging silver industry, and profits from the Comstock transferred directly to San Francisco bankers and investors.[28] Pleasant's rise to prominence in financial and philanthropic circles can be attributed in part to this general economic trend. A keen manipulator of real estate and mining stock, Pleasant also associated with members of the elite investors in the Comstock and other silver mines. Her fortune and her livelihood became linked with one banker in particular, the Scottish immigrant Thomas Bell, vice president of the Bank of California, the financial institution that amassed the greatest profits from the Comstock.[29] Pleasant and Bell had met earlier, and by the 1870s they had become financial partners when he took quarters in her new mansion.

The house that Pleasant built straddled the corner of Octavia and Bush Streets just west of the city's business district. This opulently furnished, multistory Victorian mansion inspired fantastic speculation regarding its worth. The historian Lerone Bennett values the house at $100,000 at the time of construction, sometime in 1877. This seems likely given the size of the house—more than ten rooms—and the fact that the property encompassed two city blocks.[30] Pleasant's mansion and Thomas Bell's residence in it made for intense speculation by her contemporaries. The press quickly labeled her residence the "House of Mystery" and never ceased remarking on its secrets. Long after her death in 1904 the Pleasant mansion continued to fascinate San Franciscans. In 1939 San Francisco author and newspaper columnist, Charles Dobie, wrote:

Just to pass this house inspired me with an exquisite terror. Its mystery was not the mystery of ghosts but the mystery of flesh and blood enchantment. People were reputed to live beneath its frowning mansard roof but the only person I ever saw emerge was the black witch who held them all enthralled.[31]

Typical of much popular culture that takes Pleasant as its subject, this passage associates her with witchcraft and danger.[32]

Speculation about a sexual liaison between Pleasant and Bell subsided when he married a young protégée of Pleasant's, Teresa Clingan. After 1878 the three of them, and eventually the Bell children, all lived in the house Pleasant built on Octavia Street. Pleasant was assumed by many to be the "mammy" of the household, with Thomas and Teresa Bell serving as master and mistress. This masquerade proved advantageous for Pleasant, at least for a time. Disguising herself as the household servant, Pleasant in fact managed a vast economic enterprise involving multiple properties, tenants, and investments.

Pleasant's account books from this period reveal the vast sums required to maintain the Octavia Street house. She spent exorbitant sums on supplies for the house, including lumber, water, dairy products, and meat, as well as finery like lace and jewelry.[33] San Franciscans watched Pleasant bargain and trade all over town. Customarily, Pleasant would travel in her carriage driven by coachman James Allen, "dressed in a livery of a long black coat, white breeches, and a top hat."[34] Pleasant's visits to town with liveryman and horses in tow were a familiar sight in Gilded Age San Francisco; it would become even more so as she entered into the most publicized role of her life, witness and confidante of Sarah Althea Hill.

Although Pleasant's streetcar case had generated statewide notoriety among civil rights advocates, her courtroom appearances in the 1880s would attract the attention of columnists and legal pundits across the country.[35] Sarah Althea Hill, an Irish American woman, sued William Sharon, one of the West's wealthiest men, for divorce. The resulting litigation, in which Pleasant played a central role, took on a circuslike atmosphere.[36] Pleasant's status, her place in San Francisco society, and her financial power became fodder for columnists for the rest of her life.

The first case, *Sharon v. Sharon*, hinged on the question of whether Sharon and Hill had been legally married in August 1880. Mary Ellen Pleasant testified that she had seen the marriage contract. Sarah's relationship to Pleasant proved a substantial issue for Sharon's defense team, led by William Barnes. In March 1884 Barnes's opening statement included the following declaration:

> We will show how [Sarah] visited the sanctums of fortune tellers, negroes, Germans, French and every race. We shall show how she obtained a pair of Sharon's dirty socks and had them charmed by a negro. . . . She disclosed her secrets to a colored woman and did not confide in a relative.[37]

This legal strategy—linking African Americans with the occult and using Sarah's contact with Pleasant in particular to discredit her—was the premise on which the defense built its case. Sarah Hill's choice of Pleasant as her chief confidante proved her singular lack of judgment, argued Sharon's attorneys. "Will anybody tell me," asked Barnes, "why it was that this unfortunate woman confided the secret of her marriage to not one respectable person of her color, class, or rank in life?"[38]

Pleasant's role in the divorce case carried considerable weight, as demonstrated by Sharon's efforts to discredit her. Attorneys summoned her to the witness stand on at least five occasions. Although Pleasant was accused of operating a ring of voodoo practitioners to trick Sharon into marriage, her testimony had nothing to do with potions or charms but focused on the viability of the marriage contract.

Descriptions of Pleasant's significance in the case varied; in the early days of the trial Barnes described her as peddler of "luxurious articles of female underwear."[39] After a full year of legal battles, however, Barnes reasoned that Pleasant was "the sole financier of the anti-Sharon syndicate."[40] The shift in emphasis is noteworthy; initially the defense employed slavelike imagery of a lace-peddling mammy to describe Pleasant. But by 1885 this image had been replaced by that of a crafty manipulator of the legal system.

On December 24, 1884, the judge ruled that the marriage contract was valid and Sarah was thus entitled to a divorce and alimony. He awarded Sarah $2,500 a month and $55,000 in attorneys' fees.[41] A federal decision soon overturned Sarah's brief victory, marking the end of Pleasant's and Hill's efforts to divest Sharon of his fortune.[42] Following Sharon's death in 1885, Sarah married one of her attorneys, David Terry, a former California supreme court justice. When Terry was murdered in 1889, Sarah's health rapidly declined. By 1892 journalists described her as "hopelessly insane." Pleasant attended to Sarah at the house on Octavia Street. Mrs. Sarah Terry told reporters that Pleasant's house provided her sanctuary.[43] And although Pleasant survived the Sharon trials with person and property intact, members of the Bell household were waiting in the wings to divest her of both.

In 1891 Pleasant bought Beltane, a sprawling ranch in the Sonoma Valley where she spent weekends and holidays.[44] Then in her eighties, she experienced long periods of illness, as evidenced by the house calls of her physician, Peter A. Kearney.[45] Friends and well-wishers traveled to the ranch and to her San Francisco home for regular visits. But Pleasant's relationship with her boarders and co-mortgage holders, the Bells, deteriorated in these years, as did her mask as the Bells' servant.

After nearly two decades of living in the mansard-roofed mansion on Octavia Street, the family and business enterprise of Thomas Bell, Teresa Bell, the Bell children, and Mary Ellen Pleasant collapsed. In 1897, five years after Thomas Bell had died, the eldest of the Bell children, Fred, petitioned the courts to have his mother removed as legal guardian of the children.[46] The petition charged that Teresa Bell's business affairs were "being controlled and directed by . . . M. E. Pleasant, who is a negro woman at the age of eighty-three years or thereabouts, and neither fit or a proper person to guide, control, or direct any person other than herself."[47] The petition forced Pleasant, once again, to appear before judges, reporters, and onlookers. Angered by the accusations, she told reporters what she thought of Fred's case: "[T]his suit has been brought by Fred because some enemies of ours have urged him on, and his action is too shameful to speak about."[48]

Fred Bell's legal action brought Pleasant's financial and personal relationship to the Bells under intense scrutiny for the first time. Once again her name was splashed across newspaper headlines, and once again the press scrutinized her relationship with a white woman—this time Teresa Bell. The issue of Pleasant's control over Teresa drove Fred's case from the beginning. As Fred's attorney explained, "[Fred] wants to destroy the power of 'Mammy' Pleasant and show her up to people in her true colors."[49] Previously described as the servant of the Bell household, newspaper accounts now characterized her in more sinister terms. One headline captured the new interpretation: "Porterhouse for Mammy, Soup Meat for the Family." According to one of the servants, Pleasant and Teresa Bell "fared sumptuously on Oysters, terrapin, chickens, quail, and porterhouse steaks," while the children were fed stale bread. Pleasant, explained the servant, "ran the whole house to suit herself."[50] There was more than a grain of truth to this depiction as the house in question belonged to Pleasant.

Pleasant's description of herself in this case varied little from the one she gave during the Sharon trials: she characterized herself as a servant of the Bell household. When questioned about Teresa Bell's presence, she described Mrs. Bell as her "mistress" and "the noble woman." Pleasant's reputation as a simple servant, however, repeatedly came under attack during the litigation.

The courtroom was not the only place Pleasant took center stage in the 1890s. She was also the subject of several press exposés, most notably a two-page feature article in the Sunday edition of the *San Francisco Chronicle* entitled "Queen of the Voodoos." This piece appeared as Pleasant's creditors whittled away at her fortune and successfully rendered her an "insolvent debtor" in the city's courts. In addition to describing bizarre voodoo rituals that Pleasant supposedly used on unsuspecting victims of her greed, the article questioned Pleasant's poverty, thus exacerbating her financial problems. The article, attributed to James E. Brown Jr., a former employee of Pleasant's, drew attention to Pleasant's efforts to dodge her creditors.[51] With such knowledge coming from someone close to Pleasant, it is hardly surprising that her fortune dwindled quickly in the coming years.

Pleasant responded to the various allegations as best she could. While contesting the claim that she practiced voodoo, through a letter to one of the judges in Fred Bell's lawsuit, she attempted to explain her role in the financial affairs of the Bell family. "Mr. Bell would have soon silenced those who said I had too much influence," she wrote. "I have a good deal to say about the executors and lawyer for the Bell estate—selling [the] assets to pay their own debts."[52] Determined to rescue her diminished fortune and tarnished reputation, Pleasant lashed out at the courts, lawyers, and creditors. "I have said to them, to the principals themselves[,] . . . I would rather be a corpse than a coward!" she wrote to the judge. "[N]ow this woman who has respect for the right and the truth would like to have you use your influence." The judge quickly silenced Pleasant, deeming her role in managing the financial affairs of the Bell estate inappropriate given her status as a "servant."[53] Moreover, having disguised for years her ownership of the Octavia Street house as well as mining stocks and other assets by commingling her property with the holdings of Thomas Bell, it was now impossible for her to establish her rightful claim to the mansion. After a series of subsequent lawsuits and a dramatic break with Teresa Bell, Mary Ellen Pleasant lost control of her Octavia Street house and moved to her other properties.

Pleasant lived the last five years of her life at Geneva Cottage, her residence on San Jose Road, just south of San Francisco, and in a house she owned on

Webster Street. The *San Francisco Examiner* claimed that she raised chickens and pigs at Geneva Cottage during these years as part of her effort to feign poverty.[54] In November 1903 Pleasant moved to the home of friends, Olive and Lyman Sherwood, who resided on Filbert Street. On January 11, 1904, at ten o'clock in the morning, Pleasant died at the home of her friends. Peter A. Kearney, her longtime physician, signed the death certificate. Pleasant's estate, when it was finally settled six years later, was valued at $10,000—a far cry from the millions she once owned.[55]

By the end of her life, Mary Ellen Pleasant had lost a considerable amount of property and capital to creditors and lawyers. Because of the tangled nature of the Bell and Pleasant finances and because she owned much of her property in partnership with others, the exact amount of her estate will never be known. Given that Thomas Bell was worth more than $30 million when he died in 1892—and Bell and Pleasant owned stock and property in common—we can assume that Pleasant was at least a millionaire, making her exceptional among nineteenth-century black women and certainly among black women in the West.[56]

Pleasant continues to fascinate San Franciscans and the press. This powerful financier provided fodder for novelists, filmmakers, and columnists throughout the twentieth century. Pleasant thought she had a better chance of holding on to her business enterprises by claiming the mask of mammy—the one role most white Americans recognized as appropriate for black women in Victorian America. But the few wealthy African American women of the era were easy targets for those concerned with maintaining white supremacy, and in this regard Pleasant's mask provided no protection.

NOTES

1. Lerone Bennett, "An Historical Detective Story: The Mystery of Mary Ellen Pleasant," Parts I and II, *Ebony* (April–May 1979): 90–96, 71–86.

2. Darlene Clark Hine, "Lifting the Veil, Shattering the Silence: Black Women's History in Slavery and Freedom," in *The State of Afro-American History: Past, Present, and Future*, ed. Darlene Clark Hine (Baton Rouge: Louisiana State University Press, 1986), 223–49.

3. For an incisive discussion of African American women and self-fashioning, see Nell Irvin Painter, *Sojourner Truth: A Life, a Symbol* (New York: W. W. Norton, 1996).

4. On black entrepreneurship, see Juliet E. K. Walker, "Racism, Slavery, and Free Enterprise: Black Entrepreneurship in the United States," *Business History Review* 60 (Autumn 1986): 343–82.

5. Mary Ellen Pleasant, "Memoirs and Autobiography," *Pandex of the Press* 1 (January 1902): 5.

6. For an example of slaves who disguised themselves to escape, see the chapter on William and Mary Craft in R. J. M. Blackett, *Beating against the Barriers: The Lives of Six Nineteenth-Century Afro-Americans* (Baton Rouge: Louisiana State University Press, 1986), 86–137.

7. Pleasant lived for a time in Chatham, Canada, where John Brown and other abolitionists planned the raid on Harper's Ferry. She became a part of this community and donated her time and probably her resources to Brown's cause. See Sam Davis, "How a Colored Woman Aided John Brown," *Inquirer and Mirror* 26 (December 1901); Earl Conrad, "She Was a Friend of John Brown," *Negro World Digest* (November 1940): 6–11; and J. Peter Ripley, *The Black Abolitionist Papers II* (Chapel Hill: University of North Carolina Press, 1986), 393, 398.

8. Pleasant, "Memoirs," 5.

9. Ibid., 6.

10. Barbara Linebaugh, *The African School and the Integration of Nantucket Public Schools, 1825–1847* (Boston: Afro-American Studies Center, 1978).

11. Some believe Pleasant and Smith were married in Saint Mary's Church in Boston. Pleasant claimed she sang in the choir of Saint Mary's. See Davis, "How a Colored Woman Aided John Brown."

12. *San Francisco Examiner*, October 13, 1895.

13. Bennett, "An Historical Detective Story, Part II," 72–73.

14. The sum of money bequeathed to her by her first husband is also the subject of wild speculation. Many claim that it was as much as $30,000; one source claims it was $40,000. And a San Francisco author alleged the amount was $45,000. Pleasant told a reporter that she brought $15,000 in gold coin with her from the East when she traveled to California in 1850. Even the latter amount would have been a tremendous sum for anyone to invest in the gold rush era. See J. Lloyd Conrich, "The Mammy Pleasant Legend," unpublished manuscript, no date, California Historical Society, 19; and Bennett, "An Historical Detective Story, Part II," 74.

15. *Pleasants v. North Beach and Mission Railroad Company*, Appeal, 1867, California State Archives, Sacramento. Pleasant said that after her first husband died, she went back to Nantucket to live with Edward and Phoebe Gardner. See Helen Holdredge letter to Edward Stackpole, April 9, 1951, Nantucket Historical Association. This letter, like many of Holdredge's notebooks, indicates that Holdredge had access to Pleasant's diaries or letters that are now missing or destroyed.

16. 1850 Bristol County Census, roll 309, 272; New Bedford was the destination of many fugitive slaves on the Underground Railroad, including Frederick Douglass. Douglass first took refuge at the home of David Ruggles in New York, who suggested he might find New Bedford more hospitable for fugitive slaves. See Frederick Douglass, *Narrative of the Life of Frederick Douglass* in *The Classic Slave Narratives*, ed. Henry Louis Gates Jr. (New York: Penguin, 1987), 323–26.

17. To date, one of the studies that best illuminates the intricacies of the process of conquest in California is Lisbeth Haas, *Conquests and Historical Identities in California, 1769–1936* (Berkeley: University of California Press, 1995).

18. See *John and Mary Pleasants v. NBMRR*, June 20, 1867, California State Archives, Sacramento. Several other cases of streetcar discrimination in San Francisco occurred before Pleasant's case. See *Pacific Appeal*, May 10, 1862, and March 14, 1863. When, nearly a century later, California revised its civil rights legislation, Pleasant's case would be brought to the fore. A 1958 article in the *Stanford Law Review* cited *Pleasants v. NBMRR* to demonstrate that "an aggrieved party faces an almost insurmountable burden of proof in seeking to show that a refusal to admit him to, or a discrimination in the use of facilities of, or entertainment resulted in measurable damages for which he is entitled to compensation." See Ronald P. Klein, "Equal Rights Statutes," *Stanford Law Review* 10 (March 1958): 253–73.

19. On the role of African American women as boardinghouse keepers, see Michael Coray, "Blacks in the Pacific West, 1850–1860: A View from the Census," *Nevada Historical Society Quarterly* 28 (Summer 1985): 109–10; Mikel Hogan Garcia, "Adaptation Strategies of the Los Angeles Black Community, 1883–1919" (Ph.D. dissertation, University of California, Irvine, 1985), 50; and Elizabeth H. Pleck, *Black Migration and Poverty: Boston, 1865–1900* (New York: Academic Press, 1979), 191.

20. *San Francisco City Directory*, 1869–70.

21. For a description of the plaza, see Philip J. Ethington, *The Public City: The Political Construction of Urban Life in San Francisco* (Cambridge: Cambridge University Press, 1994), 6–7.

22. Gunther Barth, *Instant Cities: Urbanization and the Rise of San Francisco and Denver* (Albuquerque: University of New Mexico Press, 1988), 298; Margaret S. Woyski, "Women and Mining in the Old West," *Journal of the West* 20 (April 1981): 44; Conrich, "The Mammy Pleasant Legend," 46.

23. The U.S. Census of 1870 lists Newton Booth as a resident of 920 Washington Street, San Francisco; Bennett, "An Historical Detective Story, Part II," 79.

24. Because of her complicated financial relationship with Thomas Bell, much of Pleasant's mining activities must be inferred from the sources. See Mary Ellen Pleasant Collections, San Francisco Public Library (SFPL) and the Bancroft Library, University of California, Berkeley.

25. For a fascinating, although fictional, account of this strategy of Pleasant's, see Frank Yerby, *Devilseed* (Garden City, N.Y.: Doubleday, 1984), 175–76.

26. For information on Pleasant's philanthropic activities, see, e.g., *Pacific Appeal*, September 10, 1870, November 19, 1870, January 1, 1871, September 2, 1871, August 30, 1873, and May 9, 1874.

27. Elsa Barkley Brown, "Womanist Consciousness: Maggie Lena Walker and the Independent Order of Saint Luke," *Signs* 14 (Spring 1989): 610–33.

28. William Issel and Robert W. Cherny, *San Francisco: Politics, Power, and Urban Development, 1865–1932* (Berkeley: University of California Press, 1986), 23.

29. Bennett describes Pleasant as "that brilliant and knowing manipulator of Western mining stock" and claims that she turned Bell into a "financial tiger." Bennett, "An Historical Detective Story, Part II," 84.

30. Bennett, "An Historical Detective Story, Part II," 84; Mary Ellen Pleasant Collection, SFPL.

31. Charles Caldwell Dobie, *San Francisco: A Pageant* (New York: D. Appleton-Century, 1939), 316.

32. See Lynn M. Hudson, "When 'Mammy' Becomes A Millionaire: Mary Ellen Pleasant, An African-American Entrepreneur" (Ph.D. dissertation, Indiana University, 1996), chap. 5.

33. Mary Ellen Pleasant Papers, Bancroft Library, University of California, Berkeley; and SFPL.

34. Interview with Charlotte Downs, Mary Ellen Pleasant Collection, SFPL. Downs knew Pleasant when she was a little girl and told Helen Holdredge, "I was in and out of the Bell house from the time it was built."

35. Robert Kroninger, *Sarah and the Senator* (Berkeley: Howell-North Books, 1964), 15. Kroninger notes that "with the aid of the new nationwide wire service," newspapers across the country followed the trials.

36. For clarity, I will refer to Sarah Althea Hill as Hill, although she claimed to be "Mrs. Sharon" and was eventually Mrs. Terry. Soon after Hill sued Sharon for divorce, resulting in *Sharon v. Sharon*, Mr. Sharon countered with a suit in federal court, *Sharon v. Hill*.

37. Transcript of W. H. L. Barnes, *Sharon v. Sharon*, San Francisco Superior Court, 1884, Bancroft Library, University of California, Berkeley.

38. Ibid.

39. Ibid.

40. Transcript of Argument of William M. Stewart, *Sharon v. Hill*, Ninth District, 1885, Bancroft Library, University of California, Berkeley.

41. Kroninger, *Sarah and the Senator*, 158.

42. See Transcript on Appeal, *Sharon v. Sharon*, California Supreme Court, 1885, California State Archives.

43. *San Francisco Chronicle*, February 14, 1892.

44. Mary Ellen Pleasant Collection, SFPL. See also Thomas and Teresa Bell papers, California Historical Society, San Francisco.

45. Teresa Bell Diary, Mary Ellen Pleasant Papers, SFPL.

46. There were six Bell children, ranging in age from twenty-two to thirteen, at the time of the trial.

47. As quoted in *San Francisco Call*, September 15, 1897.

48. *San Francisco Chronicle*, September 9, 1897.

49. Ibid.

50. Ibid., September 10 and 16, 1897.

51. Ibid., July 9, 1899.

52. Quoted in *San Francisco Call*, November 9, 1899.

53. Ibid.

54. *San Francisco Examiner*, January 12, 1904.

55. *San Francisco Call*, April 16, 1910; Conrich, "The Mammy Pleasant Legend," 177.

56. By comparison, the estate of Los Angeles entrepreneur Biddy Mason, also a black woman, was valued at $300,000 in 1896. See Lawrence B. De Graaf, "Race, Sex, and Region: Black Women in the West, 1850–1920," *Pacific Historical Review* 49 (May

1980): 285–313; see also Loren Schweninger, "Property-owning Free African-American Women in the South, 1800–1870," *Journal of Women's History* 1 (Winter 1990): 13–44; and Willard Gatewood, *Aristocrats of Color: The Black Elite, 1880–1920* (Bloomington: Indiana University Press, 1990).

A Voice from the Oppressed to the Friends of Humanity

The precarious citizenship of African American Californians generated a partially successful civil rights campaign. Because the situation for free blacks in the state—and the nation—seemed increasingly dismal, some California blacks began to explore the possibly of a mass emigration to British Columbia. By 1858 approximately four hundred blacks, about 10 percent of the state's black population, left San Francisco bound for Victoria, British Columbia, and freedom. The poem below, written by Priscilla Stewart, one of the emigrants, captures the mood of the times.

A Voice from the Oppressed to the Friends of Humanity

Composed by one of the suffering class.
Mrs. Priscilla Stewart

Look and behold our sad despair
Our hopes and prospects fled;
The tyrant slavery entered here,
And laid us all for dead.

Sweet home! When shall we find a home?
If the tyrant says that we must go
The love of gain the reason,
And if humanity dare say "No"
Then they are tried for treason.

God bless the Queen's majesty,
Her scepter and her throne,
She looked on us with sympathy
And offered us a home.

Source: Delilah Beasley, *The Negro Trail Blazers of California* (Los Angeles, 1919), 263.

Far better breathe Canadian air
Where all are free and well,
Than live in slavery's atmosphere
And wear the chains of hell.

Farewell to our native land,
We must wave the parting hand,
Never to see thee any more,
But seek a foreign land.

Farewell to our true friends,
Who've suffered dungeon and death.
Who have a claim upon our gratitude
Whilst God shall lend us breath.

May God inspire your hearts,
A Marion raise your hands;
Never desert your principles
Until you've redeemed your land.

CHAPTER 5

Rights of Passage

GENDERED-RIGHTS CONSCIOUSNESS AND THE QUEST FOR FREEDOM, SAN FRANCISCO, CALIFORNIA, 1850–1870

Barbara Y. Welke

The right to travel is a fundamental aspect of freedom. Examples abound in nineteenth-century America—immigrants fleeing the failed revolutions of 1848 in Europe and escaping by ship across the Atlantic to America, the thousands who headed west on the Oregon Trail in the 1850s. Equally cogent is the counterexample of blacks held as slaves in the American South; one marker of their lack of freedom was the restraint imposed on their movements. Outside the South, in urban America during the nineteenth century, the right to travel on public conveyances was equally crucial to freedom. Streetcars were to city size what steel was to building height. Just as steel had allowed buildings to rise more than three or four stories high, streetcars allowed cities to expand.[1] The right to ride on streetcars determined in part where a person could live, shop, work, and socialize. As geographic separation of work and family life became one component of status in urban America, exclusion from public transport blocked access to physical mobility and personal status. Exclusion from public transport was a badge of unfreedom; it narrowed the avenues of that most hallowed American value, opportunity.

Seen in these terms, "free" blacks outside the American South in the nineteenth century were not in fact free. In cities across the North, streetcar companies

adopted policies prohibiting blacks from riding on their cars.[2] More surprising
to the many blacks who had headed west in search of a frontier free of racial
hatred and bias was the speed with which the civil inequalities they suffered
under in the Northeast were replicated in western states.[3] In the years just
before, during, and after the Civil War, in courtrooms throughout the North
and West, African Americans brought lawsuits challenging company policies
that forbade them from riding on streetcars. Through these lawsuits, the right
to travel became a central, critical component of African Americans' struggle
for freedom.

Black San Franciscans' lawsuits demanding the right to equal access to public
transit in the 1860s fit into this larger movement. Throughout the nineteenth
century, the city of San Francisco had the largest black population in California,
accounting for roughly 1 percent of the city's population. It was the leading
center of black social, cultural, political, and economic life and was home to the
leading figures in the California civil rights movement. As the historian Albert
Broussard has aptly noted, "[O]rganized black protest was an integral part of
San Francisco's heritage."[4] If blacks were to participate fully in the life of the
city, the right of equal access to public transit was a practical necessity.[5]

The most striking aspect of the legal battle for access to public transit is the
extent to which it was led by black women and fought on the terrain of
respectable women's privileges in public space. In San Francisco as elsewhere,
black women brought most of the lawsuits challenging the practice of racial
exclusion in public transit. In both the courts and the white and black press,
the public dialogue over who had a right to ride on streetcars focused on
women. The exclusion of blacks from public transit—and black women's role
in challenging that exclusion—fit neatly into historians' efforts to understand
men's and women's use of and place in public urban space.[6]

My purpose here is to bring forward what has been implicit yet largely
unrecognized in the history of the black civil rights movement in California:
in their quest for freedom and civic equality, black men and women pursued
separate rights defined in the prevailing gendered-rights consciousness of the
time as male or female.[7] In this lexicon of rights, the right to vote was coded
"male," while the right to comfort and safety in public travel was coded
"female." In discussing the battle for civic equality, historians' accounts have
adopted the inclusive labels "blacks" and "the black community," yet their focus
has been primarily on rights that in fact were viewed at the time as men's rights
and the named actors in the drama overwhelming have been men.[8] Gender-
neutral references have masked the significant fact that black men's and

women's adoption of the prevailing gendered-rights consciousness was crucial to the success of the movement as a whole and was vital as well to black men and women publicly defining themselves as gendered individuals.

. . .

In its beginnings, the organized black civil rights movement in California was dominated by men and focused on achieving rights that, in nineteenth-century America, defined manhood. In two of its earliest acts of statehood, the framers of the California Constitution denied black (male) suffrage, and the legislature barred black testimony in criminal and civil suits involving whites. In nineteenth-century America participation in the political process was a defining rite of manhood.[9] To be excluded from exercising those rights was to be emasculated. African American men in California, led by men from San Francisco, responded to the testimony ban and the denial of the right to vote by establishing a political framework, known as the Convention Movement, paralleling that of white men.[10] Through their political activism, they asserted their status as gendered individuals—as men.[11] Moreover, for these men the goal that became the focus of the Convention Movement—repeal of the ban on black testimony—was seen as akin to the right of self-defense, to the right of a man to safeguard his home, his family, his business, his life.[12]

The announcements of the conventions made it clear that those expected to participate were the men of the black community. For example, the published announcement for the 1865 convention was addressed generally "To the Colored Citizens of California," but the very next line limited the meaning of the word "citizens" to black, male citizens. It read, "Men and Brothers: —You are hereby summoned."[13] By omission, black women were excluded from the terms of the invitation. The culture of the conventions was also distinctly masculine. The delegates were all male, the speeches were addressed to "gentlemen,"[14] and finally, the rights that were the focus of the conventions were seen as male rights. For example, in a speech delivered near the end of the second convention, held in 1856, the president of the convention, William H. Hall, addressed the delegates in a speech filled with references to the obligations and rights of men. "The time has arrived when we must act in accordance with the sentiment which governs other men," he stressed. And after listing the rights denied to blacks in California, he announced, "These considerations are humiliating to our manhood."[15]

Black men's battle against the ban on black testimony in civil and criminal suits involving whites achieved success in March 1863, just as the streetcar era began in San Francisco.[16] Until later in the century when cables and electricity supplied the means of locomotion, horses and mules powered streetcars. A single horse could pull only one car no more than fifteen feet long and six feet wide.[17] Given the limited means of locomotion and the fact that streetcar rides tended to be short, it is not surprising that on streetcars, in contrast to the practice in railroad and steamboat travel, there were no separate classes of travel or facilities segregated by sex.

But the lack of formal class and sex distinctions on streetcars masked widely shared assumptions about the gendered and racialized geography of urban public space. As urban growth during the nineteenth century blurred the traditional markers of status, hierarchy, and order, visual markers of difference such as gender and race assumed increased importance. In the mid-nineteenth century, city streets were largely a male domain. As the historian John Kasson explains, "[W]hen middle-class women left the confines of their home to venture out in public, they entered a realm in which they felt—or were expected to feel—particularly vulnerable."[18] In a boomtown such as San Francisco, the potential perils facing a woman in public were even more marked. As late as 1870 men in San Francisco still outnumbered women by a ratio of three to two.[19] Particularly in such a context, being recognized as a lady and enjoying the privileges that followed from that recognition was crucially important to women and to the men related to them. But a woman's status as a lady, her respectability, hinged on her careful observance in public of protocols of dress, gaze, conversation, and movement. If she failed in any detail, she risked being marked and treated as lower class, or worse, as a prostitute.[20]

The conventions regulating respectable women's movements in public space extended to public transit. Although the vast majority of streetcar passengers in this period were male, streetcars offered women a way to move inconspicuously through public space.[21] A woman could leave one female sanctum (e.g., home) and travel quickly to the protection of another (e.g., church). Moreover, while riding on a streetcar, a woman placed herself under the protection of a male conductor and driver. By the 1860s there was already a well-established obligation on the part of public carriers to protect women from offensive contacts.[22] A woman traveling by streetcar avoided not only the exhaustion and filth of dragging her long skirts through muddy city streets but also chance contacts with and "contamination" from unrespectable elements of the urban population.[23]

Blacks were excluded from the privileges of white respectability, including access to public transit. In San Francisco, as in cities throughout the North, streetcar companies adopted policies barring blacks.[24] When San Francisco's Omnibus Railroad Company and North Beach and Mission Railroad Company were organized in 1862 and 1863, both excluded black passengers. Neither company publicly announced their policy; neither put it in writing. The level of informality reflected both the sense of right and power companies felt in matters of race and the nature of corporate organization in the 1860s. The superintendents of both companies merely told their conductors that "colored persons" should not be allowed on the cars. If they got on, they should be asked to leave; if they refused, they should be put off.[25]

Streetcars shared with steamboats and railroads a distinct legal status in nineteenth-century America. Over the course of several centuries of judge-made law, an elaborate common law had developed for entities like common carriers that served public functions, existed at the behest of the state, and yet were privately owned. Streetcars, like steamboats and railroads, were "common carriers"; this legal category expressed their public role in facilitating the right to travel. Stated most generally, the common law required that, provided they had space, common carriers were required to accept all passengers who could pay the fare and to protect their passengers' comfort and safety. There were only a few narrow exceptions to this obligation to carry passengers. Carriers had the right and in some cases the obligation to exclude persons afflicted with contagious diseases, persons of known bad character, and those intent on harming other passengers or on harming the carrier's business.[26]

What had not been tested before the 1850s was whether common carriers could exclude passengers on the basis of "race." Before the San Francisco lawsuits, trial courts in several other states had held that streetcars and other common carriers were legally obligated to accept black passengers.[27] But their verdicts were not uniform, and they were not binding on courts in California; clearly, they had not prevented carriers like the North Beach and Mission and Omnibus Railroad Companies from adopting and enforcing regulations barring blacks.[28]

Within a few months after these railways began operating, the battle was joined.[29] On April 17, 1863, Charlotte Brown, the daughter of a successful black businessman in San Francisco, was forced off one of the cars of the Omnibus company. Before the year was out, she had been ejected two more times. Brown responded to each incident by bringing suit against Omnibus.[30] The month after Brown was first ejected from the Omnibus company's cars, the conductor and driver on one of the North Beach and Mission Railroad Company's cars violently ejected William Bowen, a black man, as he tried to board, even though

Bowen explained that his employer had asked him to take the streetcar and that he only wanted a place on the platform. Bowen brought a civil suit against the company and also filed a criminal assault action.[31] The timing of the incidents, coming fast on the heels of the repeal of the ban on black testimony against whites, might suggest that these were deliberate test cases. More likely, though, as the companies had never announced their policies, the incidents took the black community of San Francisco by surprise. They were not, however, unprepared. Even before the first incident in San Francisco, the black press in the city had reported incidents and lawsuits in other northern cities.[32] In any event, the lawsuits could proceed only because black men's activism in the Convention Movement had moved the California legislature to repeal the testimony ban.

Brown's and Bowen's lawsuits were followed by two more lawsuits by black women, Emma Jane Turner and Mary Ellen Pleasant, in early fall 1866 against the North Beach and Mission Railroad Company. Biographical details about Turner are limited to those in her case record: she was unmarried, could not write her name, was traveling on the cars alone at night after visiting a friend, and had "a bundle of shirts" with her, suggesting that she may have been a laundress. Mary Ellen Pleasant was well known in San Francisco at the time of the incident leading to her suit. A successful businesswoman, Pleasant had long been active in causes for the advancement of her race; she was an active abolitionist, had supported the repeal of the testimony ban, and clearly was not about to let streetcar companies in San Francisco succeed in excluding blacks from public transport.[33] Though the evidentiary record is incomplete, the sequence of events suggests that Turner's and Pleasant's cases may have been coordinated. Both suits were filed on the same day, October 3, 1866. Each involved an incident occurring the previous month.

Both sides in the battle, white efforts to exclude blacks and black efforts to win the right of passage, were fought on the terrain of female gendered rights. The legal and public debate focused primarily on the rights of respectable women to safety, comfort, and protection from contact with "unsafe" men. In the minds of many whites, though, the right to safety included freedom from contact with black women and men. When Charlotte Brown took a seat on a car of the Omnibus Railroad Company on April 17, 1863, the conductor informed her that she would have to get off because "colored persons were not allowed to ride." Three times the conductor had told her she must get off, and at each stop she had refused. Finally, when a white woman boarded the car, the conductor "ushered" Brown off.[34]

In Brown's subsequent lawsuit challenging her expulsion from the car, the company insisted on its right to exclude blacks in order to protect white women and children. Of the thousands of passengers it had carried since it began operation in December 1862, the company explained, "large numbers [were] women and children traveling without any male protection or attendant"; it was "in an especial manner bound to protect [them] from offence[,] annoyance or molestation by contact or otherwise with[in] its cars." The company insisted that the small size of its cars made exclusion the only alternative. Though the front and rear platforms on which the driver and conductor rode might appear to provide an alternative to the interior, they were small (2 by 4 feet), uncomfortable, and dangerous. In other words, all passengers rode in close proximity to one another and there was really no safe place for a passenger repulsed by the presence of a black passenger to go except off the car. Those to whom blacks were most offensive, the company insisted, were "persons of the female sex."[35] In support of this claim, the conductor testified at trial that the passenger who had objected to Brown's presence and asked that she be put off was a woman.[36]

To make its case persuasive, the streetcar company constructed an image of the sexually dangerous black man preying on innocent white girls and women.[37] The company lawyer warned the jurors—all white men—that if you let "him" on the cars, you must sleep in the same bed with "him." He played on their fears and on their duty to protect white women by highlighting the dangers to their daughters of associating with "niggers."[38] In making this argument, the company quite deliberately ignored the fact that the person who had been excluded—Charlotte Brown—was a well-dressed woman traveling alone at dusk.

Some white newspapers in San Francisco played a different variation on the theme of the dangers to white women of black access to streetcars. A cartoon published in one paper after the decision in favor of Charlotte Brown showed two modest white women pathetically crushed between two rough, dark-skinned black men and a big, equally dark-skinned black "mammy," knees spread wide, a big basket in her lap, and a bandanna on her head. The caption read: "Our artist this week gives us a glimpse of that 'good time coming,' when all the narrow distinctions of caste and color shall be abolished, and when our colored brethren shall come into the full inheritance of their rights."[39] Strikingly, whereas both black men and black women are diagrammed taking up substantial space on the limited bench, the only whites in the cartoon are women. Moreover, whereas the caption derided Brown's claim that being "escorted" off a streetcar had hurt her "sensitive feelings . . . to the amount of

$5,000," the image simultaneously implied far greater emotional harm to white women forced to share space with African American passengers (see cartoon).

In the battle for recognition of blacks' right to ride on public transit, blacks too focused on respectability and the rights of "ladies." Given the gendered geography of public space, including passage on streetcars, it is not surprising that black women demanded their right to ride on streetcars and challenged their denial of that right. In nineteenth-century America black women bore the principal burden of "proving" the respectability of their people generally.[40] Moreover, white assumptions of black women's "natural" promiscuity and the presumption that white men had the right of sexual access to black women made it especially important for black women and men alike to have the means of publicly challenging these assumptions—and of assuring black women's physical safety.[41] In forcing black women off the cars, streetcar employees forced them onto the streets, in some cases at night; no place for a "lady."[42] Exclusion or expulsion from a streetcar was a deliberate affront. Thus in demanding the rights of passage, black women were engaged in an intensely political act, and they knew it. When the Omnibus Railroad Company conductor told Charlotte Brown that she could not ride on the car because of her race, she refused to get off. She insisted that she was accustomed to taking the cars, that she was already late for an appointment, that she was tired and had a long way to go, and that she had a "right" to ride.[43]

A black woman's lawsuit challenging her expulsion or exclusion from a streetcar amounted to refusal to accept the image of her created by the streetcar company's refusal to carry her in the first place. The conductor in Mary Pleasant's case had announced loudly, so that the other passengers heard, "We don't take colored people in the cars."[44] Her lawsuit demanded acknowledgment that blacks were entitled to the same privileges as whites. A black woman bringing suit to challenge her exclusion from a streetcar made a very personal claim about her right to be accorded the respect a lady deserved in public.

Activist black men were keenly aware of the power of black women, as women, to go where they, as men, could not. In their pursuit of civil rights for African Americans generally, editors of the black press fully embraced the established lexicon of rights in which some rights were gendered male and others gendered female. They consistently spoke of the right of testimony and the right to vote as rights of manhood. They equally consistently referred to the right to be a passenger, to sit, to be carried on a streetcar as a distinctly female right. For example, an article published in mid-March 1863 in the *Pacific Appeal* angrily began with the report of the refusal of a San Francisco streetcar

THE EFFECT OF JUDGE PRATT'S DECISION.

Our artist this week gives us a glimpse of that "good time coming," when all the narrow distinctions of carte and color shall be abolished, and when our colored bretheren shall come into the full inheritance of their rights,—shall sit in the cars and the dress-circles of our theatres, with none to molest them or make them afraid. For the inauguration of this happy era, we are mainly indebted (under Providence) to Judge Pratt. Poor Charlotte Brown, in spite of the efforts made by the *Gag* to influence the jury, only got one tithe of what she demanded as a salve to her injured feelings. She said that her sensitive feelings were hurt to the amount of $5,000 by being led out of the car by a conductor, and a jury only gave her $500. Try again, Charlotte, you may do better next time; and above all don't pay the editor of the *Gag* to write editorials in your favor. It will only injure your case. You owe a lasting debt of gratitude to Judge Pratt for putting you in the way of making an honest penny. He is very partial to niggers, is the Judge, the darker the complexion the better it suits Pratt and the family. You are a *real* nigger, are you not, Charlotte? You did not use burnt cork for the purpose of gaining your point, did you? Having received $500 from the Omnibus Railroad Company, you will, of course, think it your duty to show your gratitude by patronizing them. Invest the money in car tickets and you may possibly have the luck to be turned out again.

The Effect of Judge Pratt's Decision. This political cartoon and accompanying caption published in the wake of Charlotte Brown's courtroom victory in January 1865 highlights racist animus directed at African Americans who demanded equal rights and also at whites, such as Judge Pratt, who helped them to achieve legal victories. Undated newspaper clipping, MS228A, Charlotte L. Brown. Courtesy of California Historical Society, San Francisco.

to carry "two of our most respectable females." The article noted that these well-mannered, well-dressed women had been on their way home from a visit to the lower part of the city attending a family who had suffered a death. The editor took pains to note that a man would not have required a seat in the car under the same circumstances. As to "city travel," the editor insisted, "no reputable colored man among us would attempt to intrude himself inside of a car filled with ladies." And while black men traveling to "the suburbs" on an employer's business might need to avail themselves of the advantage of taking a streetcar, carriage on the platform with the driver might meet their needs.[45]

The article set out two basic dichotomies between men and women in their natures and their use of public space. First, men were hardy, women frail. Second, men's travel was public, women's was private. Black men traveled on business at the behest of (white) employers—because they were assumed to be doing someone else's bidding their personal identity, their own status, was not at stake. Black women, however, traveled on private errands to sustain family and community. As such, the denial of carriage to a woman was a direct insult to her status, her family's status, and that of the black community as a whole. The suits themselves bear out these distinctions. The contrast between William Bowen's and Charlotte Brown's claims pointedly mark the gendered geography of streetcar travel. When Bowen was ejected, he was on an errand for his employer who had instructed him to take the cars. He repeatedly insisted that all he expected was a place on the platform.[46] In contrast, when she was ejected, Brown was on her way to visit the doctor who treated her for a chronic illness. The right she claimed in court was the right to ride in the interior of the car, to have a seat.[47]

Activist black men believed that it impugned black men's gender and class status to have black women thrown off the cars. An article appealing to white economic interests, published in the midst of Charlotte Brown's legal battle, portrayed a neatly gendered picture of the patriarchal black family. If blacks were denied carriage on streetcars, it would make it very difficult for landowners in the suburbs to sell to blacks. "What colored man," the editor asked, "would buy a homestead, or any piece of land, on the line of one of those proscriptive city railroad companies, and permit his wife to wade through the mud and be drenched by the rain, while his children wandered through the thickets to attend school?"[48] Strikingly absent from the article was any reference to how the black man of this hypothetical family would travel into the city. His actions were carefully drawn in patriarchal terms: purchasing property, refusing to permit his wife to suffer any indignity or his children to risk their safety. The article was written in terms of black male economic power. But it should also be read as saying something about the implications for manhood of powerlessness to protect black women. To be a man required not simply the economic means to provide for a family but the power to protect his wife and children, to permit or refuse permission for certain conduct. In other words, black men too had a personal stake in black women's success. Black men and women, in pursuing rights that had been gendered male or female, were identifying themselves publicly and privately as male and female.

Relying on the wedge of gender, black women's lawsuits against streetcar companies ultimately assured the right to travel of blacks generally. Court decisions made law. By entering the legal process and asking a court to state the law—here the right of blacks to travel on terms equal to those of whites—a woman was engaged in a distinctly political act. The monetary damages in the case might be paid to her, but the declaration of law was a general one that applied not simply to Charlotte Brown or Mary Pleasant, or to all black women, but to all blacks as well.

Charlotte Brown and William Bowen were the first to raise the legal issue in California courts. Emma Jane Turner and Mary Pleasant were the first to take the issue to the California supreme court. At every level, they won the legal issue their cases presented; that is, courts held that streetcars, as common carriers, were not allowed to exclude blacks on the basis of their race.[49]

These victories suggest that despite hostile coverage in segments of the white press and the streetcar companies' claims of the unanimity of "public opinion" on the need to exclude blacks, blacks clearly enjoyed strong support among important segments of the legal community. In all four cases the plaintiffs' lawyers were white; all of them successful men—"the best of the bar"—who did not have to take a case to feed their families. W. C. Burnett represented both Charlotte Brown and, two years later, Emma Jane Turner. Biographical sketches of Burnett portray a powerful, successful California pioneer.[50] The equally successful George Tyler represented Mary Ellen Pleasant.[51]

All of the judges who presided over the cases were also white men. And the personal sympathies of the trial judges as well as their reading of the law supported the plaintiffs' claims.[52] Judge Cowles, who presided in the criminal assault case brought after William Bowen was violently pushed off the platform of an Omnibus company car, tartly put the matter: "As the law now stands those who are so sensitive as to object to riding with the colored man will have to walk or ride in their own carriages with a colored man on the box driving and the wind perhaps blowing against them."[53]

Most critical to black success was the unwavering support of Judge Orville C. Pratt, an active Republican and the presiding trial judge in Charlotte Brown's suit and later in both Emma Jane Turner's and Mary Pleasant's.[54] Judge Pratt refused even to allow the streetcar companies to introduce evidence justifying their policy of racial exclusion or to show that it was customary in the city not to allow blacks to ride.[55] His support of African Americans' civil rights generated intensely negative commentary in some segments of the white press. The political cartoon that was published in the aftermath of Brown's successful suits derisively insisted that she owed Judge Pratt for her success. As the caption put it, "[H]e is very partial to niggers, is the Judge, the darker the complexion the better if it suits Pratt and the family."[56] Yet Pratt never wavered. In Turner's suit against the North Beach and Mission Railroad, Judge Pratt's directions to the jury included a long recitation against the wrongs of slavery—that "barbarous relic of the past"—and the badge of inferiority that had accompanied it for blacks.[57]

Faced with such judicial clarity, the Omnibus company apparently rescinded its policy after Brown's second successful suit.[58] The North Beach and Mission company proved more stubborn, leading to Turner's and Pleasant's lawsuits in fall 1866. At trial, based on favorable instructions to the jury from Judge Pratt, both women won substantial damages.[59] The streetcar company appealed; the California supreme court reversed both decisions.[60] The crucial issue on appeal in both cases was whether the conductor's failure to stop was based on a company policy of racial exclusion, or at least was racially motivated. In both cases, the company insisted that it did not have a policy excluding blacks. Against the word of Mary Pleasant's witness, who explained that the conductor had explicitly said that blacks were not allowed on the cars, the company placed the word of the conductor, who insisted that he had not heard anyone on board asking him to stop and had not seen a woman waiting until he was well past her. Against Emma Turner's word that the conductor had physically put his hand on her breast and pushed her away from the car, the company placed the conductor's testimony that someone had hailed him but that the person was too far from the car at the time to catch it anyway. Both conductors denied knowing the race of the person hailing the car.[61] On these facts, the California supreme court held that the two women had not made out their case of intentional exclusion based on race.

The end result in the two cases was ambiguous. California's highest court had declared that the law did not allow carriers, including streetcars, to exclude passengers on the basis of race.[62] But in reversing the trial court verdicts in favor of Turner and Pleasant, the court insisted that neither woman had proved that the company had a policy excluding blacks or that the conductors' actions had been racially motivated. Not seeing, not noticing gender or race, denying intentionality, denying prejudice—it all added up to a new approach to the "problem" of black women who were asserting their right of passage. The California supreme court's decision returned the cases to lower courts for new trials. But absent proof of a willful failure to stop and/or malice or ill will, the women were limited to "actual" damages, which here probably meant nothing. Pleasant's lawyer understood the consequence of the court's decision. In his brief to the California supreme court he had argued, "[L]et this Court once hold that all a negro can recover is nominal damages for being refused permission to ride in the cars, on account of his color, and that class of persons can never enjoy the privilege in San Francisco." Turner's and Pleasant's suits showed the limits of law. The highest court in California had stated the law that carriers could not exclude passengers on the basis of race, yet it had chosen to ignore evidence of conduct that most certainly amounted to intentional exclusion.

What is most surprising in the wake of the high court's decision was the silence that followed it. There were no additional lawsuits filed against the North Beach and Mission Railroad or other streetcar companies in San Francisco. Equally important, there were no additional incidents reported in the black press. Throughout these years, the black press had been vigilant in reporting incidences of exclusion and lawsuits challenging streetcar companies' policy of racial exclusion both in San Francisco and across the country.[63] Despite the reversal before the California supreme court of the Turner and Pleasant cases, streetcars in the city had finally acquiesced in affording African Americans the right of passage.[64]

· · ·

By the end of the nineteenth century, the black civil rights movement in California could celebrate significant achievements. But as the argument here suggests, it is important nonetheless to highlight exactly who was where, doing what, and why. Black men and women were successful in their civil rights struggle because they conformed to and spoke the language of gendered-rights consciousness of nineteenth-century America. In the written history of the black civil rights movement in California, inclusive language neutered men's and women's gendered voices and, in doing so, masked how truly keen was black understanding and acceptance of nineteenth-century American political culture. Black men and women were seeking only to enjoy the rights enjoyed by white men and women as men and women. This in itself was a significant claim. But they were not challenging the gender and class order. "Respectable" black men acted like men, treated their wives and daughters like women, and asked only for themselves and their womenfolk the rights that would naturally accrue to them according to their gender but for their race. "Respectable" black women asked only to be accorded the same rights in public transport as white women. Charlotte Brown's suit and those that followed document black women's role in attaining recognition of the right of blacks to equal access to public transit. It was a battle that would be fought in one state after another in the years just before, during, and after the Civil War.[65] In all of these battles, women, and the rights of ladies, were key. Ultimately black men and women both enjoyed rights that they fought for separately. Black men had mustered the fight against the testimony ban; women were the first to make use of the new right. Black women had mustered the fight for equality of access to public transport; men, as well as women, enjoyed the fruits of that battle.

NOTES

I wish to thank Peggy Pascoe, Linda Kerber, Barbara Corrado Pope, Laura Fair, Caroline Forell, Lisa Kloppenberg, Kirsten Fischer, the participants in the Feminist Theory Reading Group at the University of Oregon, and the editors of this volume for their generous comments and helpful critiques on this and earlier versions of this chapter.

1. See Sam B. Warner, Jr., *Streetcar Suburbs: The Process of Growth in Boston, 1870–1900* (Cambridge, Mass.: Harvard University Press, 1962); Clifton Hood, *722 Miles: The Building of the Subways and How They Transformed New York* (New York: Simon & Schuster, 1993); William D. Middleton, *Time of the Trolley* (Milwaukee: Kalmbach, 1967).

2. See, e.g., State v. Kimber, 30 Ohio Dec. 197 (Hamilton C. P. Ct. 1859); Derry v. Lowry, 6 Phil. Rep. 30 (C.P. Ct. 1865); Dorothy Sterling, ed., *We Are Your Sisters* (New York: W. W. Norton, 1984), 223–24. For a general discussion of exclusion and segregation in public transportation in the North, see Leon F. Litwack, *North of Slavery: The Negro in the Free States, 1790–1860* (Chicago: University of Chicago Press, 1961), 106–12.

3. Lawrence B. De Graaf, "Race, Sex and Region: Black Women in the American West, 1850–1920," *Pacific Historical Review* 49 (1980): 292. For an overview of racial discrimination in the West, see Quintard Taylor, *In Search of the Racial Frontier: African-Americans in the American West* (New York: W. W. Norton, 1998).

4. Albert S. Broussard, *Black San Francisco: The Struggle for Racial Equality in the West, 1900–1954* (Lawrence: University Press of Kansas, 1993), 2, 16.

5. San Francisco grew exponentially in the second half of the nineteenth century, beginning with a population of 1,000 in 1848 and reaching almost 150,000 by 1870. The

same pattern continued for the remainder of the century. By 1900 the population was 342,782, making San Francisco the largest city on the West Coast. See Broussard, *Black San Francisco*, 11.

6. The leading monograph focusing on the gendered geography of nineteenth-century public urban space is Mary P. Ryan, *Women in Public: Between Banners and Ballots, 1825–1880* (Baltimore: Johns Hopkins University Press, 1990). See also John F. Kasson, *Rudeness and Civility: Manners in Nineteenth-Century Urban America* (New York: Hill and Wang, 1990).

7. In recent years, historians have shown a growing interest in charting black women's experience and significance in the history of the American West. See Willi Coleman, "African American Women and Community Development in California, 1848–1900," in *Seeking El Dorado: African Americans in California*, ed. Lawrence B. De Graaf, Kevin Mulroy, and Quintard Taylor (Seattle: University of Washington Press, 2001), 98–125; Peggy Pascoe, "Race, Gender, and the Privileges of Property: On the Significance of Miscegenation Law in the U.S. West," in *Over the Edge: Remapping the American West*, ed. Valerie Matsumoto and Blake Allmendinger (Berkeley: University of California Press, 1999), 215–30; Taylor, *In Search of the Racial Frontier*, esp. chaps. 3, 7; and Elizabeth Jameson and Susan Armitage, eds., *Writing the Range: Race, Class, and Culture in the Women's West* (Norman: University of Oklahoma Press, 1997), which also includes an extensive bibliography. For two pioneering efforts in the field see, De Graaf, "Black Women in the American West"; and Glenda Riley, "American Daughters: Black Women in the West," *Montana: The Magazine of Western History* 38 (1988): 14–27. More generally, scholars, particularly women of color, have aggressively challenged the tendency in historical discussions of race to read "black" as meaning male and then to read "male" as standing for the whole. See, in particular, Evelyn Brooks Higginbotham, "African-American Women's History and the Metalanguage of Race," *Signs* 17 (1992): 251–76; Evelyn Brooks Higginbotham, "Beyond the Sound of Silence: Afro-American Women in History," *Gender & History* 1 (1989): 50–67; and Paula Giddings, *When and Where I Enter: The Impact of Black Women on Race and Sex in America* (New York: William Morrow, 1984).

8. Historians of the nineteenth-century civil rights movement in California have focused primarily on the battle over the extension of slavery, the barring of black testimony in cases involving whites, and the denial of black (male) suffrage. See Rudolph M. Lapp, *Blacks in Gold Rush California* (New Haven: Yale University Press, 1977); James A. Fisher, "A History of the Political and Social Development of the Black Community in California, 1850–1950" (Ph.D. dissertation, State University of New York at Stony Brook, 1971); Philip M. Montesano, "Some Aspects of the Free Negro Question in San Francisco, 1849–1870" (M.A. thesis, University of San Francisco, 1967). For the first half of the twentieth century, see Broussard, *Black San Francisco*. In discussing black men's and women's political activism in the antebellum North, James Horton notes that although women were encouraged to work for the elevation of their race, men dominated political actions including conventions. See James O. Horton, "Freedom's Yoke: Gender Conventions among Free Blacks," in Horton, *Free People of Color: Inside the African American Community* (Washington, D.C.: Smithsonian Institution Press, 1993), 115–16.

9. See Paula Baker, "The Domestication of American Politics: Women and American Political Society, 1780–1920," *American Historical Review* 89 (1984): 620–47.

10. As Rudolph Lapp notes, most black men who were active in the civil rights movement in California had experience in political organizing in the East before traveling West. See Lapp, *Blacks in Gold Rush California*, 186–91. Most scholars focusing on the post–Civil War South have argued that there as well black men dominated the formal political sphere. See Leon Litwack, *Been in the Storm So Long: The Aftermath of Slavery* (New York: Vintage Books, 1979), 502–13; Eric Foner, *Reconstruction: America's Unfinished Revolution, 1863–1877* (New York: Harper & Row, 1988), 87. For a recent challenge to this view, see Elsa Barkley Brown, "Negotiating and Transforming the Public Sphere: African American Political Life in the Transition from Slavery to Freedom," *Public Culture* 7 (1994), 107–46. Brown argues that in the immediate postwar years, black women participated politically in much the same terms as black men and saw the basic rights of citizenship granted to black men as belonging to them as well.

11. For a complete discussion of the Convention Movement, see Lapp, *Blacks in Gold Rush California*, 186–237; and James A. Fisher, "The Struggle for Negro Testimony in California, 1851–1863," *Southern California Quarterly* 51 (1969): 313–24.

12. The testimony ban was the principal impetus for the Convention Movement. Lapp, *Blacks in Gold Rush California*, 211; Broussard, *Black San Francisco*, 17. Although there were a number of egregious cases of white on black crime during the thirteen years in which the testimony ban was law, it was the murder of George W. Gordon, a widely respected and affluent black barber, played a critical role in the final push for legislative repeal of the ban. The details of the case supported black men's claim that their ability to protect their homes, their families, their property, and their lives was central to their manhood and depended on the right to testimony. For a discussion of the Gordon case, see Lapp, *Blacks in Gold Rush California*, 208–9; and Robert J. Chandler, "Friends in Time of Need: Republicans and Black Civil rights in California during the Civil Rights Era," *Arizona and the West* 24 (1982): 333–34, 340.

13. *Proceedings of the California State Convention of Colored Citizens* (San Francisco: The Elevator, 1865), 75.

14. The manly character of the conventions was true from the beginning of the Convention Movement. The only evidence that even a single woman was present at the first convention held in 1855 was a resolution of appreciation of the work of the committee offered by "Mrs. Alfred J. White." That Mrs. White placed the resolution in the hands of a man to announce, as well as the chivalric tone of his comments regarding Mrs. White and support of the "ladies," highlights the convention as dedicated to manly work. See *Proceedings of the First State Convention of the Colored Citizens of the State of California* (Sacramento: Democratic State Journal Print, 1855), 24. For evidence that women provided financial support for the delegates from their communities, see *Proceedings of the Second Annual Convention of Colored Citizens of the State of California* (San Francisco: J. H. Udell and W. Randall, Printers, 1856), 71.

15. *Proceedings of the Second Annual Convention*, 71.

16. The first streetcar had begun operating in the city in 1852 just as the battle over black civil rights in California was joined. In its first decade, though, public transit in

the city was more akin to urban stagecoaches than streetcars. There were no tracks, routes were limited, and high fares made travel beyond the means of most. Edgar N. Kahn, *Cable Car Days in San Francisco* (Stanford: Stanford University Press, 1940), 10–17.

17. See Middleton, *Time of the Trolley*, 21.

18. Kasson, *Rudeness and Civility*, 128.

19. Ryan, *Women in Public*, 15. Ryan's account focuses on San Francisco, New York, and New Orleans, from 1825 to 1880. The most important chapter for the discussion here is chapter 2, "Everyday Space: Gender and the Geography of the Public." Ryan, *Women in Public*, 58–94. The same gender imbalance existed in the African American community. As Willi Coleman notes, the ratio of men to women in San Francisco in 1860 was close to 3 to 1. See Coleman, "African American Women and Community Development," 102. See also De Graaf, "Black Women in the American West," 288.

20. Kasson, *Rudeness and Civility*, 130–31; Ryan, *Women in Public*, 68–76.

21. Although streetcar companies did not keep records showing the number of male versus female riders, the photographic record leaves little doubt that men were the vast majority of streetcars passengers. See Middleton, *Time of the Trolley*.

22. See, e.g., Chamberlain v. Chandler, 3 Mason 242, 245–46 (N.Y. 1823).

23. Ryan, *Women in Public*, 71.

24. In some cities company rules allowed blacks to ride on the platform of the cars but not in the interior. In others, as in San Francisco, company rules barred blacks from riding anywhere on the cars.

25. Complaint, Testimony of Thomas S. Dennison, Conductor and Mr. Gardner, Superintendent, Omnibus R.R. Co. (testifying for Defendant streetcar company), January 17, 1865, Record in *Charlotte L. Brown v. The Omnibus R. R. Company*, California Historical Society, San Francisco. Testimony of Mr. Morrison, Superintendent, North Beach and Mission R.R. (testifying for Defendant streetcar company), in *William Bowen v. The North Beach and Mission R.R. Company*, undated newspaper clipping, California Historical Society, San Francisco. The only San Francisco streetcar company that did not exclude black passengers in the early 1860s was the steam-powered Market Street Railroad. See Chandler, "Friends in Time of Need," 335.

26. On the common law of common carriers, see, e.g., Joseph K. Angell, *A Treatise on the Law of Carriers of Goods and Passengers by Land and by Water*, 5th ed., rev. John Lathrop (Boston, 1877), 465–77; Jencks v. Coleman, 13 F. Cas. 442 (C.C.D.R.I., 1835) (No. 7, 258); Commonwealth v. Power, 7 Metcalf 558 (Mass. 1844).

27. State v. Kimber, 30 Ohio Dec. 197 (Hamilton C.P. Ct. 1859); Derry v. Lowry, 6 Phil. Rep. 30 (C.P. Ct. 1865); Sterling, ed., *We Are Your Sisters*, 223–24; Litwack, *North of Slavery*, 111–12. The only state supreme court to address the issue of exclusion was the Michigan supreme court in Day v. Owen, 5 Mich. 520 (1858). The steamboat company involved in *Day* had a regulation barring blacks from cabin passage and allowing them only to ride as deck passengers. The court rejected Day's claim, noting that he had not been excluded from passage.

28. Each state had its own common law, or judge-made law, of common carriers. One state's holdings were not legally binding on another. Nonetheless, just as in other

areas of law, judges in one state looked respectfully to the decisions of their brethren in other states. They were not bound by them, but they often followed them, so that a "common law" in the sense of a shared law in fact developed.

29. The language of war seems apt here. If ever there was proof of the emotional proximity of the Civil War to those in the West, the evidence in these cases provides it. The newspaper article describing the criminal assault prosecution following Bowen's ejection had one subheading entitled "What They Did to the Contraband." References in the argument to the repugnance of "Copperheads, Secessionists, and old line Democrats" erased the geographic divide between South and West. In Charlotte Brown's suit against the Omnibus Company too one "feels" the war in the language of the parties. W. C. Burnett, Brown's lawyer, captioned his draft brief on Brown's behalf "Contraband Brief."

30. *Pacific Appeal*, July 11, 1863, p. 3; *Pacific Appeal*, July 18, 1863, p. 3; *Pacific Appeal*, November 21, 1863; Record in *Brown*; Chandler, "Friends in Time of Need," 336–37.

31. Undated newspaper clipping, California Historical Society, San Francisco; *Pacific Appeal*, July 11, 1863, p. 3. He won both cases, with an award of over $3,000 in damages in his civil suit.

32. *Pacific Appeal*, May 10, 1862, p. 3 (describing petition in Philadelphia); *Pacific Appeal*, May 16, 1863, p. 3 (describing 1855 suit by Elizabeth Jennings). In reporting on Bowen's criminal case, the paper also noted the suit of a woman named Sarah Fawcett in Cincinnati from two years earlier. Newspaper clipping, California Historical Society, San Francisco.

33. The challenge in charting Pleasant's life lies less in finding details than in separating fact from construction. The 1860 U.S. Manuscript Census describes Pleasant as forty years old, born in Massachusetts, black, and a servant in the household of Captain Selim Woodworth. John Pleasant, Mary Ellen Pleasant's second husband, is also listed as a servant in Captain Woodworth's household. U.S. Manuscript Census of 1860, California, San Francisco, microfilm reel 68, p. 232. It is interesting that Mary Pleasant was with Captain Woodworth's wife at the time of the incident leading to her suit. The census record conflicts in terms of Pleasant's age, birthplace, and status with other accounts of Pleasant's life. Several collections of notable American women include biographical sketches on Pleasant. See Darlene Clark Hine, Elsa Barkley Brown, and Rosalyn Terborg-Penn, eds., *Black Women in America* (Bloomington: Indiana University Press, 1993), 2:932–33; Jessie Carney Smith, ed., *Notable Black American Women* (Detroit: Gale Research, 1992), 858–62; Edward T. James, Janet Wilson James, and Paul S. Boyer, eds., *Notable American Women* (Cambridge, Mass.: Radcliffe College, 1971), 3:75–77. For a more in-depth look at Pleasant, see Lynn M. Hudson, "A New Look, or 'I'm Not Mammy to Everybody in California': Mary Ellen Pleasant, a Black Entrepreneur," *Journal of the West* 32 (1993), 37–40; and Lynn M. Hudson, "When 'Mammy' Becomes a Millionaire: Mary Ellen Pleasant, an African-American Entrepreneur" (Ph.D. dissertation, Indiana University, 1996).

34. Testimony of Charlotte Brown, Testimony of Thomas S. Denison, Conductor, January 17, 1865, Record in *Brown*.

35. Answer and Amended Answer (Omnibus R.R. Co.), Record in *Brown*.

36. Testimony of Thomas S. Denison (Conductor), Record in *Brown*.

37. Other suits followed the same pattern. In William Bowen's suit after his ejection from the platform of a car on the Omnibus Railroad Company, the company's lawyers played to jurors' personal racial prejudices, warning that if this case were decided in Bowen's favor, then "negroes would have a right to thrust themselves into the cars and seat themselves between ladies." Undated newspaper clipping, California Historical Society, San Francisco.

38. Trial Notes of W. C. Burnett (Charlotte Brown's lawyer) recording street railway's argument, Record in *Brown*.

39. Undated newspaper clipping, California Historical Society, San Francisco.

40. The antebellum black press promoted white, middle-class gender conventions, including woman's place. For an example from the black press in San Francisco, see "A Woman's Power," *Pacific Appeal*, May 30, 1863, p. 2. The particular burdens black women bore in challenging white images of black women's assumed promiscuity is the subject of a rich and growing literature. See Glenda E. Gilmore, *Gender and Jim Crow: Women and the Politics of White Supremacy in North Carolina, 1896–1920* (Chapel Hill: University of North Carolina Press, 1996); Evelyn Brooks Higginbotham, *Righteous Discontent: The Women's Movement in the Black Baptist Church, 1880–1920* (Cambridge, Mass.: Harvard University Press, 1993); Higginbotham, "Beyond the Sound of Silence"; Giddings, *When and Where I Enter*; and Horton, "Freedom's Yoke," 56.

41. See Darlene Clark Hine, "Rape and the Inner Lives of Black Women in the Middle West: Preliminary Thoughts on the Culture of Dissemblance," in Vicki L. Ruiz and Ellen Carol DuBois, *Unequal Sisters: A Multi-Cultural Reader in U.S. Women's History*, ed. Vicki L. Ruiz and Ellen Carol DuBois, 2d ed. (New York: Routledge, 1994), 342–47; Giddings, *When and Where I Enter*, 31, 49, 86–87.

42. The streets of nineteenth-century American cities at night were no place for a respectable woman. Ryan, *Women in Public*, 69–72; Kasson, *Rudeness and Civility*, 132–33.

43. Testimony of Charlotte Brown, Record in *Brown*.

44. Testimony of Lisette Woodworth (on behalf of Mary Pleasant), 67 Cal. S. Ct. Records 13-17, Transcript on Appeal in *Pleasants v. North Beach & Mission R.R.*, California State Library, Sacramento. One of the historical discrepancies in charting the facts of Mary Pleasant's life is in the matter of the spelling of her last name. She is often referred to as "Pleasant," but in the legal record an *s* appears at the end of her name. Here, I refer to her as Mary Pleasant, except in citations from the legal record.

45. *Pacific Appeal*, March 13, 1863, p. 2.

46. Undated newspaper clipping, California Historical Society, San Francisco.

47. Testimony of Charlotte Brown, Testimony of Dr. Geay, Record in *Brown*.

48. *Pacific Appeal*, May 9, 1863, p. 2.

49. Record in *Brown*; *Pacific Appeal*, July 11, 1863, p. 3 (William Bowen); Turner v. North Beach & Mission R.R., 34 Cal. 594 (1868); Pleasants v. North Beach & Mission R.R., 34 Cal. 586 (1868).

50. His wife similarly traced her lineage back to America's early colonists and was well connected in San Francisco's budding high society and charitable world. Oscar T.

Shuck, *History of the Bench and Bar of California* (Los Angeles: Commercial Printing House, 1901), 797; Bailey Millard, *History of the San Francisco Bay Region*, vol. 3 (San Francisco: American Historical Society, 1924), 24–32. Neither sketch mentions Burnett's legal work in support of black civil rights.

51. U.S. Manuscript Census of 1860, California, San Francisco County, microfilm reel 68, p. 819 (Tyler, George W.).

52. For brief biographical sketches of Judges Oliver C. Pratt and Maurice C. Blake, see Shuck, *History of the Bench and Bar of California*, 441–42, 551–52. Judge Blake, like Judge Pratt, was an active Republican. In an 1858 criminal assault case, Judge Blake allowed a black man to testify against his white assailant. See Lapp, *Blacks in Gold Rush California*, 206.

53. Undated newspaper clipping, California Historical Society, San Francisco.

54. Shuck, *History of the Bench and Bar of California*, 441–42.

55. Record in *Brown*.

56. Undated newspaper clipping, MS 228A, Charlotte L. Brown, California Historical Society, San Francisco.

57. Instructions to the Jury, Transcript on Appeal in *Turner*.

58. Although the Omnibus Railroad Company filed an appeal to the California supreme court following the trial court verdict for Brown, sometime in 1866 the company and Brown settled the case. Notice of Appeal (Omnibus R.R. Co.), February 7, 1866, Notation "Settled 1866," Record in *Brown*.

59. Turner was awarded $750; Pleasant was awarded $500. Judgment, 70 Cal. S. Ct. Records 7, Transcript on Appeal in *Turner*; Judgment, 67 Cal. S. Ct. Records 5, Transcript on Appeal in *Pleasants*.

60. *Pleasants*, 34 Cal. 586, 591 (1868); *Turner*, 34 Cal. 594, 600 (1868).

61. Testimony of Mary Pleasant, Lisette Woodworth (white passenger), and L. M. de Beusche (conductor), 67 Cal. S. Ct. Records 10–22, Transcript on Appeal in *Pleasants*; Testimony of Emma J. Turner, Edward Hughes (Conductor), 70 Cal. S. Ct. Records 9–28, Transcript on Appeal in *Turner*.

62. *Turner*, 34 Cal. 600 (1868).

63. For reports of cases outside California, see *The Elevator*, December 29, 1865, p. 3 (re Cincinnati case); September 20, 1867, p. 2 (petition in Philadelphia); October 26, 1867, p. 1 (steamboat case in Georgia).

64. In 1893 the California legislature joined other northern states that, in the wake of the U.S. Supreme Court's 1883 decision holding the Civil Rights Act of 1875 unconstitutional, passed an equal accommodation statute banning racial discrimination in public accommodations and conveyances.

65. After the Civil War the focus of litigation shifted to the American South. Although in the South the battle was fought over whether common carriers could segregate rather than exclude passengers on the basis of race, gender and the rights of respectable women remained central. For discussion of the situation in the South, the role played by black women, and the significance of their suits in the development of the law of "separate but equal," see Barbara Y. Welke, "When All the Women Were White,

and All the Blacks Were Men: Gender, Class, Race, and the Road to *Plessy*, 1855–1914," *Law and History Review* 13 (1995): 261–316; and *Recasting American Liberty: Gender, Race, Law, and the Railroad Revolution, 1865–1920* (New York: Cambridge University Press, esp. 280–322.

The Post–Civil War Era

CHAPTER 6

"Anxious Foot Soldiers"

SACRAMENTO'S BLACK WOMEN AND EDUCATION IN NINETEENTH-CENTURY CALIFORNIA

Susan Bragg

In 1871 a black Sacramento resident, Sarah, confidently predicted a victory for the Republican candidate for the office of State Superintendent of Public Instruction. Writing to the *Pacific Appeal*, a black newspaper based in San Francisco, she announced, "I expect a reform in the development of the compulsory [education] system after we elect Professor Bolander."[1] As a woman, Sarah could not vote, but she clearly saw the black civil rights movement as a joint venture between men and women. Her use of the pronoun "we," a pattern seen in the writings of other black women of the era, suggests that although tools for social justice might be gendered, both men and women shared in the struggles and success of the nineteenth-century black civil rights movement. In fact, as important as it is to understand how Victorian-era gender ideologies shaped black women's activities in early California, it is also important to recognize that the shared experiences of building communities in the West fostered a subtle but significant sense of collective identity. This spirit, reinforced through family and kinship ties, underwrote black women's activism.[2]

Despite the stereotype of nineteenth-century black California as a bastion of masculinity and bachelorhood, black men and women's allegiance to family and kin demonstrates the importance of collective bonds and duties in local black communities. These ties can be seen in the fight for black children's educational opportunities. Education was highly valued by the black community, both as a means of personal uplift and as a public privilege commonly denied. Although historians have described black men's roles in organizing statewide Colored Citizens' Conventions, petition drives, and court battles on behalf of education, women's actions, taken largely within constructed networks of friends, neighbors, and kin, have gone unexamined. The focus on formal black political activities at the state level not only obscures female activism, but the importance of black family and community needs within the civil rights movement.[3]

Recent scholarship in African American history has demonstrated that the very recognition of black womanhood, family, and respectability was highly politicized in nineteenth-century America, given the legacy of slavery and destructive racial ideologies. Claiming "true womanhood" and tending to family needs was not just a private matter but also an effort that sanctioned black women's public activities.[4] Women's nurturing roles as mothers supported their participation in schooling-oriented activism, but these same women often saw schooling in the larger context of citizenship and race pride, thus potentially blurring the boundaries between gendered "rights" and roles in the nineteenth-century civil rights movement. To recognize black women's involvement in educational reform, it is necessary to see politicized actions beyond the political convention or the demand for the ballot. As home to a large, established black population in California during the nineteenth century, Sacramento provides a fitting site for the exploration of the ways in which familial and gender conventions shaped black activism in the American West.[5]

Sacramento's black community first emerged in the early years of the California gold rush. The discovery of gold triggered a massive migration westward, with cities like Sacramento, conveniently located between the financial and shipping capital of San Francisco and the gold deposits in the Sierra Nevada, developing virtually overnight. A substantial number of blacks joined the stampede of migrants to California, and by 1850 the federal census reported that 962 blacks lived in the state.[6] Census takers in Sacramento County counted 212 blacks and mulattoes, and 195 of those black residents were men. Yet the proportion of black women to men in Sacramento rose steadily so that while black women made up about 8 percent of Sacramento's total black population in 1850, by the next decade census takers counted 160 black women in Sacramento, or just over 34 percent of the total black population. Because migration frequently takes place within networks of friends and kin, this pattern of black migration to California may have frequently been a family decision, a decision made of optimism and hope.[7]

Like the majority of migrants to California during the gold rush, black Americans certainly shared the hope of striking it rich, but more important, they may have seen the gold rush as a unique opportunity to reconstruct individual lives and family relationships in the American West. Free blacks hoped to escape the legal, social, and economic discrimination typical in more populous regions of the United States, but at least 60 percent of Sacramento's black community migrated from the South, suggesting these men and women had considerable contacts with the institution of slavery.[8] Some free southern black migrants, such as the Booth family from Baltimore, Maryland, came to California hoping for greater opportunities in a nonslave state. Edward Booth traveled to California in 1849, earning enough money mining to return to Maryland and gather up his three brothers and two sisters. While Edward, Elige, and Samuel Booth took up mining claims in the Sierra Nevada foothills, George Booth and his sisters, Ann Maria Hubbard and Harriet Booth, settled permanently in Sacramento.[9]

Yet despite California's status as a free state, some blacks came west still in bondage to white masters. Many slaves were brought to California against their will; others were attracted by promises of freedom in exchange for terms of labor or money. By 1856 Reverend Darius B. Stokes, a black activist, claimed that black Californians had spent at least $750,000 to assist family members gain freedom. The existence of slavery both in the South and the West shaped patterns of westward migration and the consciousness of all blacks in the region. The story of the Yantes family demonstrates the staggered patterns of liberation and migration of black families that may have been familiar to many members of Sacramento's black community. Henry and Persila Yantes arrived in Sacramento in the earliest years of the gold rush and were officially married by a local white Baptist minister in 1856. By the late 1850s the Yantes had saved enough money to purchase their daughters, Anna and Julia, from bondage in Missouri.[10] For families like the Yantes, the significance of freedom and reconstructing family relationships was not relegated simply to individual consciousness or "private" family life. Instead, these issues surfaced and gained additional meaning in the public relationships among black community members, as established black Sacramento residents introduced newer migrants to friends and peers through social networks and community institutions.

In fact, despite the image of black gold rush communities as a population of single males, it seems clear that families like the Yantes formed the core of

Sacramento's black community by 1860. A more equitable ratio of women to men in the black community may also have provided greater opportunities for marriage than in the white community. Black laundryman Daniel Blue proudly remembered that he and his wife, Lucinda, both originally from the Deep South, were the first "American" couple wed in Sacramento in 1849, and by 1860 the census manuscript documents many black families whose children were born in California, including the Blues, Grubbs, Clarks, Gastons, Johnsons, Fishers, McLearys, and Marshalls.[11] Even single men, who still predominated numerically in California into the later decades of the nineteenth century, should not be assumed to have identified themselves solely in the context of independent (or exclusively masculine) interests. Black Californians frequently lodged together either as boarders with an established family group or in family-run hotels catering to black clients. Some boarders may have lived with families because of an inability to provide for themselves independently, but others probably enjoyed the familial setting that boarding provided. These gendered relationships reinforced the communal experience of Sacramento's black community and formed the backdrop for individual actions.[12]

The familial atmosphere in Sacramento's nineteenth-century black community not only provided support for individuals but also helped to define the goals of the community, allowing women and children entry into public discourse. In the years after the gold rush, blacks in Sacramento and in other communities in northern California built networks of solidarity and support to resist white discrimination and prejudice. It should be no surprise that blacks' first local actions in Sacramento were to create institutions that favored family-oriented participation and expression.

In particular, black churches brought black men, women, and children together as a community and provided an institutional base for protest against racial injustice. Sacramento black community members began meeting in Daniel and Lucinda Blue's home on I Street for regular church services in 1849, formally organizing St. Andrew's African Methodist Episcopal (AME) Church a year later and building a house of worship on the corner of Seventh and G Streets. Another group of black city residents organized Siloam Baptist Church in the late 1850s, purchasing a building that formerly housed Sacramento's Jewish synagogue. These churches created a forum for community interests and provided the physical space for family-oriented activities. It is no coincidence that two northern California AME ministers, T. M. D. Ward and J. J. Moore, assumed responsibility for reporting on educational opportunities at the first California Colored Citizens' Convention in 1855. Representing the familial interests of the congregations, the ministers reminded male delegates assembled in Sacrament's St. Andrew's Church, "[U]nder God, our dependence is in our children."[13]

Although formal participation in political conventions provided black men with an opportunity to assert their rights as men, education activism needs to be seen in the larger context of community. As early as 1854 Elizabeth Thorn Scott, a widow, had begun teaching school for black children in the basement of St. Andrew's, and throughout the nineteenth century, both St. Andrew's and Siloam Baptist Church supported the community's educational needs and encouraged adult participation.[14] Scott probably drew on popular Victorian-era gender conventions that articulated teaching as an extension of female domesticity, providing a form of employment preferable to the typical low-paying, service-oriented jobs typically open to black women. But while black women gained new opportunities with the feminization of the teaching profession during the nineteenth century, black men did not entirely remove themselves from the classroom either. Education, so highly valued in the black community, continued to provide an opportunity for black men to demonstrate their professional skills while acting in public leadership roles. Within the year, Scott remarried and moved to Oakland, California, but her position was quickly taken by a newcomer to Sacramento, Jeremiah B. Sanderson. By spring 1855 Sacramento's city directory noted that twenty-two black children regularly attended his school. Sanderson had been deeply involved in racially integrated abolition efforts associated with William Lloyd Garrison in his home state of Massachusetts. In June 1855 Sanderson petitioned the Sacramento City School Board (also referred to as the Sacramento Board of Education and used interchangeably here) to support the fledgling school with public funds, setting off a heated local debate that spilled into state politics.[15]

Despite Sanderson's recognized history as an abolitionist and black civil rights leader, it should not be assumed that he acted independently. He probably used his experience as a Garrisonian abolitionist to act as a negotiator between Sacramento's black parents and the white education establishment. In the black community, parents organized the Colored School Committee, a group composed of both men and women. This organization set out to raise private funds to support the existing school for black children and gain public school moneys and thus official recognition of the school and the black community. The Colored School Committee was chaired by former slave and AME trustee George Fletcher, but the men and women who participated in the group identified themselves collectively as parents. Sacramento's black residents had previously protested injustices such as slavery in California and the state's ban on black testimony through publicized petitions, but it is striking that the first organized interaction between local blacks and city officials was to ensure black children's schooling opportunities, illustrating again the significance of familial interests in the black community.[16]

Although neither early state legislation nor local school ordinances explicitly excluded black children from attending public schools, white school officials remained ambivalent about using state money for black children's education. Sacramento school board members cautiously approved Sanderson's petition, agreeing to apportion some school funds to the separate school but only under a city charter amendment that explicitly excluded black children from attending school with white children. Later that year, state legislators clarified California's education codes, echoing Sacramento's revised charter provisions and creating de jure segregation in California's schools. Yet the charter amendment did not actually guarantee any money to the school, and in the following years, the school board debated the actual amount of taxes paid by Sacramento's black residents, refusing to pay to the school any more than the amount these residents paid in school taxes. In essence, the "colored school" was still a private school, relying on black community–generated funds. By 1860 the growth of the black community and particularly the increasing numbers of black children encouraged state lawmakers to require local school boards to provide regular funding for black children's education in segregated schools, if more than ten black children lived in a school district. Although this still denied black children in rural areas access to public schools, it ensured regular state funding of urban black children's education.[17]

Sacramento's black parents initially celebrated city officials' votes on behalf of the separate school, even with the inclusion of segregation stipulations in state and local school codes. But although the city now promised to provide some funding for the school, it was the black community, black women in particular, who sustained the struggle to educate black children in Sacramento. After repeated difficulties obtaining the promised financial support from the school board, parents returned to regular fund-raising in the black community, holding festivals and "soliciting subscriptions." A group of black women took the organizational lead, eventually using the donations to purchase a lot on the east side of O Street, between Ninth and Tenth Streets, as a permanent school site in 1858. The women, Emily Allen, Persila Yantes, Mary Joseph, Maria Caldwell, Rebecca Gibbs, and Jane Ware, transferred the deed to three male trustees for one dollar but specified that the lot must only be used for school purposes and any failure to follow these directions would result in the lot returning to the women's control.[18] With this action, black women demonstrated their own sense of power as members of the Colored School Committee: they were not silent or subordinate members of this organization but retained an interest in the product of their fund-raising efforts.

By 1859 black parents had established a permanent schoolhouse for their children and hired a white teacher, Mrs. Julia Folger, after Sanderson left the community in 1856. The Sacramento City School Board, which had rejected payments to unnamed black teachers deemed "unqualified," agreed to pay Folger a regular salary of $50 per month, thereby ensuring some stability in educational services to black children. By the following year, the *Sacramento Daily Union* reported enthusiastically on the progress of students at the school, noting the large number of black parents attending regular public examinations there.[19]

Both mothers and fathers took pride in the school, not only because it provided individual students with the opportunity to learn new skills, but also because government funding of black children's education was tacit recognition of black families and their civic rights.[20] In addition, these parents clearly saw education as a means of destroying negative racial stereotypes, a tool equally important to both boys and girls. As early as 1855, members of the Colored School Committee publicly declared that through education black children would become "intelligent and worthy men and women," and Lucinda Blue, a former washerwoman from Alabama, repeated these views later in 1862, as racial tensions mounted in the context of the Civil War. Writing to the black newspaper the *Pacific Appeal* as Sacramento's black community struggled to rebuild the schoolhouse on O street after first a winter flood and then an arson attack destroyed the original structure, Blue angrily charged,

> [A]lthough much can be done through our exertions to ameliorate our condition, much also, must come from the helping hand of a government, which, by its disavowal of the degrading influences of slavery, has acknowledged to the world, our fitness to be marshaled in the ranks of the civilized nations of the earth.[21]

Blue's response was not simply a demand for funds but for respect through the privileges of education. Blue's vocabulary is instructive: she demanded acknowledgment of the black community as a whole, instead of using gendered language that distinguished between men's or women's intellectual or cultural "fitness" and rights.

Black parents' joint participation in the Colored School Committee encouraged this collective ethos, which was also reinforced in Sacramento's separate school. Boys and girls attended classes together in the one-room schoolhouse, studying basic academic skills such as reading, spelling, geography, and arithmetic. Outside of the schoolroom, Sacramento's black adolescents continued to participate in coeducational activities; a literary institute was organized where they held debates, read compositions, and gave speeches. Yet while education was a universal value for both men and women, young black women may have been the greatest practical beneficiaries of schooling opportunities, particularly in the years immediately following the gold rush. For example, when members of the Sacramento Board of Education visited the school for spring examinations in 1860, they pronounced it "the best one that has yet been held in any of the schools this term" and bestowed achievement awards on Ellen Dorsey, Anna Yantes, and Lucy Caldwell, noting that girls made up the majority of the school's enrollment.[22]

Black parents promoted universal education, but they may have been compelled by economic circumstances to send their sons into the workforce. Initially girls stayed in school longer because they had fewer employment opportunities, particularly since Chinese immigrants dominated both the laundry and domestic service industries, the two professions typically open to black women during the nineteenth century.[23] By the mid-1860s boys' enrollment regularly matched that of girls, perhaps as family incomes and the regional economy stabilized and matured. The school provided one more benefit to young black women as well. In 1866, after receiving applications from three black female graduates of the school, the Sacramento City School Board hired Anna Yantes, a former slave and a graduate of the school, as an assistant teacher to Mrs. Folger. The school board paid Yantes less than white assistants in other city schools, but her appointment to an official position in the Sacramento City School District must have been a source of pride to parents whose children now had a black role model and leader in the classroom. That year Yantes attended the county's education convention, providing public evidence of her intention to join white women in the teaching profession.[24]

In the 1860s black women increasingly took on public roles in matters of education, although their activities have received little attention. The Civil War heightened black Californians' expectations of justice and equity and reenergized statewide political organization. Building on political networks forged during the gold rush years, black Californians increasingly demanded equal rights before the law through mass meetings and the black press. In particular, political conventions organized throughout the era provided a forum for black men to express their political views and target specific issues such as the right of legal testimony and suffrage. Yet focusing exclusively on the gendered rhetoric of "manhood rights" expressed in conventions or in editorial opinions in black newspapers obscures the underlying acknowledgment of familial relationships within male activism, as well as women's roles in shaping communal interests and goals.[25] Although women did not participate in conventions as official delegates, they attended the proceedings and in at least one case officially endorsed the actions of male participants. In fact, conventions allowed black families from all over northern California to gather together, forming durable social and political networks. Black newspapers carried notice of convention visitors, both male and female, and family interests entered the explicit political dialogue regularly during convention sessions. As early as 1856, Colored Citizens' Convention president, William H. Hall, protested that blacks in California were "deprived of protection for the safety of our families, taxed for the support of education, and yet the doors of the common school-house are closed against our children." In fact, black men may have assumed the role of the "family delegate" at these meetings, using the convention as a gendered tool to address issues of significance to the larger community.[26]

If black men used Colored Citizens' Conventions to demand civil rights such as equal educational opportunities, some black women drew on popular Victorian-era gender conventions to create their own platform. At first glance, Sacramento's black women acted within the traditional boundaries of "true womanhood." Even in this largely working-class community, nineteenth-century census takers reported that virtually all of Sacramento's married black women were "keeping house" for their families.[27] California's black press also frequently lauded female domesticity, a gendered image in contrast to editorials touting the rhetoric of manhood rights in civil rights campaigns. Black editor Peter Anderson urged women to make their homes "the seat of happiness" for their husbands in an 1863 *Pacific Appeal* column, and Sacramento's "Cleopatra" articulated a similar vision of womanhood in her 1869 letter to *The Elevator*, a black-owned newspaper published in San Francisco. "Her place is not at the ballot box," she explained, "her place is at home, attending to the young of her house, sowing the seeds of virtue and goodness in their young hearts, using her influence to make good and useful members of society."[28] Yet it was this gendered emphasis on women's nurturing abilities that created space for women in the nineteenth-century civil rights movement, both through participation in shaping communal education values and through formal activism on behalf of public schooling.

Perhaps the most typical site of female community activism was in the church-based Sabbath school, an institution claimed by women on the basis of the prevailing gender ideology that promoted women's maternal and spiritual qualities. The importance of Sabbath schools in the black community should not be underestimated, as female teachers taught children religious and moral values using the family model but also supplemented public school education. For black children who lived in the outlying districts of Sacramento County, a Sunday journey to church and participation in Sabbath school may have been the only education available.[29] By the 1860s both St. Andrew's AME Church and Siloam Baptist Church boasted thriving Sabbath schools led by black women, each with its own library. Children and their lay teachers frequently organized festivals, picnics, and readings in front of the adult congregation. St. Andrew's AME Sabbath school teacher, Annie E. Vincent, described one such celebration in an 1864 letter to the *Pacific Appeal*: "[T]he juveniles had full possession of the evening, until the late hours of 11 and 12. As far as I can learn, everyone left the church feeling they had been fully compensated for the amount required."[30] These child-centered group activities led by female teachers fostered racial pride based on education and community growth.

Experience at the church Sabbath schools frequently led black men and women into other educational activities. At least two of Sacramento's black Sabbath school teachers also taught in the state's public schools, suggesting that the black community's emphasis on education blurred the boundaries between religious and public schools. Siloam Baptist's Sabbath school teacher, Anna Yantes, taught at the local segregated school, and Annie E. Vincent, the AME Sabbath school teacher, earned a teaching certificate in San Francisco and eventually taught at a segregated school in Santa Rosa, California.[31]

In addition to the practical work of educating black children, Sacramento's black women helped to maintain public interest in education through their correspondence with black-owned newspapers, such as Peter Anderson's *Pacific Appeal* and Philip Bell's *The Elevator*, which circulated throughout northern California. These newspapers provided essential leadership in the black civil rights movement of the 1860s and 1870s but also reinforced kinship bonds between communities by carrying regular social columns and reports of family events. In fact, these newspapers may have succeeded where an 1857 paper, the

Mirror of the Times, had failed precisely because the family and social ties built since the 1850s sustained a larger population of both readers and local correspondents. Sacramento's black women took advantage of these newspapers, frequently writing letters and editorial columns, advertising local events, and even providing crucial financial support. *The Elevator*'s Sacramento correspondent, "Mary," challenged northern California's black women to collect donations on behalf of the newspaper, noting, "[T]he ladies do not neglect you as literary contributors, and I know they will not neglect you as financial contributors."[32]

The *Pacific Appeal* and *The Elevator* regularly documented black women's interests in education as well as other social activities, suggesting that their actions shaped and maintained larger community perspectives. Vincent was one of the most prolific essayists in the pages of these newspapers, clearly using the black press to rally support for her favorite cause, education. Like other black activists, Vincent promoted education as a tool for personal uplift but also as a means of demonstrating power over racism. "The only way to be happy—really and truly happy," wrote Vincent in an 1864 letter to the *Appeal*, "is to be wise, and wisdom comes through knowledge, and knowledge through education."[33] Throughout the 1860s and into the next decade, women like Vincent maintained community interest in schooling through their frequent letters to black newspapers describing Sacramento black children's participation in both the public and Sabbath school settings and promoting education as a community value. The published writings of Sacramento's women also provided important models for similar activities in other communities throughout the state, implicitly sanctioning black women's public activism.

Vincent and other black women readily joined the push to destroy segregated schools in the early 1870s, although here it is particularly instructive to pay close attention to local interests. During the 1865 Colored Citizens' Convention, male delegates first announced that while their goal was to attain access to education for all black children in California, they were also ready to mount an attack on segregated schools. Yet black leaders in the following years focused their attention on the Fifteenth Amendment to the Constitution, guaranteeing male suffrage. This goal certainly can be read in the light of a desire on the part of black men to gain equal manhood rights, but suffrage and civil rights legislation were also tools to promote familial interests, as black male delegates repeated frequently at an 1871 Stockton convention dedicated to education. Philip Bell, editor of *The Elevator*, later expressed this communal perspective in his frustration over the 1875 Supplementary Civil Rights Bill passed in the

U.S. Congress. Bell decried the deletion of a provision requiring integrated schools: "[W]e care more for the education of our children than for all these superficial advantages. The former are but the enjoyment of the day, the latter will mold the character of the rising generation."[34]

In Sacramento the black community clearly supported statewide efforts to force integration in all of California's public schools even as they acted to shore up black children's educational experiences hin the local separate school. Male delegates at the 1871 education convention agreed to support legislative attempts to integrate California's public school systems, an attempt that relied on black men's political influence through the ballot.[35] Again, women and family were not absent. When Peter Anderson visited Sacramento's Siloam Baptist Church to urge black men to support Republican candidates pledged to school reform, not only did women participate as enthusiastic audience members, but Annie E. Vincent joined him on the podium to endorse his message. Although her speech was not recorded, her presence at this political rally demonstrates that many black women pushed the boundaries of typical gendered reform activism. "Sarah," a Sacramento correspondent to the *Appeal* probably spoke for many female audience members when she announced, "[L]ike anxious foot soldiers we rest on our arms to await the day when we shall fight the great battle of our educational interest—the hope of liberty and happiness throughout the world."[36] Sarah's commentary suggests her feeling of inclusion, replicated in later published letters describing Republican conventions in Sacramento and proudly detailing black men's participation. If black men expressed their political views through conventions and the ballot, black women participated in a larger political sphere through their keen commentary on electoral events as well as their practical actions on behalf of education.[37]

Women's efforts to support educational reform became even more crucial when white lawmakers refused to desegregate California schools in 1871 and 1872. Black Californians next turned to the court system, pushing for a test case to integrate the state's public school system. Sacramento's black parents joined other communities throughout the state to raise money for the expected legal fees associated with the case. They organized a group of fourteen men and twelve women to assist the efforts of the executive committee appointed at the earlier education convention. While black men undertook a collection drive to raise money from individuals, the women drew on social and kin networks to organize a music festival and a fruit festival to raise money. By fall 1872 Sacramento's parents announced they had raised more than $100 to support the test case, just as a white lawyer, John Dwinelle, sued San Francisco grammar school principal Noah Flood for refusing to admit a black student, Mary Frances Ward, to his school.[38] Black parents throughout the state eagerly awaited the verdict only to have their hopes dashed when the California supreme court finally ruled in 1874 that segregated schools did not violate the Fourteenth Amendment, although the state must provide "separate but equal" facilities for black children. If black leaders protested the continuation of segregation, the ruling at least required rural areas to admit black children to public schools with white children if a separate class could not be maintained, and it required urban areas to provide specialized or advanced academic programs for black students.[39]

Sacramento's black parents expressed disappointment at both these failures, but their actions suggest that they expected to rely on grassroots activism to shape and ensure their children's education. Parents' first goal, expressed as early as 1867, was to replace white teachers at the segregated school with black teachers. The hiring of a new white teacher, William Crowell, had precipitated two years of crisis at the school. Attendance dropped sharply as Crowell engineered the dismissal of the black assistant teacher, Anna Yantes. Although no details explaining the disruption have survived, black parents made it clear they preferred black leadership at the school. Crowell was eventually replaced by another white teacher, who the parents accepted, but they did not fully express satisfaction with the school again until 1873, with the hiring of Sarah Jones, a black Oberlin College graduate and recent arrival to the city. Parents enthusiastically endorsed Jones, applauding her employment in the pages of the *Pacific Appeal* and attending the spring school examination in large numbers.[40] Jones's teaching abilities clearly impressed black parents, as did her presence as a strong role model for their children.

Under Jones's leadership, parents pressed the Sacramento City School Board to adhere to *Ward v. Flood*'s ruling that black children be provided equal opportunities. By the end of Jones's first term at the one-room schoolhouse, Ernest Small and Susan Bullard passed exams qualifying them to attend the city's only grammar school, and in what seems to have been an unexpected move, the white principal, A. H. McDonald, admitted the two pupils in fall 1874, thus initiating the integration of Sacramento's schools. This action touched off two years of angry debate in the Sacramento City School Board, frustrated by financial inability to live up to the "separate but equal" requirements of *Ward v. Flood* and pressured by the success of Jones's students. Jones herself entered the fray by publicly supporting integration in a letter to the *Sacramento Daily Union*. Denying reports that she favored maintaining the separate school (and thus her job), Jones wrote,

> The colored children are taught daily that they are inferior to the white, until like an old story that one tells so often he believes it to be true himself, our children think they are inferior, and the only way to disabuse their minds of this false impression, and to do away with this false theory of those narrow minded persons who teach it is to educate the negro in the same school as the white child.[41]

With full parental support, Jones and her students spent school vacations preparing for examinations so that by the next year, another four black children met the requirements to attend the grammar school. What statewide political efforts had failed to achieve, black families and a black female teacher accomplished through persistent yet practical actions.

By 1875 the Sacramento City School Board ended its public fight against black children attending the city's specialized schools alongside white children. The city's white residents and black residents seem to have reached a compromise based on internal community desires. Black students who passed advanced examinations were allowed to attend the grammar and later the city's high school, but the board maintained the separate O Street school for primary-level students, refusing a handful of requests by parents to send their children to closer neighborhood schools. Many black residents seemed to accept the segregated primary school as a means of providing black leadership and a supportive environment for their younger children.[42] When California lawmakers quietly removed provisions in state laws requiring segregated education for black children in 1880, parents continued to send their children to Jones's school. As one black Sacramento resident remembered, "I chose the colored school because I wanted to be loyal to my race."[43] In 1894 school administrators finally abolished the separate school as a matter of economy and with congratulations and praise for her years of teaching, transferred Jones to the principalship of a large, integrated primary school.[44]

Sacramento's black women, such as Sarah Jones and her earlier counterparts Lucinda Blue, Anna Yantes, Annie E. Vincent, as well as countless other women throughout California truly acted as "anxious foot soldiers" in their support of the nineteenth-century civil rights movement. Victorian gender ideology encouraged women's involvement in educational activities but placed them in seemingly subordinate roles under male leadership. Yet men's status as official political actors and group leaders should not be conflated with individualized or solely masculine-centered activism. Constructed familial and kinship alliances provided women with a sense of collective purpose in the black community, spurring their participation in a variety of civil rights activities. For nineteenth-century black Californians, community was inherently political and community included men, women, and children.

NOTES

1. *Pacific Appeal*, September 30, 1871, p. 3.

2. See Elsa Barkley Brown's important work suggesting the nature of this collective ethos in the South in two essays, "Negotiating and Transforming the Public Sphere: African American Political Life in the Transition from Slavery to Freedom," *Public Culture* 7 (1994): 107–46; and "To Catch a Vision of Freedom: Reconstructing Southern Black Women's Political History, 1865–1880," in *African American Women and the Vote, 1837–1965*, ed. Ann D. Gordon, Bettye Collier-Thomas, John H. Bracey, Arlene Voski Avakian, and Joyce Avrech Berkman (Amherst: University of Massachusetts Press, 1997), 66–99.

3. For surveys of state educational history and policy vis-à-vis minority groups, see Irving G. Hendrick, *The Education of Non-Whites in California, 1849–1970* (San Francisco: R & E Research Associates, 1977); and Charles M. Wollenberg, *All Deliberate Speed: Segregation and Exclusion in California Schools, 1855–1975* (Berkeley: University of California Press, 1976).

4. On the political nature of the African American family and gender roles, see Elsa Barkley Brown, "To Catch a Vision of Freedom"; Glenda Elizabeth Gilmore, *Gender and Jim Crow: Women and the Politics of White Supremacy in North Carolina, 1896–1920* (Chapel Hill: University of North Carolina Press, 1996); Evelyn Brooks Higginbotham, "African American Women and the Metalanguage of Race," *Signs* 17 (Winter 1992): 251–74; Shirley Carlson, "Black Ideals of Womanhood in the Late Victorian Era," *Journal of Women's History* 77 (Spring 1992): 61–73; Linda Perkins, "The Impact of the 'Cult of True Womanhood' on the Education of Black Women," *Journal of Social Issues* 39 (1983): 17–28; and Shirley J. Yee, *Black Women Abolitionists: A Study in Activism, 1828–1860* (Knoxville: University of Tennessee Press, 1992), esp. chap. 2, "Black Women and the Cult of True Womanhood."

5. Clarence Caesar, "An Historical Overview of the Development of Sacramento's Black Community, 1850–1983" (M.A. thesis, California State University, Sacramento, 1985). For preliminary studies of black women in the American West, see Lawrence B. De Graaf's "Race, Sex and Region: Black Women in the American West, 1850–1920," *Pacific Historical Review* 49 (May 1980): 285–313; and Glenda Riley, "American Daughters: Black Women in the West," *Montana: The Magazine of Western History* 38 (Spring 1988): 14–27. Both of these essays point out that further research remains to be done.

6. *The Seventh Census of the United States: 1850* (Washington, D.C.: James Armstrong, Public Printer, 1853), 969; *Population and Industry of California, by the State Census for the Year 1852* (Washington, D.C.: R. Armstrong, Public Printer, 1853), Table 1, "Population—Whites, Coloreds, Indians Domesticated, and Foreigners—1852," 982; *Population of the United States in 1860; Compiled from the Original Returns of the Eight Census* (Washington, D.C.: Government Printing Office, 1864), 23, 25, 28; and Michael S. Coray, "Blacks in the Pacific West, 1850–1860: A View from the Census," *Nevada Historical Society Quarterly* 28 (Summer 1985): 98–99. See also Rudolph Lapp, *Blacks in Gold Rush California* (New Haven: Yale University Press, 1977); Douglas Henry Daniels, *Pioneer Urbanites: A Social and Cultural History of Black San Francisco* (Berkeley: University of California Press, 1990); and James A. Fisher, "A History of the Political and Social Development of the Black Community in California, 1850–1950" (Ph.D. dissertation, State University of New York at Stony Brook, 1972). For a useful discussion of the California gold rush, see Malcolm J. Rohrbough, *Days of Gold: The California Gold Rush and the American Nation* (Berkeley: University of California Press, 1997). On Sacramento, see John W. Reps, *The Forgotten Frontier: Urban Planning in the American West before 1890* (Columbia: University of Missouri Press, 1981), 60–61.

7. See also Michael S. Coray, "Blacks in the Pacific West, 1850–1860: A View from the Census," *Nevada Historical Society Quarterly* 28 (Summer 1985): 98–99. Delilah L. Beasley's early work, *The Negro Trail Blazers of California* (Los Angeles, 1919; rpt. New York: G. K. Hall, 1998), provides the fullest coverage of black women.

8. Coray, "Blacks in the Pacific West, 1850–1860," 98–99; Florida-born George Proctor serves to illustrate both the desperation and the hope of black migrants to California. Although Proctor was free, he migrated to Sonora, California, hoping to raise enough money to purchase his wife's and his children's freedom. Proctor lost hope after the hotel he operated burned in 1852, and his family was sold at auction two years later. See Proctor's story in Lee H. Warner, *Free Men in an Age of Servitude: Three Generations of a Black Family* (Lexington: University Press of Kentucky, 1992), 71–79.

9. According to the 1860 state census, 67 percent of the 160 black women in Sacramento previously lived in the South. See *Population of the United States in 1860*, 23, 25, 28. Regarding the Booth family, see Beasley, *The Negro Trail Blazers of California*, 115–16; and the 1852 California State Census, microform index compiled by the Daughters of the American Revolution, Genealogical Records Committee, 1934–35.

10. "The Scavenger's Depot: Interesting Statistics of the Colored Population" in the *Daily Evening Bulletin*, September 16, 1856, p. 2. For a similar assertion by a German traveler, see Carl Meyer, *Bound for Sacramento: Travel Pictures of a Returned Wanderer*, trans. Ruth Frye Axe (Claremont, Calif.: Saunders Studio Press, 1938), 144–45. On the issue of slavery in California, see Lucille Eaves, *A History of California Labor Legislation* (Berkeley: University Press, 1910), 82–104; and Lapp, *Blacks in Gold Rush California*, 64–77, 132–34. The story of the Yantes family was reported in the *Sacramento Daily Union*, November 1, 1859, p. 2; August 15, 1874, p. 5. Note that the family name is sometimes spelled "Yantis."

11. On the Blues, see Thompson and West, *History of Sacramento County, California*, 105; Sacramento County Marriage Records, Reel 332, Sacramento County

Recorders Office, Daniel Blue to Lucinda Lung, August 9, 1850, p. 1, Record 2. See *Population of the United States in 1860*, passim, for numerous references to black families.

12. The historians John Modell and Tamara K. Hareven suggest that the common practice of boarding created "surrogate families." See Modell and Hareven, "Urbanization and the Malleable Household: An Examination of Boarding and Lodging in American Families," in *Family and Kin in Urban Communities, 1700–1930*, ed. Tamara K. Hareven (New York: New Viewpoints, 1977), 164–86; and Tamara K. Hareven, "The History of the Family and the Complexity of Social Change," *American Historical Review* 96 (February 1991): 105–6. See also Susan Armitage's perceptive discussion of kinship networks in "Women and Men in Western History: A Stereoptical Vision," *Western Historical Quarterly* 16 (October 1985): 384–85.

13. See Moore and Ward's speech on behalf of education in *Proceedings of the First State Convention of the Colored Citizens of the State of California* (Sacramento: Democratic State Journal Print, 1855; rpt. San Francisco: R & E Research Associates, 1969), 25. Regarding early notices of black churches, see Thompson and West, *History of Sacramento County, California*, 105, 107; *Sacramento Transcript*, December 16, 1850, p. 2. For two works that explore the critical connections between education and religion in the antebellum black community, see Janet Duitsman Cornelius, *When I Can Read My Title Clear: Literacy, Slavery, and Religion in the Antebellum South* (Columbia: University of South Carolina Press, 1991); and David E. Swift, *Black Prophets of Justice: Activist Clergy before the Civil War* (Baton Rouge: Louisiana State University Press, 1989). Elsa Barkley Brown eloquently argues that during Reconstruction, southern black churches fostered collective relationships based on kinship and caring, in "To Catch a Vision of Freedom," 67–68.

14. Samuel Colville, ed., *Samuel Colville's City Directory of Sacramento* (San Francisco: Monson and Valentine, Book & Job Printers, 1854), 79; Beasley, *The Negro Trailblazers of California*, 174, 177. Beasley reports that after Scott married ex-miner Isaac Flood and moved to Oakland in 1857, she opened the first school for black children in that region.

15. Samuel Colville, ed., *Colville's Sacramento Directory* (Sacramento: James Anthony & Co., Book and Job Printers, 1855), 72. Regarding Sanderson, see William Wells Brown, "Jeremiah Burke Sanderson," in *The Black Man, His Antecedents, His Genius, and His Achievements* (New York: Thomas Hamilton, 1863; rpt. New York: Johnson Reprint Corporation, 1969), 91–92; Rudolph M. Lapp, "Jeremiah B. Sanderson: Early California Negro Leader," in *Journal of Negro History* 52 (October 1968): 321–25; and Beasley, *The Negro Trail Blazers of California*, 163–64, 168–69. Regarding black involvement in Garrisonian abolition, see James Oliver Horton, *Free People of Color: Inside the African American Community* (Washington, D.C.: Smithsonian Institution Press, 1993), 46–48. Although his petition has not survived, see reports of this document in Minutes, Sacramento City School Board, June 19, 1855, Sacramento Archives and Museum Collection Center.

16. *Sacramento Daily Union*, October 24, 1855, p. 2. For a brief description of George Fletcher, see his brother Barney Fletcher's obituary in the *San Francisco Alta Times*, November 4, 1884, p. 5. Regarding earlier protests against slavery and the ban on black

testimony, see Lapp, *Blacks in Gold Rush California*. Women's roles in these early protests have yet to be fully explored.

17. See a full discussion of these changes in Susan Bragg, "'Knowledge is Power': Sacramento Blacks and the Public Schools, 1850–1894" (M.A. thesis, California State University, Sacramento, 1997), 21–32.

18. At least one black father took part in the fund-raising. The *Sacramento Daily Union* reported Daniel "Blew" (probably Daniel Blue) appealing for donations in a notice printed April 3, 1858, p. 2. See other notices of fund-raisers organized by women in the *Union*, April 8, 1858, p. 3; October 1, 1859, p. 3. The purchase of the lot is recorded in Sacramento County Land Sales Records and Indexes, Sacramento County Recorder's Office, Deeds Book W, 243 B44, 331.

19. Minutes, Sacramento City School Board, June 27, 1857; October 31, 1857; October 31, 1859. Regarding reports of the school, see *Sacramento Daily Union*, April 23, 1860, p. 3; December 17, 1860, p. 5; and Minutes, Sacramento City School Board, December 3, 1860.

20. There is a large body of literature that explores the nature of public schooling and the motivation of educators. For a sample of relevant works on the history of common schooling, see Pamela Barnhouse Walters, "Who Should Be Schooled: The Politics of Class, Race, and Ethnicity," in *The Political Construction of Education: The State, School Expansion, and Economic Change*, ed. Bruce Fuller and Richard Robinson (New York: Praeger, 1992), 173–87; Carl F. Kaestle, *Pillars of the Republic: Common Schools and American Society, 1780–1860* (New York: Hill and Wang, 1983); and David Tyack, *The One Best System: A History of American Urban Education* (Cambridge, Mass.: Harvard University Press, 1974).

21. *Sacramento Daily Union*, October 24, 1855, p. 2. Blue's letter, dated December 23, 1862, was published in the *Pacific Appeal*, January 10, 1863, p. 3. See *Pacific Appeal*, December 20, 1862, p. 3, for the original editorial, "Colored Schools," reprinted from the *Christian Recorder*, an Ohio newspaper.

22. *Pacific Appeal*, August 16, 1862, p. 3. A brief reference to a "Ladies and Gentlemen's Literary Sociable Club" in 1871 suggests that these mixed-sex organizations were a lasting feature of Sacramento's black community. See *Pacific Appeal*, April 15, 1871, p. 3.

23. The *Union*'s reporter noted that boys did not attend school because of their need "to earn their bread." See reports of the examination in the *Sacramento Daily Union*, April 23, 1860, p. 3.

24. Minutes, Sacramento City School Board, March 26, 1866.

25. For an example of the gendered political language employed by male editors, see *The Elevator*, October 20, 1865, p. 2. Regarding the masculine rhetoric of political expression, see James O. Horton, "Violence, Protest, and Identity: Black Manhood in Antebellum America," in Horton, *Free People of Color*, 80–97; and Glenda Gilmore, "Race and Manhood," in Gilmore, *Gender and Jim Crow*, 61-90.

26. See typical examples of both political and social commentary in accounts of the 1857 convention in the *Mirror of the Times*, December 12, 1857, p. 2; and the 1871 Educational Convention in *Pacific Appeal*, November 25, 1871, p. 2. For Hall's speech, see

Proceedings of the Second Annual Convention of Colored Citizens of the State of California, 71. See also a reference to Mrs. Alfred J. White's resolution thanking members of the Business Committee in *Proceedings of the First State Convention of the Colored Citizens of the State of California* (Sacramento: Democratic State Journal Print, 1855; rpt. San Francisco: R & E Research Associates, 1969), 24. The minutes of the 1855, 1856, and 1865 conventions, all held in Sacramento at St. Andrew's AME Church are reprinted in *Proceedings of the Conventions of the Colored Citizens of the State of California* (San Francisco: R & E Research Associates, 1969).

27. Certainly, married women's labor in family businesses was underreported, but the lack of outside employment among Sacramento's nineteenth-century black women is interesting (and worthy of greater research) in light of the fact that economic discrimination typically forced black married women in other regions into the labor force. See James Oliver Horton, "Freedom's Yoke: Gender Conventions among Antebellum Free Blacks," *Feminist Studies* 12 (Spring 1996): 59–62; and Sharon Harley, "For the Good of Family and Race: Gender, Work, and Domestic Roles in the Black Community, 1880-1930," *Signs* 15 (1990): 342–43.

28. "A Woman's Power," *Pacific Appeal*, May 30, 1863, p. 2; *The Elevator*, July 2, 1869, pp. 2–3. James Horton describes similar gender proscriptions in the antebellum northern black press in "Freedom's Yoke," 102–6.

29. See Anne M. Boylan's useful work, *Sunday School: The Formation of an Institution, 1790–1880* (New Haven: Yale University Press, 1988), 114–26, regarding domestic ideology, and pp. 22–59, on providing academic education for minority children; and James D. Anderson, *The Education of Blacks in the South, 1860–1935* (Chapel Hill: University of North Carolina Press, 1988), 12–13.

30. *Pacific Appeal*, March 26, 1864, p. 3; *The Elevator*, May 7, 1869, p. 3. See other reports of Sacramento Sabbath school activities in the *Pacific Appeal*, May 16, 1862, p. 3; August 29, 1863, p. 3; November 28, 1863, p. 3; September 19, 1873, p. 2. See accounts of books and members of local Sabbath schools in the minutes of the 1865 Colored Citizens' Convention in *Proceedings of the Conventions of the Colored Citizens of the State of California*, 85.

31. *The Elevator*, June 9, 1865, p. 2; February 16, 1866, p. 2; *Pacific Appeal*, November 26, 1870, p. 2; August 21, 1872, p. 3. See the *Sacramento Daily Union*, January 1, 1874, p. 5, for a listing of Annie Vassels (nee Yantes) as a longtime Siloam Baptist Sabbath school teacher.

32. *The Elevator*, February 14, 1868, p. 2. See also *The Elevator*, May 1, 1868, p. 2.

33. For other essays by Vincent, see *Pacific Appeal*, May 2, 1862, pp. 2–3; June 21, 1862, p. 3; May 23, 1863, p. 3; January 2, 1864, p. 3.

34. *The Elevator*, December 26, 1874, p. 3. See also Peter Anderson's similar commentary in *Pacific Appeal*, January 9, 1875, p. 2.

35. *Pacific Appeal*, November 23, 1871, p. 2.

36. *Pacific Appeal*, August 26, 1871, p. 1; October 7, 1871, p. 3. See another sample of Sarah's commentary on Republican Party activities in *Pacific Appeal*, September 2, 1871, p. 1.

37. Brown, "To Catch the Vision of Freedom," 74.

38. *Ward v. Flood*, 48 California 5283, 56–57; *The Elevator*, March 7, 1874, p. 2; *Pacific Appeal*, March 7, 1874, p. 2.

39. See *The Elevator*, April 27, 1872, p. 2, for a recounting of legislative reform failures.

40. Regarding teachers at the O Street school, see Minutes, Sacramento City School Board, May 1, 1867; April 27, 1868; June 28, 1869; August 31, 1871; August 28, 1871; April 12, 1873; *Pacific Appeal*, April 19, 1873, p. 2; April 26, 1873, p. 2; *Sacramento Daily Union*, June 27, 1873, p. 3.

41. *Sacramento Daily Union*, April 29, 1874, p. 3.

42. *Sacramento Daily Union*, June 26, 1874, p. 3; *The Elevator*, March 31, 1877, p. 3.

43. *Sacramento Observer*, November 1873, LL-72; Minutes, Sacramento City School Board, October 4, 1894; November 7, 1894.

44. Minutes, Sacramento City School Board, October 3, 1894.

Willianna Hickman's Nicodemus Saga

Willianna Hickman, an Exoduster from Kentucky, was thirty-one when she traveled with her minister husband, their six children, and one hundred forty other colonists to the all-black settlement of Nicodemus in west Kansas. They got off the railroad at Ellis, Kansas, some thirty miles away, on March 3, 1878. In the vignette below she describes the last part of the journey to Nicodemus.

I had some trouble getting housed as my children broke out with measles on the way. We dwelled at a farm house that night. The next night members of the colony had succeeded in stretching a tent. This was our first experience of staying in a tent. We remained in the camp about two weeks. Several deaths occurred among the children while we were there.

We left there for Nicodemus, traveling overland with horses and wagons. We were two days on the way, with no roads to direct us save deer trails and buffalo wallows. We traveled by compass. At night the men built bonfires and sat around them, firing guns to keep the wild animals from coming near. We reached Nicodemus about 3 o'clock on the second day.

When we got in sight of Nicodemus the men shouted, "There is Nicodemus." Being very sick I hailed this news with gladness. I looked with all the eyes I had. I said, "Where is Nicodemus? I don't see it." My husband pointed out various smokes coming out of the ground and said, "That is Nicodemus." The families lived in dugouts. The scenery to me was not at all inviting and I began to cry.

From there we went to our homestead fourteen miles west of Nicodemus. Rev. S. M. Lee carried us to the farm in his wagon and as usual there was no road and we used a compass. I was asleep in the wagon bed with the children and was awakened by the blowing of horns. Our horns were answered by horns in the distance and the firing of guns, being those of my brother Austin, and a friend, Lewis Smith. They had been keeping house for us on our new homestead. Driving in the direction of the gunfiring, we reached the top of the hill where we could see the light of the fire they had built to direct our way.

Source: Dorothy Sterling, ed., *We Are Your Sisters: Black Women in the Nineteenth Century* (New York: W. W. Norton, 1984), 375–76.

Days, weeks, months, and years passed and I became reconciled to my home. We improved the farm and lived their nearly twenty years, making visits to Nicodemus to attend church, entertainments, and other celebrations. My three daughters were much loved school teachers in Nicodemus and vicinity.

§~~~§

Homesteading on the Plains:
The Ava Speese Day Story

The Kinkaid Homestead Act of 1904, which threw open thousands of acres of the Sand Hills region of northwestern Nebraska, provided an opportunity for the only significant African American homesteading in the state. Recognizing the arid condition of the land, the federal government provided homestead claims of 640 rather than 160 acres. The first African American to file a claim, Clem Deaver, arrived in 1904. Other blacks, primarily from Omaha, soon followed, and by 1910 twenty-four families filed claim to 14,000 acres in Cherry County. Eight years later 185 blacks claimed 40,000 acres around a small all-black community named DeWitty, after a local African American business owner. Yet by the early 1920s black farm families began leaving the isolated region for Denver, Omaha, or Lincoln. Ava Speese Day provides the most detailed accounts of this homesteading community. Her recollections have been called a black "Little House on the Prairie" because of their richly evocative description of her Nebraska childhood.

The Negro Homesteaders in the Sandhills were led there by my mother's father, Charles Meehan. He grew up in Detroit and Round Eau, Ontario, Canada, where he met and married Hester Freeman, born and raised in Canada. They heard of land available in Nebraska so went there, settling near Overton, where my mother, Rosetta, was born. When they heard about the Kinkaid Act, grandfather and several others investigated and filed claims northwest of Brownlee, along the North Loup River.

In the spring of 1907 he led the first emigrant train to Cherry County, accompanied by William Crawford and George Brown. He drove one of his three wagons, his son Den drove another and my mother, Rosetta, drove the third. She took care of her own team, greased the wagon wheels, and she was just turned sixteen. Uncle Bill rode with George Brown. He was fourteen. Grandpa's homestead was about twelve miles upriver from Brownlee on the north side of the river. Uncle Den was upriver two miles. Across from him was the Emanuel home, and another mile up was Jim Hatter. Two miles more was A. P. Curtis, and further up the Griffiths.

Source: Ava Speese Day, "The Ava Speese Day Story," in *Sod House Memories*, 3 vols., ed. Frances Jacobs Alberts (Hastings, Neb.: Sod House Society, 1972), 3:261–75.

Several miles on were Bert and Ida Morgan. William Crawford homesteaded about a mile down river from Meehans, and George Brown a mile east. His son, Maurice, who married Aunt Gertie, was farther east.... Other negro families took Kinkaids farther down from the river until there were forty or more. There were the Price family, the Praythers, Bill Fords, Josh Emanuel, DeWitty. Jim Dewitty ran the store and post office, and after he left Uncle Dan Meehan was postmaster, and changed the name from DeWitty to Audacious...

Dad and Mom lived near Westerville for a year and then moved to Torrington, Wyoming, moving back to the Sandhills in November 1915. At that time I was three years old. We lived with grandpa and grandma Meehan the first winter till our house could be built.

I remember them cutting sod for it. They laid the sod like we do brick today, overlapping layers. The door frames were made of 2 x 12's. This home was across the river from grandpa's on Uncle Ed's homestead that we rented for a few years. ... I could watch our house go up, our sod house. What a thrill on the occasions when we all rode the lumber wagon across to take a look up close. Before we moved in we knew where each piece of furniture would sit. Our first sod house was one large room. It was partitioned off in sections with curtains to make bedrooms. Later most everyone added a sod kitchen, joining them by using a window as the door to the new room. We felt we had a whole new house again.... It was heaven, and we enjoyed it.

We had two big problems, the dirt and the flies. Summertimes we twisted news-papers and lit the tip. Holding this carefully it was swept close to the ceiling, which was made of brownish or pinkish building paper. The flame burned the wings off the flies and then they were swept up and burned. We only did this when dad was home. If the paper ceiling had caught fire, but it didn't. Otherwise we all waved clothes and drove them out. Then there were the sheets of grey fly paper you poured water on and the poison seeped out. And large sheets of sticky fly paper that gathered flies. Grandpa Meehan added a crowning touch to his soddy, he plas-tered the entire inside, no one had a home as easy to keep clean as grandma....

The negro pioneers worked hard, besides raising plenty of corn, beans and what vegetables they could, everyone raised cattle. It was too sandy for grain so the answer was cattle. If you did not have enough land you rented range land. We had range cattle and about sixty head of brood mares.... We raised mules, and when they were broken to drive, brought a good price on the Omaha market.

One of my earliest memories is a trail herd.... It was a sight to see them coming out of the hills on down the river.... They traveled on open range where this was possible. Sometimes the entire three miles within our sight was a long line of cattle....

We attended one room frame schools. There was a coal bin attached on back and the older boys kept the coal scuttle filled from the bin.... The backlot held two outhouses. If teacher caught us throwing spitballs we had to stand in a corner, or she spanked our hand with a ruler. It was a pretty bad offense of yours if you got spanked, teacher sent a note home with you and you got another spanking....

The negro teachers we had in Nebraska were Irene Brewer[,] ... Fern Walker[,] ... Esther Shores[,] ... and Uncle Bill Meehan. They were all good teachers but of course Uncle Bill was our favorite.... Our school was Riverview, District 113.... The School Superintendent preached two things to us, that teachers were underpaid, and that Knowledge is Power....

During summer there would always be a big picnic at 'Daddy Hannahs' place. This would usually be in August on the first Sunday. There would be speeches and eats and rodeo.... Social life was very much a part of the community. There were dances, I mean parties held at homes. A great number of these forty families were excellent musicians so who was to provide music was no problem.... Our family was fortunate, we had a cottage organ. You pumped the pedals to force air through the reeds. Dad used to play Sunday evenings and we all sang.... We had fun around the organ, wore out two of them and a piano....Looking back it seems that getting our 80 [acres] was the beginning of the end for us in Nebraska. There was one thing after another.... In March 1925, we left the Sand Hills for Pierre, South Dakota.... This account is factual, and I did not realize it would be so long, but, a way of life is not short. No, a way of life is not short.

CHAPTER 7

Women of the Great Falls African Methodist Episcopal Church, 1870–1910

Peggy Riley

The history of African Americans in the West, long marginalized, is emerging as a dynamic field, in part because of interest in the "New Western History," which recognizes the multiethnic nature of western settlement, and in part because of a growing recognition that blacks were active participants in the westward movement.[1] This is not to deny the realities of discrimination, Jim Crow laws, and inequalities of treatment and opportunity but to acknowledge that despite these obstacles African American westerners maintained social, religious, and cultural identity, were often reasonably prosperous, raised families, educated their children, and built communities. This was as true in Montana as in other parts of the West. Although the African American population in Montana was and is a small percentage of the total population, African Americans actively participated in building communities.

The story of black communities in Montana is a fascinating one, although limited by sources. Secondary sources are few, and primary sources are divided into three basic categories: census data, public records, and private records. Several studies have analyzed manuscript censuses for valuable and enlightening information.[2] The public record comprises newspapers for the most part. Three newspapers were published by black Montanans around the turn of the century; but other local newspapers reported news about the black citizenry.[3] Newspapers, however, cover primarily what are traditionally men's concerns, business and politics, not the daily domestic lives and mundane activities, traditional women's concerns that are the foundations of communities.

In addition to newspapers, another public record exists for Great Falls, Montana: *Great Falls Yesterday*, a Works Progress Administration (WPA) compilation of biographical sketches of pioneering citizens, containing the stories of a number of early black settlers, both men and women.[4] Still, the information on African American activity is skimpy compared to the plethora of material available on white settlers.

Private records such as letters, diaries, journals, minutes of club and church meetings, and oral histories are the most difficult to access, as they are often kept by families or local institutions, stashed in attics or basements or scattered among descendants or church members. Yet these sources can often provide insights into the activities that bind members of a community in affection and common interests—church socials, bake sales and other fund-raising activities, musicales, club meetings—activities primarily in the women's sphere that, combined with a solid grounding in home and family, enable communities to grow and prosper.

It is often through women's stories that we can better understand the histories of communities, including black communities in the West, yet it is exactly these stories that are largely untold. As Lawrence B. De Graaf argues in a seminal article published in 1980, black women remain an invisible segment in the history of western society despite their many accomplishments.[5] More recently, Glenda Riley has demonstrated that black women are still nearly invisible in the historical record and argues that not including black women's stories unbalances western history.[6] However, Riley's article was published in 1988 and still little work has been done to balance the record, even though the stories of black women in the West rival anything in history texts or the popular media. The stories of the African American women of Great Falls show that black women helped to found western communities and bore children who carried on their work. The lives of the women who helped to found and build the community centered on the Union Bethel African Methodist Episcopal (AME) Church in Great Falls, Montana, broadens our understanding of the impact that black women had in shaping the history, culture, and economies of the American West.[7]

THE FOUNDERS

The city of Great Falls was established in 1883 by Paris Gibson, who recognized the potential of the site, near the Great Falls of the Missouri River, for the development of hydroelectric power. His town's success was ensured when eastern interests decided to link mines in Butte, smelters in Anaconda, and refineries in Great Falls by railroad. Gibson also attracted local capitalists who invested in city real estate and business blocks, built flour mills, and established banks.[8] The town grew so rapidly that its total population of 4,750 in 1890 exploded to 14,930 by 1900.[9] By the turn of the century, the Great Falls economy provided both business and domestic service jobs that drew African American settlers to the area: the men worked primarily as porters, cooks, barbers, bartenders, and laborers in 1900. Some single mothers worked as laundrywomen or domestic servants. Few of the wives worked outside of the home.[10]

Even earlier, in 1884, while Paris Gibson was busily preparing the Great Falls site plan he would file on September 30 with the Choteau County Clerk and Recorder, African American pioneers in the area were forming an AME congregation.[11] The congregation was small, probably fewer than twenty, but determined to establish its own place of worship and community center. Two women, Tennessee Finn Hagin and Mamie Courtney, approached Gibson about the possibility of obtaining land to build a church. He agreed to sell the congregation a site in the low, swampy area of town, south of the downtown business area. The Great Falls Water, Power and Townsite Company transferred the warranty deed for the property to the trustees of the Union Bethel AME Church on January 26, 1891. The property was mortgaged twice in the early years: once for $800 and once for $560. (Since that time the church property has never been mortgaged, a tribute to the women and men who worked tirelessly to keep their church the center of community life.) When the mortgages were paid, the trustees of the church, Edward Simms, William M. Morgan, and A. W. Ray, were issued the abstract deed on March 2, 1895.[12] Although the women had taken the initiative to obtain the church property, it is men's names that appear in the public record.

We know very little about these founders of the Union Bethel AME Church in Great Falls. Curiously, neither Hagin nor Courtney appear in the manuscript census for 1900; however, Hagin, a native of Kentucky, is listed as a fifty-four-year-old restaurant cook in the 1910 census. Edward Simms is recorded in the 1900 census as a forty-four-year-old native of Arkansas and father of a large family; his occupation is given as club steward. By 1910 he owned a shoe-shining parlor, and two of his daughters were working as "chambermaids in a house of ill-repute." One of the daughters, Mollie, married Roy Winburn, a shop porter, sometime before the 1920 census and remained active in the Union Bethel AME Church community until she died in 1946.[13]

Though we know little about the founding members of the church, we can glean something about the Great Falls African American community from the census. By 1900, sixteen years after the founding of the church, the community numbered 128, a tiny percentage of Great Falls's total population of almost 15,000. The black population was evenly divided between males and females. Except for a few individuals scattered throughout the city working in domestic service, most African Americans lived on the south side of town, in the neighborhood of the church. The neighborhood was by no means segregated. On one street alone, residents hailed from England, Sweden, Kentucky, Canada, Scotland, Germany, Nebraska, and California. It was a working-class, family neighborhood, including at least fifteen black families. Many of these families' young children had been born in Montana, suggesting that young black married couples had come to Great Falls searching for better lives for themselves and their growing families.

Although few wives worked for wages, they certainly worked for their community, a community that revolved around Union Bethel. When Hagin and Courtney approached Paris Gibson about land for their church, they listed sixteen people as founders and organizers of the church, ten of whom were women.[14] These women played a determining role in the establishment of their church and their community, laying the foundation for the women of the next generation who would build on their work.

THE BUILDERS

According to De Graaf, black women in the American West constituted less than 1 percent of the female population. He suggests that a cultural pattern emerged that was very different from that in the South, that "black women in the West . . . considered themselves to be an elite," able and willing to break with their traditional culture.[15] A break with traditional culture suggests a willingness to create a new culture, one reflecting current circumstances. Because they were a small population concentrated in urban areas, black women might have felt the strain of isolation but instead took advantage of the opportunity to create, through black communities, a culture that may be unique to the West.

From a preliminary study of manuscript census material, Susan Armitage and Deborah Wilbert have found suggestions that black women were "significant forces in local economies and community building." Armitage and Wilbert also note how rarely documents exist for dispossessed groups such as black women.[16] It is fortunate indeed that some documents survive for the women of Great Falls, women such as Marie Ellis, Mattie Welch, and Emma Smith who exemplify the contributions of club women, homemakers, and churchwomen. Through their stories we can gain some understanding of the impact of black women on the history of Montana and of the West.

Club Woman: Marie Dutrieuille Ellis

Marie Dutrieuille Ellis moved with her mother to Great Falls after her father's death in 1911. Her mother, Maria Adams Dutrieuille, has a fascinating history of her own. Maria's sister, Mary Adams, was cook for General and Mrs. George Custer at Fort Lincoln. Maria joined her sister to work as housemaid for the Custers, arriving in Fort Lincoln in 1875. When the Custer house was closed after the Battle of the Little Bighorn, the Adams sisters worked in Miles City, Montana, and Bismarck, North Dakota. In 1878 they arrived in Fort Benton, Montana, a booming port town on the Missouri, after hearing about opportunities for work. Maria worked as a laundress until she met John Lambert "Duke" Dutrieuille, probably in Fort Benton where he had established a barbershop in 1879. They were married in Helena in 1880 and lived in Fort Benton and Helena. By 1900 Maria and Duke were residing in Belt, raising their two children, Frank and Marie. After Duke's death in 1911, Maria moved to Great Falls with her children and remained there until her death in 1939.[17] The Dutrieuilles must have been warmly welcomed by the AME church community when they arrived. Marie Ellis was an active and devoted leader at the church and in the community for as long as she lived in Great Falls.

Marie married Theodore Ellis, who worked as a janitor in a drugstore, in 1914. In 1918, by now the mother of two small children, Marie was a member of the Red Cross Auxiliary, joining Tennie Hagin, one of the church founders; Mrs. L. Horsey, a minister's wife; and Katie Knott, Lillian McFarlin, and Susie McCracken, longtime active members of the AME church. These women were also members of the Dunbar Art and Study Club, named for Paul Laurence Dunbar, "a Negro poet who portrayed 'life among the lowly.'" Marie Ellis founded the club in 1920 and served as its first president.[18]

The Dunbar Art and Study Club was the local manifestation of the emergence of black women's clubs in the early twentieth century. Similar clubs existed in Helena, Billings, and Butte. Like white women's clubs, they were grounded in middle-class values, particularly education, material progress, and the importance of the home and woman's moral influence in it. However, the black women's club movement differed in that its primary concerns were meeting the needs of the black community—promoting racial self-help and raising the standards of women and families to counter prejudice and accusations of immorality. The National Association of Colored Women's motto, "Lifting as we climb," reflects the commitment of black club women to improve the welfare of all black people, regardless of class, region, or educational level.

That Marie Ellis was instrumental in the founding of the Dunbar Club, "a fellowship of women whose aim is to further education, to broaden contacts and to work in unity for the community," illustrates her commitment to building community among African American residents of Great Falls. That the membership of the club was drawn primarily from the Union Bethel congregation illustrates the importance of the church as the keystone for the community and as the training ground for the women's club movement. "The club movement among black women owed its very existence to the groundwork of organization skill and leadership training gained through women's church societies," notes the historian Evelyn Brooks Higginbotham.[19] Through Ellis's efforts in establishing the Dunbar Club, the black women of Great Falls became a force in their community for social service and racial self-help, joining in the work of the nationwide National Association of Colored Women.

The Dunbar Club met regularly in members' homes rather than the church, which was used for larger gatherings, but it is clear that the church remained at its center, providing a strong bond for the membership.[20] Meetings opened and closed with prayer and often song, a chaplain was regularly elected as one of the officers, and club projects included supplying the church with tables and chairs, flatware, and dishes. Its secular activities included collecting donations for the needy and providing college scholarships for young women. The Dunbar Club also reached out to the larger African American communities in Montana. It joined the Montana Federation of Colored Women's Clubs in 1922, one year after the federation was founded, and regularly raised funds to send representatives to statewide meetings. In 1923 Oscar McFarlin, husband of member Lillian McFarlin, visited the club in his capacity as president of the local chapter of the National Association for the Advancement of Colored People (NAACP) "and made very interesting remarks in regards of cooperation [of the] NAACP with the club with its local work."[21] As its cooperation with the NAACP suggests, the Dunbar Club showed an early interest in improving the position of African Americans in Great Falls. A club historian notes that "the early minutes make reference to such projects as a civil rights bill for Montana; opening of the public swimming pool to Negroes[;] and protesting discrimination against Negro youngsters at the ice skating rink."[22]

Marie Ellis's commitment to the Dunbar Club and to her community was repaid in kind. When her husband drowned in a tragic hunting accident in 1924, church and club members came to Mrs. Ellis's aid: "Be it resolved, That this body, the members of Dunbar Art and Study Club send a letter of condolence and the sum of (5.00) five dollars to Mrs. Ellis in her bereavement." The club was an important part of Ellis's life and a comfort in her sorrow; soon after her husband's death, she hosted a meeting at her home.[23]

Marie Ellis, widowed and with three children to raise and support, worked briefly in domestic service, one of the few jobs open to black women in the West. Before her marriage, in Belt, when her father was ill, she had taken in sewing to help support herself and her family. Later she was well known in the Great Falls community for her sewing and baking skills and eventually taught these crafts in WPA classes.[24] Perhaps she drew on these talents in the 1920s and 1930s to help support her children. In any event, she did not give up her community commitments. In addition to her work with the Dunbar Art and Study Club, Ellis was an active member of the Women's Missionary Mite Society, a group that supported the church and its missionary efforts through both spiritual and fund-raising activities.[25] She participated in the Union Bethel AME Sunday School, in which all three of her children were active members, and she served on the church's Board of Trustees.[26]

Details of Marie Ellis's later life are sketchy. She married James Ingram sometime before 1940, many years after the death of her first husband, and eventually moved to California to join a daughter who lived there.[27] Like her mother, Maria Adams Dutrieuille, Marie Ellis survived tragedy and hard times, raised a family, and helped to build a lasting community. "Yes, Grandmother and mother were unusually strong," remembers Maria Raybon, Marie's daughter, reflecting on their commitment to their families, their people, and their community. "Yes—they were invincible characters."[28]

Homemaker: Mattie Byers Novotny Welch

Mattie Welch, a childhood friend of Marie Ellis's, was also an active member of Union Bethel and, like Marie, came from a family of Montana pioneers. Her aunt, Mattie Bell Castner, had been born into slavery in 1855. After emancipation, she worked in domestic service and as a hotel maid. She heard of opportunities in the West, so in 1876 she came to Fort Benton. She worked as a laundress at the Overland Hotel, eventually owning and operating her own laundry. She must have met Maria Adams, who also worked as a laundress, sometime in 1878 or 1879; perhaps Maria worked for her. In 1879 Mattie Bell married John K. Castner, a white freighter, and shortly thereafter moved to Belt, where together the Castners built the settlement's first log cabin. Their cabin became the stage stop for the Great Falls–Lewiston line and grew into a flourishing hotel and restaurant.

The interracial marriage of John and Mattie Castner, despite Montana miscegenation laws (which were not repealed until late in the twentieth century), apparently did not hinder their achievements. Mattie became a successful businesswoman in her own right, running the hotel and restaurant and stocking her ranch in the nearby Highwood Mountains while John owned and operated the first commercial coal mine in Montana.[29]

It is probable that the Castners and Dutrieuilles were good friends. John Castner and Duke Dutrieuille appear together in a photograph in the *Belt Valley History*; Duke had opened a barbershop, Duke's Place, on Castner Street in Belt, ostensibly to take advantage of the coal mining boom.[30] Duke and Maria moved from Helena to Belt to be with their old friends from Fort Benton. Their shared experiences created a special bond between Maria and Mattie. Both Maria and Mattie came from the South, Maria from Kentucky and Mattie from North Carolina. Both had worked as laundresses in Fort Benton. And as two of only six blacks in Belt out of a population of more than three thousand, their African American descent may have fostered a sense of sisterhood between them.[31] In any event, Mattie and Maria were longtime friends. Mattie visited Maria at least once while the Dutrieuilles were living in Helena. And the two shared adventures in Belt that reinforced their bond.

On a trip to Fort Benton where she sold her homegrown vegetables, Mattie, accompanied by her adopted baby son, Albert, and Maria, encountered Indians who stopped the wagon she drove and took all of the vegetables and one of the horses. Mattie rode the remaining horse back to Belt, got another horse, and returned to take Albert and Maria home.[32]

Mattie Castner made two trips to North Carolina to try to find members of her family, of whom there were few records: they had been sold. However, on her first trip she located a sister and brother-in-law, Mr. and Mrs. Byers, and later sent for them to join her in Belt. They returned to North Carolina in 1889 because of Mrs. Byers's ill health. In 1897 Castner made a second trip and brought her niece and namesake, thirteen-year-old Mattie Byers, back with her. Young Mattie attended school in Belt and graduated from the eighth grade. Like her aunt, Mattie married a white man, J. L. Novotny, in 1900. Although Mattie Castner was integrated into the almost all-white community in Belt, when J. L. and Mattie Novotny and their family moved to Great Falls in 1911, they were absorbed into the black community centered on Union Bethel. The Novotnys had moved to Great Falls hoping their children would benefit from the better educational opportunities available there.[33] That same year, Maria Dutrieuille and her children moved to Great Falls.

After J. L. Novotny died, Mattie married a Mr. Welch; the dates are not certain. Mattie's name does not appear in the 1920 census or in the Union Bethel records until the 1930s. In the 1930s Mattie was a member of the church and its Women's Missionary Mite Society.[34] Like Marie Ellis's children, two of Mattie Welch's children, Mary and Jacqueline Novotny, were active enrolled members of the Bethel AME Sunday School.[35]

What Mattie Welch did between 1911, when she moved to Great Falls, and 1937, when she is listed as a member of the Missionary Mite Society, is not a matter of record. However, according to one source, Mattie bore twenty-two children, nine of whom survived into adulthood. Focusing her energies on home and family, Mattie exemplifies many black women's commitment to what Higginbotham describes as the "politics of respectability." "Respectability provided a discursive common ground in its concern for sexual purity, child rearing, habits of cleanliness and order, and overall self-improvement."[36] Many black women in Great Falls, like Mattie Welch, seem to have embraced this philosophy. They were involved in church work and in club work. They insisted their children get a good education: by 1920 every African American in Great Falls ten years and older knew how to read and write.[37] Mothers made sure their children were neat and clean. Lucille Smith Thompson, a friend of Mattie Welch's children, remembered that she was not allowed to leave the yard unless her hair was combed and her face washed. Families lived in neat frame houses in the neighborhood near the church, sent their children to school and to Sunday school, and established a sense of community and identity through their church and the activities centered there. The positive influence of the home and family, these women felt, would help to refute negative racist stereotypes that followed African Americans even to Montana.

Although it is clear that these stereotypes existed in Great Falls, we do not know the extent of racism in the area. In 1894 the Colorado Conference of the AME Church held its annual session in Helena and visited Great Falls. The presiding bishop, the Right Reverend James A. Handy, made a "telling speech" in which he congratulated the people of Great Falls on what they had done but urged them on to higher attainments. He counseled them to embrace their opportunities and get money, land, and educate themselves. Handy declared, "[O]ur fathers learned us to sing 'you may have all the world—give me Jesus'— Now the white folks have taken us at our word—they have taken all the world, and we have little but Jesus. If you have sung that song, quit singing it." His speech was well received, as there were others who had spoken along the same lines.[38]

That Handy's speech was "well received" suggests the people of Great Falls were familiar with its implications (and had good senses of humor), but it also expresses the determination of church members to overcome racial restrictions and their recognition of the importance of "overall self-improvement." The very fact that Union Bethel AME Church was established at such an early date suggests an African American population that was socially segregated from mainstream culture. Therefore, the AME church served a dual purpose: it operated as a religious sanctuary and fulfilled the social aspirations of the black community. Its long history as the first public institution over which blacks exercised control ensured its place as the heart of the community. "The black church—open to both secular and religious groups in the community—came to signify public space," Higginbotham writes.[39] The church, then, in both its religious and its secular manifestation, provided a forum for its congregation, a physical base for its work through the Dunbar Club, the young people's ACE League, the missionary society, and other groups to establish a community dedicated to improving the status of its people.

Despite the racial constraints, a spirit of cooperation between the black and white communities seemed to prevail in relationship to the church. For example, in 1891 Silas Beachly, the only white man to spend winter 1883 in the Great Falls area and later the first Sunday school superintendent in Great Falls, donated $2 for the construction of the AME church.[40] And in 1917, when church members engaged in a fund-raising campaign to augment the $1,400 they had for a new church building, the new pastor, Reverend G. E. Horsey, and the congregation depended on their "white Christian brethren and neighbors" for help.[41] Evidently their hopes were met. The new church was dedicated in September of that year.[42]

Religious cooperation notwithstanding, Lucille Thompson Smith recalled that Mattie Welch's children and other African American children in Great Falls were subject to racial taunting at school:

> God made the nigger
> Made 'em in the night
> Made 'em in a hurry
> And forgot to paint them white.

However, the black children gave as good as they got, retorting:

> God made the white trash
> Made 'em in a shack
> Made 'em in a hurry
> And forgot to paint them black.[43]

The strengths of their homes, their church, and their community instilled in these children a sense of pride and identity. They were not easily intimidated.

Mattie Welch, like most western women, led a busy life. She raised a large family. Nine children survived to adulthood. Sadly, two of her grown sons died: John Laurence, as the result of injuries suffered in an airplane accident while he was training for the aviation service in Florida in 1928; Herbert, burned to death fighting forest fires in 1931.[44] However, Mattie continued to contribute to her community through her church-related activities. She made lifelong friends, endured family tragedies, and with her family made her mark on western history. Her aunt, Mattie Castner, was a Montana pioneer; her daughter, Mary Novotny Berry, remained in Great Falls after the other children had scattered, carrying on the family connection with Union Bethel and the Great Falls community.

Churchwoman: Emma Riley Smith

Emma Riley Smith, a contemporary of Marie Ellis and Mattie Welch, moved to Great Falls with her young family in the early 1920s; her youngest child, Morris, was born in Great Falls in 1923. Mrs. Smith's husband, Martin, went to work as a cook on the Great Northern Railroad. Emma Smith went to work helping to build the Union Bethel AME Church and its community.

Like Marie Ellis and Mattie Welch, Emma Smith brought a wealth of history and experience with her. Her father, James Wesley Riley, had been a farmer in Arkansas. "My great-grandfather had always urged my father to return to Africa. It was a wish he had that he could never fulfill, but he talked about it to my father," Emma remembered in later years. "My father was fourteen years old when freedom was declared, and my mother was four years old. When I was fourteen years old, my father sold his little farm and took my mother, my brother and me to Monrovia, Liberia, West Africa."[45] Soon after their arrival, a sister, Thelma, was born.

Emma Smith lived in Liberia for fifteen years. She and the other children helped with the family farm: "We planted the small [coffee] trees. And we picked coffee. We raised potatoes, and we raised ginger and rice." She remembered vividly and fondly the native African and Americo-Liberian foods, clothing, and cultures from her experience in Africa. Her parents and brother died before Thelma was fifteen. Emma recalled, "Then I got a yearning to come back to America to see my relatives, my grandmothers was living. But I didn't want to stay. It was my intention of returning to Liberia. And so when [Thelma] was fifteen years old, she and I came back to America to visit, and here I am until now. I never had a chance to get back."

Emma stayed in New Jersey and Pennsylvania for a few months before going on to Arkansas to visit with relatives. Her relatives welcomed her with open arms and wanted her to stay in Arkansas, but Emma had other plans: "I had seen other places, and I didn't exactly like the way the Negro was treated. . . . I says 'I couldn't live here and take care of my sister and send her to school,' I said. 'There's better places in America to live,' I said, than here, I said, and 'I'm going to find them.'" So Emma left Arkansas and went to a friend in Cheyenne, Wyoming, where she met a woman from Montana who assured her that she could find work there. In 1913 Emma arrived in Montana and stayed. "After I got settled in Montana, I wouldn't like to exchange places with no state that I have visited, and I think I'll stay here until the end, God willing."[46]

God was willing. Emma met her husband, Martin Smith, in Butte in 1913, and their first child, Madeline, was born there. Later they moved to Lewiston where Smith worked as a cook for the Milwaukee Railroad. When he transferred to the Great Northern Railroad, the growing family, by now including three more children, moved to Great Falls.

Emma Smith, like Marie Ellis and Mattie Welch, was cordially received into the community and Union Bethel Church. By 1927 Emma had been nominated and elected conference secretary for the church's Board of Trustees, a position she held for almost thirty years.[47] During this time, she participated in the mundane but essential tasks of keeping the church going: endless bouts of fundraising to pay for coal, lights, and repairs. Along with her fellow trustees, she planned church socials, dinners, baby contests, and "rallies" to help raise money. As secretary, Emma extended the Board of Trustees' thanks for donations from the Dunbar Club, the Women's Missionary Mite Society, and the Willing Workers Club and private contributions from church and community members.[48]

Emma's fund-raising efforts extended beyond her activities for the Board of Trustees. She served as president of the Women's Missionary Mite Society almost continuously from 1937 to 1967. For the few years during which she did not hold that position, she was an active member, often leading prayers and songs, occasionally giving reports to the society on the activities of the missionaries in Africa and, as always, engaged in fund-raising. The Missionary Mite Society gave bake sales, raffled handmade quilts (Mrs. Smith was an excellent quilter), and sold chances on ham, sugar, and cheese. The society also sponsored dinners (menu for a dinner in 1937: chitterlings, slaw, coffee, cornbread, baked apple), birthday parties, ice-cream socials, and "entertainments," musical evenings in the homes of members. The proceeds went to support the church and its missionary efforts and to assist the needy. The members of the society also participated in Bible reading and discussion. They studied the missionary program, including missionary activity in the West. On one occasion, Mrs. Nixon, the pastor's wife and president of the society, read "on home missions from the book *Last of the Old West*"; on another, a member read a paper about the Whitmans, pioneering missionaries to Washington who were killed by Indians.[49] Emma Smith's tireless efforts on behalf of the Missionary Mite Society and the AME church illustrates vividly the church's place in the community.

During a number of her terms as president of the Missionary Mite Society, Mrs. Smith was assisted by Marie Ellis as vice president. The two women also served as superintendent and assistant superintendent of the Sunday School. Their leadership was passed on to their children. When a young people's organization, the ACE League, was formed in 1935, Ted Ellis was elected president; Lucille Smith, secretary; Mildred Ellis, corresponding secretary; Jacqueline Novotny (Mattie Welch's daughter), organist; Morris Smith, librarian; and Martin Smith, reporter.[50]

The wider community of Great Falls recognized Mrs. Smith's leadership when she was nominated Mother of the Year in 1967. Both of her sons had served in the military during World War II. Her daughter, Madeline Smith Haskins, worked as a secretary for the state legislature in California. Her other two daughters, Alma Smith Jacobs and Lucille Smith Thompson, were librarians.[51] Mrs. Jacobs was head of the Great Falls Public Library and later worked for the State Library in Helena. She was named Woman of the Year in Great Falls in 1957 and was president of the Montana Federation of Colored Women's Clubs.[52] Mrs. Thompson was a reference librarian at Montana State University in Bozeman. Thanks to Mrs. Jacobs and Mrs. Thompson, who recognized their historical value, their mother's papers and records of her years of service to the Great Falls AME church and community were preserved.

LEGACY

Higginbotham, in her landmark study of the role of black churchwomen, quotes W. E. B. Du Bois: "Black women (and women whose grandmothers were black) are . . . the main pillars of those social settlements which we call churches."[53] Union Bethel AME Church was and is a social as well as a religious settlement. The community established in and through the church nurtured pride, self-identification, and empowerment among its members and their children. And the women who helped to found and build that community wove together threads of American and western history, such as the Battle of the Little Bighorn, pioneer settlement of a western town, the back-to-Africa movement, along with threads of black American women's history: their work as club women, homemakers, and churchwomen to establish a place for themselves and their families in an often hostile dominant culture. Those threads have spun a continuous line from the founders of the church, Tennie Hagin and Mamie Courtney, to its builders, their friends and sister church members Marie Dutrieuille Ellis, Mattie Byers Novotny Welch, and Emma Riley Smith, to the children of these three women and to Eva Reed and Kathy Reed.

The second generation of Great Falls African Americans, the children of the 1920s and 1930s whose parents worked as domestic servants, janitors, porters, and laborers, achieved successful careers as librarians, teachers, firefighters, secretaries, and pilots. Others continued the work of the founders and builders, maintaining the church and its community right down to the present. Still others moved away from Montana to take advantage of opportunities on the West Coast, especially when jobs opened up during World War II. The self-esteem instilled by the builders of the AME community made it possible for the next generation to meet their aspirations, to be lifted as their predecessors climbed.

These women may indeed have been elite, as De Graaf suggests, but surely elite in the sense that they were courageous, purposeful, willing workers. Their stories and their work for the Great Falls AME community help to illuminate the role of black women in the West. Kenneth Wiggins Porter argues that "only after grassroots studies of the Negro in all regions and states are available can any valid generalizations as to racial policies and practices become possible."[54] This has been a grassroots study, a study of a few black women in one small western town. Their experiences suggest that an examination of the histories and records of other western communities will reveal other stories of black women whose wealth of experience, knowledge, dedication, and commitment demonstrate how communities can encourage and inspire their children and how African American women have contributed to and participated in the settling of the American West.

NOTES

1. For an excellent overview of the history of blacks in the west, see Quintard Taylor, *In Search of the Racial Frontier: African Americans in the American West, 1528–1990* (New York: W. W. Norton, 1998); and "From Esteban to Rodney King: Five Centuries of African American History in the West" and the accompanying "Bibliographic Essay on the African American West" in *Montana: The Magazine of Western History* 46 (Winter 1996): 2–23. For an overview of the establishment of black communities, see Taylor's "The Emergence of Black Communities in the Pacific Northwest: 1865–1910," *Journal of Negro History* 64 (Fall 1979): 342–51.

2. See, e.g., Elmer Rusco, *"Good Time Coming?" Black Nevadans in the Nineteenth Century* (Westport, Conn.: Greenwood Press, 1975). Although this book does not consider Montana, it is a good example of how census data can be used in historical research. See also Christian McMillen, "Border State Terror and the Genesis of the African-American Community in Deer Lodge and Choteau Counties, Montana, 1870–1890," *Journal of Negro History* 79 (Spring 1994): 212–47.

3. See William L. Lang, "The Nearly Forgotten Blacks of Last Chance Gulch, 1900–1912," *Pacific Northwest Quarterly* 70 (April 1979): 50-57. My thanks to Quintard Taylor for bringing this article to my attention. It is interesting that the Helena newspapers Lang discusses either "maintained a journalistic silence" about the black population or found only "notorious incidents" newsworthy. In contrast, the *Great Falls Tribune* included news stories about AME church activities and obituaries regularly. See also Rex C. Myers, "Montana's Negro Newspapers, 1894–1911," *Montana Journalism Review* 16 (1973): 17–22.

4. Works Progress Administration, *Great Falls Yesterday* (N.p., 1939). The biographical sketches of Great Falls's black pioneers are included as a matter of course and with evident pride and interest, another interesting contrast to the Helena history as related by Lang. Certainly the WPA book came along a generation later, but it still significantly precedes the civil rights movement and modern sensibilities.

5. Lawrence B. De Graaf, "Race, Sex and Region: Black Women in the American West, 1850–1920," *Pacific Historical Review* 49 (May 1980): 285–311.

6. Glenda Riley, "American Daughters: Black Women in the West," *Montana: The Magazine of Western History* 38 (Spring 1988): 14–27.

7. While I was working on this chapter, I had the good fortune to have the help of Lucille Smith Thompson, retired librarian from Montana State University, whose mother, Emma Riley Smith, was a longtime active member of the Great Falls AME Church. Lucille and her sister, Alma Smith Jacobs, preserved the church papers their mother had in her possession. Lucille generously gave me permission to read and copy these papers. Even more generously, she gave me her time, support, and encouragement, reminiscing with me about her years growing up in Great Falls as a member of the AME community. Lucille died in February 1996. I hope this chapter would have pleased her. She was intensely interested in Montana's black people and their history. Alan Thompson, Lucille's son, donated the AME church papers to the Montana Historical Society, Helena, at Lucille's request, where they are currently being processed. I will cite these papers as the Smith/Thompson papers.

8. Richard B. Roeder, "A Settlement on the Plains: Paris Gibson and the Building of Great Falls," *Montana: The Magazine of Western History* 42 (Autumn 1992): 4–19.

9. *Eleventh Census of the United States, 1890: Population of the United States*, vol. 1.1 (Washington, D.C.: Department of the Census, 1891); *Twelfth Census of the United States, 1900: Population*, pt. 1, Montana State University Library, Bozeman.

10. "Twelfth U.S. Manuscript Census, 1900: Montana; Cascade County, Great Falls," Montana State University Library, Bozeman.

11. Roeder, "A Settlement on the Plains," 7.

12. For the founding of the church, see "1884–1991, over 100 Years of Christian Service," published by the Union Bethel African Methodist Episcopal Church of Great Falls on the occasion of its centennial celebration; "The Cornerstone Laid," *Great Falls Tribune*, January 21, 1917, p. 6. See also Smith/Thompson papers.

13. "Twelfth, Thirteenth, and Fourteenth U.S. Manuscript Censuses (1900, 1910, 1920): Montana, Cascade County, Great Falls." Obituary for Millie Simms Winburn, *Great Falls Tribune*, January 24, 1946, 10.

14. Smith/Thompson papers. Lined sheet in Mrs. Smith's hand, dated February 18, 1940, lists sixteen people "and others" as the original members of the church.

15. De Graaf, "Race, Sex and Region," 289.

16. Susan H. Armitage and Deborah Gallacci Wilbert, "Black Women in the Pacific Northwest: A Survey and Research Prospectus," in *Women in Pacific Northwest History: An Anthology*, ed. Karen J. Blair (Seattle: University of Washington Press, 1988), 136–51. For communities as social and support networks, see Sue Armitage, Theresa Banfield, and Sarah Jacobus, "Black Women and Their Communities in Colorado," *Frontiers* 2 (1977): 36–40.

17. "Twelfth U.S. Manuscript Census, 1900: Montana; Cascade County, Belt." For Maria Adams Dutrieuille, see WPA, *Great Falls Yesterday*; Dutrieuille Papers, Montana Historical Society Archives, Helena; Joel Overholser, private papers, Schwinden Library, Fort Benton, Montana; Ethel Castner Kennedy and Eva Lesell Stober, *Belt Valley History*, Project of Alma Chapter No. 110 O.E.S.–Masonic Lodge No. 137 A.F. & A.M. (n.p., n.d.); John S. Manion, "Last Statement to Custer," Monroe County, Michigan: Library System,

1983. I have been unable to locate a copy of or information about *Cradled in Dixie* by Florence B. Franklin. An article about this book, which tells Maria Dutrieuille's story, appeared in the *Great Falls Tribune* on June 24, 1956.

18. Alma Smith Jacobs, "History of the Dunbar Art and Study Club, Great Falls," n.d., Smith/Thompson papers. For information on Theodore Ellis, see "Fourteenth U.S. Manuscript Census, 1920: Montana; Cascade County, Great Falls." A copy of the invitation for Marie's wedding is with the Dutrieuille papers, Montana Historical Society, Helena. Curiously, the census lists Theodore Ellis's place of origin as New Mexico, but the wedding invitation reports his birthplace as Salt Lake City.

19. Evelyn Brooks Higginbotham, *Righteous Discontent: The Women's Movement in the Black Baptist Church, 1880–1920* (Cambridge, Mass.: Harvard University Press, 1993), 17. I am grateful to Frances Jones-Sneed for alerting me to the importance of this book. For the black women's club movement, see also Paula Giddings, *When and Where I Enter: The Impact of Black Women on Race and Sex in America* (New York: Bantam Books, 1984), 95–117.

20. Minutes of the Dunbar Art and Study Club, 1920–24; August 25, 1920; Smith/Thompson papers.

21. Dunbar Minutes, August 8, 1923.

22. Jacobs, "History of the Dunbar Art and Study Club." Unfortunately, the minutes to which Mrs. Jacobs refers were not with the Smith/Thompson papers.

23. Dunbar Minutes, April 17, 1924; and May 20, 1924.

24. Lucille Smith Thompson, personal communication, June 1995.

25. Minutes of the Women's Missionary Mite Society, October 1937–November 1939, Smith/Thompson papers.

26. Minutes of the AME Church Board of Trustees, 1930–52, Smith/Thompson papers.

27. Her name appears as Marie Ellis Ingram on a list of church members dated 1940. Minutes of the AME Church Board of Trustees, Smith/Thompson papers.

28. Letter from Maria Raybon to Mrs. Baucus, Dutrieuille Papers, Montana Historical Society, Helena.

29. For Mattie Castner, see Kennedy and Stober, *Belt Valley History*, 21–22; and WPA, *Great Falls Yesterday*, 74–75.

30. WPA, *Great Falls Yesterday*, 74–75.

31. The other African Americans in the community were Castner's niece, two employees at the hotel, and a local barber. See *Belt Valley History*; and "Twelfth U.S. Manuscript Census 1900: Montana, Cascade County, Belt."

32. WPA, *Great Falls Yesterday*, 74.

33. Ibid., 74–75, 196.

34. Minutes of the Missionary Mite Society meetings, 1937, and minutes of the AME Church Board of Trustees, 1938, Smith/Thompson papers.

35. Bethel AME Sunday School Record, July 29, 1934, to September 6, 1936, Smith/Thompson papers.

36. Higginbotham, *Righteous Discontent*, 139.

37. *Fourteenth Census of the United States, 1920: Population*, pt. 1.

38. *Minutes of the Eighth Annual Session of the Colorado Conference of the African M.E. Church, Held in Helena, Montana, October 11, 1894* (Albuquerque, New Mex.: Edmund G. Ross, Book and Job Printer, n.d.), 28–29.

39. Higginbotham, *Righteous Discontent*, 7.

40. *Great Falls Tribune*, June 9, 1891, p. 5; WPA, *Great Falls Yesterday*, 31–32.

41. *Great Falls Tribune*, January 21, 1917, p. 6.

42. *Great Falls Tribune*, September 9, 1917, p. 7.

43. Lucille Smith Thompson, personal communication, June 1995.

44. WPA, *Great Falls Yesterday*, 196.

45. Mrs. Emma Smith's story of her trip to Liberia, recorded by her daughter Alma Smith Jacobs, undated, ca. 1973, Smith/Thompson papers. For the back-to-Africa movement, see Edwin S. Redkey, *Black Exodus: Black Nationalist and Back-to-Africa Movements, 1890–1910* (New Haven: Yale University Press, 1969).

46. Emma Smith, oral history, recorded in Great Falls in 1970. Original in possession of Emma Smith's grandson, Alan Thompson, of Helena, Montana.

47. Minutes of the AME Church Board of Trustees meetings, 1927, Smith/Thompson papers.

48. Minutes of the AME Church Board of Trustees meetings, 1924–27 and 1930–56, Smith/Thompson papers.

49. Minutes of the Women's Missionary Mite Society meetings, 1937–39, Smith/Thompson papers.

50. Minutes of the ACE League meetings, October 6, 1935, to May 17, 1937, Smith/Thompson papers.

51. *Great Falls Tribune*, March 12, 1967, p. 13.

52. News Release, Montana State College, Bozeman, August 6, 1962. Copy with Smith/Thompson papers.

53. Higginbotham, *Righteous Discontent*, 1.

54. Kenneth Wiggins Porter, foreword to Rusco, *"Good Time Coming?"* xiv.

Kate D. Chapman Describes Blacks in Yankton, Dakota Territory

In April 1889, seven months before Dakota Territory became the states of North and South Dakota, nineteen-year-old Kate D. Chapman, destined to be one of the few black female journalists in the nation, wrote about the small African American community in her hometown of Yankton. Her account suggests that African Americans could survive and even prosper in regions where their numbers were few (according to the 1890 U.S. Census, Yankton had 59 blacks and South Dakota had 540).

Yankton has a mixed population of five thousand inhabitants, about sixty of whom are Afro-Americans, who are all more or less in a prosperous condition. The schools, churches and hotels are thrown open to all regardless to color, and . . . the feeling that exists between the two races is friendly in the extreme. . . .

The colored people pay taxes on fully $22,000 worth of property. The majority of them came from the Southern States only a few years ago, and by their industry have earned for themselves homes and the respect of all. One man, Mr. Amos Lewis, who came here ten years ago with nothing except a knowledge of plastering, now owns $5,000 worth of real estate, saying nothing of his fine team and other personal property.

Another man who is on the road to wealth, is Mr. James Parsons, who formerly kept a restaurant at this place; he is worth about $3,000 in cash and [has] property [worth] about $2,000. . . .

J. B. Shaw, the city constable, is a progressive colored man and is worth about $1,500. He has a daughter who will be famous some day in the world of music. . . .

C. T. Chapman [Kate Chapman's father] is a cook by trade, and has thoroughly mastered his profession. He has a home valued at $2,500. He owns also a fine breed of hunting dogs valued at from $50 to $100.

Henry Robinson, who owns an elegant barber shop, situated on the principal street, has several white hands working under him, and has property worth about $2,500.

Source: Willard B. Gatewood Jr., "Kate D. Chapman Reports on 'The Yankton Colored People,' 1889," *South Dakota History* 7 (Winter 1976): 32–35.

Another fine man belonging to the Afro-American race is Thomas Sturgiss, an excellent mechanic, who employs his idle hours in distributing good literature among the race. His home is valued at $1,000.

Washington Stokes, who now owns a $1,000 home says that he borrowed the money to pay the fare of himself and his wife when he came here from Eufaula, Alabama, and now is doing well. . . .

Mrs. Amy Davis, a sprightly little widow has by her own exertions acquired $1,500 worth of property.

Mrs. Towns is also an industrious widow, owning $1,800 worth of real estate.

Mr. Fred Baker, assistant druggist in one of the largest drug stores, is a property holder in the south, and is worth about $800 in cash. He has been in Yankton about three years, and thinks it [is] just the place for poor colored people who want to get a fair show in the world.

Mrs. Proteau, whose husband, a Frenchman, perished in the blizzard last winter, up about Pierre, Dakota, owns a home worth $800. . . .

The church, a branch of the A. M. E. connection, is valued at $2,000, and has a membership of twenty persons. A Masonic Lodge is also in existence. The people are socially inclined and extend a hearty welcome to all who come. When we think of the crowded tenement houses, loathsome streets, foul air, bitter prejudice many of our people have to endure in the south, we are forced by the love we bear them to say, for the sake of health, wealth and freedom, come west. Dakota has been well named the 'Beulah Land,' for such she had proved to those of our people who have ventured, despite the prediction that they would certainly 'freeze to death,' to come to the Territory of Dakota.

Hoping you will visit the colored Yanktonians some fine day, I close with a line . . . from the brilliant Pope: "Worth makes the man, and want of it the fellow; The rest is all but leather and prunella."

A Black Woman on the Montana Frontier

From 1888 to 1931 Sarah Gammon Bickford owned and managed the Virginia City Water Company, which serviced Virginia City, Montana. A partial account of her remarkable life is provided by her daughter, Mabel Bickford Jenkins.

Sarah Gammon arrived in Virginia City, Montana, a rough, frontier gold mining community in 1871. Born a slave on December 25, 1855 in North Carolina, Sarah was raised by an aunt in Knoxville, Tennessee after her parents were sold away. When she was fifteen Sarah and her Aunt accompanied the family of Judge William Murphy overland from Tennessee to Virginia City, where Murphy, a Confederate veteran, was slated to serve as a Magistrate.

Sarah first worked as a chambermaid in one of the hotels and later married William Brown, one of the gold miners. Three children were born to the marriage but only one, Eva, survived. William Brown died in 1877 and three years later Sarah married Stephen Bickford, a white miner from Maine who was twenty years older than the widow.

In 1888 the Bickfords bought two-thirds of the Virginia City water system which brought water drinking down from surrounding mountains through wooden logs. The Bickfords substituted iron pipes for the wooden logs which allowed indoor plumbing. Later they added hydrants along the street.

Sarah Bickford, acknowledged as Virginia City's first "career woman," managed the books for the system, billing customers and controlling expenditures. She also ran the Bickford farm on the eastern edge of the city. There with her four children by Stephen Bickford, she cultivated vegetables and poultry including ducks which were sold to the small colony of Chinese miners in Virginia City.

When Stephen Bickford died in 1900 Sarah became the sole owner and manager of the water plant and farm. Although she was aided by her oldest daughter, Virginia, she nevertheless enrolled in a Business Management course from a correspondence school in Scranton, Pennsylvania, to become more profi-

---

Source: Mabel Bickford Jenkins, "Stephen E. and Sarah G. Bickford: Pioneers of Madison County, Montana," unpublished paper, 1971, 1–9.

cient in the affairs of her business. Feeling more confident in her ability to manage the company she bought out the other third of the water business from Harry Cohn, making her the sole owner. Eventually she acquired additional springs to meet the demands of the growing town. She also became its first philanthropist, purchasing and maintaining at her own expense, several historic buildings in Virginia City. She moved her office into the Hangman's Building, the largest and oldest building in town, made famous by Virginia City's Vigilantes who in 1870 hanged five outlaws from a beam of the building while it was under construction. The office was the home of what Bickford now called the Virginia City Water Company. Sarah Gammon Bickford continued to manage the Company until her death in Virginia City in 1931.

CHAPTER 8

"Is There No Blessing for Me?"

JANE ELIZABETH MANNING JAMES, A MORMON
AFRICAN AMERICAN WOMAN

Ronald G. Coleman

An African American woman named Jane Elizabeth Manning James was among the early pioneer residents of Utah, a state settled primarily by members of the Church of Jesus Christ of Latter-day Saints (LDS). The Saints were seeking an isolated refuge from the persecution and violence experienced at earlier settlements in New York, Ohio, Missouri, and Illinois. Jane Elizabeth's life embodies the intersection of religion, race, and gender in the nineteenth century, as well as its implications for the western frontier region.

Jane Elizabeth was one of a small number of blacks who felt sufficiently compelled by the message of Mormonism to join this new faith organized officially by Joseph Smith Jr. on April 6, 1830, in Fayette, New York. Early Saints, primarily from New England and the Middle Atlantic states, believed Smith was God's prophet and his teachings the "Restored Gospel of Jesus Christ." Church members accepted Smith's claim of authority to "organize a lay priesthood, gather 'the honest in heart,' and establish communities dedicated to Christian principles." As a result of the proselytizing fervor of LDS missionaries, fourteen years after its formal organization, membership in the Mormon Church numbered thirty-five thousand. Only a few of these early converts were African American. Jane Elizabeth Manning James was among that number.[1]

Born in 1813 in Wilton, Connecticut, Jane Elizabeth Manning was one of five children of Isaac and Phillis Manning, both of whom were free blacks. At an early age, Jane Elizabeth was sent to work in the home of Joseph Flitch, a successful Wilton area farmer. During her years with the Flitch family, Jane Elizabeth worked as a domestic servant, cooking, washing, ironing, and doing general housework. In 1837 Jane became pregnant and returned to her mother's home. On March 1, 1838, she gave birth to a son, Sylvester, whose father was said to be a white minister in either the Presbyterian or Methodist denomination. Leaving Sylvester in the care of her mother, Jane Elizabeth returned to work in the Flitch household.[2]

At the age of fourteen, Jane Elizabeth became a member of the local Presbyterian church, perhaps as a result of the Flitch family's influence. However, a spiritual void remained for the young woman, who would recall years later, "[I]t seemed to me there was something more that I was looking for." This would change when, in 1842, she heard Charles Wesley Wandell, a Mormon missionary proselytizing in the area. Although her Presbyterian pastor told Jane Elizabeth not to attend the Latter-day Saints meeting, she went nonetheless and left the meeting convinced that she heard the "true gospel." One week later she was baptized and confirmed a member of the Church of Jesus Christ of Latter-day Saints. Three weeks after her baptism, while kneeling in prayer, Jane Elizabeth started speaking in tongues, startling family members who were in the next room. Soon afterward several of them also converted to Mormonism.[3]

One year after her conversion, Jane Elizabeth Manning and several family members decided to travel with fellow Saints to Nauvoo, Illinois, the gathering place for LDS members. They were led by Wandell, the Mormon elder whose earlier message had prompted Jane Elizabeth's conversion and baptism. The party traveled by canal from Wilton to Buffalo, New York, where the black Saints, unable to pay their fare beyond that point, left the party and began the eight-hundred-mile journey to Nauvoo on foot. Their fellow Mormons were unable or unwilling to come to their aid with the necessary funds.[4]

Black Saints bound for Nauvoo in 1843 felt the physical hardships of sore, cracked, and bleeding feet, which thousands of other Mormons experienced four years later while crossing the plains and Rocky Mountains. But they faced the additional peril of being stopped and interrogated about their status: were they alleged runaway slaves or free women and men? If they were the former, they could be immediately arrested. Jane Elizabeth and her party confronted their greatest fears on arriving in Peoria, Illinois. Local authorities detained them and asked for papers to verify their status as free persons. The group informed the local officials that they had always been free. Apparently, Jane Elizabeth and her party were convincing, and they were allowed to continue to Nauvoo.[5]

From Peoria, the party walked day and night, undeterred by natural obstacles or the elements. As Jane Elizabeth later recalled in her autobiography, "[We] went on our] way rejoicing, singing hymns and thanking God for his infinite goodness and mercy to us, blessing us as he had, protecting us from all harm, answering our prayers and healing our feet." In La Harp, thirty miles from Nauvoo, the group met a family with a sick child who was said by Mormon elders to be beyond hope. However, the black Saints, perhaps with their spirits lifted as a result of their own perceived blessings, "administered," and the child's health improved dramatically.[6]

Arriving in Nauvoo in November 1843, the black Mormons faced "all kinds of hardship, trial and rebuff," until they arrived at the home of Orson Spencer who directed them to Joseph Smith's residence, or "the mansion" as it was called. Emma Smith, Joseph's wife, invited the group in, and that evening Joseph Smith asked Jane Elizabeth to share the story of their journey and experiences with several guests at the mansion. Jane Elizabeth gave a detailed description of their journey. At the end, she records Joseph Smith as having slapped the knee of John Bernhisel, a friend and physician, and saying, "Doctor, isn't that faith." Smith asked Jane Elizabeth to stay on as a household servant.[7]

Living and working in the Smith household was a special and meaningful experience for Jane Elizabeth—one she would remember all her life. In her autobiography she recalled having never seen anything like the robes worn by Joseph Smith, which she was given to wash. "I looked at them and wondered," she recalled. "I pondered over them and thought about them so earnestly that the spirit made manifest to me that they pertained to the new name that is given the saints that the world knows not of."[8]

Jane Elizabeth felt privileged to know that Lucy Smith, Joseph's mother, had trusted her to handle a bundle of clothes that contained Urim and Thumim, the sacred stones that Mormons believed Joseph Smith used to translate the *Book of Mormon*.[9] Later in life, Jane regretted not responding favorably to Emma Smith's invitations to be adopted into Joseph and Emma Smith's family as a child. "[The Smiths] were always good and kind to me," she acknowledged. But she declined Emma's invitation because, she said, "I did not understand or know what it meant.... I did not know my own mind. I did not comprehend."[10]

In 1844, as tensions between Mormons and non-Mormons increased in Illinois, Smith closed the mansion. With Joseph Smith's approval, Jane Elizabeth and her sister Angeline went to nearby Burlington in search of work. During the three-week period when the Manning sisters were away, Joseph and his brother Hyrum were murdered while prisoners in the Carthage jail. On her return to Nauvoo, Jane wrote of the sorrow and agony that had befallen the community of Saints following the death of their prophet.[11]

Homeless again, Jane Elizabeth went to live with and work for Brigham Young's family soon after he assumed the leadership of the Latter-day Saints. She remained there until Young began to make preparations to relocate the Saints to a place free of anti-Mormon influences. The leadership chose the Great Basin region on the western side of the Rocky Mountains. The remote Salt Lake Valley would be the Great Basin Zion, the site for the Saints to gather and commence with the work of building the kingdom of God on earth.[12]

While residing with Brigham Young's family, Jane Elizabeth married Isaac James, a black Latter day-Saint who relocated to Nauvoo after joining the Mormon Church in Monmouth, New Jersey. Isaac resided at Nauvoo when the Mannings arrived in late 1843. It is unknown how long Isaac and Jane Elizabeth had known each other before deciding to marry. Following Brigham Young's departure from Nauvoo in February 1846, Jane Elizabeth lived in the Reynolds Cahoon home. It is unclear if Isaac, her new husband, also resided there. However, her son, Sylvester, remained with Jane Elizabeth's mother, Phillis, in Nauvoo.[13]

Jane Elizabeth stayed briefly at the Cahoons'. Along with her husband, she joined fellow Mormons who abandoned Nauvoo and crossed the Mississippi River to temporary locations in Iowa and Nebraska in anticipation of a journey west. Although Jane Elizabeth's relatives had journeyed with her to Nauvoo and remained members of the LDS Church during Joseph Smith's lifetime, only Jane Elizabeth's brother, named Isaac like her husband, eventually moved west. Isaac came to Utah forty-five years after his sister and brother-in-law settled in the Great Basin Zion.

In June 1846 Jane Elizabeth gave birth to a second son, Silas, at the family's temporary homesite, Keg Creek, Iowa. One year later the James family began the journey to Utah as members of Captain Ira Eldredge's overland company. Jane's autobiography described the overland journey as without any serious mishaps, except for the stampeding of some of the party's cattle. Perhaps the passage of years had minimized the hardships that other Mormon emigrants vividly recalled—inadequate forage for livestock, finding suitable fords for river crossings, and the sudden blinding dust storms common to the plains.

The James family and other members of Ira Eldredge's group reached the Salt Lake Valley on September 19, 1847, two months after the arrival of the vanguard party led by Brigham Young. The Jameses were not the first African

American settlers to arrive in Utah. They were, however, the first free blacks to enter the valley. They joined approximately 1,500 Saints who reached the Salt Lake Valley by December 1847. By winter 1847–48, the population was approximately 1,650, only 6 of whom were black.[14]

The settlers constructed log cabins, planted crops, and dug irrigation ditches. The early years of settlement were difficult for the fledgling community of Mormons gathered in Salt Lake Valley. Although winter 1847–48 was not particularly harsh, there was a shortage of food, a situation exacerbated when late frosts damaged the garden vegetables and winter wheat that settlers were looking to have that spring. The situation was complicated further in May and June 1848 by the invasion of massive numbers of crickets that ravaged the land. The settlers fought the invaders, using brooms, sticks, shovels, trenches, and gunnysacks, without much success. The unexpected arrival of white-winged seagulls that devoured the invading crickets was taken to be a direct blessing from God—an answer to prayers.[15]

At the end of 1848 the non-Indian population was 4,200, and of this number 50 were black. With the exception of the James family and one or two others, all were slaves. The presence of more than forty slaves in the Great Basin region was directly connected to the emigration of a small number of slave-owning Mormon converts from the South, including one group called the Mississippi Saints. Many of these emigrants and their slaves settled in the southeastern section of Salt Lake Valley named Holladay-Cottonwood. The second winter was longer and colder, requiring rationing of the food supply at three-fourths of a pound of breadstuff per day for each person. Many of the settlers ate sego lily roots, thistle tops, and roots. Mormon leaders asked those with surplus food to bring it in for distribution to others. A spirit of mutual aid and cooperation prevailed in the community based on shared religious ties and the realization that misfortune could strike anyone at any time.[16]

Isaac and Jane Elizabeth James were intimately involved in the network of mutuality and reciprocity that characterized the Mormon settlement during the early years in Utah. Jane Elizabeth remembered suffering from cold and hunger and the pain of hearing her young children ask for bread. In 1849 Eliza Lyman found herself without the means to make bread for her family. Lyman noted in her journal, "Jane James, the colored woman let me have two pounds of flour, it being half of what she had."[17]

Isaac and Jane Elizabeth resided in the southeast corner of Salt Lake Valley's First Ward, a rural, underpopulated, impoverished area. Initially, the family engaged in farming and was able to establish a subsistence livelihood. Like most

Mormon women in the First Ward, Jane Elizabeth made the family clothing. Isaac and Jane Elizabeth had six more children between 1848 and 1860, including one stillborn. During this period, the financial resources of the family improved demonstrably. In 1856 the James family property holdings included a time-piece, a land claim and improvements, and other possessions. By 1860, in addition to the land claim and family dwelling, Isaac and Jane Elizabeth had acquired household furnishings, a cart, an ox, a horse, a cow, and three hogs. Five years later the cart and ox were gone and in their place were a new wagon, three horses, and a small flock of sheep. The family possessions were valued at $1,100. By this point the James family was more prosperous than most of its neighbors. Four households in the First Ward held more property than the Jameses; thirty-one held less.[18]

The Jameses' financial stability was shattered by 1870. Difficulties with Jane Elizabeth led Isaac to leave the family home, ending nearly twenty-five years of marriage. After selling part of his share of the family realty to Jane Elizabeth for $500, Isaac left Utah. In 1872 Isaac James sold the balance of his share in the First Ward property for $200 to Feramorz Little, a prominent LDS leader and local businessman.[19]

Shortly after the divorce from Isaac, Jane Elizabeth exchanged her property in the First Ward for a lot with a two-story home located in the Eighth Ward. Never again did Jane Elizabeth realize the financial stability that the family enjoyed before her marriage ended. Her reduced property placed her among the poorest of the Eighth Ward residents. Her primary concern following the divorce was maintaining and caring for the family members still residing with her. The 1870 James household consisted of Jane Elizabeth, two daughters, two sons, and one granddaughter. The family planted a small garden, Silas and Jessie worked as laborers, and Jane Elizabeth did domestic work while also making and selling soap.

Despite her poverty, Jane Elizabeth continued to share her few resources with relatives and fellow Saints. In 1872 she gave her daughter Maria part of her Eighth Ward homesite so that Maria and her husband could build a residence. Years later Jane Elizabeth turned over another section of her homesite to three of her grandchildren. On occasion the children took advantage of their mother's generosity. When daughter Ellen faced a financial crisis, Jane Elizabeth transferred the entire Eighth Ward homesite to her. Ellen used the title as security for a loan and relocated to Los Angeles. Later she transferred the homesite back to Jane Elizabeth without repaying the loan, thereby imposing an additional financial burden on her mother.[20]

Jane Elizabeth joined the LDS Women's Relief Society shortly after moving to the Eighth Ward. She contributed financially to the building of temples in other Utah communities, including St. George, Manti, and Logan. She also helped to support special projects, such as a Lamanite Mission—a proselytizing effort among American Indians in a designated area—a fund-raising fair for the Deseret Hospital, and an excursion to Liberty Park for senior citizens and contributed to the People's Party, the LDS political organization in Utah.[21]

Four years after ending her marriage with Isaac, Jane Elizabeth wed Franklin Perkins, who came from Missouri to Bountiful, Utah, in 1848. Franklin was a slave of Reuben Perkins, a southern convert. After gaining his freedom during the Civil War, Franklin and several of the former Perkins slaves moved from Davis County to Salt Lake County. Franklin's daughter, Mary Ann, had married Jane Elizabeth's son, Sylvester, which probably brought Jane Elizabeth and Franklin together. Jane Elizabeth took Franklin's surname and is listed in Mormon Church records and some legal documents from August 1874 to April 1876 as Jane E. Perkins. The marriage lasted less than two years, after which she resumed using James, her former married name.[22]

In addition to two failed marriages, Jane Elizabeth endured the loss of three of her children between 1871 and 1874. Silas, her second child, died of consumption in 1872 at the age of twenty-five. Two daughters died in childbirth—Mary Ann in 1871 at the age of twenty-two and Miriam in 1874 at the age of twenty-four.[23] In 1880 Jane Elizabeth James's household included only a son, Jessie, two granddaughters, and herself. Her listed occupation was laundress.[24]

Soon after the loss of her children, Jane Elizabeth became part of a widening circle of African American Mormons, interacting with other black Eighth Ward LDS families. These residents were the first blacks other than family members that Jane Elizabeth had lived in close proximity to since coming to Utah in 1847. Typical of her new acquaintances was Samuel Chambers, a former slave who converted to the Mormon Church in Mississippi before the Civil War. Chambers, his wife, Amanda, and son, Peter, along with Amanda's brother, Edward Leggroan, and his wife and three children relocated to Utah in 1870. Soon after arriving in Salt Lake City, the two LDS families moved to houses side by side in the Eighth Ward. Jane Elizabeth and the members of the Chambers and Leggroan families knew one another and attended religious services and other activities at the local ward house. Their shared experiences of race, religion, and bondage helped to form lines of communication, familiarity, reciprocity, romance, courtship, and marriage in this small African American population.[25]

Twenty years after leaving Salt Lake City, Isaac James returned. He and Jane Elizabeth may have resolved some of the differences that had led to their divorce. Isaac's membership in the Church of Jesus Christ of Latter-day Saints was reactivated, and when he died in 1891, the funeral services were held at Jane Elizabeth's home. A few years later Jane Elizabeth asked that Isaac James be included in her request for an ordinance of adoption, which, if approved, would mean they would be bound as a family in the afterlife. Two years after Isaac James died, Jane Elizabeth's brother, Isaac Manning, moved to Salt Lake City. His wife and daughter were dead, and he had not seen his sister for forty-five years. Isaac Manning's membership in the Mormon Church was also reactivated, and he resided with Jane Elizabeth in the home on Fifth East.[26]

The pain of losing loved ones, however, continued to burden Jane Elizabeth. Following the death of her husband, she lost a son, Jessie, age thirty-seven, in 1894; and a daughter, Vilate, age thirty-seven, in 1897. At the time Jane Elizabeth dictated her autobiography in 1893, only eight of her eighteen grandchildren were alive. Jessie's death posed a financial hardship as well as an emotional one for Jane Elizabeth. He had worked as a laborer and porter, contributing to the family income. Jane Elizabeth continued to work even though she was more than eighty years old. The family income was now supplemented by Isaac Manning's earnings from employment as a laborer, plasterer, and carpet cleaner. Isaac was seventy-eight when he relocated to Salt Lake City; he continued to work well past his eightieth birthday. In addition, Jane Elizabeth received small amounts of money at various times from her daughter Ellen, now in Nevada. Sylvester James provided his mother with fruits and vegetables from his garden. Jane Elizabeth also received merchandise and small amounts of cash periodically from the Eighth Ward Relief Society.[27]

Despite insufficient income and personal setbacks, Jane Elizabeth maintained her dignity and sense of self-worth throughout her life, due in part to her long-standing membership in the LDS Church and the belief that she had followed the gospel to the best of her ability. Proud to be a pioneer of 1847, Jane Elizabeth, her son Sylvester, and Green Flake, one of three black members of Brigham Young's vanguard party, participated in the 1897 fifty-year celebration of the arrival of the Mormon pioneers in Salt Lake Valley.[28]

Although Jane Elizabeth James fervently believed she was a model member of the LDS Church, she was also well aware of the restrictions placed on her because of her race and gender. Mormon theological teachings held that blacks were descendants of Ham whose curse by his father, Noah, denied him and his seed the priesthood. Blacks were also said by some Mormon leaders to be the descendants of Cain and thus the heirs of God's displeasure with Cain for slaying his brother, Abel. Still other Saints described blacks as descendants of the people of Canaan who, in their unrighteousness, became despised and had a curse placed on them.[29] Such nineteenth-century beliefs about inherent black wickedness were hardly unique to Mormonism. They were widely shared among theologians of various denominations and were the foundation for the "biblical defense" of Southern slavery.[30]

Given this significant belief system, church involvement for Mormon blacks was subject to various restrictions. After 1849 African American males were ineligible for the priesthood, a central tenet of Mormon life. Black Mormons, male and female, could not have temple marriages or receive endowments, two rituals that are prerequisites to the Mormon concept of worthiness. Denial of endowments was especially crucial. Mormons believed such endowments were necessary to enter the highest degree of their tripartite celestial kingdom. Without endowments, African Americans were assigned to the lower levels of the multitiered kingdom of the afterlife.[31]

Jane Elizabeth's concerns about the religious prohibitions sanctioned by LDS leaders became paramount in her mind as she aged and began to contemplate death. The demise of prominent church leaders such as Brigham Young, John Taylor, and Wilford Woodruff, along with the loss of three adult children in the 1870s, a former husband, and two other children in the 1890s, undoubtedly intensified her concerns about her place in the afterlife.[32] Beginning in December 1884, Jane Elizabeth attempted periodically to persuade church leaders to grant her endowments requests, which, she believed, offered her hope for attaining exhaltation, the highest level of the celestial kingdom in the afterlife.

Jane Elizabeth dictated a letter to LDS president John Taylor following a visit to his home in 1884 to talk about her salvation. Acknowledging her awareness and acceptance of LDS theological beliefs about black Mormons, she declared, "I realize my race and color & cant [sic] expect my Endowments as those who are white." Jane Elizabeth argued, however, that the teachings found in the *Pearl of Great Price*, one of four sacred Mormon books, provided some relief for those of her color. She cited the passage that records a conversation between God and Abraham in which God promised, "[I]n thy seed after thee shall be all the families of the earth be blessed." Jane Elizabeth interpreted this scripture as allowing her membership in the "families of the earth," acknowledging, in effect, that she and all of humankind were natural heirs of Abraham and thus entitled to "the life eternal." Having endeavored to meet all requirements of the gospel, Jane Elizabeth asked, "[I]s there no blessing for me[?]"[33]

In her letter to President Taylor, Jane Elizabeth briefly recounted her life story. She also emphasized Emma Smith's invitation to be adopted into the Smith family as a child and her failure to comprehend the meaning at the time the offer was made. At the end of her letter, Jane Elizabeth asked Taylor to present her case and request to the other members of the First Presidency, hoping they would grant her request for adoption into Joseph and Emma Smith's family.[34]

Church leaders did not grant Jane Elizabeth's request for adoption. On January 16, 1888, she received a letter from Angus M. Cannon, president of the Salt Lake Stake, which gave her permission to enter the temple to be "baptized and confirmed for your dead kindred," that is, to have deceased ancestors baptized. But Cannon refused to extend endowments, adding, "[Y]ou must be content with this privilege, awaiting further instructions from the Lord to his servants."[35]

Jane Elizabeth was not content to wait on the Lord. On February 7, 1890, a letter dictated by Jane Elizabeth was sent to Joseph F. Smith, the nephew of the deceased church founder, Joseph Smith. The younger Smith was a counselor to Wilford Woodruff, LDS Church president. In the letter, Jane Elizabeth once again renewed her request for adoption into Joseph Smith's family and recalled her close ties with Smith's uncle. Jane Elizabeth also inquired if it was possible for her to be sealed to Walker Lewis, an African American Mormon convert who had been dead for at least thirty-five years. Lewis, a barber in Lowell, Massachusetts, had joined the Latter-day Saints during the early 1840s and had become a church elder. Jane Elizabeth believed that being sealed to Walker Lewis, who had been admitted into the priesthood before the prohibition was imposed on African American males, would assist her in gaining the endowments she desired. She also inquired about the possibility of obtaining endowments for her deceased family members, as she now had approval to have her dead baptized.[36]

Sometime during 1893, feeling the pains of old age and failing eyesight, Jane Elizabeth asked Elizabeth J. D. Roundy to write her autobiography, which was to be read at her funeral. *The Autobiography of Jane E. Manning James* was dictated when Jane Elizabeth was increasingly concerned about her place in the afterlife as well as the way her life would be recorded and interpreted for posterity and her fellow Saints. She believed it best to avoid discussing any incidents that might be construed to raise concerns regarding her "worthiness" within the LDS community. She certainly did not want to give Mormon leaders any reasons for denying the requests she was making during this period.[37]

Jane Elizabeth met with President Wilford Woodruff during early fall 1894, asking to obtain her endowments in the temple. The Mormon leader blessed Jane Elizabeth for her long-standing, unwavering faithfulness to the gospel, but he also reminded her that as a descendant of Cain, she remained disadvantaged. In denying Jane Elizabeth's request, Woodruff said, "[T]his I would not do as it was against the Law of God. As Cain killed Abel, all the seed of Cain would have to wait for redemption."[38]

Undeterred, Jane Elizabeth appealed to the First Presidency one year later. President Woodruff informed the members of the Quorum of Twelve, that "Sister Jane James, a negress of long standing in the church had asked him for permission to receive her endowments and that he and his Counselors told her that they could see no way by which they could accede to her wishes."[39] At a January 1902 meeting of the Quorum of Twelve, the subject of Jane Elizabeth and her endowments was again brought up. The First Presidency was unwilling to approve Jane Elizabeth's request to be sealed or granted her endowments. However, they allowed her to be adopted into the Joseph Smith family as a servant. Jane Elizabeth refused to be placated by these gestures from the LDS leaders. She continued to pursue her endowments.[40]

Hopeful that the new president might be favorably disposed to her request, Jane Elizabeth dictated a letter to Joseph F. Smith in August 1903. Again she asked for authorization to obtain endowments and to complete the work she had started for her deceased kindred. She asked to meet with President Smith to talk about her requests. It is unknown whether Smith responded to Jane Elizabeth's request for a meeting. It is clear, however, that the church leadership agreed on the subject of the denial of the priesthood to blacks and related matters. They concurred with Angus M. Cannon who said, "[T]o let down the bars in the least on this question would only tend to complications, and . . . it is perhaps better to let all such cases alone, believing, of course, that the Lord would deal fairly with them."[41]

Jane Elizabeth James never understood the continued denial of her church entitlements. Her autobiography reveals a stubborn adherence to her church even when it ignored her pleas. "My faith in the Gospel & Jesus Christ of Latter-day Saints is as strong today, nay, it is if possible stronger than it was the Day I was first baptized. I pay my tithes and offerings, keep the word of wisdom, I go to bed early and rise early, I try in my feeble way to set a good example to all."[42]

On April 16, 1908, Jane Elizabeth Manning James died at the age of ninety-five. Her death was announced in a front-page article in the church-owned

Deseret News. The article included a photograph of Jane Elizabeth and her brother Isaac and the caption "Servant in Family of Prophet Joseph Smith at Nauvoo Passes Away Today." The writer noted that the sister and brother converted to the Mormon religion early in the 1840s and that they had been servants to the Smith family. They were described as remaining "loyal and true to his memory." Jane Elizabeth died at home, following a fall and gradual deterioration in health. Praising her for her faith and faithfulness, the reporter concluded by observing, "[M]any will regret to learn this kind and generous soul has passed from earth."[43]

Funeral services were held on April 21 at the Eighth Ward meetinghouse where Jane Elizabeth had been an active participant for nearly forty years. A large number of people were in attendance, including many African Americans. A tribute was made to Jane Elizabeth's "undaunted faith and goodness of heart." Elizabeth J. D. Roundy read the autobiography Jane Elizabeth had dictated approximately fifteen years earlier. Bishop Oscar F. Hunter presided over the services that also included Bishop T. A. Clawson and LDS president Joseph F. Smith among other speakers. President Smith predicted Jane Elizabeth Manning James "would in the resurrection attain the longings of her soul."[44]

Black-white relations in Utah during the nineteenth and early twentieth century featured a paternalism that governed the interactions between Euro-Americans and African Americans. Stereotypical images of blacks based on the widely assumed superior-subordinate relationship between the two groups shaped religious as well as secular interaction. Mormon and non-Mormon Utah whites subscribed to these views. A close reading of the newspaper accounts of Jane Elizabeth's death and the remarks of President Joseph F. Smith and earlier LDS leaders, such as Brigham Young, Wilford Woodruff, and Angus Cannon, demonstrate this point. This paternalism flowed easily from the patriarchal nature of the LDS Church and the theocracy its leaders developed during the nineteenth century in New York, Ohio, Illinois, and eventually Utah.[45]

Some black Mormons contributed to this paternalistic relationship through the ways in which they interacted with white Utahns. They assumed a passive role as a strategy to achieve their goals and, in a sense, mask their true feelings or intentions. The life of Jane Elizabeth Manning James reflects this strategy. As a young free woman of color, she grew up in an environment virtually devoid of interactions with blacks beyond her immediate family. This appears to have been a characteristic of Jane Elizabeth's entire life, whether in Wilton, Connecticut, Nauvoo, Illinois, or Salt Lake City, Utah. Apparently she felt spiritually unfulfilled until she heard the proselytizing message of a Mormon missionary. Jane Elizabeth adhered to her new faith despite its restrictions and the personal rebuffs she suffered from some fellow Mormons through five decades of her life.[46]

Perhaps her acceptance of the Church of Latter-day Saints grew from Jane Elizabeth's close relationship with the church founder, Joseph Smith. As the Smith family servant, she maintained a proximity with the Prophet few other Mormons could claim. Yet she was also completely dependent on Smith for her employment as well as her status in the Mormon faith. The quality of that personal experience, with its paternalistic overtones, no doubt mitigated against the antiblack tenets of the faith and in later life helped her to face the continuing denial of the endowments to which she felt entitled. Jane Elizabeth James's months in Joseph and Emma Smith's home constituted, in her mind, a special tie to the LDS Church. Many years after Smith's death she described the LDS Church founder as "the finest man [she] ever saw on earth."[47] This direct interaction with Smith and a familiarity with other early LDS leaders, along with a personal internalization of Mormon theology, sustained the quiet dignity that characterized Jane Elizabeth's life.

Despite her unwavering belief in Mormonism, Jane Elizabeth was not oblivious to her membership in a proscribed race. Her racial consciousness, however, did not extend beyond her family and some fellow black Saints. There is, for example, very little evidence of her interaction with the growing population of non-Mormon blacks in Salt Lake City by the 1880s and 1890s. Much of Jane Elizabeth's time was spent providing for herself and other family members, especially after the departure of Isaac James from the household in 1870. Financial necessity combined with church activities left little time for other outside interests beyond some LDS Church work.[48]

Jane Elizabeth's numerous appeals to LDS leaders during the last twenty-five years of her life can be viewed as the indomitable spirit of a woman who was determined to reap the promises of a religion she embraced body and soul. Hers was not a quest for a singular place in the afterlife. She was also attempting to secure a place for Isaac, her deceased former husband, and her brother of the same name, as well as her children and other family members. In this, Jane Elizabeth Manning James was seeking to do what white Saints were permitted to do as a normal part of being deemed a "worthy" church member. That she failed says much more about LDS rigid adherence to racial proscriptions than to any flaw in her character.[49]

The First Presidency of the Church of Jesus Christ of Latter-day Saints lifted the 129-year priesthood ban on African American males on June 7, 1978, nearly seventy years after Jane Elizabeth Manning James died. The church refused, however, to rescind the ban for women of any color. One year later Jane Elizabeth Manning James received her endowments. Because she had no living descendants who were still active members of the LDS Church to perform the required temple rites on her behalf, a group of "special friends" consisting of black and white Saints conducted a ceremony at the temple in Salt Lake City where her endowments were received by proxy.[50] A faithful Saint in the nineteenth century, Jane Elizabeth Manning James was finally welcomed into the highest level of the LDS celestial kingdom.

NOTES

1. Leonard J. Arrington and Davis Bitton, *The Mormon Experience: A History of the Latter-day Saints* (New York: Vintage Books, 1980), 2, 21–22. The original name given to the church on April 6, 1830, was the Church of Jesus Christ. Some members called it the Church of Christ, and the names were used interchangeably. By 1834 the name was changed to the Church of Latter-day Saints, a name that ended in 1838 when the present name was adopted. On African American membership, see Newell G. Bringhurst, *Saints, Slaves, and Blacks: The Changing Place of Black People within Mormonism* (Westport, Conn.: Greenwood Press, 1981), 38.

2. Henry J. Wolfinger, "A Test of Faith: Jane Elizabeth James and the Origins of the Utah Black Community," in *Social Accommodation in Utah*, ed. Clark Knowlton (Salt Lake City: American West Center, University of Utah, 1975), 127, 155, 157. It is difficult to verify the year Jane was born. According to her brother Isaac, she was born in 1813. See *Autobiography of Jane E. Manning James*, 8–9, LDS Archives, Church History Department; *Journal of Church History*, June 21, 1847.

3. James, *Autobiography*, 1.

4. Wolfinger, "Test of Faith," 129, 158; James, *Autobiography*, 1. According to Jane's autobiography, she and her family left Wilton in 1840. This is not true since she did not convert until 1842 and traveled to Nauvoo in 1843. James, *Autobiography*, 1. Jane also said they were unable to raise the additional money needed to pay their fare. Folk tradition says that the black Saints were prevented from traveling on the boat because of their color. Interview with Darius Gray, president of the Genesis Group, a support group for black Mormons in Utah. None of the white Saints who accompanied Jane Elizabeth and her party from Wilton to Buffalo felt compelled to travel with the black Saints on foot to Nauvoo.

5. James, *Autobiography*, 2. A group of blacks traveling through Ohio, Indiana, and Illinois near the midpoint of the nineteenth century would have raised questions in the minds of local white residents as well as law enforcement officers. It is surprising that the group was not stopped before reaching Peoria. For examples of antiblack restrictions in the Midwest, see Eugene H. Berwanger, *The Frontier against Slavery:*

Western Anti-Negro Prejudice and the Slavery Extension Controversy (Urbana: University of Illinois Press, 1967), 30–59.

6. James, *Autobiography*, 2–3. Latter-day Saints believe that a combination of prayer, blessings, and anointing with special oils can improve the health of a sick person. Administrations are normally performed by elders of the church. It was not unusual, however, for a woman to administer in the early church, especially if the sick person had been anointed earlier by an elder. My colleague, Professor Dean May and his wife, Dr. Cheryll May, helped me to understand this aspect of LDS culture. See Bruce R. McConkie, *Mormon Doctrine* (Salt Lake City: Bookcraft 1966), 21–23.

7. James, *Autobiography*, 3. Jane Elizabeth James did not specifically describe the "hardships and trials" they first experienced in Nauvoo. Perhaps it had something to do with the antiblack statutes that the Mormon city had adopted. See Bringhurst, *Saints, Slaves, and Blacks*, 88–99.

8. James, *Autobiography*, 5–6.

9. There is no record of Joseph Smith having Urim and Thummim in his possession in Nauvoo. The bundle that Jane was told contained Urim and Thummim probably contained the seer stone that was in Smith's possession and for many years was sometimes referred to as Urim and Thummim. See McConkie, *Mormon Doctrine*, 818–19. This information was also provided by Dr. D. Michael Quinn, an independent scholar who specializes in LDS history.

10. James, *Autobiography*, 6. Adoption was important to the LDS conception of salvation. At the time that Emma Smith asked Jane Elizabeth if she wanted to be adopted into the Smith family, salvation in its highest degree was linked to family ties. The families were believed to be eternal units that would remain intact in the afterlife. In her autobiography, Jane Elizabeth said she did not understand what Emma was offering her through adoption as a child. She certainly understood the meaning by 1884, the year she started to contact Mormon officials seeking to be adopted into the Smith family. As a member of the family, Jane Elizabeth believed she would have access to participate in temple rituals reserved for all "worthy" Saints. For a detailed discussion of Mormon beliefs on adoption, see Gordon Irving, "The Law of Adoption: One Phase of the Development of the Mormon Concept of Salvation, 1830–1900," *Brigham Young University Studies* 14 (Spring 1974): 291–314.

11. See James, *Autobiography*, 6; and Arrington and Bitton, *The Mormon Experience*, 81.

12. James, *Autobiography*, 6; Arrington and Bitton, *The Mormon Experience*, 95–96.

13. Wolfinger, "Test of Faith," 158; James, *Autobiography*, 6.

14. James, *Autobiography*, 6–7. See also Kent S. Brown, Donald Q. Cannon, and Richard H. Jackson, eds., *Historical Atlas of Mormonism* (New York: Simon and Schuster, 1994), 75; *Journal of Church History*, June 21, 1847; and Wolfinger, "Test of Faith," 130. Wolfinger says the James family may have arrived on September 19, 1847. Jane Elizabeth's autobiography says they arrived on September 22. The six blacks were the James family along with Oscar Crosby and Hark Lay, two of the three blacks who were in Brigham Young's advance party that arrived in Salt Lake in July 1847.

15. James B. Allen and Glen M. Leonard, *The Story of the Latter-day Saints* (Salt Lake City: Deseret Book Company, 1976), 248–51; Arlington and Davis, *The Mormon Experience*, 113–17; Leonard J. Arrington, *Great Basin Kingdom: An Economic History of the Latter day-Saints, 1830–1890* (Lincoln: University of Nebraska Press, a Bison Book, 1966), 57–60.

16. Arrington, *Great Basin Kingdom*, 50, 57–60; Ronald G. Coleman, "A History of Blacks in Utah, 1825–1910" (Ph.D. dissertation, University of Utah, 1980), 34–36, 69; Wolfinger, "Test of Faith," 131.

17. See James, *Autobiography*, 7; Wolfinger, "A Test of Faith," 131, 141; Kate Carter, *The Story of the Negro Pioneer* (Salt Lake City: Daughters of the Utah Pioneers, 1965), 9–10.

18. Wolfinger, "A Test of Faith," 132, 160–61.

19. Ibid., 133, 161.

20. Ibid., 134, 139–40.

21. Ibid., 135. LDS theological writings say American Indians are descendants of one of the lost tribes of Israel. Throughout the centuries, the Lamanites, as they were called, had lost their former righteousness and degenerated into an uncivilized state of existence. Mormons believed American Indians could be redeemed. See Floyd O'Neil and Stanford J. Lyman, "Of Pride and Politics: Brigham Young as Indian Superintendent," *Utah Historical Quarterly* 46 (1978): 237–41.

22. Wolfinger, "A Test of Faith," 133, 161; Carter, *Negro Pioneer*, 28.

23. Wolfinger, "A Test of Faith," 138–39.

24. Federal Census, Utah Territory, 1880, U.S. Census Office, Tenth Census Population Schedule, Utah, 1880. Microfilm copies of the holograph 1880 schedule are available at the Marriott Library, University of Utah, Salt Lake City. A son, Jessie, is not listed as residing in Jane's 1880 household. Jessie sometimes worked as a porter and may not have been home at the time the census was taken. Wolfinger, "Test of Faith," 139, indicates that Jessie was living with his mother.

25. Other black families also lived side by side in South Cottonwood, the Mill Creek Area, and the Ninth Ward. See William G. Hartley, "Samuel D. Chambers," *New Era* 4 (June 1974): 47–49; Utah Territory Census, Salt Lake County, 1870, 1880; and Wolfinger, "A Test of Faith," 142–43.

26. See Wolfinger, "A Test of Faith," 133; and Zina D. H. Young to Apostle Joseph F. Smith, January 15, 1894, Document 4, in Wolfinger, "A Test of Faith," 150.

27. Wolfinger, "A Test of Faith," 138–39.

28. Utah Semi-Centennial Commission, comp., *The Book of the Pioneers*, 2 vols. (Salt Lake City: Utah Semi-Centennial Commission, 1897), vol. 1, 242, 368–69.

29. For information on the historical development of the Latter-day Saints' ban against black males and the implications of the ban, see Bringhurst, *Saints, Slaves, and Blacks*; and Lester E. Bush Jr., "Mormonism's Negro Doctrine: An Historical Overview," *Dialogue: A Journal of Mormon Thought* 8 (1973): 11–68. Also see Lester E. Bush Jr. and Armand L. Mauss, eds., *Neither White nor Black: Mormon Scholars Confront the Race Issues in a Universal Church* (Midvale, Utah: Signature Books, 1984).

30. Bringhurst, *Saints, Slaves, and Blacks*, 41–45; Eric C. McKittrick, ed., *Slavery Defended: The Views of the Old South* (Englewood Cliffs, N.J.: Prentice Hall, 1963), 86–98.

31. David John Buerger, *The Mysteries of Godliness: A History of Mormon Temple Worship* (San Francisco: Smith Research Associates, 1994), preface, 58–61, 97–131. Endowments are special blessings given in LDS temple ceremonies to "worthy" Mormons who are then considered "endowed with power from on high." The participants receive instructions pertaining to God's plans for mankind on earth in order to be ready for the celestial kingdom in the afterlife. See McConkie, *Mormon Doctrine*, 225–28. The first written information on the denial of the priesthood to blacks was made by Brigham Young in February 1849. See Bush, "Mormonism's Negro Doctrine," 70. The historian Ronald Esplin believes that the priesthood ban originated with Joseph Smith, although Esplin does not provide a specific date. See Ronald K. Esplin, "Brigham Young and Priesthood Denial to the Blacks: An Alternate View," *Brigham Young University Studies* 19 (1979): 399–402.

32. Jane Elizabeth's autobiography was originally written in 1893. Only Brigham Young and three of her adult children had died before 1894. The subsequent deaths of the others mentioned in her autobiography means the autobiography was modified after the death of Lorenzo Snow in October 1901. See Wolfinger, "Test of Faith," 170.

33. Quote appears in Jane E. James to President John Taylor, December 27, 1884, Document No. 1, in Wolfinger, "A Test of Faith," 147–48. For background on the scripture that serves as the basis for Jane E. James's argument, see the Book of Abraham, chap. 2, verse 11, *The Pearl of Great Price: A Selection from the Revelations, Translations and Narrations of Joseph Smith, Published by The Church of Jesus Christ of Latter-day Saints* (Salt Lake City: The Church of Jesus Christ of Latter-day Saints, 1955). Latter-day Saints theological beliefs are based on the Bible, the *Book of Mormon*, the *Doctrine and Covenants,* and *The Pearl of Great Price.*

34. Wolfinger, "A Test of Faith," 147–48. The First Presidency consists of the president of the LDS Church and his two counselors. They are the highest council in the church and make all final decisions on "controversial" spiritual issues. See McConkie, *Mormon Doctrine*, 283.

35. Angus M. Cannon, President of [the] Salt Lake Stake, to Jane E. James, June 16, 1888, Document No. 2, in Wolfinger, "A Test of Faith," 148–49. Jane was authorized to enter the LDS temple to do baptisms for her deceased family members. Ordinances are performed by proxy for deceased family members. Latter-day Saints believe that the ordinances serve as a means for the deceased to obtain salvation even though they were not baptized during their lifetime. See McConkie, *Mormon Doctrine*, 72–73.

36. Jane E. James to Apostle Joseph F. Smith, February 7, 1890, Document No. 3, in Wolfinger, "Test of Faith," 148–49. Sealings are special ordinances that ensure the continuity of spousal and family unions in the afterlife. Latter-day Saints believe that the ordinances performed in LDS temples by priesthood holders are the result of God's mercy and justice for righteous living persons and by proxy for the deceased. Children born of parents who were married in the temple are considered sealed to their parents at birth. Married couples who were not initially married in the temple may go through the temple ordinances at a later time. Their children may subsequently be sealed to

them after the children receive their temple ordinances. See McConkie, *Mormon Doctrine*, 684.

There is no indication that Jane Elizabeth ever met Lewis or corresponded with him. Perhaps Jane Elizabeth, having some knowledge of the existence of another black elder, prayed and, in her own mind, believed that Walker Lewis wanted her sealed to him for time and eternity. Apparently this was shortly before Isaac James returned to Salt Lake after an absence of nearly two decades. Elijah Abel was baptized in 1832, and in 1836 he became an elder in the Melchizedek priesthood, the higher of two priesthood levels in the Mormon Church. Abel, along with his wife, Mary Ann, and three children moved from Ohio to Utah in 1853. Abel continued to be an active Saint, and as late as 1877 he received notice that he was still a member of the Third Quorum of Seventies, a group of priesthood holders designated to perform certain duties. This may have surprised Abel as President Brigham Young had not approved Abel's earlier requests to have his wife and children sealed to him. During Brigham Young's tenure as president, denial of priesthood was applied to all black male Saints. In addition, Young prohibited black participation in temple ceremonies. Black women were ineligible to do what other "worthy" women could do as a matter of regular course—"only be in 'good standing' to gain access to the temple." Young believed that blacks were cursed because they were descendants of Cain. Jane Elizabeth was probably aware of Young's rejection of Abel's request and consequently did not consider the possibility of being sealed to Abel, who died in 1884, shortly before Jane Elizabeth contacted President John Taylor regarding her endowments. For information on Elijah Abel, see Bringhurst, "Elijah Abel and the Changing Status of Blacks within Mormonism," 130–48; and Lester F. Bush, "Mormonism's Negro Doctrine: An Historical Overview," in Bush and Mauss, *Neither White nor Black*, 77.

37. The act of omission in autobiography is not uncommon. One of the functions of omission is to reinforce the impression in the reader's mind of the salient points the author wishes to make. See Charles T. Davis, "From Experience to Eloquence: Richard Wright's Black Boy as Art," in *African American Autobiography: A Collection of Critical Essays*, ed. William L. Andrews (Englewood Cliffs, N.J.: Prentice-Hall, 1993), 142–45. In Jane Elizabeth's case, it is clear that by omitting direct references to the divorces and circumstances of Sylvester's birth, she is attempting to demonstrate that her life had no blemishes that should cause anyone to doubt her faithfulness and worthiness as a Latter-day Saint.

38. *Journals of Wilford Woodruff*, October 16, 1894, entry, Document No. 5, in Wolfinger, "A Test of Faith," 150. See also Mathias Cowley, *Wilford Woodruff: History of His Life and Labors*, (Salt Lake City: Deseret News, 1909), 587. The Quorum of Twelve consists of twelve high priests, who, in Mormon theology, are referred to as the twelve apostles. The Quorum of Twelve is second only to the First Presidency in authority over LDS theological issues. In the event of the death of the president, the First Presidency is dissolved and the Quorum of Twelve assumes leadership until a new president is selected. See McConkie, *Mormon Doctrine*, 597–98.

39. "Excerpts from the Weekly Council Meetings of the Quorum of Twelve Apostles, Rights of the Negro in the Church, 1849–1940," George Albert Smith Papers, Special

Collections, Marriott Library, University of Utah. See also "Minutes of a Meeting of the Council of Twelve Apostles, August 22, 1895," Document No. 6, in Wolfinger, "A Test of Faith," 150.

40. "Minutes of a Meeting of the Council of Twelve Apostles, January 2, 1902," Document No. 7, in Wolfinger, "Test of Faith," 151.

41. Lester E. Bush, *Compilation on the Negro in Mormonism*, 186–87, Special Collections, Harold B. Lee Library, Brigham Young University Library (1970).

42. James, *Autobiography*, 8.

43. *Deseret News*, April 16, 1908, p. 1.

44. *Deseret News*, April 21, 1908, p. 4; Cowley, *Wilford Woodruff*, 587.

45. Bringhurst, *Saints, Slaves, and Blacks*, 69–70, 86, 98; Bush, "Mormonism's Negro Doctrine," 79.

46. An entire body of literature, from the folk songs and folktales of the slaves and early autobiographical writings of Olaudah Equiano (Gustavus Vassa), Frederick Douglass, Booker T. Washington to the masterpieces of Maya Angelou, Richard Wright, Malcolm X, and Angela Davis, reveals this trope of "mastering the form of the mask." See Houston A. Baker, *Modernism and the Harlem Renaissance* (Chicago: University of Chicago Press, 1987), 15–37, where he discusses Booker T. Washington's oratorical skills in relations to the minstrel's mask that he often donned. Baker argues that Washington's "mind is undoubtedly always fixed on some intended gain, on a mastery of stories and their telling that leads to Afro American advancement" (pp. 31–32).

47. Wolfinger, "A Test of Faith," 136.

48. Ibid. Wolfinger said that although Jane Elizabeth was a culturally devout Mormon, she also "remained racially conscious ... indirectly rather than directly." Wolfinger cites Jane Elizabeth's awareness and support of Joseph Smith's prophecy on the impending end of slavery as an example of her race consciousness. Jane Elizabeth said, "[T]hings come to pass what he prophesied about the colored race being freed. Things that he said has come to pass. I did not hear that, but I knew of it." Rather than an example of a racially conscious person, the passage suggests that Jane Elizabeth was a person who believed strongly in the prophetic powers of Joseph Smith and used his prophecy regarding the end of slavery to authenticate Smith as prophet, seer, and revelator. Jane Elizabeth was racially conscious but for reasons other than a strong sense of racial awareness and pride. By 1890 the Salt Lake County black population was 240, of which 75 percent were not LDS. Non-Mormon employment opportunities in transportation, the military, and mining were the primary reasons for African American settlement. See Coleman, "A History of Blacks in Utah," 77–80, 223.

49. Jane Elizabeth did baptisms for deceased family members as well as ask that Isaac James and Isaac Manning be adopted along with herself into the Smith family.

50. *Salt Lake Tribune*, June 10, 1978, p. 1. The "special friends" were Mary Lucille Perkins Bankhead, Ruffin Bridgeforth, Lowell Bennion, and Linda and Jack Newell. I based the 129 years of black priesthood denial on the 1849 date when the priesthood policy was stated by Brigham Young. See Bush, "Mormonism's Negro Doctrine," 70.

The Early Twentieth Century

CHAPTER 9

"The Mountains Were Free and We Loved Them"

DR. RUTH FLOWERS OF BOULDER, COLORADO

Susan Armitage

Ruth Cave Flowers, born in Colorado Springs in 1902, was a distinguished educator who received Harvard University's Teacher of the Year Award in 1969 and the Bicentennial Mother of Achievement award from the state of Colorado in 1975. She began her notable career in unpromising circumstances. Her parents were divorced before she was born, and her mother died when she was eleven, leaving Ruth and her sister, Dorothy, in the care of their sixty-year-old grandmother, Minnesota Waters, who was struggling to make her own living. In the oral history contained in the following pages, Flowers describes how she, her sister, and her grandmother lived and worked in the small university town of Boulder, Colorado, during the years 1917 to 1924.[1] In this community marked by segregation and discrimination, Flowers forged her determination, commitment, and enduring love of the mountains.

In 1924 Ruth Cave became the first African American woman to graduate from the University of Colorado. However, discrimination prevented her from finding a position in the West, and she was forced to leave Boulder for the segregated South to find a teaching job. She taught French and Latin at Claflin College in South Carolina from 1924 to 1928 and returned to Boulder in 1929–30 to care for her grandmother and get an M.A. from the University of Colorado in French and education. She then moved to Washington, D.C., and taught at Dunbar High School from 1931 to 1945. Her grandmother died in 1943, but Cave kept her Boulder house, returning to it when she could. She attended Robert F. Terrell Law School at night and received her law degree in 1945. In 1937 she married a fellow law student, Harold Flowers, with whom she later practiced law and had a son. They were divorced in 1949, and Flowers went on to complete work on a Ph.D. in foreign languages and literature from Catholic University of America in Washington, D.C., in 1951. From 1951 to 1959 she was an associate professor of Spanish at North Carolina College in Durham. In 1959 she and her son, Harold, returned to Boulder to live, and she was hired as the head of the foreign languages department at the new Fairview High School, a position she held until her retirement in 1967. In her retirement, she tutored reading in a Boulder elementary school, gave talks throughout the school system on African American culture, and gave public talks and interviews about her memories of the black community in Boulder. The community that she remembers was dissolved by World War II, when most residents left for better jobs on the West Coast. Dr. Flowers's clear-eyed recollections are the fullest account that exists of the prewar period. She brings her best skills as a teacher to her thorough and unsparing description of the social and economic prejudice in Boulder at that time. She aimed to raise public consciousness about race relations, and, as she wryly put it, "I feel a duty to let people know their fair city is not always as fair as they believe it to be." She died in Boulder in 1980 at the age of seventy-seven.

· · ·

After the death of their mother, Ruth Cave Flowers and her sister Dorothy were raised by their maternal grandmother, who lived in the famous mining town of Cripple Creek, Colorado. However, Cripple Creek was a dying town, and Mrs. Waters had difficulty finding jobs and supporting them. Flowers recalls:

I remember, in Cripple Creek—she had just about gotten to the end of her string, as far as being able to find any way of feeding us. So she put out a little word in the community, that there were two girls for adoption. So she would have us clean up the front room, and put on our pretty white dresses, and combed our hair, and put ribbons in it, and brought out our trunk with our few belongings, and have us sitting on the trunk. So here began coming various people. They'd look at me—"She's too puny." They'd look at Dorothy—"She looks sullen." But there were several that were willing to take one of us, but nobody was willing to take both of us. So Grandma got mad, and with a few choice words that I wouldn't care to repeat, she opened the door and invited them all out. And then she closed the door, and said, "Take off your clothes put on your regular clothes, put the trunk back in there, and somehow, we'll make it."

In desperation, Mrs. Waters sent the two teenage girls ahead to the university town of Boulder, where she thought they could all find work. Dr. Flowers's memories of Boulder begin with her trip from Cripple Creek, along with her sister, to enter high school.

My earliest memories? Well, they would go back to 1917 when I first came here; January of 1917. My sister and I were send down here from Cripple Creek by our grandmother, to get in school. We were supposed to try and find some work, and help her get down here in March.

When we got down here in January, we didn't know anybody but an old man who had been living in Cripple Creek. He had sent us our fare and he found a room for us to stay up here on this street. Monday was the first day of the second semester of high school here. When we presented ourselves that morning at the high school, with our transcripts from Cripple Creek, we were not admitted. The rule at that time was that you had to be a resident of Boulder for six months in order to be able to register in the high school, or pay a tuition of $75.00 apiece. That let us out. Then we were told, also, that you had to buy your books. Nothing was free. They didn't furnish anything.

We sat out on the steps of the high school, not knowing what to do. So then my sister (she's taller than I am), she said, "Well, let's go find some work." So we started out and began knocking on doors to see if anybody needed any help. My sister got a job right away. He was the mayor of the town, and they hired her right away. Well, I knocked on quite a number of doors, and I didn't get anything. I was quite small, a lot smaller than she was. I was 14 at the time. She was 15. And I didn't get anything. So I came on back down on this street, and the second house from 19th St. was a little hand laundry, run by a Negro woman. She hired me to iron. I think I got about 10 to 15 cents an hour, ironing men's shirts. So I did that. We did get together enough money and sent for Grandma, and she came the last of March.

When Grandma came down in March, she went to see if we could have a house to rent. We'd have to be renting, because we didn't have any money. We were told by the real estate firm, that unless we could get a house on the south side of Water St. or either side of Goss St., between 19th and 23rd, we might as well forget it. Because they rented or sold no property [to Negroes], except for that.

Luckily, there was one vacant house, the second from the corner at 19th and Water. We rented that. There was nothing really good about the house. The land sloped down, and that meant that you got all the water around. But we had a nice garden at the back, and lots of fruit trees. Everybody had two or three fruit trees. And we had grass and we had flowers. We fixed it up the best we could inside. My sister had the upstairs bedroom. Grandma and I had the other bedroom upstairs. We slept together. Then we had a living room, a very big kitchen, and then another bedroom, downstairs, in case someone should come. We called it a spare bedroom. Other than the inconveniences, it was just an old house.

Cripple Creek had been a wide-open, tolerant town, but Boulder was not. In contrast to the myth of the freedom of the West, Flowers found restrictions everywhere.

The first day we came down, on Saturday (to back up just a little ways) we had a couple or three nickels, and we went to get an ice cream cone while we were walking around trying to find someplace to work. We were refused service. You couldn't go in any restaurant, any hot dog stand, any ice cream parlor, any movies,—you could go no place—absolutely no place. No Negro student—no Negro person, student or not, could go anywhere here. It was [a] shock, because we hadn't been accustomed to that.

You know these pretty homes on Mapleton? They were mostly built by rich people who came from Oklahoma or Texas. They brought their own servants with them, most of them, and they brought up all the businesses—that means the theaters, that means the restaurants, and that means *all* the businesses. They just bought out everything. Consequently, when they bought out everything, they said—O.K.—no Negroes in any theaters, no Negroes in any restaurants—no Negroes anywhere.

In the face of this persistent discrimination, the black community was not without its own resources.

I was counting the families that were on these blocks. There were fifty [Negro] families that lived in this area. Of the fifty families I counted, there were sixty children. We were all concentrated right here. And at the time that we came here, there may have been about fifteen young people of our age. We used to go to the Baptist Church—its meetings were at 4 o'clock in the afternoon, the Methodist Church was 8 o'clock in the evening. So we would go to both churches, and sing in the choirs at both churches. There was—it was a very nice feeling at that time—a feeling of togetherness, which made it not too bad.

What I was trying to say about the neighborhood was—you couldn't get an ice cream cone or anything like that. So, what they did—various families would have ice cream socials. And they would put their tables outdoors, you know, and the whole neighborhood would come, and we had a social. We couldn't go to the movies, so what we did was to go to various homes. Among the various young people who were here when I came, the majority of them were musically talented. Very, very musically talented. Practically all of the youngsters could play the piano. They could play the saxophone, they could play the trumpet. They could play the violin. So, we would get together. I've got pictures even in my scrapbook here of singing around the piano. My sister could play the piano a little bit. I couldn't and neither one of us could sing. That didn't make any difference, you know. Off a key and off a tune, but we still sang! Then, we would sing, play games, we would dance—except for a few church members who wouldn't allow any dancing—but those that did, we would go to those places and do a little dancing. This was in the various private homes—practically every weekend, we'd do something like that.

For the young black people of Boulder, the freedom of the mountains (wild and undeveloped but laced with hiking trails) was a genuine escape from white pressure. Flowers recalls that sometimes the trip to freedom began with a small act of defiance—sitting on the grass in Chautauqua Park.

Then the other thing that we did, since we couldn't go anywhere, was to go hiking. We hiked, in, I think, every canyon, and every part of the hills. We would simply start on 9th St. and walk up. Well, you'd go up to Chautauqua [park]. We could swing on the swings up there if there were no white people there. If there were white people, we couldn't swing in the swings, but they couldn't keep you from sitting on the grass. Usually we didn't stop in the Chautauqua, because of the ugly looks that we got. But we would go up Bluebell Canyon, and carry our lunches and go up Flagstaff all the time. The older people wouldn't object. We'd take a great big heavy skillet like Grandma would have, and a great big coffee pot like grandma would also have. And from the various families we'd get some coffee and some rolls and a little bit of meat, you know. We'd leave about 7 o'clock in the evening, and get to the top of whatever hill we were trying to climb about 10 o'clock—we would carry a lantern—and build a fire. We always carried our firewood—the paper and the wood. We'd try to stop some place where there was a stream, you see, for our coffee, and we would cook these steaks. We called them steaks—they were these little steaks that you call rib steaks—and put them on the bread, and make a sandwich, and have the strong coffee. We'd set up there in the mountains and play the ukulele, or the banjo or something, and then start back down and get back home about 2:00. Nobody ever asked us what we did—or if we behaved ourselves. Grandma just made one statement and after that she never bothered us. She said—"You know how to behave; you'd better behave." And I think probably everybody else did the same. So in the summertime, we were in the mountains all of the time. The mountains were free and we loved them.

Mountain trips were wonderful, but the daily reality for Flowers and her family was work.

After Grandma came down here, she got a job right away. She was a short order cook out of this world. She had the privilege of hiring a dishwasher, so she hired me. And we worked there until I finished high school. You see, what I had to do—I had to get up at 6:30 in the morning,—go in the back way, and open it up, and get everything ready for Grandma. She would come in at 7:30 or 8:00. Then I would come at noon, and wash up all the dishes that they had stacked there, and then get back down to the high school before the next class. I think we had an hour off. Then I would go back after school and I had to stay there until about 8:30, because I had to mop the restaurant before I left. So then I was studying from about 9:00 at night to 1:00 or 2:00 in the morning. My sister had better hours, she was still working for the same mayor. Well, that solved our eating problem, and gave us enough money to pay the rent on the house.

Back to the community here—I told you there were about sixty families, I counted this morning, and about sixty youngsters, going from little ones up to our age, and about fifteen, of course, who were about our age. Now, of these sixty families, I counted, there were only twenty men—fathers—who were here when we got here, the reason being that before the town became what it did become, there were three hotels and they had hired Negro waiters. So there had been work for men at that time. But after the hotels closed, there was no work; no work for Negro men at all. Now, two or three of them could work [as] section hands, on the railroad. They were track walkers. Then, the only other work that [they] could get would be maybe a janitor job, and a sideline would be shining shoes. So the only men who remained here were the older men, those who couldn't leave. When somebody asked me whether Boulder was a matriarchal society, as far as our race was concerned, I said "yes"—it was by necessity a matriarchal society. Because the younger men who could get out, and all of the boys, who became 16 or 17, they all left Boulder. Many of them went to Denver. You could get work in Denver. The rest of them, of course, worked on the railroad—dining car porters, and sleeping car porters, and so forth. And they would run from Chicago. When they had any time off, they would come back home. But I'm talking about those who really lived here with their families.

So it left the women to support their families, and to look after their families and to raise their families and to work. So, counting up and down, see, it was just the same situation as with Grandma and me and my sister. The men were just not here. Many of the men were dead. Then, I was figuring in the next ten years, I think there were only ten left. The rest had either died off or had gone entirely away. So, the Negro women, of course, were the support of the church, the backbone of the church, the backbone of the family, they were the backbone of the social life, everything.

They could only get two kinds of work—the kind that I got and my sister got—washing and ironing, or general housework. Cooking, of course, with the exception of being in the sorority or fraternity houses, was combined with the general housework. We had quite a few of the women who cooked in the fraternity and sorority houses. That, of course, was a full-time job.

The boys couldn't get any work. No work at all. Most of the boys dropped out of school in the 9th grade. A few of them got to the 10th, but most of them didn't, and I'll give you the reason for that, too. As far as the girls were concerned, they all worked. Either they did washing and ironing at home, which is what I did (and I did that all the way through college 'cause I couldn't arrange my schedule so I could do anything else, you see)—or they did general housework. So when we got to the 12th grade at Boulder High School, there was just my sister and I left in school. There was only one boy behind us in the 11th grade.

One of the Flowerses' hardest struggles was to receive an education. A racist high school principal refused to allow her and many other black students to march in the commencement procession or to cross the platform to receive a diploma as the white students did. In fact, he fabricated a story to prevent her from graduating at all. But because Flowers had all the necessary courses for college admission, the denial did not prevent her from making the journey "up the hill" to the University of Colorado above the town of Boulder.

I'm positive, almost, that the principal of the high school must have been a Ku Klux Klan [member]. Certainly, he was a racist. So what happened when the students entered, they'd have a rough time of it. Not that they were stupid. We didn't have many stupid people here. Kids were talented and most of them were smart. But they had difficulty in the 9th grade. Now, the boys, seeing the other boys out playing baseball, and they couldn't play, they quit at the end of the 9th grade. They said that what's the use—what's the need of trying to go? They weren't interested in just going to classes. Boys are interested in playing, and they couldn't even play on the playground, you see. So they dropped out. Then when you got to the 10th grade—if you made it to the 10th grade—you were discouraged to go any further. You were told you were too stupid, there was no need of going, you can't get anywhere, you can't get in the university. All kinds of reasons were given to you. Some by the faculty, most of them by the principal, you see. If you got to the 11th grade, they didn't really bother you, because they knew what was going to happen when you got to the 12th grade. I didn't know, and my sister didn't know, and the boy behind us, in the next grade, didn't know. So, we got through the 11th grade, my sister and I, and got in the 12th grade. Both of us had tried very hard to make up that semester that we missed, so we would graduate at the time that we should have graduated. So, we took six subjects, all the way through, from the second semester of the 9th grade until we got to the 12th grade, just trying to make up. When we got to the 12th grade, my sister didn't feel like she could take seven subjects. But I took seven subjects. And the only way I was able to take seven subjects was because one very nice teacher taught me solid geometry during lunch. So, came about two days before graduation, my sister knew she couldn't graduate, because she was minus one point. She would have to come back that next September, which she intended to do. However, about two days before graduation, the principal sent for me and said, "You can't graduate." I said, "I can't? I've got 16 units." He said, "But you don't have 16 units. We just erased one of them." I said, "What did you erase?" He said, "We erased your physics mark. You didn't complete one of the experiments." I know I had completed the experiment, but they claimed they didn't find it. He said, "You're not going to graduate."

Well, of course, tears were all over the place, you know. So I went and found Grandma, down here at 1912 Water, and I said, "Grandma, the principal said I can't graduate. Will you come up and talk to him." O.K. She went up and talked to him. And I don't know what went on in the office. I was locked out, of course. Pretty soon the door opened in the office. The door slammed and Grandma stomped out and went on home. I'm right behind her. She was still steaming, you know. So, she said that the principal said, "I take the word of my teacher, not the word of your daughter. The teacher is always right."

So I didn't graduate. But I had the right fifteen units to get in the university, and that's all they required. He was so sure that I didn't have the right fifteen units, but I had them. I wasn't going to do anything that summer. I was so discouraged. A senior fellow who was up there working in the fraternity house came down—he was a friend of mine—and he said, "You're going up there and register." I said, "I don't want any more school. I'm sick of it. I wasn't treated fairly, I'm just not going on." He just took me by the hand, and carried me—pulled me all the way up to the registrar's office, registered me, and then left me. And so, of course, I finished in the four years.

But my sister, after she saw me crying that day, said, "I am not going to ever put my foot in that high school again." She'd been going with a fellow from Manitou Springs, and she went on down, and he came up and asked Grandma for her hand. They got married. They went on down to Manitou Springs, and she never finished high school.

But I still didn't know what was going on, until the next year. When I was a freshman up at the university, the boy who was behind me, who was a very smart boy, got to the senior year, had his sixteen units, they wouldn't let him graduate. And graduation time came—he didn't graduate.

His mother and aunt were working for some very influential white people. They decided to have an investigation, and they went to see what was going on at the high school; why no child ever got beyond the 10th grade, usually, why most of them didn't get beyond the 9th grade, why those who wanted to go to high school had to be sent to Kansas or to Missouri. That's where most of these kids (they didn't stop at the 9th grade or the 10th grade—practically all of them finished high school) finished the university, not here, but in Kansas. In the high school in Kansas, they had to go to a segregated high school, because, you see, Kansas was segregated.

Anyway, this committee went to the high school to talk to the principal, and he said, "While I am principal here, no Negro student is going to cross the platform at Macky Auditorium and receive a diploma from me." So, he mailed the diploma to this boy. The boy came up here to the university, too, but he mailed the diploma to him. He was not going to see a Negro on that platform. Of course, he was fired right then. Then the next girl, who was then in the 9th grade, graduated in 1924, the same year I graduated from the university, was the first Negro to ever cross the stage at Macky Auditorium in a high school graduation.

Flowers's determination was homegrown, as her mature recollection of her grand-mother's harsh encouragement illustrates.

When I went up there [to the University of Colorado] in 1920, I was the first Negro girl. Grandma just expected me to go on [to college]. That idea was implanted on me in Cripple Creek. But now, Grandma did this: she didn't say anything about going to school, but she would do the best she could to help you, if she could. But the main thing was, if I came home and complained about some class being difficult, or show her some test that I had failed, Grandma would just look at me with those gray eyes of hers, and she'd say, "Anybody pass?" And I'd say "yeah" and she'd say, "What's wrong with you?" No smile or nothing, you know. "I don't know," she'd say, "I don't ever want to see that again." And I'd try hard not to let her see that again, you know. But that was her way of encouraging you. I have sat up in this room—that next room, which was the kitchen—all night long from the time I started until the sun rose, with my feet in the oven, trying to get through some of the books we had.

Grandma always said, "Don't come to me with any problems. You got problems, you solve them yourself." She was trying to make us independent. If she hadn't done that, we never could have come down here by ourselves, we probably would have ended up in the gutter somewhere.

Although Flowers successfully made the journey "up the hill" to the university, she was not welcome there.

There was no [Negro] girls at the University of Colorado. When I went up there in 1920, I was the first Negro girl. You could go to the classes at the University, but you couldn't participate in anything, whatsoever, except the YMCA. I was in languages, and I could go to the language club meetings. But that was all. But if there were any social affairs, of course you couldn't go. You couldn't stay in the dorms, you couldn't eat on the Hill. The [Negro] students who went up there could not get a sandwich anyplace on the Hill. They had to trot all the way down here to Goss Street to eat. They ate every place that they lived so if Grandma had wanted to, we could have put four or five of them in here. They put them under stairwells, they put them every place. They had no place to go. That situation existed until 1943.

Throughout her college years, Flowers had to continue her work-related journeys up and down the Hill.

But, you see, when Grandma took us, she was almost 70. So when she became 65—I believe 66—I believe they let her stay until she was 66, then she lost her job up there at the Allen's Cafe.

It was my second quarter at the University, and it was difficult, and of course I no longer had the dishwashing job. So I had to work on the Hill. I would do the same thing, I'd go to a restaurant between classes and dish wash. I couldn't cook, of course. And I didn't have time. Grandma was not feeling well, and I had the additional job of trying to look after her. I was still doing washing and ironing, plus the work that I had to do on the Hill. At noon, I went over and washed dishes at some of the places. Sometimes I served parties at night. I didn't have too much extra time but I managed.

Washing and ironing was tedious—you had to carry it up on the Hill—that was the job that I despised. You carried it always in suitcases, usually, in order not to get it mussed up. So, you'd get the suitcase of clothes from the student, put them in the suitcase, you'd carry it home, you'd wash and iron the clothes in the suitcase, put them in the suitcase, and carry it back up there.

During my last year up at the University I worked for President and Mrs. Norlin. Mrs. Norlin just created the job for me, when she found out the hard time I was having, just doing washing and so forth, and knowing that Grandma was sick, and it really was an awful chore. I was really beat. So she just imagined that she needed an upstairs girl—and she had me make myself a little costume. I made myself a little black dress with a white collar, and a little gray dress with a white collar. And I had a little fancy apron. I opened the door. They had an awful lot of company—being the president—I waited on the table, for them. I dusted upstairs. She had two cooks, so I really wasn't needed. But I washed the dishes and that sort of thing. She always made sure, that if anything was left over, I would take it home to Grandma. That didn't please the two cooks too much, because they had the same thing in mind. Mrs. Norlin would come out and say, "Ruth will take whatever is left home." But I didn't take every-thing, I just took enough for Grandma.

It was then that Grandma just decided let's try to find a lot, and start building a house. We found this lot, and then Grandma hired a carpenter who would be considered, now, a retired senior citizen. She was a pretty good carpenter. So she and the carpenter put up this [house], and I helped when-ever I could. I'm not a carpenter, but I could help. So we got it built. There was just this room and the next room, there, and, of course, a porch. If you look on the outside, you can see that they're two different sections. There was this section. This was a porch, here. Grandma used to, after I started teaching and would send her some money, she would save the money, and try to have a surprise for me—maybe a sleeping porch, or something, you know. And that was the way the house was built. That's why it's built in such a strange way.

When Ruth Flowers achieved her goal and graduated from the University of Colorado in 1924, she could not find work. In the 1920s it was rare for black women to be employed as schoolteachers in the West. And so new journeys, spanning a period of thirty-five years, began for her, to Claflin College, South Carolina; to Dunbar High School in Washington D.C., where she also earned a law degree from Howard University and a Ph.D. from the Catholic University of America; and to North Carolina College in Durham. During all those years, she repeatedly returned to Boulder and her grandmother's house.

I came home every summer. I never missed a summer from the time I graduated until Grandma died. Four times, I took the year off, without pay, and looked after her. And then during the Second World War when this work became available in California, we had an exodus from here. As soon as the shipyards opened up, then the Negro people just left in droves. Because usually their older son, or their father or somebody, had already gone out there and found a job. And then pretty soon, they would leave and all get together, mostly in California. See those people made more money in one month than they had seen in a year. And the women found out they could do something else beside washing and ironing. They could use all kinds of instruments on those planes. They had a whole new horizon open to them. Now, as far as the people who used to be here—they've either all died out; most of them have died out—like Grandma and all the people that we used to run around with. I don't think anybody ever came back to live. I'm about the only one who came home.

NOTES

1. This oral history was conducted by Theresa Banfield for the Boulder Women's Oral History Project in 1977 and edited for this chapter by Susan Armitage with the assistance of Harold Flowers of Denver, Colorado. The full transcript of the interview with Dr. Flowers is deposited at the Carnegie Library branch of the Boulder Public Library.

☙ ～～～ ❧

Nettie J. Asberry: African American
Club Woman in the Pacific Northwest

By the early twentieth century African American women had organized clubs throughout the
West that provided a multitude of self-help or charitable services in a larger agenda of "racial
uplift." Tacoma's Nettie Asberry illustrates how club work supported black women's public
activism in a variety of forms.

On August 9, 1917, black club women from across Washington State convened
to affiliate their local clubs with the National Association of Colored Women
(NACW). They met in Spokane at the home of Mrs. George Clay, with the intention "to furnish evidence of Material, Mental, and Moral progress made by our
people." In truth, black women in Washington could already take credit for years
of service in their communities. For club women like Tacoma's Nettie J. Asberry as
well as her peers throughout the region, clubs provided a means to participate in
their communities. All of the clubs, whether they were formed around reading
groups or art, also included charity work in their charters. Although Washington's
black women had founded several organizations by 1917, affiliation with the
national group must have bolstered their collective sense of purpose.

Asberry launched the Clover Leaf Art Club in 1908, after learning that the
Alaska-Yukon-Pacific Exposition (AYPE), to be held in Seattle the following year,
planned to construct a women's building to display the "handiwork and handi-
craft" of Washington women. As she later wrote, "A group of us here in Tacoma
became inspired with the idea of making a display of the work of colored women
of this community." Procuring the exhibit space was difficult, so to pay for the
space, the Clover Leaf Art Club sold "colored dolls." Club members won a gold
medal for the exhibit, as well as individual awards for their work, and Asberry later
reminisced, "From that history making venture, the women took on new life and
spirit." Although black women's clubs had been founded before 1908, they proliferated after the Clover Leaf Art Club's public success. Mrs. V. A. Freeman of

---

Source: Karla Kelling, "Nettie Asberry and Washington State Black Women's Clubs in the Early 20th
Century," unpublished manuscript, 1999.

Longview, Washington, recalled a visit from Asberry to meet with the black families in town and urge local women to form their own clubs. Freeman soon started a book club and study club, and her daughter received a scholarship to Reed College through the Washington State Federation of Colored Women's Clubs—a scholarship supported through the sale of cookbooks and other creative forms of fund-raising.

Like club women throughout the nation, Washington's club women participated not only in charitable and social activities in their communities but also in more direct forms of political activism. Even as she supported herself by giving music lessons, Asberry found time to organize the Tacoma branch of the National Association for the Advancement of Colored People (NAACP) in 1915 and participated in the Tacoma Inter-Racial Council. Other black women joined Asberry in their enthusiasm for civil rights activism, even firing off telegrams to Congress demanding federal intervention to prevent lynching. The Women's Political and Civil Alliance of Seattle urged one congressman to stop the "barbaric" and "heinous" lynch mobs, writing, "We are petitioning your far-reaching influence in Congress in behalf of this race of maltreated American Citizens."

By the time Washington's black women's clubs officially allied with the NACW, they were already committed to the organization's motto, "Lifting as We Climb." This spirit is exemplified by Seattle's Women's Home and Foreign Mission Society, first organized in 1902. Along with promoting a "spirit of helpfulness" and contributing money to their church, black women members also sought to "secure employment of colored people." Such charitable work imbued black women with a sense of community spirit and racial pride. Nettie J. Asberry reiterated the accomplishments of club work when she reported to the *Seattle Post Intelligencer* in 1926 on the promotion of Negro History Week. As she explained, "It would be uplifting to the colored children to know that their mothers and fathers helped make America what it is today."

Sarah Jones and her class, 1882. Courtesy of the Clarissa H. Wildy Collection, Sacramento Archives and Museum Collection Center.

Lucinda and Nancy Jane Todd. Courtesy of the Kansas Collection, University of Kansas Libraries.

Mary Ellen Pleasant. Courtesy of the Schomburg Collection, New York Public Library.

Clara Luper and the Oklahoma City Youth Council chose Katz Drugstore as the site for their first demonstration in 1958. Copyright, The Oklahoma Publishing Company.

Luper led the Youth Council in demonstrations such as this one at Green's Drug Store until a city ordinance banning demonstration was passed in 1964. Courtesy of the Oklahoma Historical Society.

Members of the Great Falls AME Church gathered in front of the church, ca. late 1920s. Marie Dutrieuille Ellis is at the far right of the photo. Lucille Smith Thompson is the little girl, left front center, in a white dress with her hands in her lap. Next to her on the left is her brother, Martin. Mary Novotny, daughter of Mattie Byers Novotny, is on the far left, partially hidden. Courtesy of Alan Thompson.

Maria Adams Dutrieuille, once a housemaid to George Armstrong Custer, was an early member of the Great Falls AME Church. Courtesy of the Montana Historical Society.

African American Loretta Red Bird, who married into the Flathead Tribe, appears on horseback. Courtesy of the Mansfield Library, University of Montana.

Jane E. James and other Utah pioneers at the 1897 Jubilee Celebration of the 1847 arrival of Mormon pioneers in Salt Lake City. Courtesy of the LDS Archives.

CHAPTER 10

Susie Revels Cayton, Beatrice Morrow Cannady, and the Campaign for Social Justice in the Pacific Northwest

Quintard Taylor

In 1920 nearly six thousand African American women called the Pacific Northwest home. They could be found in towns and cities across the region, including Helena, Montana, Pendleton, Oregon, Pocatello, Idaho, and Spokane, Washington, but approximately 40 percent lived in two cities, Seattle and Portland. Despite their long residence in the Pacific Northwest, these women have not been heard because of the small populations, because of the paucity of documentary sources on their lives, and because regional historians have only recently shown interest in their role in shaping the social, cultural, and political history of the region.[1]

Among those African American women were two remarkably gifted social activists, Susie Revels Cayton of Seattle and Beatrice Morrow Cannady of Portland. As wives, mothers, and working women employed outside the home, Cayton and Cannady experienced lives much like many western working-class women. As college-educated newspaper editors, however, both women were members of a small African American middle class. Cayton's background as daughter of the first African American senator in the nation's history and Cannady's as the first black woman to practice law in Oregon ensured that each would hold a revered place of civic and social leadership in their respective communities. Despite their similarities, these African American women followed two distinctly different paths, Cayton as a Communist Party organizer and Cannady as an official in the National Association for the Advancement of Colored People (NAACP), in their campaigns for social justice and racial equality in the West.

Both Cayton and Cannady were migrants, arriving in Seattle and Portland in 1896 and 1910, respectively. Much like the thousands of others streaming into the Pacific Northwest from elsewhere in the United States as well as from Asia and Europe, their views on race and region remained inchoate, evolving and subject to periodic reassessment. The two women espoused the widely shared idea that the Pacific Northwest offered greater freedom to African Americans than the South or much of the eastern third of the nation. Yet given their own often painful experiences with bigotry in Washington and Oregon, they, and probably most other African American women of the era, were clearly not yet ready to declare, as had NAACP founder W. E. B. Du Bois, in his 1913 visit to the Pacific Northwest, that "the [regional] fight against race prejudice has been . . . triumphant."[2]

If both women acknowledged an identification with the Pacific Northwest, their respective ages, health, and politics influenced their ability to disseminate their messages beyond Seattle and Portland. Susie Cayton, who became an activist only in her sixties, focused her energies almost exclusively on working-class issues in Seattle. The combination of advancing age and diabetes, as well as her Marxist message, precluded Cayton's extensive travel throughout the region in the 1930s. Cannady, twenty years younger and in much better health, traveled easily to small cities and towns across Oregon and Washington as well to New York, Chicago, Philadelphia, and Los Angeles to promote her regional campaign for racial equality. Their combined activities were a powerful reminder that in the matter of race regional exceptionalism did not apply to the West.

• • •

There is little in Susie Revels Cayton's background that suggested the political path she would eventually follow. She was born Susie Sumner Revels in 1870, the daughter of Hiram Rhoades Revels, the first African American U.S. senator in the nation's history. Revels, a minister in the African Methodist Episcopal (AME) Church and the first president of Alcorn University, was selected senator by the Mississippi legislature the year his daughter was born.[3]

Susie Revels spent her first two years in Washington, D.C., and the next decade on the Alcorn campus. She became a teacher at the age of sixteen, working in a one-room rural Mississippi school while attending Rust College.

Following a courtship by correspondence, Susie Revels traveled to Seattle to marry Horace Cayton on July 12, 1896. A fellow Mississippian ten years her senior, Horace Cayton had studied with her father at Alcorn and arrived in Seattle in 1889 after working in Nicodemus, Kansas, and Ogden, Utah. The Caytons had much in common: both were college graduates, teachers, writers, intellectuals, and evolving journalists.[4]

Horace Cayton worked briefly as a political reporter for the *Seattle Post-Intelligencer* before founding the Seattle *Republican* in 1894. Unlike other "African American" newspapers of the period, the *Republican* carried political news for the entire city and by 1900 had the second largest circulation in Seattle. In 1903 the Caytons resided in an elite Seattle neighborhood and were the wealthiest, most prominent African American couple in the Pacific Northwest.[5]

By the beginning of the twentieth century, Susie Revels Cayton was the associate editor of the *Republican*, where she was responsible for articles on religion and "women's features." She also wrote the newspaper's editorials and published the *Republican* when her husband was out of town. Her views, as reflected in the editorials during this period, were virtually identical to those of her husband, who considered himself a Theodore Roosevelt Republican. In 1909 Horace Cayton acknowledged on the front page of the *Republican* his debt to Susie when he said the newspaper's success was "not partially due, but . . . sometimes . . . wholly due" to her efforts.[6]

True to her gender and social class, Susie Revels Cayton engaged in "social uplift" work designed to educate and morally reform African American working-class women and provide services to the community. It was the latter ideal that prompted Cayton in 1906 to found the Dorcus Charity Club, one of the major social uplift organizations in pre–World War II black Seattle. The club was formed in response to an urgent request for assistance in placing abandoned African American twin baby girls afflicted with rickets. Unable to find a private home to place them and unsure of what action to take, Children's Home officials released the girls to the county hospital, which in turn sent them to Medical Lake, an institution for the mentally ill. As a last resort, Medical Lake officials contacted Susie Revels Cayton, and she and three other black women, Letitia A. Graves, Alice S. Presto, and Hester Ray, recognizing this as one of a number of such cases, organized the Dorcus Charity Club. The twins were placed with a foster home located by Cayton, and three years later the club continued to provide their full support, "until a suitable home [could] be found for them."[7]

Susie Cayton's life took a sharp turn when in 1913 the Seattle *Republican* failed. Whether the paper's demise came because of shifting consumer tastes that the Caytons failed to anticipate or because the grisly account of a southern lynching drove away white readers, the Cayton's lifestyle declined dramatically, and they lived on the edge of poverty for the next three decades. The Caytons soon vacated their elegant home for an apartment in a rooming house they owned. Despite their meager resources, Susie Cayton, at the age of forty-three, withdrew from her business and social activities to care for her four children, who ranged in age from six to sixteen. By 1919 she reentered the employment market only to find that despite her college education, the only work available to her was as a "domestic." In the summers she and her children gathered berries, and she watched her daughter Madge work as a waitress in small black Seattle restaurants despite her 1925 degree in international business from the University of Washington.[8]

The family's declining fortunes had the unintended consequence of liberating Susie Cayton from her husband's vision of class relations and social progress. Unlike Horace, who insisted on maintaining proper class boundaries even after the family's fall from prosperity, Susie Cayton challenged social pretense. The treatment of working-class people in the Cayton employ suggests one such example. While Horace felt their Japanese servant, Nish, and Mr. Fontello, the garbage collector at the family's rooming house, should be "kept in their place," Susie argued that Nish was a source for learning Japanese and described Mr. Fontello as "one of the most intelligent men [she had] ever met," defiantly declaring, "[A]nd I will continue to talk with him for as long as I please." Moreover, unlike her husband, Susie had what her biographer called "a love and democratic acceptance of blackness," which allowed her to be much more comfortable around dark-skinned African Americans than Horace was.[9]

After Horace's death in 1940, Susie Cayton revealingly wrote of how she could continue to support someone with whom she often had significant disagreement: "Since it was impossible to fully unite my efforts with my husband's . . . I would join him wholeheartedly whenever the opportunity presented itself, steelhandedly pushing my own project yet comforting him when he wished it and loving him always."[10]

Through the 1920s Susie Cayton came into contact with working-class Seattle—white, Asian American, Native American, and black—and heard their grievances. She also eagerly followed the political conversion of her youngest son, Revels, who, after intense reading during his yearlong convalescence from a life-threatening illness in 1925, embraced Marxism: "[B]y the time I got off that porch I was a socialist. . . . I found it reasonable and sensible . . . that the only way blacks were going to get free would be in conjunction with the working class." Four years later, on the night of his high school graduation in

1929, Revels was not with his class but on Pioneer Square listening to speakers indicting capitalist exploitation of the working class.[11]

By the early 1930s Susie Cayton openly differed with her husband, Horace, in her reaction to political events in depression-era Seattle. If Horace Cayton looked longingly backward at the individual freedom represented by Seattle's frontier past, Susie's vision broadened as she looked forward to a more egalitarian future in an industrial democracy. At some point in the mid-1930s, around the time of her sixty-fifth birthday, she followed her son into the Communist Party, declaring, much to the consternation of her husband, "[W]e are now an international family."[12]

Although challenged by age and diabetes, Susie Cayton became more politically active in the 1930s than at any other period in her life. She assisted Revels in organizing a Madison Street branch of the Committee to Free the Scottsboro Boys. For some time she was the only woman member of the Skid Road Unemployed Council and served as its secretary, earning the name "Mother Cayton" from the organization's mostly white male workers. On another occasion, she formed a sewing circle among African American women that produced quilts for the homeless but also provided a forum for political discussions. Cayton called this process "educating the neighborhood."[13]

Susie Revels Cayton became well known to visiting black leftist intellectuals such as Langston Hughes and Paul Robeson. Her introduction to Robeson was directly attributable to her growing reputation in Party circles. On one occasion the famed concert singer and Left political activist arrived at the Cayton's Seattle home unannounced to an astounded household and declared, "I'm Paul Robeson, and I'm on a concert tour here, and so many people have told me about you that I just wanted to come up and see you."[14]

In a December 1936 letter to her daughter Madge, Susie revealed both an active schedule and her ideological commitment to the cause of Marxism.

> I will give you some idea of my activities and nothing but shortage of car fare ever keeps me from pursuing them. Monday night: P.W.U. Local, A.F. of L. . . . meets in one of the Minor School portables. (Walking distance.) Tuesday night: The Negro Workers Council, meets in a portable at the Horace Mann School. I'm Vice President and our President is out of the city at this time. Wednesday night: stay in and read late. Thursday: Party Unit always meets. (Some times walking distance, some times not.) Friday night: Stay home or visit in the neighborhood. Saturday: The Harriet Tubman Club meets. . . . Sunday night: The Worker's Forum, 94

Main Street. Besides I try to attend the Legislative Council which meets every first and third Monday in the month, also the P.T.A. at Garfield, which meets every third Thursday in the month. Of course, there are mass meetings, dances and what not that come in at times. I'm having the time of my life and at the same time making some contribution to the working class, I hope.[15]

Cayton continued to work for the causes of the Communist Party throughout the remainder of the 1930s in Seattle and then in Chicago where she relocated in 1942. At seventy-three, in one of her last acts, Cayton "held court" in her bed as Richard Wright, Langston Hughes, and other celebrities came to see her. On the night of her death, July 28, 1943, dozens of Chicagoans joined the Communist Party in her honor. Unlike her husband, Horace, who never deserted the Republican Party and subsequently became increasingly disillusioned just before his death in 1940, Cayton died a proud member of the Communist Party. Susie Revels Cayton's ashes, like those of Horace in 1940, were spread over the waters of Puget Sound.[16]

• • •

Beatrice Morrow Cannady also envisioned a new world of social justice. Her instrument for effecting that justice was the NAACP. Beatrice Hulon Morrow was born in Littig, Texas, on January 9, 1890, one of fourteen children. She attended Wiley College in Marshall, Texas, and after graduation became a teacher in Oklahoma. After a brief period at the University of Chicago, where she studied music, Beatrice Morrow arrived in Portland, Oregon, in 1910 and two years later married Edward Daniel Cannady, a waiter at a downtown hotel. By World War I Beatrice Cannady was a respected member of Portland's small African American community. She was listed as an "active patriotic worker" who served as president of the Colonel [Charles] Young War Savings Society. Cannady was also developing a national reputation, as reflected in her invitation to speak at the National Association of Women's Clubs convention in Denver where she proposed resolutions be sent to President Woodrow Wilson asserting the national organization's "whole hearted cooperation and support to the United States and their [sic] allies."[17]

In 1919, at the age of twenty-nine and with two sons, George and Ivan, at home, Cannady enrolled in the Northwestern College of Law in Portland. Three years later she became the first African American woman to graduate from the law school and one of only two women in a class of twenty-two. She was admitted to the Oregon Bar in 1922, thereupon becoming the first black woman to practice law in the state. Recalling her graduation ceremony years later, Cannady described how she "was asked to take her friends away so as to avoid embarrassment." She also described her reaction to the request: "[F]or the first time during the whole course of study I was reminded of my color. Of course, I do not forget such experiences, and no one can fully appreciate the distress unless they have suffered in the same way."[18]

Cannady was one of 165 founding members of the Portland NAACP in December 1914. However, she quickly emerged as its most powerful voice. When in 1916 D. W. Griffith's controversial, anti-black film, *The Birth of a Nation*, was slated to be shown in Portland, Cannady and other representatives of the local NAACP appeared before the city council to protest its showing in local theaters. In response, the Portland City Council enacted an ordinance that prohibited the showing of any film that, in its view, provoked racial hatred. The ban made Portland one of a handful of cities in the nation to respond decisively to black protests concerning the film. Subsequent attempts to circumvent the law and show the film in 1922, 1926, and 1931 were similarly unsuccessful after Cannady and other black and white community leaders objected. Eleanor B. Colwell, secretary of the Portland Board of Motion Picture Censors, wrote in 1929, "[I]t was entirely due to [Cannady's] effort that *The Birth of a Nation* and similar films were refused exhibition here."[19]

The Portland NAACP's campaign against *The Birth of a Nation* earned Cannady a high profile in Los Angeles in 1928 during the organization's nineteenth national convention, the first held on the West Coast. Personally invited by NAACP Executive Secretary James Weldon Johnson, Cannady was the only major convention speaker who did not hold a national NAACP office. Cannady's address, "Negro Womanhood: A Power in the Development of the Race and Nation," followed W. E. B. Du Bois's convention keynote speech. Cannady was also selected, along with Du Bois, Robert Bagnell, William Pickens, and Mary White Ovington, to address selected Los Angeles area churches on the work of the organization and race relations in the United States.[20]

Beatrice Cannady shaped local black community opinion through her role as editor of the city's leading African American newspaper, the Portland *Advocate*, founded in 1903 by three Portland African Americans, Edward Rutherford, McCants Stewart, and her future husband, Edward Cannady. She became assistant editor in 1912 and remained affiliated with the paper until 1934, eventually becoming its editor and owner by 1929. Cannady used the *Advocate* to challenge the discrimination routinely practiced in Portland during the 1920s and 1930s by restaurants, hotels, and movie theaters and to lobby for state civil rights legislation. Her efforts were not always confined to written protests. On one occasion in 1928, Cannady was able to obtain seats in the main section of Portland's Oriental Theater after refusing to be relegated to the segregated balcony. She described the anguish of these constant and intermittently successful challenges of segregation in an editorial entitled "Some of the Joys of Being Colored."[21]

Such victories were partial consolation for the continuous difficulty the African American community faced in obtaining state civil rights legislation. Cannady knew that frustration when in 1919 she helped to craft the first civil rights bill presented to the Oregon state legislature. The bill would have provided for full access to public accommodations without distinction based on race or color. After intense debate the measure was defeated on the last day of the legislative session.[22]

Beatrice Cannady was successful, however, in her efforts to repeal the notorious "black laws" of Oregon. The discriminatory measures embedded in the first state constitution, enacted in 1858, prohibited African Americans from settling in Oregon while simultaneously denying voting rights to "blacks, Chinese and mulattoes" already resident in the state. Although both measures were technically voided by the post–Civil War Fourteenth and Fifteenth Amendments to the United States Constitution, their continued presence in the state constitution was viewed by Oregon's African Americans, and by many white Oregonians opposed to antidiscrimination laws, as symbols of the European American populace's attitudes toward black Oregonians. Statewide ballot measures that would have repealed the black laws were narrowly defeated in 1893, 1900, and 1916.[23]

Cannady mounted a fourth campaign beginning in winter 1925 to repeal the measures. Urging her black and white fellow citizens to inform themselves about the laws and declaring the campaign "a splendid opportunity for some missionary work," she called on churches, fraternal societies, women's clubs, and other civil and social organizations to become active on behalf of repeal.[24] For six weeks before the election, the *Advocate* ran pro-repeal editorials and urged sympathetic white organizations to support its efforts. The highly publicized campaign of the *Advocate* prompted other newspapers, including the Corvallis *Gazette-Times*, the Albany *Democrat Herald*, and the Eugene *Guard*, to support repeal. The *Guard* claimed the measures were "the shame of Oregon." When the statewide ballots were tallied on November 2, the vote for repeal of the black laws was 108,332 to 64,954.[25]

Beatrice Cannady dominated the activities of the NAACP through the 1920s. She led the organization in successfully challenging school segregation in Vernonia, Oregon, and Longview, Washington. When black children were denied access to the public schools in these towns, Cannady intervened by organizing chapters of the NAACP to challenge local segregation. Cannady personally interceded with Vernonia town and logging company officials to ensure that the community's African American children would have access to the local public schools. Once they entered the local schools, the African American students were quickly incorporated into academic and extracurricular activities. According to the recollections of a local resident, one black student was soon after elected student body president.[26]

Viewing herself as an unofficial racial ambassador, Cannady also wrote articles and gave lectures (more than one hundred by 1927) on African American history and racial prejudice. She frequently exploited the new medium of radio to spread her message of racial egalitarianism and justice. In 1927, during what was then known as Negro History Week, she gave radio talks on the three leading stations in Portland, KGW, KXL, and KOIN. "What we need is not a history of selected races or nations," she declared in a broadcast over KGW, "but the history of the world void of national bias, race hate and religious prejudice. . . . Let truth destroy the dividing prejudice of nationality and teach universal love without distinction of race [and] rank." In 1929 Cannady was nominated for the Harmon Award in Race Relations from the Harmon Foundation in New York City for her efforts to promote racial understanding and specifically for persuading the Portland Board to Education to require courses on African American history in the city's high schools.[27]

Cannady lectured in various venues throughout the Pacific Northwest, including Salem, McMinnville, Newberg, Corvallis, and Eugene. When she was scheduled to speak at Willamette University in a class on race relations, Clare Jasper, a member of Beta Chi Sorority, requested that she stay at their sorority house. "The girls are all anxious to meet you and talk with you. [Please] come in time for dinner the evening before and then spend the night with us. We have to get up early, for our class meets at 7:45." Irene H. Gerlinger, assistant campaign director of the Portland Community Chest, however had a special assignment for Cannady as guest speaker, which served as a reminder that even those who presumed to support racial equality often harbored attitudes informed by invidious stereotypes. "Probably only a handful of people would come out to meetings," declared Gerlinger, "that were not enlivened by something entertaining, so . . . I am depending upon you and your friends to get singers; for we can get hundreds of people out to our meetings if we can tell them that negro spirituels [sic] will be sung."28

When Cannady arrived to speak to five hundred students at the Arleta Vacation Bible School in Portland in 1923, at the invitation of Alice Handsaker, chairman of the Fellowship for Better Inter-Racial Relations, she found the building surrounded by Ku Klux Klan members passing out racist literature. Undaunted, Cannady calmly walked past the protesters and delivered her scheduled address, pleading "eloquently for justice and fair play for her race," according to Handsaker, who then added, "[I]t gives me such pleasure to bear this witness to her achievements and as an Anglo-Saxon of pure blood, I deem it an honor to be associated with her work." Four years later Cannady's speech before two hundred delegates of the Oregon Federation of Women's Clubs meeting in Bend, persuaded the statewide group to endorse an antilynching resolution. The resolution noted that one black man was lynched in Braggadocia, Missouri, on May 23, during the time the convention was meeting.29

Cannady's interracial ambassadorship often entailed direct interaction with individuals throughout Oregon. Maintaining a library of three hundred volumes of literature and history by and about African Americans, as well as a complete file of leading black publications such as the NAACP's *Crisis*, the Urban League publication *Opportunity*, and the socialist newspaper, the *Messenger*, Cannady allowed interested youth and adults to gather by her living room fireplace to read or to borrow items as needed. Word of Cannady's library spread across the state, and in 1927 she received requests from high school students in Bend seeking information on the black population in the Pacific Northwest and from Mrs. P. S. Davidson of Prineville for a copy of Alain Locke's *The New Negro*. Davidson indicated that the volume was not in the state library and wrote, "I thought you might have it." Cannady sent not only *The New Negro* but Langston Hughes's *The Weary Blues*, James Weldon Johnson's *Anthology of Negro Verse*, and several copies of *Crisis* and *Opportunity*, with an accompanying letter indicating her "special pleasure to furnish you material regarding the Negro." She then asked, "[Please return the books and periodicals] as soon as they have served the purpose, as I have numerous calls similar to the one from you."30 Improving race relations, according to Cannady, also meant bringing leading African American artists and intellectuals to white Oregon audiences, "to offset the unjust propaganda disseminated . . . by the newspaper press of the country." In 1919 she arranged the speaking engagement of William Pickens, then dean of Morgan College for Negroes in Baltimore and a member of the Executive Committee of the NAACP. Welcoming addresses for Pickens came from Portland mayor George L. Baker and Oregon governor Ben W. Olcott, who "flew over" from Salem in an airplane to greet the NAACP official. Other prominent artists and activists introduced to Oregonians by Cannady included concert singer Roland Hayes, composer and musician J. Rosemond Johnson, Montana-born author Taylor Gordon, opera singer Florence Cole Talbert, newspaper editor and labor union leader A. Philip Randolph, NAACP executive Robert W. Bagnell, and Addie W. Hunton, a national official with the YWCA.[31]

Cannady's activism extended far beyond the NAACP's quest for African American civil rights. She served at various times as a member of the Oregon Prison Association, the Near East Relief Organization, and the Oregon State Federation of Colored Women. She also served on one national board, the Commission on the Church and Race Relations for the Federal Council of the Churches of Christ in America, headquartered in New York City. Other commission members included its chair, AME Zion bishop George C. Clement, prominent African American sociologist George E. Haynes, and Dr. Will W. Alexander, executive director of the Council on Interracial Cooperation, a group of southern white social activists. Cannady's work as a peace activist prompted her membership in the Oregon Committee on the Cause and Cure of War. In 1929 she wrote an open letter to newly elected Oregon congressman Frederick F. Korell, supporting his proposal before the Inter-Parliamentary Union in Washington, D.C., calling for the complete embargo of the export of arms and munitions.[32]

Interest in Africa's history and future led Cannady to join the Pan African Congress, a group of black intellectuals founded by W. E. B. Du Bois in 1919 to work for the liberation of the world's most colonized continent. Cannady joined the organization soon afterward, and in February 1927 she represented Oregon at its national convention in New York City. En route Cannady stopped in Chicago, where she received a tour of the *Chicago Defender* facilities, the nation's largest African American newspaper, from its owner, Robert S. Abbott. Nine months later Cannady organized a miniature Pan African Conference at the Portland Public Library. Featured speakers included Nettie Asberry, a leader of the Colored Women's Clubs in Tacoma, Ken Nagazawa, a Japanese poet and playwright, Charles A. Rice, superintendent of Portland Public Schools, and Mrs. D. A. Graham, wife of the president of Monrovia College in Liberia. Dr. Norman F. Coleman, president of Reed College, and Marshal Dana, editor of the *Oregon Daily Journal*, completed the list of speakers.[33]

That only one of the conference speakers, Mrs. Graham, had any direct ties to Africa is not necessarily surprising considering the dearth of students or political leaders from that continent in the Pacific Northwest. What is surprising, however, are the resolutions that flowed from the two-day gathering, none of which specifically addressed the African condition. Marshal Dana set the tone by focusing on interracial cooperation in Portland and the United States. He in fact used his address to call for a Pan-Pacific Interracial Conference, declaring "the colors, white, brown, yellow and black, must be harmonized before the era of the Pacific can succeed. The races must learn to live together in human brotherhood, common aspiration and peace. There must be understanding and gratitude." In keeping with that theme, the Portland Pan-African Congress requested that the Portland School District place volumes of the *Journal of Negro History* in school libraries, opposed racially discriminatory legislation, and commended Connecticut senator Hiram Bingham for refusing to enter a discriminatory social club. The conference then closed with papers describing internationally famous persons of African ancestry and international problems.[34]

Beatrice Cannady had her critics. Some NAACP members felt she used the organization and the *Advocate* for personal advancement. Others cautioned against her individualistic approach to African American grievances, arguing that her actions often precluded a more deliberate, organizational response. As a consequence of these charges, the branch was reorganized in 1923 to curtail her power as branch president, and in the following years, disgruntled members continued to ask for Cannady's resignation or for intervention by the national organization. The national headquarters, however, refused to take any action against Cannady and in fact commended her for organizing branches in neighboring communities and for "bringing to better understanding the two races . . . in that part of the country"[35]

Beatrice Cannady received her sharpest rebuke from community spokespersons, including members of the NAACP, over her criticism of the popular but segregated Portland YWCA. In 1921 the black branch of the Portland YWCA was established in a portable structure on the corner of Williams Avenue and Tillamook Street. Five years later work commenced on a new, permanent building on the site, funded primarily by a gift of $12,000 from Mrs. E. S. Collins, a white woman active in YWCA affairs. African American opposition to the segregated facility emerged almost immediately, fueled by rumors that the gift originated with the Ku Klux Klan. Some white Portlanders also opposed the facility, fearing the siting of a social service institution serving a predominantly

African American clientele near their homes would depress property values. The white opponents failed, however, in their bid to persuade the city council to deny a building permit after the city attorney reminded council members that they could not deny a building permit simply on the basis of race.[36]

Cannady's objections to the facility stood in contrast to both black and white opponents and reflected the dilemma common to many civil rights activists committed to integration. "Segregation is the root of all evil," she had written in 1926, "for when people do not know one another, they are suspicious and distrustful of one another. Only by contact of the races will ever an understanding be reached." Although she recognized the desperately needed benefits, services, and support the YWCA would provide to African American Portland, Cannady could not, on principle, endorse a segregated facility while calling on the rest of the community to abolish such segregation, even if her position meant alienating significant segments of African American Portland.[37]

The Williams Avenue YWCA was constructed and emerged as a center of community activities despite the concerns of the various opponents, including Cannady. The facility had a gymnasium and an auditorium with a stage, a kitchen, an office, a lounge, and locker rooms and showers for both boys and girls. Local black organizations raised $1,300 to furnish the building. The Williams YWCA sponsored clubs for grade and high school girls as well as classes in Spanish, sewing, Bible studies, musical programs, dancing, games, exhibits featuring black artists, and activities celebrating community holidays and commemorations such as Negro History Week.[38]

Although most of the previous two decades of her life had been devoted to the politics of civil rights, Cannady entered the political arena formally only once in her career. In 1932 she ran unsuccessfully for the office of state representative from District 5, Multnomah County. Two years later Cannady left Portland permanently for Los Angeles, California.[39]

There is no evidence that Susie Revels Cayton and Beatrice Morrow Cannady ever met. Yet the Portland activist equally could have spoken for her Seattle counterpart when she declared,

> I believe that if we could be allowed to express or to demonstrate our "human-ness" there would be less prejudice. . . . We want our children educated, we want to feel safe in our homes, we want to be able to worship God peacefully in our churches, and want to be allowed to maintain a standard of life that is an American standard. No one knows how difficult it is to do this under the conditions prevailing in the country.[40]

• • •

Susie Revels Cayton and Beatrice Morrow Cannady represent, then, two of many unheralded activists in the Pacific Northwest who translated their lived experiences into expressions of hope for a better world. Their histories, like those of other African American Pacific Northwesterners, illustrate the persistent campaign for racial and social justice. Generations of regional historians have unfortunately dismissed stories of African American women like Cayton and Cannady as unimportant to the central narrative of the region. Yet the experiences and activities of these courageous women illustrate the African American contribution to the development of social and political thought in Washington and Oregon. The Cayton and Cannady stories remind us that the quest for social justice transcends racial, gender, and regional boundaries.

NOTES

1. For works on twentieth-century African American women in the Pacific Northwest, see Susan H. Armitage and Deborah Gallacci Wilbert, "Black Women in the Pacific Northwest: A Survey and Research Prospectus," in *Women in Pacific Northwest History: An Anthology*, ed. Karen Blair (Seattle: University of Washington Press, 1988), 135–51; Evelyn Crowell, "Twentieth-Century Black Woman in Oregon," *Journal of African and Black American Studies* 1 (Summer 1973): 13–15; and Kathryn Hall Bogle, "Katherine Hall Bogle on the African American Experience in Wartime Portland," *Oregon Historical Quarterly* 93 (Winter 1992): 404. For general African American histories that discuss Pacific Northwest black women, see Esther Hall Mumford, *Seattle's Black Victorians: 1852–1901* (Seattle: Ananse Press, 1980); Elizabeth McLagan, *A Peculiar Paradise: A History of Blacks in Oregon, 1788–1940* (Portland: Georgian Press, 1980); Mamie O. Oliver, *Idaho Ebony: The Afro-American Presence in Idaho State History* (Boise: Idaho State Historical Society, 1982); and Quintard Taylor, *The Forging of a Black Community: Seattle's Central District from 1870 to the Civil Rights Era* (Seattle: University of Washington Press, 1994). See also Glenda Riley, "American Daughters: Black Women in the West," *Montana: The Magazine of Western History* 38 (Spring 1988): 14–27; and Lawrence B. De Graaf, "Race, Sex and Region: Black Women in the American West, 1850–1920," *Pacific Historical Review* 49 (May 1980): 285–313, for western regional surveys.

2. W. E. B. Du Bois, "The Great Northwest," *Crisis* 6 (September 1913): 238.

3. See Richard Stanley Hobbs, "The Cayton Legacy: Two Generations of a Black Family, 1859–1976" (Ph.D. dissertation, University of Washington, 1989), 44–45.

4. Ibid., 49–55.

5. See Taylor, *Forging*, 19–20; and Hobbs, "The Cayton Legacy," 25–41, 101, 117–19.

6. The quotation is from the Seattle *Republican*, July 23, 1909, p. 1. Locally Cayton was allied with former U.S. senator John L. Wilson, the King County Republican "boss"

who controlled the *Seattle Post-Intelligencer* between 1899 and 1910. See Hobbs, "The Cayton Legacy," 110–12.

7. See Seattle *Republican*, "Northwest Negro Prosperity Number," 15, no. 11 (June 1909): 21; and Horace L. Cayton, *Long Old Road: An Autobiography* (Seattle: University of Washington Press, 1963), 6–7. For a description of black social clubs across the nation, see Willi Coleman, "Keeping the Faith and Disturbing the Peace: Black Women from Anti-Slavery to Women's Suffrage" (Ph.D. dissertation, University of California, Irvine, 1982), 70–77, 83–85; and Julius Nimmons, "Social Reform and Moral Uplift in the Black Community, 1890–1910: Social Settlements, Temperance, and Social Purity" (Ph.D. dissertation, Howard University, 1981), 77–82. See Karen J. Blair, *The Clubwoman as Feminist: True Womanhood Redefined, 1868–1914* (New York: Holmes & Meier, 1980), 39–56, for a description of the role of native-born middle-class white women in creating comparable organizations.

8. Hobbs, "The Cayton Legacy," 138–41, 183, 209; Taylor, *Forging*, 61.

9. The first quotation appears in Hobbs, "The Cayton Legacy," 190. See also p. 193.

10. Ibid., 314.

11. See Hobbs, "The Cayton Legacy," 233; quotation on p. 231.

12. Ibid., 251.

13. Ibid., 250–52.

14. Ibid., 251.

15. Susie Revels Cayton to Madge Cayton, n.d., quoted in Hobbs, "The Cayton Legacy," 311.

16. Ibid., 312–15.

17. Quoted in *Portland Oregonian*, undated clipping, Beatrice Cannady Scrapbook, p. 61, Beatrice Cannady Papers, Oregon Historical Society.

18. See Beatrice Cannady Biography, p. 2, Beatrice Cannady Papers.

19. See letter by Colwell in Beatrice Cannady Papers. See also McLagan, *A Peculiar Paradise*, 123, 134–35.

20. See James Weldon Johnson to Cannady, February 11, 1928; and Beatrice Cannady Scrapbook, p. 40, Beatrice Cannady Papers.

21. *Portland Advocate*, December 8, 1928, p. 3. See also McLagan, *A Peculiar Paradise*, 111, 131.

22. McLagan, *A Peculiar Paradise*, 164–65.

23. Franz M. Schneider, "The 'Black Laws' of Oregon" (M.A. thesis, University of Santa Clara, 1970), 81–82.

24. *Portland Advocate*, February 21, 1925, p. 4.

25. See Schneider, "The 'Black Laws' of Oregon," 93–95, 99. For examples of the newspaper campaign for repeal, see *Portland Advocate*, July 31, 1926, p. 4; August 14, 1926, p. 4; August 28, 1926, p. 4. See also the *Eugene Guard*, October 8, 1926, p. 4.

26. McLagan, *A Peculiar Paradise*, 123, 140–41; Schneider, "The 'Black Laws' of Oregon," 72.

27. The quotation appears in the *Philadelphia Tribune*, March 12, 1927, p. 1. Endorsements of Cannady's nomination were advanced by Levi T. Pennington, president of Pacific College in Newberg, Oregon; Sadie Orr Dunbar of the Oregon General

Federation of Women's Clubs; Sceva Bright Laughlin, Department of Economics and Sociology, Willamette University; Bernard Mobile, professor of political science, Reed College; Portland pastors W. R. Lovell, First AME Zion Community Church; Daniel G. Hill, Bethel AME Church; Millie R. Trumbull, president of the Oregon Prison Association; and Franklin Griffith, president of Portland Electric Power Company. Robert W. Bagnell, national director of branches of the NAACP also endorsed Cannady. All letters of endorsement are found in the Cannady Papers.

28. For the first quotation, see Clare Jasper to Beatrice Cannady, May 19, 1927. The second is in Mrs. G. T. Gerlinger to Cannady, August 25, 1928, Cannady Papers.

29. Alice Handsaker to Cannady, n.d., Cannady Papers. On the Women's Clubs resolution, see clipping in the Cannady Papers. Cannady also persuaded Willamette University students in 1926 to pass a resolution urging enactment of the Dyer Anti-Lynching Bill following her presentation on campus. See *California Voice*, May 7, 1926, p. 1. The clipping is in the Cannady Scrapbook.

30. See Mrs. P. S. Davidson to Cannady, January 10, 1927, Cannady to Davidson, January 14, 1927, Beatrice Cannady Papers.

31. The Pickens lecture is detailed in *Portland Oregonian*, July 26, 1919. See also Beatrice Cannady Scrapbook, pp. 78–82, Beatrice Cannady Papers.

32. Cannady to Congressman Frederick F. Korell, n.d., Cannady Papers.

33. See *Portland Oregonian*, February 6, 1927, p. 10; November 19, 1927, p. 9.

34. Ibid. See also Beatrice Cannady Scrapbook, pp. 67–75, Beatrice Cannady Papers.

35. The quotation appears in a letter from Robert W. Bagnell, National Director of Branches, NAACP, to the Harmon Award Commission, Harmon Foundation, New York City, August 19, 1929, Cannady Papers. See also McLagan, *A Peculiar Paradise*, 123.

36. McLagan, *A Peculiar Paradise*, 121.

37. The quotation is from Cannady's response to a call for help in combating the creation of a racially segregated school in Maxville, Oregon. See Cannady to J. L. Stewart, November 17, 1926, Cannady Papers.

38. Ibid.

39. On the Cannady legislative campaign, see *Portland Advocate*, April 9, 1932, p. 1; April 30, 1932, p. 1; May 28, 1932, p. 1.

40. Cannady Scrapbook, p. 4, Beatrice Cannady Papers.

Marcus Garvey: A Seattle Woman Remembers

In September 1976 Juanita Warfield Porter was interviewed as part of an oral history project sponsored by the state of Washington. Proctor, a Seattle native who at that time was sixty-four years old, discussed among other subjects her parents' membership in the Universal Negro Improvement Association (UNIA) in that city. She was ten years old when UNIA founder Marcus Garvey visited Seattle in 1922. In the passage below she describes that visit and the activities of the Seattle division.

On Sunday morning after Sunday School at First A.M.E. Church we Warfield children walked down 14th Avenue to the UNIA Hall where they'd have meetings for the kids. . . . Sometimes we kids wouldn't want to stay. 'Course, we'd have to stay until my parents came to the meeting. After they came my mother and the other ladies used to fix a big dinner for us kids and then they'd have their meeting. I can remember the large dining room, they had this long table.

My mother was one of the Black Cross Nurses. There were about 50 to 100 women that belonged to the Black Cross Nurses. They practiced first aid and stuff like that. They used to march in the parades, like the Memorial Day Parade, and Fourth of July Parade. And they'd dress in their beautiful white uniforms with the black cross on the forehead, and on the arm a red, black and green sash. And my dad, and the men wore the red, black and green sash across their chest.

[Were your mother and father officers in the UNIA?] Well no, they were more of working members, you know, mostly they were very faithful members, because they went every Sunday and they would practice marching. They had march sessions, you know, on Wednesday evenings. I remember sometimes they would take us kids to them and they would practice their march. And then on Fridays they had choir rehearsal. See, they even had choirs too.

I remember Marcus Garvey coming here. We met [him] at the Union Station, and all the Black Cross Nurses and the men were all there [in uniform] to greet him. And I was the little girl that they gave the flowers to give to him. I thought

Source: Juanita Warfield Proctor Interview, September 22, 1975. Transcript at the Manuscripts and Archives Division, University of Washington Library, Seattle.

he was going to be a big tall man. He looked big in the pictures, and when I went to give him the flowers he was almost as short as I was.

He spoke at the Washington Hall on 14th and Fir. As for his speech, you know, with kids, when we're kids we don't pay any attention to what they were talking about. They were trying to teach us about Africa, that we should know more about Africa. I remember that, and they were working to . . . free . . . Liberia. And I remember my mother and father talking about Marcus Garvey was getting this ship up to send black people back to Africa, the ones that wanted to go.

CHAPTER 11

"Try Being a Black Woman!"

JOBS IN DENVER, 1900–1970

Moya B. Hansen

"Negroes did not participate in the settlement of the West." The sociologist Gunnar Myrdal made this astonishing statement in his highly regarded 1944 work, *An American Dilemma: The Negro Problem and Modern Democracy.*[1] Certainly it was true that only a small percentage of the western population was African American, and recent studies have shown that large numbers of African Americans did not migrate west until World War II when war production plants needed a sizable number of laborers for the war effort.[2] Over the past thirty years, scholars have recognized the importance of African American settlement in the West, yet their studies have left the Rocky Mountain region largely unexplored.[3] In completed studies, African American women have been greatly overshadowed by African American men—mountain men, miners, cowboys, soldiers, and others who played pioneering roles in the region. Because studies indicate that people commonly migrate to areas of economic opportunity, my interest here is to look at the opportunities offered black women in Denver, Colorado—the Rocky Mountain region's largest center of black population.[4]

The belief widely held after the Civil War that the American West was a region of limitless opportunity disappointed many people, men and women, white and black. In its early decades, the Rocky Mountain states, particularly

Colorado, experienced the boom-and-bust cycles common to other areas founded on mining economies. The speculative nature of precious metals brought miners and suppliers rushing to a prospective bonanza. If the potential proved real, railroads, smelters, and businesses arrived quickly—often too quickly. Overspeculation resulted, and those who failed to establish themselves in the market moved on. By 1880 Denver had become a common destination for those who had failed in the mining camps.[5]

The discovery of gold in 1858 fueled Colorado's first decade of exuberant growth. During that period, Denver was only a supply town with a population of slightly more than 4,700. In 1870, however, two major railroads, the Union Pacific and the Kansas Pacific, brought rails into Denver, and by 1880 the town was the terminus for several small narrow-gauge lines that shipped supplies to mountain mining towns and brought ores back to Denver smelters. Before the turn of the century, jobs with these Colorado mines and railroads attracted a larger black population than any other Rocky Mountain state.[6] The 1880 census indicates that black men had migrated to counties where mining and railroading were primary occupations.[7] The speculative nature of those occupations usually attracted single men; married men often left their families behind, so that as late as 1890, Denver—an established urban metropolis of more than 106,000 people—had nearly twice as many black men as black women.[8] Demographics changed by 1900, however, and black women outnumbered black men 2,042 to 1,881.[9] This dramatic shift in black population (from 2,808 to 1,881 men and from 1,482 to 2,042 women) very likely resulted from the 1893 Silver Panic that closed silver mines and decreased the need for railroad operations between the mountain mines and Denver smelters. Single black men moved on or married, and married men brought their families to Denver where their wives found work—along with other employed women—as live-in domestics or household help.

By 1900 slightly less than half of all working women (45.7 percent) were employed in the domestic or personal service field. Yet while only 34.8 percent of Denver's native-born white women and 68 percent of foreign-born white women were employed in this manner, a full 93 percent of working black women were so employed. Despite this high percentage, surprisingly few black women worked as laundresses; more typically, they were "servants or waitresses." In other parts of the country, laundry was considered black women's work, yet less than 3 percent of Denver's black women did laundry.[10] Kate Little, a former slave who moved to Denver in 1880, explained, "[T]he Chinese did most of the washing at that time and it was not until the later Nineties when they had made many of the Chinamen leave town because of the Alliance [*sic*] with white women that the colored women were able to get much washing to do." Though it is difficult to imagine that anyone would be eager to take on laundry work, Denver suffered a decade of hard times following the Silver Panic of 1893, the very years that so many black women moved to Colorado.[11]

One problem common to all women who helped to support families was a Victorian social theory that carried over into the early twentieth century. The theory held that the manner in which any society treated its women was a prime indicator of its place in the evolutionary hierarchy—evolutionary hierarchies being all the rage after Darwin's publication of the *Origin of the Species.* As the historian Cynthia Eagle Russet writes,

> At the apex of the social order stood the societies of contemporary western Europe and America—whose distinguishing sexual character-istic . . . was the exemption of women from productive labor, that they might better devote themselves to the bearing and rearing of children. At the foot stood the primitive cultures of Africa, Asia, and the Amer-icas, whose women, slaves to their men in all but name, toiled unceas-ingly at the most arduous physical tasks.[12]

It seemed obvious to the evolutionary social theorists (if not to the many American and European women whose productive labor helped to keep their families fed) that only in primitive cultures did women work and that women's "progress" resulted from emancipation from productive labor. Social theorists also defined sexual and racial characteristics in hierarchical terms, placing women below men and people of color below Caucasians. People of color were thought to be like children, and black people were thought to resemble very young children, incapable of doing anything other than simple work.[13] Furthermore, popular social theory held that black people, like children, lacked the moral sensibilities of an adult and their unchecked passions led them to sexual promiscuity. Consequently, black communities had reason to support the gender-defined jobs of women as cooks, household servants, laundresses, beauticians, and waitresses. Even though it resulted in low-status and low-paying jobs for their women, "sex segregation" helped to protect black women, married or single, from charges of immorality.

Prostitution certainly existed in the black community, but no statistical evidence supports the notion that black women turned to prostitution as a means of support in greater numbers than did white women. Because census records do not include the world's oldest profession, the only place that the "brides of the multitude" appear is on police blotters. Before the turn of the century, drinking, gambling, and prostitution were legal in Denver, so police arrested prostitutes mainly for drunk or disorderly conduct. Black prostitutes were frequently subject to arrests and bookings by police because Denver's madams did not hire black women other than as servants, and black prostitutes, operating independently out of cribs, lacked the protection that a house and madam provided.[14] Although people of both races looked down on prostitutes, the white community did not believe that white prostitutes reflected poorly on the entire race. Black prostitutes, however, raised concerns in the black community because they served as proof to white people that black people were morally inferior.[15]

Though nineteenth-century social attitudes toward women's roles carried over into the early twentieth century, job and career opportunities for white women improved. Denver continued to grow, and white employers became increasingly amenable to hiring white women as secretaries, bookkeepers, store clerks, teachers, principals, nurses, librarians, and newspaper reporters. Most of these avenues remained closed to black women, however. As late as 1930, Denver Public Schools (DPS) would not hire black teachers, the city hired no black librarians, and black nurses could not work in white hospitals. The American Woodmen Life Insurance Company, a black-owned business, first hired black women as clerical help when it moved to Denver in 1911. White businesses refused to hire black clerical help until the civil rights movement of the 1960s. Consequently, domestic service, laundry, and cooking remained the primary employment avenues for Denver's black women.[16]

Comparatively, however, Denver's black community was in an enviable position in the early decades of the twentieth century when Jim Crow laws became more severe and public lynching became more frequent in other parts of the country. The National Association for the Advancement of Colored People's (NAACP's) *Crisis* reported on Denver's African American community in 1923: "Out of the West comes the report of 6,500 colored people who work and play and have their being side by side with 25,000 whites and both races are content and happy. It is a relief in the midst of our vexing racial problems to read of such a Utopia."[17] The author of the article complimented Denver's black citizens on their churches, homes, businesses, professionals, YMCA and YWCA, and Boy Scout troop and the cooperation received from the "White friends of Black Denver." The support of "white friends" such as Governor O. H. Shoup, former Colorado governor William E. Sweet, Judge Ben Lindsay, school principal Lila M. O'Boyle, and Opportunity School founder Emily Griffith seemed a positive statement in the light of recent Ku Klux Klan activities in Denver's expanding black neighborhoods.[18] Black Denverites could congratulate themselves that their schools were not segregated, that they did not ride at the backs of streetcars or in separate train cars, and that poll taxes, literacy tests, and property ownership played no part in their eligibility to vote. Denver's black women had actively engaged in promoting Republican Party candidates through the Colored Women's Republican Club starting in 1894, when all Colorado women had received the right to vote.[19] Yet the daughters and granddaughters of these women would face an increasingly difficult struggle for equality in the workplace.

Women such as Marie Anderson Greenwood, Marguerite Grant Baker, and Jennie Walker Rucker clearly remember the work their mothers performed for white women. They recall equally well the support their mothers gave them in wanting more for themselves. Marie was an only child who moved to Denver at the age of twelve with her parents in 1924. Her father worked as a janitor, and her mother took in laundry. Her father's job occasionally allowed the family to live in an apartment building where he worked but always in the basement where it was dark and dreary. Marie recalls, "All I heard, all my life, was 'You're going to have an education. You're not going to work like we have had to work. You're going to have an education.'"[20] As a child watching her mother sweat over other women's laundry, Marie vowed that she would indeed get an education and find a job that would allow her to buy her parents a home.

Marguerite Baker, born in 1919, grew up during the depression and remembers accompanying her mother to work for a family when she was still in grade school. Marguerite's employer wanted her to wait on her daughters. Marguerite refused. When reprimanding her for obstinance, the woman told Marguerite that her only livelihood could be working for other people. Marguerite recalled, "'Oh, no,' I said, 'I'm going to school and I'm going to do something better than this. . . . I'll not spend my time working for white people! No!' In fact, that's when I told her 'I'm going home now!'" The woman asked Marguerite's mother if she didn't have better control over her daughter. "My mother said no, she couldn't make me do something I didn't want to do."[21]

The boll weevil drove Jennie Rucker's parents, George and Lucy Walker, from Texas to Pueblo, Colorado, in 1923. George Walker's job with the steel mills proved unsatisfactory, and the family moved on to Denver where he found better-paying, regular work with the Union Pacific Railroad cleaning coaches. Jennie, just a year old when her family came to Colorado, remembered seeing her mother only on Thursdays and Sundays because she lived with the people she cooked for during the week. Though her mother's work some-times allowed her to live at home, Jennie remembered that she left the house early in the morning and arrived home late at night. During an interview, Jennie noted that a home on Sixteenth and Holly where her mother had cooked for many years was for sale. "I'd like to see that house," she said. "I'd just like to see that kitchen where my mother worked for those white folks all those years."[22] But Jennie's mother wanted more for her daughter. "We were supposed to get a college education," Jennie recalled. In high school, when Jennie tried to sign up for shorthand and typing, the school counselor told her that she would never find a job as a secretary and advised her to sign up for cooking. Jennie reported this to her mother. Lucy said, "You tell the teacher to teach you shorthand and typing. I'll teach you how to cook and sew!"[23]

The depression took its toll on all workers, but black women found them-selves at a serious disadvantage. In Denver their numbers in the workforce dropped from 1,610 to 1,183. Though the drop can be accounted for in part by the fact that the 1930 census recorded working women over the age of ten and the 1940 census recorded working women over the age of fourteen, this change could scarcely account for the loss of 427 workers. Contrary to Marguerite Baker's recollection that "almost everybody had somebody to work for them," the number of domestic workers dropped in both real numbers—from 11,993 to 4,735—and as a percentage of workforce—from 31.8 to 13.1 percent. Black women lost a total of 450 jobs as domestics, while 292 more white women took their places.[24]

Despite a decade of overall job losses for Denver women, 359 additional cler-ical positions had opened by 1940. Black women filled only seven of those new positions, bringing their total numbers to forty-seven. Two black telephone operators were hired during the decade—the first in Denver's long history of telephone service (Denver had one of the first telephone systems in the country in 1879). Black women held only a few professional positions between 1900 and 1940, but the door opened just a crack during the 1930s when the redoubtable principal of Whittier Elementary, Lila O'Boyle, insisted that she wanted to hire a black teacher. Although nine black women counted themselves as teachers in the 1930 census, none of them taught in Denver Public Schools.[25] Few white high school teachers or counselors encouraged black girls to go on to college, let alone aspire to teach.

As Marie Anderson Greenwood neared the end of her sophomore year at East High School in 1929, this lesson was driven home when the girls' adviser summoned her to the office. Marie recalled being afraid that she had somehow violated the rules and was in trouble. Her fears escalated when she reported to the adviser's office and was ignored for what seemed an eternity. At last, when the adviser brusquely asked what she wanted, Marie replied that she had been told to report to her. The counselor thumbed through a stack of papers until she found Marie's name. She said, "'Oh, well, we were checking the upper ten percent of the class to see what their plans are after high school so that if they are going to college we'll be sure they get what they want.' Well, it had never crossed that lady's mind that the only black child in the whole sophomore class might be in the upper ten percent." When Marie told the adviser that she planned to go to college, the teacher informed her that she would be wasting her father's money as the only work she could do would be in another woman's kitchen. Marie said, "It hurt so badly that I just told her, 'Well, I am going to college,' and I wheeled around . . . and went straight to the girls' lavatory and . . . I cried, and I beat the walls."[26]

Fortunately for Marie, her family moved, and the next fall she enrolled at Denver's West High School. The girl's high school adviser encouraged Marie to try for a National Merit Scholarship, an annual scholarship awarded to the top four students in the graduating class. Though Marie's grades had slipped when she attended East High School, she persevered, won the scholarship, and Colorado State College of Education (currently the University of Northern Colorado) in Greeley accepted her in fall 1931. Marie knew she could not teach in Denver, but she hoped to find a job in the South. In the early years of the depression, even that prospect seemed slim. "When I graduated, there was no money at all. . . . I didn't have enough money to even buy stationery to send out applications," Marie said. But again luck was on her side. O'Boyle had offered Marie a job at Whittier Elementary the year before she graduated. Though women could teach in Colorado's public school system prior to graduation, Marie decided she needed to earn her degree, and another black teacher took the job. Marie's astonishment at being contacted a second time scarcely matched her astonishment when she received her letter of appointment from the school board. "Twelve hundred dollars a year! A hundred dollars a month was a fortune! . . . It was just like a miracle!"[27] Though Marie was not the first black teacher hired to teach by the DPS, she was the first black teacher to secure tenure.

While many black women sought Works Progress Administration (WPA) work during the depression, Marguerite Grant Baker's mother held a steady job with the William Gray Evans family, enabling Marguerite to attend the Emily Griffith Opportunity School, where she studied to become a dietitian.[28]

Endorsed by the Denver school board, Opportunity School was unique when it was founded in Denver in 1915. It offered day and evening vocational and academic courses to people of all ages, races, and ethnicities, free of charge. The entire community supported the school, and numerous young black women received vocational training at a price they could afford.[29] Despite her training, Marguerite could not find a job as a dietitian and unwillingly returned to domestic work. No other opportunities presented themselves until World War II brought wartime industry to Denver.

Albert S. Broussard's study of black San Francisco, Quintard Taylor's study of black Seattle, and Shirley Ann Wilson Moore's examination of the black community in Richmond, California, show the effect of the World War II years on the Pacific Coast.[30] Although Denver's inland location did not lend itself to the large-scale, wartime manufacturing efforts that turned Seattle, Los Angeles, and the San Francisco Bay Area into destination points for the African American population, the Remington Arms Denver Ordinance Plant, Kaiser Company, and the Rocky Mountain Arsenal employed approximately thirty-five thousand civilians.[31] President Frankin Roosevelt's Executive Order 8802, issued in response to A. Philip Randolph's threatened 1941 "March on Washington," meant that black men and women in Denver would be hired in these defense industry plants and other firms with defense contracts. Marguerite Grant Baker gladly went to work in the cafeteria at the Remington plant and for the first time in her life received wages comparable to those paid white women. Oleta Crain, a college graduate, remembered her employment at the Remington plant in a less favorable light, however. Oleta recalled that black women could either work as service operators (janitorial or cafeteria service) or in the lead shop. Oleta was first hired as a service worker and then managed to transfer to the lead plant because of her education. She remembered working only with men and having to walk two blocks to the cafeteria and a separate restroom.[32]

Jennie Walker Rucker also worked in the Remington cafeteria in summer 1941, following her freshman year at the University of Colorado. When a deacon at her church informed church members that Roosevelt had ordered the removal of photographs from Civil Service exams, Jennie decided to take the shorthand and typing exams. When she scored a 97 on the tests, she knew her mother had been justified in insisting that Jennie be allowed to take the classes in high school. Immediately after the bombing of Pearl Harbor in December 1941, the Civil Service office notified all women who had scored well on their exams to report to Washington, D.C.

When Jennie arrived in Washington, she discovered she was one of about six hundred black stenographers who had passed the test. None of them was assigned to a job, however, and she sat there along with the other black stenographers, from December 14 until the end of May, drawing a salary that amounted to $1,440 a year. As the war effort mounted, the government finally assigned Jennie to work with the Corps of Engineers. "They created these long pools, rooms, with typewriters, banks, rows of typewriters," she said. Someone brought in the work and handed it to the foreman who passed it out to the women. "They wouldn't assign you to an office."[33]

Denver's military installations—Fitzsimmons Army Hospital, Fort Logan, Lowry Air Base, and Buckley Naval Air Station—employed a sizable number of civilian workers.[34] Though Jacqueline Miller Chambers was too young to start working during the war, she recalled that her grandmother was a cook at the Fitzsimmons Officer's Club, a job preferable to cooking in a white woman's home.[35] Government jobs entailed regular hours, and black women enjoyed freedom from the whims of domestic employers.

Though the government did not station black cavalry and infantry units in Denver, numerous black soldiers passed through the city. State laws notwithstanding, Denver's hotels and restaurants would not provide services to blacks, so black soldiers sought accommodations in the Five Points area. As a result, more black women found jobs as waitresses and some became proprietors of their own restaurants. One of Denver's wartime female entrepreneurs made an obvious appeal to visiting military men by naming her establishment "Mable's Navy and Soldier Hot Dog and Chile Garden."[36]

The end of the war signaled the end of many occupational opportunities for women, white as well as black. For black women, however, doors opened by the federal government during the war often slammed shut. The Federal Employment Protection Commission Regulations, which did not enjoy either presidential or legislative support, were largely ignored.[37] When Jennie Rucker decided to return to the West after seven years in Washington, D.C., she called the Corps of Engineers in Omaha, Nebraska, about a stenographer's job that had been announced. Assured via a telephone call that the job was open, Jennie left immediately for Omaha. But when she walked in the door and said, "I'm here about the job," the woman at the desk replied, "We don't have any charwomen's jobs open." Jennie's indignation over this response was apparent: "Now, I said, 'I came for the stenographer's job.' 'Oh no, we don't hire colored in our office jobs.' And that was that!" Oleta Crain, who had left her Remington job to enlist as the first black woman from Denver in the Woman's Army Corps, remained in the military. Marguerite Baker, who had moved into a production job at the Remington plant, lost that job but was hired as a cook in the special diets kitchen at Fitzsimmons Army Hospital, a job in which she could at last use her training as a dietitian.

For Denver's black working women, the war years brought many demographic changes. The number of African American women over the age of fourteen nearly doubled in that decade, and the number of other minority women rose nine times. The white female population over the age of fourteen increased only five-tenths of 1 percent. But as a percentage of those who worked, the number of white women nearly doubled. The percentage of black working women increased significantly, but women of "other" races decreased as a percentage of the female workforce.[38]

During the 1940s, the number of women in clerical jobs more than doubled, from 11,035 to 24,823. As a proportion of jobs available to women, clerical work rose from 30.5 percent in 1940 to nearly 36 percent in 1950. And while the number of white women clerical workers grew by 6.1 percent and women of other races by 11.3 percent, black clerical workers' numbers increased by only 2.7 percent. The category "Domestic Service Worker/Private Household Worker" also shows significant change. Those jobs declined in real numbers, from 4,753 to 3,785, and as a proportion of jobs held by women, they decreased from 13.1 percent in 1940 to only 5.5 percent in 1950. White women had filled 86 percent of those jobs in 1940 but held only 75.6 percent of the total ten years later. Black women, who had lost jobs as domestics during the depression, filled 13.5 percent of those jobs in 1940 but climbed back up to 22.8 percent in 1950. The number of black women employed in the category "Operatives and Kindred Workers" increased both in real numbers and as a percentage between 1940 and 1950. Thus it would appear that not all black women lost their jobs in the manufacturing sector after the war. Similarly, the number of black women employed in the professions rose in real numbers and in percentages between 1940 and 1950. On balance, however, the trend in employment opportunities for black women in Denver did not reflect the trend in opportunities for white women.

The increased diversity of jobs filled by women during the war raised Denver's black women's hopes that any education they earned would help them find a job locally. Before 1941 none of Colorado's state universities allowed black women into their nursing programs, and the 1940 census lists only one black nurse in Denver. A breakthrough occurred in 1941 when the University of Colorado School of Nursing accepted Zipporah Parks Hammond into its program.[39] Immediately after the war, Rose Hospital, a privately funded facility built in memory of General Maurice Rose, opened its doors to black and Jewish doctors and nurses. That opportunity attracted twenty-eight new black nurses to Denver by 1950.

Another door that opened to Denver's educated black women during the 1940s was in the field of librarianship. The 1940 census shows no black librarians in Denver, and the 1950 census lists eight. Pauline Short Robinson became Denver Public Library's (DPL's) first black librarian before her graduation from the University of Denver (DU) Library School, despite assurances from DPL supervisor Cora Cook that there would "never be a professional Negro working in the Denver Public Library."[40] Pauline's grandfather Charlie taught her to read even before she entered grade school in Gay, Oklahoma. After graduating from high school in Lawton, Oklahoma, Pauline moved to Denver where she lived with two aunts and worked as a domestic. She made enough money to pay for her living expenses while she reenrolled in high school at Emily Griffith. Although she longed to become a lawyer, she saw no way to go to college even though her excellent grades at Opportunity School earned her a half-tuition scholarship to the University of Denver in 1935. Unfortunately, her cooking and cleaning job paid scarcely enough to support her, let alone cover the other half of DU's tuition.[41] The school counselor advised her that the National Youth Administration might pay the other half and helped her to fill out the application forms. Pauline also found a job at the Community Vocational Center library in Five Points, the heart of Denver's black community. The library received Denver Public Library's cast-off books—those marked "NLP," meaning "no longer property of Denver Public Library." Many of the library's visitors were children who came in after school because the library was heated. Pauline discovered that she enjoyed teaching children to read and set out to obtain books that would teach them about their African American heritage. Because the Five Points library had no budget, Pauline had to purchase them herself. She rounded up enough apples to make one hundred apple pies, which she peddled door-to-door. Her efforts garnered $40—enough to buy both the children's books and African American newspapers from other cities, as well as monthly issues of the NAACP publication, *Crisis*.

At the end of her junior year in college, Pauline applied to and was accepted by the DU Law School, but she had married in 1940 and family economics dictated that she work full time. When she returned to complete her undergraduate degree in education, a counselor discouraged her from attending law school. As she approached her student teaching, she expressed the desire to teach in Denver's secondary schools. A professor told her that Denver's public school system would not hire black teachers to teach classes above the first-grade level. Very soon after that, Cole informed her that DPL would not hire a black librarian. That was the last straw for Pauline, and she immediately applied to DU's library school. She continued to work at the Community Vocational Library until her graduation in 1943, when she left Denver to follow her husband who was serving in the army. She returned in 1945 to discover that Community Vocational's circulation had dropped drastically, that the children's reading program had been discontinued, and that DPL planned to close the facility. Pauline's presence spurred the Five Points community to action and principals of the area's elementary schools spearheaded an effort to create a new library. DPL responded by building the Cosmopolitan branch library in the heart of Five Points and appointing Pauline its first librarian.[42] Jennie Rucker, who returned to Denver after the war, recalled the black community's pride in Pauline's achievement and attributed the change in attitude to the entry into politics of O. T. "Sonny" Lawson, an African American business leader and community activist.[43] Jennie, a later graduate of DU's library school, had no recollection of any black librarians other than Pauline working for DPL or in the Denver public schools in 1950. The other seven women who listed themselves as librarians in the 1950 census may have been clerks rather than graduates from a library sciences program.

One employment source that had grown during the war and become a significant factor in the Denver economy during the 1950s was the federal government. Pacific Coast cities had attracted wartime industry and experienced a subsequent decline in employment when the war ended. In Denver the Remington arms plant, Kaiser Company, and Rocky Mountain Arsenal had employed only thirty-five thousand people between them. After the war the government converted the Remington plant into the Federal Center, a facility that housed regional branches of federal agencies and employed far more people than the munitions plant. Denver's military installations—Lowry, Buckley, and Fitzsimons—still hired civilian employees, and Denver received an additional boost when the government relocated the Air Force Finance Center from St. Louis to Denver in the late 1940s.[44] These factors, more than the war itself, brought numerous black people to Denver before the end of the decade. Though the Federal Employment Protection Committee had not received presidential or legislative support of its rules, an attitudinal shift had begun during the war that allowed some black women to find work and equal pay in government jobs. Ten women were employed by the postal service, fifty-three in federal public administration, and thirty-nine in state or local public administration.[45] The census figures unfortunately reveal nothing about whether these jobs were janitorial, clerical, or administrative.

Denver's rapid growth throughout the 1950s resulted from new and growing businesses and corporations. But census figures for both men and women show that minorities were not equally represented in the professions or in management, clerical, or sales positions. They did not fit the white-collar image of administrators, managers, sales personnel, advertising people, investment counselors, bank tellers, or clerical support staff, regardless of their education or qualifications.[46] Clerical positions offered by far the largest number of jobs available to women by 1960. Thirty-eight percent of the 125,563 jobs held by women were in clerical fields.[47] For black women, however, clerical positions provided only 16.8 percent of their jobs, and 25 percent were still employed as private household workers. In 1930 domestic work comprised 27.1 percent of the jobs available to all women; in 1960 only 6.7 percent of women's jobs fell into the "Private Household Worker" category. In 1930, 27.1 percent of native-born white women, 48.5 percent of foreign-born white women, and 88.8 percent of the city's black women worked as domestics. The drop to 25 percent over a thirty-year period becomes fairly significant.

At the opposite end of the employment spectrum, the percentage of all women employed in professional services that required a college degree or specialized training had remained fairly constant, falling from 14.9 percent in 1940 to 14 percent in 1950, then rising to 14.5 percent in 1960. For professional black women in Denver, the gains were significant. In 1940, less than 4.0 percent had been employed in the professions. The 1950 census shows a gain of almost 2.0 percent, but in 1960 more than 9.0 percent of Denver's black women were professionally employed. Teachers and nurses accounted for the greatest numbers of professional women. By the end of the 1930s, the decade that Marie Greenwood became DPS's first tenured black teacher, seven more black teachers had been hired. By 1950, 48 women were teaching and by 1960, 126 black women were employed as elementary or secondary school teachers. Though this appears an impressive leap in numbers, black women still faced discrimination as they struggled to realize their dreams.

Ruth Cousins Briscoe and her husband moved to Denver from St. Louis in 1951 when the air force relocated her husband to Denver's Air Force Finance Center. Ruth's husband was an expert typist and took excellent shorthand. Because his clerical job at the Finance Center did not pay enough to make ends meet, he soon took a second job at a pharmacy at night. When it became obvious that Ruth would need to work also, she applied for a job with Denver Public Schools. Though she had taught school in St. Louis, DPS would not hire her. Ruth decided to take advantage of the Finance Center's IBM training and worked as a key punch operator. She stayed alert, however, to changes in Denver Public School's hiring practices. As Denver's black population rose, DPS opened more jobs to black teachers. Ruth applied again for a teaching job, but what followed was something she described as "the horror story" of her life.[48] The school personnel office told her that the schools could not hire her because of her weight.

> So I went home and I said, "Well, I've got to have this job" . . . so I decided that I would go to the doctor, go on a diet. So I went on a diet and within ten months I lost eighty pounds. So I went back again to be examined. And then they said, well, this time they said . . . you've just got excessive hair on your body, your face and . . . we don't like that.

Ruth returned to the doctor who helped her solve that problem but also told her, "Don't imagine they're not using this an excuse not to hire you." Ruth applied a third time and was rejected, but she was eventually hired by DPS as a substitute teacher. A year later she received a contract. But, as Ruth recounts, black elementary school teachers could teach only at one of three schools in the Five Points area. Ruth recalled them saying, "'This is where you can go,' so I chose Gilpin. And that's where I went."[49]

Reflecting the changes that were occurring in the 1950s, Pat Baker Lewis had no trouble being hired by DPS in 1959. Pat's problems occurred earlier when she decided she was not getting the education she needed to be admitted to college. She switched from Denver's Manual High School to Cathedral High School, only to discover that the nuns did not encourage the aspirations of young black women. Following an aptitude test, Pat's counselor told her the test results indicated she could be a factory worker. "I told the nun . . . 'I'm not going to be a factory worker.' She said, according to these tests that's what your aptitude is. . . . I said, 'I'm going to college.' She said, 'well, according to this, you don't have the aptitude for college. . . .' She did say, she said, 'someday you might be able to be a helper in the kindergarten.'"[50]

Nonetheless, Pat received encouragement from both her mother and her grandmother. Pat's mother, Marguerite Baker, the second black woman hired to cook in Denver's public schools (Manual High School), learned of a summer job with the YMCA camp outside of Granby, Colorado. On arrival she found that she could have two helpers and promptly hired her daughter and her niece.

The two girls stashed their summer wages into college savings accounts. After enrolling in college, Pat continued to work, traveling between Greeley and Denver by bus to do laundry for the Evans family on the weekends.

> The one good thing about the way I was raised is that I learned to work, so that when it was time to work, I knew how. When my grandmother got sick, I knew how to iron shirts, I knew how to wash clothes, you know. I guess I just took it for granted that's the way everybody lived. . . . I always knew that I wasn't going to do that for the rest of my life. . . . In our family, if you said, you know, I want to be the president, they said sure. . . . There was never this black people can't do this or black people can't do that . . . so I never felt limited in my dreams.

Pat was hired by Denver Public Schools before she graduated from college. She was aware, however, that "they had their quotas. . . . There were 4,000 teachers and 400 minorities [minority teachers]. . . . They still have a quota."[51]

By 1956 the nation's white-collar workers outnumbered blue-collar workers; the number of salaried middle-class workers rose 61 percent, and the largest number of newly created jobs were in the service rather than the industrial sector.[52] Denver's long history of "clean" industry made it particularly amenable to service sector companies such as medical and dental research laboratories, environmental research agencies, geologic and aerospace development, and engineering technology companies. By the end of the 1960s, the Denver metropolitan area had become home to offices for Ball Brothers Research Corporation, Martin Marietta Aerospace Corporation, Beech Aircraft Corporation, the National Center for Atmospheric Research, IBM, Hewlett Packard, Johns-Manville, Sunstrand Corporation, and Honeywell.[53] But black men and women had difficulty entering managerial, supervisory, and clerical positions with the companies driving the area's economy.

This situation contributed to the social unrest that swept Denver in the early 1960s. For years, Denver's African American residents considered their lifestyle and their educational and work opportunities superior to anything that might be found in other parts of the country. A number of African Americans, newly arrived after the war, could see more clearly the discrimination that existed. Many newcomers were World War II veterans who had begun to resent the constraints placed on black citizens who had fought for their country but still suffered from discrimination in the workplace, in educational institutions, in housing, and in the courts. The city's growing prosperity eluded many of them as a newly affluent white population moved to the suburbs, leaving Denver schools with a decreasing tax base and de facto segregation. Denver's bulging postwar black population was confronted with restrictive housing covenants that kept black people in congested and decaying neighborhoods with inadequate schools and city services—this despite Colorado's having passed the nation's first Fair Housing Act in 1957.[54] These were among the reasons that Jim Reynolds, his wife, Alice, and their three daughters, Ruth Briscoe Denny, and a small, racially mixed group of other Denverites came together to form the Denver chapter of James Farmer's Congress on Racial Equality (CORE). Skip Reynolds Crownhart, Jim and Alice's eldest daughter, had grown up with the type of racial discrimination that angered so many black people during and after World War II. Born in 1941, Skip remembered the major and minor injustices and blatant discrimination that led a number of African Americans to join CORE and push for equality in the workplace, housing, schools, and the judicial system. As a sophomore at the University of Denver, Skip was among the first to join the newly formed CORE in 1961, walking picket lines with other CORE members. When her fears threatened to overwhelm her she turned to her father for encouragement: "I talked to my dad one time about being afraid because a lot of times I was afraid through all of this. I mean, probably fear doesn't even begin to cover it. . . . [H]e said, 'It's all right to be afraid, but it's not all right to let it rule your life.'"[55]

Skip's outspoken activism jeopardized her social standing in the community. She recalled that a number of her university friends called her "insane." Nonetheless, she persevered, turning her energy to direct action, picketing, boycotting, and publicly exposing the discriminatory hiring practices of Denver businesses.[56] CORE specifically targeted Denver's downtown retail stores, grocery stores, cab companies, and public utility companies. Gradually, the organization's efforts paid off. After graduation, for example, Skip was hired in the accounting office at Mountain Bell, the local telephone company, which enjoyed a low reputation in the black community for its discriminatory employment policies. On being called to a meeting with a supervisor who had a reputation for hostility to blacks, Skip remembered telling a coworker, "I will probably come out of there crying, but she will too." That did in fact happen, but Skip's supervisor did not fire her. Despite having risked her social standing, her job, and her dignity, Skip hoped—as did many black people who participated in the civil rights movement—that life would be better for her children. "If they were capable of doing something, they would truly do it and color would not make the difference."[57]

The actions of the civil rights activists made a difference for black women in the workplace. One of the most striking changes of the decade lay in the number of black women who held positions as secretaries, bookkeepers, and related clerical help. Their numbers jumped from 1,091 to 2,486.[58] Another notable change can be found in the category of professional and technical workers. During the decade, their numbers more than doubled and increased in percentage points. Of equal importance was the change in the number of domestic workers: they decreased in real numbers from 1,190 to 853 and in proportion from 22 to 10 percent. They could thank Skip Crownhart, Ruth Denny, Pat Lewis, Marguerite Baker, Jennie Rucker, Pauline Robinson, Marie Greenwood, and others like them for efforts on their behalf.

Though none of the women interviewed for this study would admit to having done anything out of the ordinary, they all acknowledged a determination to make a place for themselves, their children, and other minority women in a city and a region where discrimination supposedly did not exist. None of them would suggest that the playing field has been leveled, and most expressed a concern over legislation that would abolish affirmative action. "If you think it's tough being a woman, you ought to try being a black woman," Skip Reynolds Crownhart noted. Yet the determination they showed greatly enlarged job and career opportunities for several generations of women of color and continues to inspire others who will find by their example the will and conviction to do as they have done.

NOTES

1. Gunnar Myrdal, *An American Dilemma: The Negro Problem and American Democracy* (New York: Harper & Brothers, 1944), 186.

2. Albert S. Broussard, "Strange Territory, Familiar Leadership: The Impact of World War II on San Francisco's Black Community," *California History* 65 (March 1986): 18–24; Albert S. Broussard, *Black San Francisco: The Struggle for Racial Equality in the West, 1900–1954* (Lawrence: University Press of Kansas, 1993), 143–46, 149, 151–52; Daniel M. Johnson and Rex R. Campbell, *Black Migration in American: A Social Demographic History* (Durham: Duke University Press, 1981); Shirley Ann Wilson Moore, *To Place Our Deeds: The African American Community in Richmond, California, 1910–1963* (Berkeley: University of California Press, 2000), 40–93; Quintard Taylor, *The Forging of a Black Community: Seattle's Central District from 1870 through the Civil Rights Era* (Seattle: University of Washington Press, 1994), 159–63, 165; Quintard Taylor, "The Great Migration: The Afro-American Communities of Seattle and Portland during the 1940s,"

Arizona and the West 24 (Summer 1981): 2–23; Quintard Taylor, *In Search of the Racial Frontier: African Americans in the American West, 1528–1990* (New York: W. W. Norton, 1998), 251–54, 261–64.

3. The Rocky Mountain range extends from the state of Montana through Wyoming and Colorado and into New Mexico.

4. For comparative census figures of the western territories, states, and cities, see Taylor, *In Search of the Racial Frontier*, 104, 193, 223, 279, 286–87, 314. For an examination of black migration patterns in the Rocky Mountain West, see Johnson and Campbell, *Black Migration in America*, 6, 60, 67, 69, 130, 139, 160.

5. Andrew Gulliford, *Boomtown Blues: Colorado Oil Shale, 1885–1985* (Niwot: University Press of Colorado, 1989), 5–83. The first chapter of Gulliford's book reviews the boom-bust mining cycles of Colorado's western slope. Though his time frame is later than the early gold mining years, Gulliford describes the cycle well.

6. U.S. Census Bureau, *Eleventh Census of the United States: 1890* (Washington, D.C.: Government Printing Office, 1890), Table 19, "Growth and Distribution of the Black Population in the Mountain States," 588–89. See also "Progress of the Nation," p. cvi. Colorado had the greatest number of mines among the Mountain states, followed by Montana. Utah's African American population was inhibited by the attitude of its Mormon population.

7. U.S. Census Bureau, *Statistics of the Population of the United States at the Tenth Census, June 1, 1880* (Washington, D.C.: Government Printing Office, 1883), Table V, 382–83; Table VI, 416. With the exception of Colorado Springs, mining or smelters contributed to the economy of the town. Colorado Springs was the creation of William Jackson Palmer, owner and founder of the Denver & Rio Grande Railroad.

8. U.S. Census Bureau, *Eleventh Census of the United States: 1890*, Table 19, 588–89. Black men outnumbered black women 2,808 to 1,482. The same held true for "foreign born," with migrant men outnumbering women 55,911 to 28,079. Denver's black population quadrupled between 1880 and 1890, with the largest number of black migrants arriving from Missouri (520), Kentucky (233), and Kansas (134)—possibly as result of Denver's black leaders' attempt to bring Exodusters to Colorado after Kansas closed its borders to black people in 1879. *Statistics of the Population at the Tenth Census*, Table 12, 488–89. Also, see Nell Irvin Painter, *Exodusters: Black Migration to Kansas after Reconstruction* (New York: Alfred A. Knopf, 1977), for an account of the black migration to Kansas.

9. For a study of early demographics among western African American women, see Lawrence B. De Graaf, "Race, Sex and Region: Black Women in the American West, 1850–1920," *Pacific Historical Review* 49 (1980): 185–313. See also Lyle W. Dorsett, *The Queen City: A History of Denver* (Boulder, Colo.: Pruett, 1977), 104.

10. Jacqueline Jones, *Labor of Love, Labor of Sorrow: Black Women, Work, and the Family from Slavery to the Present* (New York: Basic Books, 1985), 125.

11. Writer's Program, Colorado Negro Pioneers, "Interviews, 1936–1942," Colorado Historical Society Works Progress Administration holding, bound manuscript, p. 37; Dorsett, *The Queen City*, 101–3. The Chinese population was not welcome in Colorado. The majority were male and worked in laundries, as waiters in restaurants, or as janitors or servants. By 1890 the Bureau of Labor Statistics of Colorado reported that more

than 1,000 Denverites could be employed if the Chinese were not in the laundry business. Kate Little's statement about the expulsion of the Chinese is not documented, but census statistics show that the Chinese population dropped from almost 1,000 in 1890 to 306 in 1900.

12. Cynthia Eagle Russett, *Sexual Science: The Victorian Construction of Womanhood* (Cambridge, Mass.: Harvard University Press, 1989), 131.

13. Ibid., 51–52. Like children, black people theoretically exhibited a lack of willpower, a feeble attention span, a weak capacity for abstraction, imitativeness, lack of originality, impulsiveness, and general emotionalism.

14. Clark Secrist, *Hell's Belles: Denver's Brides of the Multitudes* (Aurora, Colo.: Hindsight Historical Publications, 1996), 277–78. Although Denver reformers passed legislation against gambling and prostitution in 1904, the town's gamblers and prostitutes enjoyed the protection of Mayor Robert Speer and the police force in return for money that was used to help execute the mayor's City Beautiful program.

15. Myrdal, *An American Dilemma*, 328, 655, 838–39, 974, 976–77, 1268.

16. Moya Hansen, "Pebbles on the Shore: Economic Opportunity in Five Points, 1920–1950," 1993 unpublished paper on file at the Colorado Historical Society, Denver, 10–13, 16–18.

17. Jessie Fauset, "Out of the West," *Crisis* 17 (November 1923): 11.

18. Ibid.

19. Linda Faye Dickson, "Lifting as We Climb: African American Women's Clubs of Denver, 1890–1925," *Essays in Colorado History* 13 (1992): 72.

20. Marie Anderson Greenwood, Interview by Moya Hansen, January 15, 1993. Tape on file at the Stephen H. Hart Library, Colorado Historical Society, Denver.

21. Marguerite Grant Baker, Interview by Moya Hansen, August 18, 1996.

22. Jennie Rucker, Interview by Moya Hansen, January 21, 1996.

23. Ibid.

24. U.S. Census Bureau. *Fifteenth Census of the United States, 1930*, vol. 7, Table 12, "Males and Females 10 Years Old and Over in Selected Occupations by Color, Nativity, and Age, for Denver, 1930," Con. 246 (Washington, D.C.: Government Printing Office, 1933); U.S. Census Bureau, *Sixteenth Census of the United States: 1940 Population*, vol. 3, pt. 2, "Race and Age of Employed Persons (Except on Public Emergency Work) and of Experienced Workers Seeking Work, by Occupation and Sex, for the State, and for Cities of 1000,000 or More: 1940," Con. 393.

25. Marie Anderson Greenwood, Interview by Moya Hansen, November 20, 1992.

26. Ibid.

27. Ibid.

28. William Gray Evans was the son of territorial governor John Evans. Although Evans died in 1924, his two daughters, Josephine and Katharine, and his sister Anne continue to live in the large family home at 1310 Bannock, and they employed a cook, a gardener, and a laundress throughout the depression.

29. Dorsett, *The Queen City*, 164–67.

30. Broussard, *Black San Francisco*, 133–34; Taylor, *The Forging of a Black Community*, 159–60; Taylor, *In Search of the Racial Frontier*, 251–53; Moore, *To Place Our Deeds*, 71–93.

31. Dorsett, *The Queen City*, 238.

32. Marcia Tremmel Goldstein, "Breaking Down Barriers: The Denver YWCA and the Phyllis Wheatley Branch, 1940 to 1949," *Historical Studies Journal: University of Colorado at Denver* 1 (Spring 1995): 43.

33. Jennie Rucker, Interview by Moya Hansen, January 21, 1996.

34. Dorsett, *The Queen City*, 238.

35. For a study of black women's attitudes toward living and working in white women's homes, see Elizabeth Clark-Lewis, *Living In, Living Out: African American Domestics in Washington, D.C., 1910–1940* (Washington, D.C.: Smithsonian Institution Press, 1994).

36. *Colorado Statesman*, September 25, 1944, 3. See also Moya Hansen, "Entitled to Full and Equal Enjoyment: Leisure and Entertainment in the Denver Black Community, 1900 to 1930," *Historical Studies Journal: University of Colorado at Denver* 10 (Spring 1993): 47–77; and Hansen, "Pebbles on the Shore," 27–28.

37. William H. Chafe, *The Unfinished Journey: America since World War II*, 2d ed. (New York: Oxford University Press, 1991), 19. See pp. 18–25 for Chafe's account of the war's effect on employment of American minorities.

38. Table 3, "Race and Age of Employed Persons (Except on Public Emergency Work), and of Experienced Workers Seeking Work, by Occupation and Sex, for the State, and for Cities of 100,000 or More: 1940," *Sixteenth Census of the United States*, vol. 3, pt. 2, 393; U.S. Bureau of the Census, Table 77, "Race and Class of Worker of Employed Persons, by Occupation and Sex, for the State and for Standard Metropolitan Areas of 100,000 or More: 1950, *Seventeenth Decennial Census of the United States, Census of Population: 1950* (Washington, D.C.: Government Printing Office, 1952), 147.

39. Joan Reese, "Two Enemies to Fight: Blacks Battle for Equality in Two World Wars," *Colorado Heritage* 1 (1990): 14. Zipporah was the only black woman out of 1,600 student nurses in Colorado who were automatically made members of the U.S. Nurse Corps during the war. Despite the government's emergency call for 10,000 qualified nurses in 1945, Zipporah could only be assigned by the federal government to serve in an all-black unit.

40. Steve Jackson, "By the Book," *Westword*, September 6–12, 1995, p. 22.

41. A number of Denver's black high school graduates attended the University of Denver, a private institution founded as a Methodist university by territorial governor John Evans. Although the state universities did not discriminate in the enrollment of black students, they refused to house them in the dormitories. As a result, many black college students found it more comfortable and convenient to live at home and attend DU.

42. Jackson, "By the Book," 14–16, 18, 20, 22, 23. Denver Public Library named a new branch library after Pauline Short Robinson in 1995.

43. Jennie Rucker, Telephone interview by Moya Hansen, February 16, 1997. O. T. "Sonny" Lawson and Hulett Maxwell opened the Radio Pharmacy in Five Points in 1923. Sonny entered Denver politics in the 1930s when racial discrimination coupled with the depression put the African American population at a serious economic disadvantage. "Last hired, first fired" was an adage that held true even in federally funded relief jobs.

44. Late in the nineteenth century Denver's commerce recognized the federal government's importance chamber of to urban development. The location of Fort Lyon (1898), Fitzsimons Army Hospital (1918), and Lowry Aviation Field (1924) in Denver resulted from intense efforts on the part of the local chamber to attract government facilities. During the 1930s, the chamber launched a campaign, known as the "Little Capital of the United States" or the "second capital" campaign, to bring more federal agencies to Denver, hoping to offset the effects of the drought and the decline in tourism. Federal office employment figures reflected its success—from 2,000 in 1930 to 6,500 in 1941 and 16,456 in 1946. Although it is not readily apparent from census figures just which federal agencies might have employed black women, the increase in black female clerical workers from 49 to 161 between 1940 and 1950 indicates that some may have found government jobs.

45. *Seventeenth Decennial Census*, vol. 6, Table 77, "Race and Class of Worker of Employed Persons by Industry and Sex, for the State and for Standard Metropolitan Areas of 100,000 or More: 1950," 6–147.

46. Publication of the City and County of Denver, *Community Renewal Program*, City and County of Denver, Denver, Colorado, 1962, 19.

47. U.S. Bureau of the Census, *Eighteenth Census of Populations: 1960, Detailed Characteristics, Colorado* (Washington, D.C.: Government Printing Office, 1962), vol. 7, Table 122, "Occupation of the Experienced Civilian Labor Force by Color, of the Employed by Race and Class of Worker, and of Persons not in Labor Force with Work Experience, by Sex, for the State and for Standard Metropolitan Statistical Areas of 250,000 or More: 1960," Con. 7-301.

48. Ruth Cousins Denny, Interview by Moya Hansen, May 29, 1995.

49. Ibid.

50. Marguerite Grant Baker and Pat Baker Lewis, Interview by Moya Hansen, August 18, 1996.

51. Ibid.

52. Chafe, *The Unfinished Journey*, 114–15.

53. Dorsett, *The Queen City*, 262.

54. Ibid.

55. Skip Reynolds Crownhart, Videotaped interview by Moya Hansen, April 21, 1996.

56. Ibid.

57. Ibid.

58. U.S. Bureau of the Census, *Nineteenth Census of the Population: 1970* (Washington, D.C.: Government Printing Office, 1973), vol. 1, Characteristics of the Population, pt. 7, Colorado, Table 17, "Occupation of Employed Persons by Class of Worker, Race, and Sex: 1970," Con. 7-515.

Hattie McDaniel Wins an Oscar

In February 1940 the Academy of Motion Picture Arts and Sciences presented an Oscar to an African American actor for the first time in its history when it selected Hattie McDaniel as Best Supporting Actress for her role as Mammy in *Gone With the Wind*.

On the big night, February 29, 1940, the Academy Award presentations were held in the Coconut Grove ballroom of Hollywood's Ambassador Hotel, before an audience of 12,000 people. As Hattie arrived late at the ballroom on the arm of Wonderful Smith many people jumped to their feet to applaud her. Hattie wore an aqua blue evening dress, an ermine wrap, and wore gardenias in her hair with a diamond clasp, her purse dappled with rhinestones. She sat through most of the ceremonies at David O. Selznick's table.

After a seemingly interminable wait, Hattie's name was called as the winner of the Oscar for Best Supporting Actress. When Frank Capra and Faye Bainter made the announcement, the crowd went wild. As one observer noted, "The ovation that [Hattie] received will go down in history as one of the greatest ever accorded any performer in the annals of the industry. En masse, the entire audience, stars in every place, stood and cheered their beloved Hattie McDaniel. Tears came to Mammy's eyes as she made her way to the stage to accept the award."

Accepting the award, she said, "Fellow members of the motion picture industry, guests, this is one of the happiest moments of my life, and I want to thank each of you who had a part in selecting me for one of the awards for your kindness. It makes me feel very humble, and I shall always hold it as a beacon for anything that I may do in the future. I sincerely hope that I shall always be a credit to my race, and to the motion picture industry. My heart is too full to express just how I feel, so may I say to each and every one of you, Thank You and God Bless You. . . ."

Many in the audience, like Hattie, were weeping for joy. Olivia de Havilland, who herself had been nominated as the best supporting actress for portraying Melanie Wilkes[,] . . . said later that "Hattie was entitled to that award. . . . But on

---

Source: Carlton Jackson, *Hattie: The Life of Hattie McDaniel* (Lanham, Md.: Madison Books, 1990), 51–53.

Academy Awards night, I found I couldn't stay at the table another minute. I had to be alone; so I wandered out to the kitchen at the Ambassador Hotel and cried."

For two weeks after the Academy Awards de Havilland later asserted, she was "convinced there was no God." Then she changed her mind: "One morning I woke up in more ways than one, filled with delight that I lived in a world where God was certainly present, and where justice had indeed been done. . . . I suddenly felt very proud . . . that I belonged to a profession which honored a black woman who merited this [the Academy Award], in a time when other groups had neither the honesty nor the courage to do the same sort of thing."

CHAPTER 12

From Peola to Carmen

FREDI WASHINGTON, DOROTHY DANDRIGE, AND HOLLYWOOD'S PORTRAYAL OF THE TRAGIC MULATTO

Alicia I. Rodríquez-Estrada

Early in my career it was suggested that I might get further and make a bigger contribution by passing as French or something exotic. But there was no way I could do that, feeling the way I do. First, I'm too honest, and second, I felt you do not have to be white to be good. I've spent most of my life trying to prove that to people who thought otherwise.[1]

FREDI WASHINGTON, 1978

What was I? That outdated "tragic mulatto" of earlier fiction? Oddly enough, there remains some validity in this concept, in a society not yet integrated. I wasn't fully accepted in either world, white or black.[2]

DOROTHY DANDRIDGE, 1965

The African American actors Fredi Washington and Dorothy Dandridge questioned and problematized their positions across the terrain of race, identity, and stardom in twentieth-century American society. Washington's light skin allowed her to pass if she so chose. Yet for her, passing was unthinkable, and thus she found her career opportunities on screen and stage during the 1930s and 1940s limited at best. Dorothy Dandridge managed to attain some of the star status denied to Washington twenty years earlier while at the same time encountering racism in the industry. Once told she exhibited a "blend of the world's skin tones," Dandridge found herself between two worlds, and more than anything, she sought acceptance in both.[3]

Although Washington's and Dandridge's personal lives differed and they came of age twenty years apart, they both encountered the double paradox faced by many light-skinned black people: whites considered them too light to be black and too dark to be white. Their acting careers were stalled or hampered by limited opportunities. But to understand the history of these women, we must first examine the images of the mulatto in history and literature and the significant role these images had in shaping the portrayal of black women on and off the screen in the United States. By reclaiming Washington's and Dandridge's place in African American history and film history, we illuminate the problematization of race and color in the film industry.

The genesis of the exotic or "tragic" mulatto paradigm is deeply embedded in the nation's antebellum past. The historian Deborah Gray White argues that much of the race and sex ideology that provides the foundation for that paradigm evolved during the era of slavery. Female slaves were often raped or taken as mistresses by their owners. Relations with their masters were at times consensual but more often forced. The children born of these liaisons and rapes took their mothers' slave status. Some masters sold their own mulatto children to fellow slave owners to appease their wives and or other family members; others sold them for profit. A few slaveholders who acknowledged their mulatto children might send them north where they could be free. South Carolina planter Elijah Willis ordered the executor of his estate to sell his property and send his slave mistress, Amy, and their children to Ohio, emancipate them, and buy them land. Unfortunately, an owner's wishes were not always followed, as in the case of Henry Grimké. Grimké left instructions that on his death his slave–common law wife and their children should be taken care of by his son Montague, who disregarded his father's wishes and sold his half brothers.[4]

The offspring of a Euro-American and a mulatta was considered a quadroon, or one-fourth black, and the offspring of a Euro-American and a quadroon, an octoroon, or one-eighth black. According to Joel Williamson, the 1850 census counted 406,000 mulattoes among 3,639,000 "Negroes," indicating they constituted 11.2 percent of the black population, or 1.8 percent of the national total. Slightly over one-third of these mulattoes, 137,000 lived in the lower South. Throughout the lower South, particularly in Charleston, South Carolina, and New Orleans, Louisiana, the elite free mulattoes established a caste of their own and lived in urban areas, becoming artisans and businesspeople.[5]

In New Orleans, some free mulatto and octoroon women participated in *placage*, or arranged relationships with white men. These contracts included allowances to set up housekeeping in an elegant home, clothes, and an education for any children that might result from the relationship. The arrangement could last months, even years. As these mixed racial people became light and lighter in complexion, many chose to "pass" as European Americans, "crossing the race line and winning acceptance as white in the white world." Others passed part time, at work or while traveling or attending the theater or restaurants, a process known as situational passing. Those who chose to pass all the time often severed communication with family members darker than themselves. Shirley Taylor Haizlip writes in *The Sweeter the Juice: A Family Memoir in Black and White* that this was exactly what her mother's older siblings had done.[6]

Despite the growing presence of biracial people in the United States, the prevalent thinking on race in the nineteenth and early twentieth century denied the existence of the mulatto. Booker T. Washington put it succinctly in 1900: "It is a fact that, if a person is known to have one per cent of African blood in his veins, he ceases to be a white man. The ninety-nine per cent of Caucasian blood does not weigh by the side of one per cent of African blood. The white blood counts for nothing. The person is a Negro every time." These racial beliefs permeated nineteenth-century fiction, a powerful influence on early American film. Scholars have traced the appearance of the first mulatto in American literature back to James Fenimore Cooper's depiction of Cora Munro in his 1826 novel, *The Last of the Mohicans*.[7]

In their novels *Iola Leroy* (1892) and *Contending Forces* (1900), the African American authors Frances Ellen Watkins Harper and Pauline Elizabeth Hopkins used female mulatto characters to voice their dissatisfaction with the disenfranchisement of African Americans in both the North and the South. In the twentieth century, Jessie Redmon Fauset and Nella Larsen continued this theme. Fauset began her career as a literary critic for the *Crisis*. In all four of her novels, *There Is Confusion* (1924), *Plum Bun: A Novel without a Moral* (1929), *The Chinaberry Tree: A Novel of American Life* (1931), and *Comedy: American Style* (1933), Fauset focuses on how destructive passing and racism are to the African American woman. Larsen penned two novels, *Quicksand* (1928) and *Passing* (1929), both depicting mulattoes struggling with their social identities. Despite their sensitive portrayals of biracial people, the novels failed to challenge the popularly held view of troubled racially ambiguous characters.[8]

Early depictions of African American life on the stage reinforced the image of the tragic mulatto. The first black female character to appear on an American stage was depicted by a white actress in William Miln's *All in a Bustle* in 1798 in New York. African Americans attempted to establish their own theaters as early as 1822 but were soon forced to make way for white actors in blackface minstrel shows. Only in the late 1860s did black performers produce minstrel shows for white audiences. In 1890 the blackface minstrel tradition underwent a dramatic change with the production of the *Creole Show*, featuring "light-skinned dancers." The *Creole Show* differed from earlier productions by setting the action in the city rather than the rural areas depicted in earlier minstrel shows. The troupe traveled from Boston to Chicago for the World's Fair in 1893 and ended in New York City on Broadway. The popularity of the *Creole Show* allowed other nonblackface, all-black musicals to succeed. Yet "despite its contributions, the *Creole Show* performed a disservice to black women performers: it helped to foster and preserve the 'lightskinned woman' image over the years, which tended to exclude 'dark-skinned' black women from certain roles."9 Other shows appeared, including those staged at the legendary Cotton Club in Harlem, which soon became known for its light mulattoes and "high yellow" chorus line. Both Fredi Washington and Lena Horne received their early training there.

Washington should be considered one of the first black dramatic actors, along with Hattie McDaniel and Louise Beavers, in early-twentieth-century film. Whereas Washington played the "tragic mulatto," McDaniel and Beavers portrayed the beloved "Mammy." Characteristics for the "Mammy" included dark skin color, large size, and loyalty to her white employers. Not surprisingly, "Mammy" lacked any hint of sex appeal. According to the scholar Catherine Clinton, the Mammy was the creation of white Southerners after Emancipation. Clinton argues that the Mammy stereotype served "to redeem the relationship between black women and white men within slave society in response to the antislavery attack from the North during the antebellum era, and to embellish it with nostalgia in the postbellum period." In other words, the "Mammy" image was intended to represent what was good about slavery. Thus, according to the theater historian Patricia Turner, "the actress who played *Gone With the Wind*'s mammy, Hattie McDaniel, became the first African American to win an Academy Award for playing a truly fictional character, a character shaped and molded by nostalgia merchants eager to create a past that never was."10 The experiences of Fredi Washington and other African American actors in Hollywood illustrates the way in which both legal and social codes constructed and distorted images of people of color in the United States. Hollywood reproduced and solidified stereotyped images, which reflected the values of most white Americans. Significantly, section II, Rule 6, of the 1930 Motion Picture Production Code (Hays Code), which outlined U.S. movie content from 1934 until the mid-1960s stated, "[M]iscegenation (sex relation between the white and black races) is forbidden." Just as nineteenth-century civil rights activists Anna Julia Cooper and Ida Barnett Wells described miscegenation laws and lynching in the South as maintaining white economic and political power over African American males, the Production Code kept African American women and men from representing their history, a history that included the raping and lynching of African American people.

How did the movie industry influence the social construction of race and gender for African American women? According to Neal Gabler, author of *An Empire of Their Own*, immigrants who desperately wanted to emulate "America's founding fathers," and "New England-Wall-Street-Middle West money" used Hollywood and the film industry to accomplish that goal.[11] Depicting the ideals of the elite included treating African Americans as second-class citizens. Drawing on a literary tradition in which whites portrayed African Africans in stereotypical ways, filmmakers perpetuated these "mulatto" and "Mammy" caricatures.

The historian Carlos E. Cortés demonstrates how Hollywood in the late 1920s clearly defined terms of white and nonwhite. Unlike Latino characters, who could be designated either "colored" or "white," all African Americans were "colored."[12] Designating African American citizens as "colored" allowed Hollywood filmmakers to continue to represent them as second-class citizens. The most well known Latina actors during the 1930s were Dolores Del Rio and Lupe Velez. Both emigrated from Mexico in the 1920s, and both made the transition into talkies. However, both found their careers restricted by certain stereotypes. Del Rio came to Hollywood under the tutelage of her husband, Jaime Martínez del Río and a director, Edwin Carewe, allowing herself to become known for her beauty and "exotic" portrayals. Velez, however, was relegated to a "Mexican spitfire" persona, which she became good at and well known for, especially during her Mexican Spitfire Series (1938–43).[13]

Fredi Washington was born in Savannah, Georgia, on December 13, 1903. When she was thirteen, her mother died, forcing her father to place her and her sister, Isabel, in the Sisters of the Blessed Sacrament Home for African American and Native American children in Cornwell Heights, Pennsylvania. There Fredi and Isabel underwent Catholic training, as well as academic and vocational instruction. A few years later Washington moved to New York to live with her grandmother and attend high school. She soon dropped out and found work in a dress company stockroom earning $17 a week. She heard about auditions for the stage production of *Shuffle Along* while working as a book-keeper for W. C. Handy's Black Swan Record Company. Although she had no experience, she landed a spot in the chorus, receiving $35 a week. She toured with the company from 1924 to 1926. She then worked as a dancer at New York's Club Alabam, where the producer Lee Shubert found her and suggested she audition for Jim Tully and Frank Dazey's 1926 play, *Black Boy*. Appearing oppo-site Paul Robeson, Washington portrayed Irene, a fair-skinned girl who decides to pass for white. According to an article in the *San Francisco News*, "Wash-ington passed [so] successfully . . . that a number of playgoers protested to the management about her love scenes with Mr. Robeson."[14]

Washington then left the United States with Al Moiret in 1927 and formed the dance duo, "Moiret and Fredi." They toured clubs in Paris, Monte Carlo, London, and Berlin for two years. Washington eventually returned to New York, where she appeared in Cab Calloway and Duke Ellington's short film, *Black and Tan Fantasy* (1929) and the stage productions *Hot Chocolates* (1929), *Sweet Chariot* (1930), *Singin' the Blues* (1931), and *Run, Little Chillun* (1933).[15]

Washington made only four feature films, but her few roles won her a following among African Americans. Furthermore, these roles problematized issues of color, identity, and race. The film scholar Donald Bogle noted that Washington's race worked against her, citing her role in *The Emperor Jones* (1933). After seeing rushes of the independently produced film, the Hays Office demanded that the scenes with Washington and Robeson be reshot, fearing the public would mistakenly identify her as white. "With Hays warning that the sequences would eventually be cut if the required changes weren't made, the producers reluctantly applied dark makeup to Washington for daily shoots."[16]

Washington recognized that her color affected the roles offered her. She once remarked in a 1935 *Pittsburgh Courier* interview that she wished she had the coloring of African American actress Nina Mae McKinney, feeling she would have greater opportunities if she were darker. The *Courier* opined, "Miss Wash-ington is a colored girl and must work as a colored actress. But as a matter of fact, she is not colored. Her skin is white. . . . She is too colored for white pictures and too white for colored pictures."[17]

In 1933 Washington received the coveted role of Peola in Fannie Hurst's novel, *Imitation of Life*, winning over three hundred other actors. The film was released by Universal in 1934. The story centers on two widowed mothers, Bea Pullman (Claudette Colbert) and Aunt Delilah (Louise Beavers), who pool their resources to raise their daughters, Jesse and Peola. Aunt Delilah takes care of the home and the girls while Miss Bea works outside the home selling syrup. However, Miss Bea has a difficult time as a salesperson. One day Aunt Delilah shares her family pancake recipe with Miss Bea, who markets it for millions. She offers 20 percent of the company to Aunt Delilah, who declines the offer because she wants to take care of Miss Bea and Jesse. Heartache follows when Peola refuses to be submissive like her mother and chooses to pass so that she has the same opportunities as European Americans. The movie ends with Peola returning home after her mother dies of a broken heart.[18]

From the film's inception, the sexuality and miscegenation depicted in it prompted public concern, causing the industry to establish the Motion Pictures Production Code in 1933. Soon afterward, William H. Hays and his assistant, Joseph Breen, began monitoring the production of all film content. Beginning in March 1934, memoranda begin to circulate about *Imitation of Life*. Hays sent a note to Breen, telling him he was aware of the potential controversy surrounding the film. Two days later Breen responded, assuring Hays that he was in close contact with Universal Studios and was strongly encouraging them to abandon the film:

> We had a number of conferences with the studio, stating our belief that a story of this type was in violation of the spirit of the Code clause that forbids the treatment of miscegenation on screen. Hence we stated definitely that it seemed the kind of picture which would be inadmissible under the Code. The studio is giving the matter some further thought, and the latest report is that they have shelved the story temporarily.

The Hays Office was not in full agreement on the potential problem of *Imitation of Life*. Maurice McKenzie, another staff member, informed Breen that he felt the lynching scene in the script was the principal problem, rather than miscegenation. According to McKenzie, "[T]he act of miscegenation occurred so remotely in the ancestry of the character that it need not concern us. The girl's father and mother are both Negroes though the father had white blood which gives the girl the appearance of a white person." The actual offense of a relationship between a "white" and black person was not being committed, so no actual code was being violated. Apparently Breen was swayed by this argument and gave final approval of the film that November.[19]

In a 1978 interview, Washington outlined her feelings about the role of Peola. "I had to fight the writers on lines like: 'if only I had been born white.' They didn't seem to realize that a decent life, not white skin, was the issue." Many people from the African American community seemed to agree with Washington. A

December 1934 issue of *Literary Digest* reported, "[T]he real story[,] . . . merely hinted at, never really contemplated, is that of the beautiful and rebellious daughter of the loyal Negro friend. She is light-skinned, sensitive, tempestuous, she grows bitterly indignant when she sees that the white girl with whom she has been reared is getting all the fine things of life, while she is subjected to humiliation and unhappiness."[20]

With the release of the film, Washington received numerous letters from fans and moviegoers who shared their thoughts on her portrayal and the issue of passing. One Euro-American woman from Massachusetts commented that the movie failed to follow the story line of the book, in which Peola successfully marries a white man and passes. She recognized the difficulties for African Americans in society: "I think that if I were colored, but looked white, I should try to pass." A young African American man from Illinois also wrote to Washington expressing his opinion on the subject: "I like the part that you played because I am colored and I think every person that looks as . . . white as you did . . . should pass for white[,] not because I believe that they are better than colored people[,] but I believe your chances are better if you could pass for white."[21] It is not clear whether Washington responded personally to these letters, but she cared enough to keep them.

Washington admitted in newspaper interviews that she passed but solely for economic reasons. In a November 1935 edition of the *Afro American*, a reporter wrote, "Off-stage, Fredi doesn't have a craving to be white, like Fannie Hurst's Peola did. Oh, yes, being fair, she will take advantage of her color when it means getting more for her money, better accommodations, access to places from which she might be barred if they knew, but she doesn't do this to be smart or uppish."[22] Nine years later, in an interview with the *Chicago Defender*, Washington again reinforced this sentiment, in what could be best described as situational passing. The *Defender*'s reporter, Earl Conrad, asked her some questions regarding passing:

> CONRAD: " . . . [D]o you have any trouble passing in the white world[?] . . . [W]hat happens when you go into a white hotel or restaurant?"
> WASHINGTON: "I just go in, if it's a hotel [I] get a room; or a restaurant, I eat."
> CONRAD: "Well, then you passed."
> WASHINGTON: "Well, I suppose you might call it that, but I don't think about it one way or the other. If a place is open to the public[,] that means anyone who can pay the tariff."[23]

Washington had numerous offers to step over the color line, but that would have meant leaving behind her family and friends. She often recalled how millionaire Otto Kahn offered to send her to an elite theater–dance school if she changed her name and agreed to pass as a Frenchwoman. She thanked him for the offer but declined. Unlike the members of Shirley Haizlip's family who felt "they could do more, have more, travel more, be happier," Washington had a firm sense of her own identity and of her obligations to the African American community.[24]

Both Haizlip and Washington discuss how economics could tip the scale in favor of passing. Washington understood financial hardship. She dropped out of high school to help her family. She also quit her job as a bookkeeper, once she learned she could earn more money as a chorus line dancer. In her 1978 interview, Washington recounted how chorus members were courted by "backstage Johnnies," most of whom were white. Even when she married Lawrence Brown, a trombonist with Duke Ellington's band, in 1933, she continued to work. According to the historian Jacqueline Jones, black women had very few career options during the depression. They could work as sharecroppers, domestics, or unskilled factory workers.[25] Rather than work as a domestic or in a factory, Washington chose to act.

Washington became politically active when in 1937, with Noble Sissle, W. C. Handy, and Dick Campbell, she helped Alan Corelli to lay the foundation for the Negro Actors Guild of America. The aims of the organization were as follows:

1. To uphold the honorable and sacred traditions of the race.
2. To elevate, foster, and promote good fellowship and the spiritual welfare of the Negro actors and actresses connected with all branches of the theatrical profession.
3. To create and develop better understanding between laity and people of the theater.
4. To render genuine service throughout the country to the actor and actress in time of financial assistance to its members in the theater.
5. To champion and uphold the high standards of decency on stage in other theatrical fields; and to appear and support those who adhere to its standards.
6. To provide for the specific need of the Negroes in the particular circumstances arising from the nature of theatrical conditions.

Washington served as executive director and secretary of the Negro Actors Guild, supervising welfare work on behalf of guild membership. She remained executive secretary until she returned to the stage to star in *Mamba's Daughters* with Ethel Waters in 1939.[26] She later served as administrative secretary for the Joint Committee of Actors Equity & Theater League, working on hotel accommodations for African American actors throughout the United States.

Washington also wrote for the Harlem newspaper, *People's Voice*. Although she had failed to finish high school, she became an eloquent and passionate journalist. Washington's articles reflected the thought of many black performers who wished to see changes made in the entertainment industry. She suggested short movies that would educate white audiences on the realities of African American life. She wrote, "The history of the Negro race is a fertile and unexplored field. Full length pictures should not be attempted at this time. That would be too risky and expensive; but short subjects could be done on a minimum budget and sold to chain[s] as well as independent theaters, which in turn would assure [the] producer . . . [of] maximum patronage."[27]

Washington did not obtain a long-term contract with any studio, but less than ten years after her first film in Hollywood, Lena Horne was signed by MGM. Horne had been singing on the nightclub circuit, first with Charlie Barnett's band in 1940 and then on her own at Café Society Downtown in New York City, until she was persuaded to move to Hollywood. MGM placed her in front of a pillar and let her sing, eliminating her part when the films were shown in the South. Soon after, Dorothy Dandridge began her film career as a child performer. Like Washington and Horne before her, Dandridge encountered obstacles in the film industry but also found opportunities that had been denied Washington and Horne.

Separated from her husband, Cyril Dandridge, Ruby Dandridge gave birth to her second child, Dorothy, on November 9, 1922, in Cleveland, Ohio. At a young age, Ruby realized that her two daughters had talent and began taking them on the road to perform in church revivals and other venues all over the South. Known as the "Wonder Children," Vivian and Dorothy sang, danced, recited poetry, and did acrobatics.[28] When the depression hit, Ruby scraped the necessary money together and with her two daughters and a family friend boarded a bus bound for Los Angeles, where she believed there might be better opportunities for African Americans. For the first time, Dorothy and her sister attended school but were frequently pulled out to appear in films and benefits. In 1934, with her sister, Vivian, and a third girl, Etta Jones, they formed the singing trio, the Dandridge Sisters. They performed with Jimmie Lunceford's Orchestra and Cab Calloway at the Cotton Club. They also traveled to England, where they performed in London at the Palladium.[29]

While part of the Dandridge Sisters, Dorothy met Harold Nicholas of the dancing Nicholas Brothers. It was 1936 and the Dandridge Sisters had been hired to perform at the legendary Cotton Club. Harold courted Dorothy for almost five years, and they were married on September 6, 1942. Two years later, she gave birth to a girl they named Harolyn. However, Dandridge's marriage was in trouble from the first day. Harold traveled and enjoyed the entertainment lifestyle, which included extramarital affairs. A second tragedy struck Dorothy when she discovered her daughter had suffered brain damage at birth. In an attempt to keep her marriage together, Dandridge left Harolyn with caregivers while she traveled with Harold. However, she eventually filed for divorce.[30]

With her marriage over, Dandridge realized she had to return to work. Phil Moore, a composer-arranger, coached Dorothy and helped her to find her own singing style, with Desi Arnaz's band at the Mocambo. While Dorothy performed her nightclub act, she also received small parts in two 1951 films, *Tarzan's Peril* and *The Harlem Globetrotters*. But in 1953 she got the break she wanted. MGM offered her the female lead, costarring with Harry Belafonte, in an all-black film, *Bright Road*. The film and Dandridge received excellent reviews. MGM head Louis B. Mayer promised Dandridge that if she worked hard and listened to the studio, he would make her a star.[31]

Not long after the release of *Bright Road*, Otto Preminger announced he would be directing *Carmen Jones*, based on the famous Bizet opera, *Carmen*. Dandridge decided to audition for the role of Carmen. At their first meeting, Preminger felt Dorothy was totally wrong for the part. He offered her the second female role of the good girl Cindy Lou. Dandridge felt she could pull off the role of Carmen and went back to Preminger for a second audition dressed in a tight skirt, low-cut blouse, dark eye makeup, and in character for the part of Carmen. Preminger exclaimed, "It's Carmen!"[32]

Preminger resituated the opera in the South. The main character, Carmen Jones, works in a parachute factory on an army base in Jacksonville, Florida. Her involvement in a fight leads to her arrest. Harry Belafonte's character, "Joe," is responsible for delivering her to a nearby prison. Instead Carmen convinces Joe to desert the army and run away with her. They run off to Chicago, where Carmen eventually leaves him for a boxer, Husky Miller (Joe Adams). Joe, crazed with jealousy, finds and murders her.[33]

Carmen Jones rocketed Dorothy Dandridge to fame. Receiving rave reviews, she was nominated for an Academy Award in the Best Actress category and Best Actress by the Hollywood Foreign Press Association. Twentieth Century-Fox's president, Darryl Zanuck, signed her to a three-year contract, worth

$75,000 a year. The contract was "nonexclusive," meaning Dandridge could make pictures with other studios.[34] Hollywood still could not or would not make more films that included black actors.

Sadly, Zanuck could find no scripts for Dorothy. She returned to her night-club act, traveling across the globe. It was not until 1957 that she was offered another film role. David O. Selznick cast Dandridge in *Island in the Sun,* in her first interracial film relationship. Playing opposite John Justin, Dandridge portrayed Margo Seaton, a Santa Marta native who falls for Denis Archer (Justin), an English civil servant. At the conclusion of the film, the two leave for England, where they believe they can have a life together. The interracial story line involved love scenes between Dandridge and Justin, as well as between Harry Belafonte and Joan Fontaine. In fact, under the headline "To Kiss or Not to Kiss," *Ebony* speculated as to whether Belafonte or Dandridge would be allowed to kiss their white costars. However, Selznick feared the ratings board, so Dandridge and Justin only held hands and danced together.[35]

Dandridge's other films include *Tamango,* a 1957 European film in which she played an African slave girl (mulatto) who was loved by a white sea captain, Curt Jurgens. That same year she appeared in *The Decks Ran Red,* opposite James Mason and Stuart Whitman. In this film she portrayed the wife of a ship's Maori cook. In 1960 Dandridge played a vague "exotic" opposite Trevor Howard in Malaga. Each film included an interracial love theme, but each time the directors succumbed to the pressures of the producers and studios and refrained from displaying a kiss or any intimacy between Dandridge and her costars.[36]

In her personal life, Dandridge found herself in numerous relationships, usually with white men. These relationships were always kept a secret but included Gerald Mayer, Peter Lawford, Frederick March, and other men whom Dandridge met during her nightclub engagements. These men offered her financial security, but they could not or would not offer what Dandridge wanted most, marriage. Finally, one man did offer it—Jack Denison, a maitre d' at the Hotel El Rancho in Las Vegas. On June 22, 1959, Dandridge and Denison married. Unfortunately, on their wedding night he informed her of his finan-cial problems. Her earnings from nightclub acts and films brought in about $250,000 a year. Dandridge found out Denison expected her to support him, as well as make some unsound investments. The marriage lasted four years. She divorced him and filed for bankruptcy in April 1963.[37]

By the end of her marriage to Denison, Dandridge had lost much of her self-confidence and had begun to use alcohol and pills to help herself. She had seen psychiatrists since she discovered her daughter was mentally disabled. Her manager, Earl Mills, convinced her to travel to Mexico to a health ranch, where he claims they became lovers and Dandridge began to recover. By September 1965 she had a singing engagement in New York and two movie deals in Mexico. Sadly, she never completed any of these projects. Mills found her dead in her apartment on September 8, 1965. At first the cause of death could not be determined, but the coroner later announced that Dandridge had died from an overdose of Trofanil, an antidepressant.[38]

Many scholars and writers have described Dorothy Dandridge's life as tragic. Even Dandridge herself tends to depict her life as one filled with sadness and regret. She recognized how her relationships with white men ran parallel with history and the experiences of other African American women. She wrote,

> On the lower levels, in the South, the black woman was often the classic "kept woman" in a cabin. Today she might be in an apartment, or more likely she is simply visited from time to time, but in any case she is sexually used. I went up the ladder of American public life, but only to get the same treatment up there where the bank accounts might be bigger or the reputations greater, but the attitudes were the same. I learned that the same thing applied to me as to any good-looking washwoman or houseworker in Mississippi: you can be used but don't expect to be received publicly and legally as a wife. Nothing that I had . . . beauty, money, recognition as an artist—was sufficient to break through the powerful psychological bind of racist thinking.[39]

Dandridge's observations resonate today. It would take many more years before more realistic portrayals of African Americans appeared on the screen. And even today, critics find that earlier stereotypes of African Americans have simply been traded for contemporary ones. Moreover, it would also take a similar number of years for interracial marriages and relationships to become acceptable.

Dandridge presented an image of African American women that had not been seen before onscreen. However, that image—the African American woman as a sexual and "tragic" being—was a contrivance by and for white Americans. Her role in *Carmen Jones* and subsequent films perpetuated roles already preconceived by white audiences. Although she recognized the limitations of her screen persona imposed by movie executives and a biased public, she also attempted to present a new image, that of a beautiful black woman for African American audiences.

Almost thirty years after Dandridge's death, Fredi Washington passed away in 1994 at the age of ninety. Notices of her death appeared in *Time*, the *Los Angeles Times*, the *New York Times*, *Variety*, and the *Guardian*. Veronica Chambers of the *New York Times Magazine* wrote sympathetically of Washington's troubled career, stating that she understood "that the tragic mulatto was not so much about a light-skinned black who wanted to be white as it was about a black person who lusted for the life chances that whiteness once signified."[40]

Although Washington did not obtain the star status of Dorothy Dandridge, her career should nonetheless be remembered. Had Fredi Washington been born twenty years later, would she have attained the stardom of Lena Horne or Dorothy Dandridge? We will never know. Washington worked in Hollywood during a time when African Americans appeared only as maids and servants, whereas the changing post–World War II racial climate helped to propel Dandridge to stardom. Also, like Lena Horne, Dandridge's singing ability and the opportunity to star in all-black films brought her to the notice of American audiences. Dandridge's early work in *The Harlem Globetrotters*, *Bright Road*, and *Carmen Jones* placed her in the spotlight in ways that were impossible for Washington a few decades earlier.

Understanding that racial identity was socially constructed and not biologically determined empowered Fredi Washington to seek other avenues in which to support herself and make changes in the entertainment industry for African American entertainers. From all indications, Washington felt little bitterness about her short film career. Refusing to pass, she identified strongly with the African American community. Dorothy Dandridge never had the option of passing, but she often found herself designated as the "exotic." Although Fredi Washington and Dorothy Dandridge took very different paths, their lives followed a similar trajectory in that both were African American women who wanted to act but who could use their talents only when it suited the agendas of Hollywood filmmakers. The "tragedy" of their lives was not that they were mulatto women but that their acting potential was never fully realized.

NOTES

An earlier version of this chapter was presented at the 1995 Western Historical Association Conference in Denver, Colorado, and was funded in part by a 1995 Sara Jackson Award. I would like to thank Rita Roberts for encouraging this research, Vicki L. Ruiz for reading drafts, and David T. Estrada for his constant support.

1. Norman Jean Darden, "Oh, Sister! Fredi Washington Relives '30 Razzmatazz," *Essence* (September 1978): 105.

2. Dorothy Dandridge and Earl Conrad, *Everything and Nothing: The Dorothy Dandridge Tragedy* (New York: Abelard, 1970), 155.

3. Ibid., 204. See also Donald Bogle, *Dorothy Dandridge: A Biography* (New York: Amistad, 1997).

4. Deborah Gray White, *Ar'n't I a Woman? Female Slaves in the Plantation South* (New York: W. W. Norton, 1985), 27. One of the most well known accounts of this type of relationship is Melton A. McLaurin, *Celia: A Slave* (Athens: University of Georgia Press, 1991). Brenda Stevenson argues that some slave women may have responded to such incentives as food, clothing, and better housing as well as emancipation in exchange for sexual favors. See Brenda Stevenson, *Life in Black and White: Family and Community in the Slave South* (New York: Oxford University Press, 1996), 240. It should be noted that sexual relationships between African American men and white women existed at this time also. See Paul S. Spickard, *Mixed Blood: Intermarriage and Ethnic Identity in Twentieth-Century America* (Madison: University of Wisconsin Press, 1989), 242–44; Martha Hodes, *White Women, Black Men: Illicit Sex in the Nineteenth Century* (New Haven: Yale University Press, 1997); James Kinney, *Amalgamation! Race, Sex, and Rhetoric in the Nineteenth-Century American Novel* (Westport, Conn.: Greenwood Press, 1985); and Catherine Clinton, *The Plantation Mistress: Woman's World in the Old South* (New York: Pantheon Books, 1982), 214.

5. Joel Williamson, *New People: Miscegenation and Mulattos in the United States* (New York: New York University Press, 1980), 24–25; Spickard, *Mixed Blood*, 247. See also John G. Mencke, *Mulattos and Race Mixture: American Attitudes and Images, 1865–1918* (Ann Arbor, Mich.: UMI Research Press, 1979), 11; and Willard B. Gatewood, *Aristocrats of Color: The Black Elite, 1880–1929* (Bloomington: Indiana University Press, 1990), 13.

6. Spickard, *Mixed Blood*, 243; and Williamson, *New People*, 100. Shirley Taylor Haizlip, *The Sweeter the Juice: A Family Memoir in Black and White* (New York: Simon and Schuster, 1994).

7. Mencke, *Mulattos and Race Mixture*, 141. Quote taken from Mencke, p. 37, originally cited in Booker T. Washington, *The Future of the American Negro* (Boston: Small, Maynard & Company, 1900), 158; Sterling Brown, *The Negro in American Fiction* (Albany, N.Y.: J. B. Lyon, 1937; rpt. Port Washington, N.Y.: Kennikat Press, 1958), 8.

8. Frances Ellen Watkins Harper, *Iola Leroy, or Shadows Uplifted* (Philadelphia: Garrigues Brothers, 1892); Pauline E. Hopkins, *Contending Forces: A Romance Illustrative of Negro Life North and South* (1900; rpt. New York: Oxford University Press, 1988). See also Wells Brown, *Clotel, or The President's Daughter* (1835); Frank J. Webb, *The Garries and Their Friends* (1857); and Charles W. Chestnutt, *The House Behind the Cedars* (1900). Nella Larsen, *Quicksand and Passing*, ed. Deborah McDowell (New Brunswick, N.J.: Rutgers University Press, 1986).

9. Jo A. Tanner, *Dusky Maidens: The Odyssey of the Early Black Dramatic Actress* (Westport, Conn.: Greenwood Press, 1992), 8, 14, 132; Allen Woll, *Black Musical Theater: From Coontown to Dreamgirls* (Baton Rouge: Louisiana State University Press, 1989), 4.

10. Clinton, *The Plantation Mistress*, 201–2; and Patricia A. Turner, *Ceramic Uncles & Celluloid Mammies: Black Images and Their Influence on Culture* (New York: Anchor Books, 1994), 44.

11. Neal Gabler, *An Empire of Their Own: How the Jews Invented Hollywood* (New York: Anchor Books, 1988), 5.

12. Cortés defines "color" as "individuals who have been categorized as non-white in American history." See Cortés, "Hollywood Interracial Love," 39n2.

13. Alicia I. Rodríquez-Estrada, "Dolores Del Rio and Lupe Velez: Images On and Off the Screen, 1925–1944," in *Writing the Range: Race, Class and Culture in the Women's West*, ed. Elizabeth Jameson and Susan Armitage (Norman: University of Oklahoma Press, 1997), 475–92. Del Rio and Velez had more options than Washington or Dandridge but only in regard to their color. They still had to contend with film studios' stereotypes of Mexican women. Del Rio and Velez found few roles that would allow them to portray nonstereotypical ethnic women.

14. Little is known about her parents, Robert T. and Hattie V. Washington, except that her father was a postal employee. Fredi arrived at the home on February 1, 1917, and her sister, Isabel, joined her five months later on July 5, 1917. Letter dated August 15, 1997, from Sister Maria E. McCall, archivist, Sisters of the Blessed Sacrament, Bensalem, Pennsylvania. Josephine Baker also got her break in *Shuffle Along*, when she convinced the director to let her go on in place of a sick chorus girl. The crowd adored her and she became a permanent member of the cast. She was originally not cast because the director thought she was too "dark." Baker later went to Europe, where she became internationally known. See Kathy Russell, Midge Wilson, and Ronald Hall, *The Color Complex: The Politics of Skin Color among African Americans* (New York: Harcourt Brace Jovanovich, 1992). See also Phyllis Rose, *Jazz Cleopatra: Josephine Baker in Her Time* (New York: Doubleday, 1989); and Jean-Claude Baker and Chris Chase, *Josephine: The Hungry Heart* (New York: Random House, 1993). Martin Bauml Duberman, *Paul Robeson* (New York: Alfred A. Knopf, 1988), 103. Washington appeared under the stage name Edith Warren. See *San Francisco News*, October 10, 1942. Unfortunately, the play did not receive good reviews and closed after several weeks.

15. In the short film, Ms. Washington portrays herself, a dancer with a heart condition. Broke, she agrees to perform but collapses during the performance and is carried out. She dies as Duke Ellington and his band play "Black and Tan Fantasy" for her. See *Variety*, November 6, 1929. Plots of *Singin' the Blues* and *Run, Little Chillun* can be found in Woll, *Black Musical Theater*, 151–52, 157–58. See also Bernard L. Peterson Jr., *A Century of Musicals* (Westport, Conn.: Greenwood Press, 1993).

16. Duberman, *Paul Robeson*, 168. During my research, I found no evidence in the Production Code Administrative Archives (PCAA) for *The Emperor Jones* that required scenes with Ms. Washington be reshot. In a letter from Dr. Duberman, dated September 9, 1997, he states that Ms. Washington revealed this in a telephone interview.

17. *Chicago Defender*, February 28, 1935.

18. Description and plot taken from author's viewing of the film *Imitation of Life* (1934).

19. I. Auster to Joseph Breen, March 13, 1934, Production Code Administrative Archives (PCAA) *Imitation of Life* file; Joseph Breen to Will Hays, March 22, 1934, PCAA *Imitation of Life* file; Maurice McKenzie to Joseph Breen, April 3, 1934, PCAA *Imitation of Life* file; and Joseph Breen to Harry Zehner, November 14, 1934, PCAA *Imitation of Life* file. Found in the Margaret Herrick Library, Academy Motion Picture Arts and Sciences, Beverly Hills, California.

20. Darden, "Oh, Sister!" 105; *Literary Digest*, December 8, 1934.

21. In the novel, Peola has herself sterilized, ensuring that her husband never finds out her race. See Fannie Hurst, *Imitation of Life* (New York: P. F. Collier & Son, 1933), 300. First letter dated March 10, 1935, and second letter dated March 5, 1935, Fredi Washington Collection at Amistad Research Center at Tulane University, New Orleans, Louisiana.

22. *Afro American*, November 16, 1935.

23. *Chicago Defender*, October 16, 1945.

24. *Daily Compass*, December 22, 1949. See also Haizlip, *The Sweeter the Juice*, 71.

25. Darden, "Oh, Sister!" 106. See also *Ebony*, "Cotton Club Girls" (April 1949): 34, 36, 38. Jacqueline Jones, *Labor of Love, Labor of Sorrow: Black Women, Work and the Family, from Slavery to the Present* (New York: Vintage Books, 1985), 196–97.

26. Jonathan Dewberry, "Black Actors United: The Negro Actors Guild of America, 1937–1982" (Ph.D. dissertation, New York University, 1988), 55–57. As a member of the Actors Equity Association, Washington served as deputy officer during the run of *Mamba's Daughters*.

27. A résumé Washington submitted to the Personnel Department of CBS in 1950 indicates that she took a six-week course at the Egri School of Dramatic Writing. Fredi Washington Collection at Amistad Research Center. *People's Voice*, May 8, 1943.

28. Donald Bogle, "The Dorothy Dandridge Story," *Essence* (October 1984): 100. See also Bogle, *Dorothy Dandridge*, 17–21.

29. Bogle, *Dorothy Dandridge*, 54–70. See also Dandridge and Conrad, *Everything and Nothing*, 86–87.

30. Bogle, *Dorothy Dandridge*, 104, 129–34.

31. Ibid., 227.

32. Otto Preminger, *Otto Preminger: An Autobiography* (New York: Doubleday, 1977), 138.

33. Description and plot taken from author's viewing of film.

34. Offered the role of Tumptin in *The King and I*, Dandridge turned it down.

35. "To Kiss or Not to Kiss," *Ebony* (July 1957): 33. In the film, Harry Belafonte portrayed an island labor leader who becomes involved with Joan Fontaine. See also Thomas Cripps, *Making Movies Black: The Hollywood Message Movie from World War II to the Civil Rights Era* (New York: Oxford University Press, 1993), 263–65.

36. Bogle, *Dorothy Dandridge*, 381, 404, 437–38. John Berry, the director of *Tamango*, agreed to two film versions of the interracial relationship, with the European version displaying a kiss between Dandridge and her costar Curt Jurgens. In *The Decks Ran Red*, Stuart Whitman's character forces Dandridge's character to kiss him. As Bogle notes, although this kiss was not done in a passionate manner, it was Hollywood's first interracial kiss onscreen.

37. Bogle, *Dorothy Dandridge,* 434. See also James Spada, *Peter Lawford: The Man Who Kept the Secrets* (New York: Bantam Books, 1991), 137–38; *Citizen News,* April 1, 1963; and "Why Do Stars Go Broke?" *Ebony* (July 1963): 84–86, 88–89.

38. Earl Mills, *Dorothy Dandridge* (Los Angeles: Holloway House, 1970), 227. See also Bogle, *Dorothy Dandridge,* 534–35. Bogle interviewed many of Dandridge's friends, and they dispute Mills's claims that he and Dandridge became lovers. *New York Times,* September 9, 1965; *Los Angeles Times,* September 9, 1965; and *Los Angeles Herald Examiner,* September 9, 1965.

39. Dandridge and Conrad, *Everything and Nothing,* 207–8.

40. Veronica Chambers, "Fredi Washington: The Tragic Mulatto," *New York Times Magazine,* January 1, 1995.

World War II

Lyn Childs Confronts a Racist Act

Lyn Childs, a black San Francisco shipyard worker, describes how she came to the defense of a Filipino employee on the ship she was repairing. Her account also discusses the reaction from her supervisor.

I was working down in the hold of the ship and there were about six Filipino men ... and this big white guy went over and started to kick this poor Filipino and none of the Black men that was working down there in the hold with him said one word to this guy. And I sat there and was getting madder and madder by the minute. I sprang to my feet, turned on my torch, and I had a flame about six to seven feet out in front of me, and I walked up to him and I said (you want me to say the real language?) I said to him,

"You so-in-so. If you go lift one more foot, I'll cut your guts out." That was my exact words. I was so mad with him.

Then he started to tell me that he had been trained in boot camp that any national group who was dark skinned was beneath all White People. So he started to cry. I felt sorry for him, because he was crying, really crying. He was frightened, and I was frightened. I didn't know what I was doing, so in the end I turned my torch off and I sat down on the steps with him.

About that time the intercom on board the ship started to announce,

"Lyn Childs, report to Colonel Hickman immediately."

So I said, "I guess this is it." So I went up to Colonel Hickman's office, and behind me came all these men, and I said,

"Where are you guys going?"

They said, "We're going with you."

When we got to the office [Colonel Hickman] said, "I just wanted to see Lyn Childs," and they said, "You'll see all of us, because we were all down there. We all did not have the guts enough to do what she did, [but] we're with her."

Colonel Hickman said, "Come into this office."

Source: Paul R. Spickard, "Work and Hope: African American Women in Southern California during World War II," *Journal of the West* 32 (July 1993): 74–75.

He had one of the guards take me into the office real fast and closed the door real fast and kept them out, and he said,

"What kind of communist activity are you carrying on down there?"

I said, "A communist! What is that?"

He said, "You know what I am talking about. You're a communist."

I said, "A communist! Forget you! The kind of treatment that man was putting on the Filipinos, and to come to their rescue. Then I am the biggest communist you ever seen in your life. That is great. I am a communist."

He said, "Don't say that so loud."

I said, "Well, you asked me was I a communist. You're saying I am. I'm saying I'm a . . ."

"Shh! Shh! Shh! Hush! Don't say that so loud." Then he said, "I think you ought to get back to work."

"Well, you called me. Why did you call me?"

"Never mind what I called you for," he said. "Go back to work."

Etta Germany Writes to the President

African American migrants who found work in West Coast shipyards encountered hostile unions, which, after unsuccessful attempts to bar their employment, resorted to segregating them (and white women) in auxiliary locals. Etta Germany, a black shipyard worker in Richmond, California, wrote directly to President Franklin D. Roosevelt to protest the discrimination directed against her and other African American shipyard workers.

Mr. President
Honorable Sir,

I wish to call your attention to a very disgraceful and UnAmerican situation that now exists in the Boilermakers and Welders Union Local 513 of Richmond, California. I am a Negro girl. Three weeks ago I and lots of others enrolled in the National Defense Training Classes to become welders. I applied for a job at the yards several times. But each time myself and others of my race were give the run around. . . . [Be]cause of being Negro I was not allowed to join the Union. Now Mr. President there are a great many Negroes in Defense Training as myself who upon completion of the course will be subjected to the same treatment as myself. . . . We are all doing what we can to assist in winning the war. I sincerely feel that this is no time for our very own fellow citizens to use discrimination of this type. . . .

Mrs. Etta Germany

Source: Selected Documents from the Records of the Committee on Fair Employment Practice Field Records, Region 12, Reel 108, Complaints Against Boilermakers File, National Archives, Pacific Sierra Region (Region 12), San Bruno, California.

CHAPTER 13

"Women Made the Community"

AFRICAN AMERICAN MIGRANT WOMEN AND THE CULTURAL TRANSFORMATION OF THE SAN FRANCISCO EAST BAY AREA

Gretchen Lemke-Santangelo

In winter 1943, just as the early morning sun was beginning to chase the damp chill from the air, Ethel Tillman, her ten children, and her elderly aunt could hardly contain their excitement. There, in the tired, worn colored waiting room of the Vicksburg, Mississippi, station, they anxiously awaited the train that would carry them to a new life in California. Ethel's husband, Fred, had made the trip in fall 1942 after hearing about plentiful, well-paying jobs in the San Francisco East Bay Area. His gamble had been worthwhile. He easily found work as a pipefitter at the Mare Island shipyards in Vallejo and soon saved enough money to send for his family and secure a relatively spacious apartment in a nearby war housing project.

Ethel's mind was at ease as she waited for the train that would reunite her family. She had known her husband since childhood and deeply trusted his judgment. She had also spent the past four months preparing for the move, carefully weighing what to bring and what to leave behind. A "grapevine" of women friends who had already moved west wrote that cooking ware was in short supply because of the wartime demand for metal. So Ethel packed pots and pans along with clothes and bedding. She also filled crates with home-canned pickles, preserves, fruits, and vegetables—a summer's worth of labor that would nourish both body and soul on the tastes and aromas of her Mississippi garden. Finally, Ethel took particular care in packing family heirlooms, those material reminders of the past that would preserve her children's connection to the South: a cast iron pot and Wedgwood serving platter that had belonged to Ethel's great-great-grandmother, a regal, strong-willed woman who had been born in Africa and lived her life in slavery; and a smokehouse lock that belonged to her great-grandfather, a German immigrant who loved, married, and purchased the freedom of this African woman's daughter.

In the end, however, Ethel packed more than household items and tangible reminders of the past. She brought "home" with her, transplanting the very skills, values, and traditions that allowed generations of black Southerners to survive the humiliations and hardships of slavery and Jim Crow. By 1943 Ethel was a grown woman who had fully mastered the arts of building and sustaining family and community life. She, like countless women before her, was a practiced folk healer, a skilled seamstress and quilter, a knowledgeable parent, gardener, and cook, and a storehouse of family history and communal lore. More important, she knew how to press her skills into the service of others, to share with those in need so that she too could depend on assistance during hard times.

Generosity and hospitality were second nature to her, essential for survival but also central to Ethel's spiritual identity as a sanctified Christian. Following her conversion at age twelve, Ethel embraced the church as her second home, the place where cultural traditions like family loyalty, reciprocity, charity, hard work, respect for elders, self-help, and racial solidarity were learned and refined. Under the tutelage of older church women or "mothers," she soon acquired the organizing and networking skills that sustained this and other community-based institutions. In the process, she became a woman with firm, convictions: "[F]irst for God, second for my fellow man, and third for my family."[1]

As she stood at the Vicksburg station, Ethel had no way of knowing that her cultural belongings—her southernness—would become the foundation for a new life in the East Bay. But as surely as the sun rose on that wintry Mississippi morning, Ethel's helping ethic and commitment to institution building, all pieces of a southern cultural legacy that allowed her forebears to resist the social and economic costs of Jim Crow, would not only become the basis for family and collective survival, but permanently alter the East Bay's cultural landscape.

Ethel and her family, as they would soon recognize, were part of a larger historical drama that unfolded in the early 1940s when war industrialists such as Henry Kaiser, flush with huge federal defense contracts, transformed the

Bay Area into the nation's premier shipbuilding center. Word of employment opportunities traveled fast, spread by labor recruiters, railroad workers, employment bureaus, newspapers, and word of mouth. Although federal spending on the war effort and Roosevelt's Executive Order prohibiting discrimination in defense industries transformed the East Bay into a virtual Canaan for black workers, most came for more than jobs. A majority of African American migrants were young and ambitious, facing futures clouded by the ugly realities of Jim Crow segregation and white violence. For them, the West Coast defense boom provided a rare historical advantage, one that offered escape from the limits imposed on the lives of their parents and grandparents. Maya Angelou, who arrived in the Bay Area during the war, put it this way: "[W]hite kids were going to have a chance to become Galileos and Madame Curies and Edisons and Gauguins, and our boys (the girls weren't even in on it) would try to be Jesse Owenses and Joe Louises. . . . We were maids and farmers, handymen and washerwomen, and anything higher that we aspired to was farcical and presumptuous."[2]

Between 1940 and 1945 thousands of working-class African Americans, most from Texas, Louisiana, Mississippi, Arkansas, and Oklahoma, migrated to the East Bay Area in search of both economic and social freedom. As a consequence, the area's black population grew significantly, up to fivefold in many communities. In Richmond, for example, the African American population grew from 270 in 1940 to 10,000 in 1945. Similarly, Oakland's black population grew from 8,462 to more than 37,000 during the same period.[3]

With the exception of black business leaders and a small core of civil rights activists who recognized the economic and political advantages of this demographic shift, most established residents—white and black—viewed people like the Tillmans as undesirable and unassimilable guest workers. White oldtimers, joined by poor and working-class white migrants who embraced "whiteness" as the currency of their own assimilation, reinforced and extended the discriminatory practices long used to keep native black residents in a subordinate position.[4]

Thus racial barriers actually proliferated during the war years. Restrictive covenants and discriminatory real estate and lending practices confined African American migrants to the oldest, least desirable sections of East Bay cities, producing severe overcrowding and de facto school segregation. Even federally funded war housing, administered by local housing authorities, was allocated on a segregated and racially preferential basis. Employment discrimination and workplace racial harassment were widespread, even in industries that received federal defense contracts. Several labor unions, most notoriously the Boilermaker's, steadfastly refused to admit black members or created second-class, Jim Crow auxiliaries. Finally, numerous hotel, restaurant, and bar owners refused to serve black patrons, posting signs that announced, "We Refuse Service to Negroes."[5]

Migrants' outsider status was reinforced by established black residents who were alarmed over rising racial tensions and restrictions. Whites, it appeared, made little distinction between black newcomers and old-timers as they shored up the foundations of racial privilege. Marguerite Williams, for example, recalled that "there wasn't that feeling that 'people were your enemy' before the war." However, migrants "had an ingrown dislike of white people," which she maintained led to racial conflict. "It seemed like overnight people on the street would be fighting. You would go into the store downtown and the [white] people wouldn't want to wait on you. That bothered me because I wasn't used to that."[6]

Many old-time black residents responded to the migrant influx by highlighting class and cultural distinctions between themselves and newcomers. California native Emmaline Benedict fully accepted white depictions of migrants as uninhibited, immoral, dirty, and ignorant, explaining, "I remember one family. They moved in and that thing [their apartment] got to smelling. They didn't know a thing about plumbing or anything else, you know. And they were using the bathtub for the toilet and washing their face in the real toilet."[7] Virginia Cravanas, another established resident, recalled, "[W]e in California didn't know anything about black foods. That was brought out here by the southerners. They also brought in new music. And every street corner had a storefront church. Their religion was different from ours. Ours was quiet. Theirs was holiness. As soon as a preacher felt he could preach a better sermon, a new church would spring up." Although Virginia believed that such differences reflected poorly on her community, she retrospectively observed that black newcomers possessed a sense of entitlement that had been nourished by the prodemocracy rhetoric of the times:

> Before the war blacks had to do for themselves. In California we didn't have anything. We just got the crumbs. . . . We resented the influx because we thought we were doing the right thing. But we weren't doing a thing. We were really the bottom of the bucket, working as stock clerks and maids. Newcomers came in and called attention to what we were denied. When they came out here, they felt this was the land of milk and honey,

and they were going to get some because they never had anything
anyway.[8]

Working-class migrants like the Tillmans did indeed use their southern heritage
of self-help and institution building to dismantle some of the East Bay's more
tangible racial barriers and secure a dominant role in local politics. Just as
significantly, newcomers transformed the region's culture, forcing vastly outnumbered old-time black residents to assimilate to their tastes and preferences
and defeating whites' efforts to contain the dynamism of the wartime black
diaspora. Even before the war ended, the Tillmans' cultural belongings were
widely scattered, appearing as southern foods prominently displayed on market
shelves; rich Mississippi and Louisiana accents murmuring out on the fishing
pier and rolling like thunder from storefront churches; okra and blackeyed peas
rising over garden fences; and the scent of greens and cornbread curling out
of women's kitchens.

Ironically, efforts to maintain racial barriers and define newcomers as
foreign and unassimilable only served to reinforce the power of southern
working-class culture. Just as existing residents and white migrants generated
hostile stereotypes to secure their position in the new, war-driven social order,
black migrants used positive representations of their southernness to forge a
common identity, maintain family stability, and establish permanent communities. Rather than abandon their distinctiveness on the historically remote
chance of obtaining acceptance, migrants thus drew on their cultural resources
to establish new homes and resist the prejudice and discrimination that threatened to dislodge them.

To be sure, there were significant cultural differences among southern
African Americans: linguistic, culinary, and artistic traditions, religious affiliations, and folk beliefs that migrants cultivated and preserved once they arrived
in the East Bay. Many migrants came from the same towns, cities, and states,
or shared common customs and values that prompted them to migrate in
groups or seek out compatriots on arrival. The Tillmans, for example, readily
discovered and joined a social and service-oriented organization founded by
former Vicksburg residents and just as quickly located a southern Baptist
church that closely resembled their Mississippi congregation. Similarly, women
from Louisiana, sharing distinct food preferences, speech patterns, and Catholicism, readily reclaimed their common bonds at markets, churches, and war
housing projects. Crafts, too, often reflected regional differences. Most migrant
women knew how to quilt, and their artistry reflected a common aesthetic

tradition rooted in the African past. However, the "Britches" quilt, made from strips of discarded clothing and "executed on a larger scale and with coarser fabric than other African American quilts," came west with migrants from Texas.[9] These variations nested within a broader framework of shared cultural practices and values: a common kinship system, spiritual orientation, aesthetic sensibility, oral tradition, drive for self-determination and independence, and commitment to institution building.

Most migrants maintained the southern black folkways that their enslaved ancestors forged from Central and West African, European, and Native American traditions—a cultural composite that allowed women and men to assert collective and individual autonomy from white control and to survive and resist the racial and economic exploitation of slavery. Following emancipation, folk culture lived on, particularly among the poor and working class whose economic position provided little insulation from the hardships of Jim Crow and fewer opportunities and incentives to adopt the cultural belongings of the white middle class and elite.

In the East Bay, this common cultural fabric grew stronger over time as the second and third generation mixed and mingled, and as all migrants, regardless of their regional distinctions, were regarded as unassimilable and undesirable. However, southern folk culture, forged out of a common historical experience and mediated by class, never completely subsumed regional differences. They can still be found in church, in speech patterns, in restaurants and kitchens, and in East Bay jazz and blues clubs.

Both men and women transplanted and reproduced their southern cultural traditions. Women, however, frequently identified themselves as culture "bearers"—a role that grew out of their unpaid labor as wives, mothers, and church workers. While men's status hinged on paid labor, or the provider role, women primarily derived authority and self-esteem as family and community caregivers. Echoing a common sentiment among working-class women, one migrant commented that "caring and sharing . . . doing for your family and other people too" was what gave her life structure and meaning.[10]

The caregiving role was complimented and at times complicated by women's paid labor. Most migrant women worked for wages, directly contributing to the financial stability of their families and supplying essential resources for fledgling churches, self-help institutions, political campaigns, and informal caregiving activities. However, women faced numerous pressures to minimize the significance of their paid labor, and emphasize their caregiving role. The East Bay's employment structure afforded greater economic opportunities than the

South's, but migrant women still occupied the lowest rungs of the occupational hierarchy. Relegated to the least desirable, lowest-paying jobs, women turned to caregiving as an alternative source of status and identity.

Moreover, in a society that equated male virtue with breadwinner status while simultaneously depriving black men of economic opportunities, women often chose to minimize their financial contributions to family income. Thus while women's paid labor was integral to family and community survival, "caring and sharing . . . doing for your family and other people too," was defined as "real" work. Their "minimizing," however, often masked the complex interdependence of married couples. Migrant women and men did what needed to be done to raise their families. For example, many couples arranged their work schedules to accommodate shared child care arrangements, even if this meant working different shifts and rarely having time together. Similarly, breadwinner status did not relieve most men of broader obligations to their communities. Men took active roles in their churches and civic and social organizations and as mentors to the younger generation. However, women—at least in ideal terms—were still identified as the primary nurturers of family and community.

Once in the East Bay Area, women's "caring and sharing" took a variety of forms but fell into three mutually reinforcing categories described by Ethel Tillman: doing for God, fellow man, and family. Initially, most women focused on the familial challenges associated with a major move such as the physical work of locating, cleaning, repairing, and furnishing a new home; the emotional labor of managing family adjustment to new surroundings; the immediate demands of child care, laundry, meal preparation, personal hygiene, and house-cleaning; and securing access to essential goods and services such as markets, schools, banks, medical care, recreation facilities, and churches.

To accomplish these orientation tasks, migrant women relied on their ability to forge new relationships with other migrants, or on friendships and family ties that they had conscientiously maintained over time and distance. Myrtle Eaton, for example, moved to Richmond in 1943 with her new husband after a woman friend offered them temporary shelter: "[W]ithout Priscilla we wouldn't have known just which way to go or the ways and means to get a place to live. Priscilla was one of the main ones that caused us to manage to stop in Richmond and remain here."[11]

Marlene Lewis, in contrast, depended on her family connections to make a smooth transition. Her brother-in-law and sister, Ruth, moved to the East Bay early in the war and found housing in one of West Oakland's grand old Victorians. Ruth soon restored the house and extended a welcome to Marlene, Marlene's husband, and another sibling. Estelle Peoples also drew on long-distance family ties to facilitate her move, explaining, "I sent [my husband] out here a couple of months before I came. . . . I said, 'you go first and see how you like it, because my people are going to be nice to you.' Then I came two months later, because I wanted to get my bills and things paid up." These examples not only illustrate the care that women took to maintain established relationships, but their central role in sustaining the migration—an ever-widening circle that frequently encompassed extensive networks of family and friends.[12]

Other women found help from strangers. Ethel Tillman, for example, joined a church as soon as she settled in a Vallejo war housing project and began extending assistance to "dozens of other families[,] . . . putting them up until they could find a house and a job." Ethel, who was working full time in the shipyards and struggling to keep up with her household chores, generously recalled, "[W]e have fond memories of the different people who came through—family, strangers, couples and children, single men and women."[13]

But women like Ethel did more than provide material assistance and emotional support. They also encouraged shy, overwhelmed newcomers to assert themselves in their new surroundings. Theresa Waller, for instance, arrived in the East Bay with high expectations but a strong measure of fear over how far she could stretch unfamiliar racial boundaries. Her migrant mentor helped her find housing and a job. "[She] had experienced discrimination and was set on not putting up with it here. But I held back. I didn't want any confusion because where I came from, no matter whose fault it was, we were always to blame. It's nothing you can say to make officials think that you're telling the truth or were mistreated. So you just shut your mouth and let it end just as quick as it can. Seeing my friend be assertive helped me let loose and go into any place I felt like going into."[14]

Once acclimated, women drew on their southern traditions to maintain a stable family life and cement new friendships. Drawing people together in the boomtown atmosphere of the wartime East Bay was no easy task. But the kitchen table, laden with southern foods, proved a reliable old friend. Ethel Tillman, whose childhood was enriched by a large circle of extended kin who gathered weekly around her aunt's or mother's table, used her cooking skills to "gather" friends and family in her Vallejo kitchen. She and her aunt, who "were good cooks . . . and would share with neighbors anything [they] had," actively reestablished their culinary traditions by searching markets for familiar foods and experimenting with substitutes. Arriving early in the war, Ethel "decided we just had to have some cornbread" and used Cream of Wheat as a substitute until local shopkeepers adapted to her tastes.[15]

Oma June Scott, who came later, recalled, "[M]oving out here did not change our eating habits. Stores had everything we had in Texas, and an even better selection of fruits and vegetables." Indeed, Oma June's culinary reper- toire expanded when she settled on the border of Oakland's historic Italian neighborhood. "[Although] they moved out when we started to move in . . . I learned to cook spaghetti thanks to the Italian mothers at the PTA." Such cross- ethnic contact, however fleeting, points to a more complex and lasting process of cultural diffusion. Just as Oma June acquired new tastes and preferences, others, often unconsciously, adopted hers.[16]

Women's cooking also reinforced regional connections among migrants. Cornelia Duverney and Carmelia Chauvin, raised in New Orleans, recall huge family and neighborhood meals of gumbo, stuffed crabs, potato salad, and fried chicken served in their backyard: "[A]unts and uncles came over, Mama would cook, and we would have a good time in our little place." When the family relo- cated to an Alameda war housing project, "guys from the base who were from Louisiana would come over and Mama would cook, and there would be beer and dancing." In this manner, migrants from the same state, town, or city reestab- lished common bonds of identity that endured long after the war ended.[17]

Many migrant women, even those who gladly abandoned rural life, took great pride in placing homegrown food on their tables and sharing their produce with friends and neighbors. Those who came from farm families recall how their parents would share with those in need or cement friendships through the exchange of produce. Ruth Cherry, for example, said, "[F]riends back home would help each other out if one person ran out. What you have, I have. What would hurt one, would hurt the other. Hospitality they call it, but it was the only way we made it through." Similarly, Onnie Lee Logan, a black midwife from Alabama, recalled, "[W]e had three big gardens. . . . Mother didn't give 'em time to come. She would take 'em meal, flour, piece of meat, whatever. . . . Love, care, and share, that's what we did. We had it and my daddy and mother they shared with the ones that didn't have it."[18]

Even at the risk of reinforcing unflattering stereotypes that depicted migrants as backward country folk, women transplanted their gardening heritage in the East Bay. Cornelia James, who came west as a child from Arkansas, remembers how her mother and a cousin planted a vegetable garden at their Richmond war housing project. "Mother helped people out by sharing garden produce with anyone who wanted any." Ethel Tillman and her aunt who moved to Berkeley after the war, "raised a vegetable garden and planted enough to take care of other families. Always did canning. Would can garden produce and seasonal fruits." Thus Ethel, who refused to part with her cache of Mississippi produce on that winter day in 1943, ultimately parlayed her gardening heritage into a stable source of nourishment for family and friends. Just as significantly, she and other migrant women viewed gardening as part of their helping ethic, designating it "public work"—labor that, like cooking, took place in the home but reproduced southern black working-class culture and maintained supportive social relations.[19]

Women's quilts, like their gardens, decorated migrant homes with the colors and patterns of the South. Back home, most women, eager to join in the warmth and lively conversation generated during quilting bees, learned to sew at an early age. Pecolia Warner, from Mississippi, recalled, "[W]e was in the country then, and no house was very far apart. So Mama would have them at our house, or she would go to my auntie's or cousin's, and she would help them quilt. I was a little girl, but I'd be following her, because I wanted to learn how to do that. I used to say, 'If I ever get grown, I'm going to quilt myself.'" At times, quilting also involved charity. After Pecolia learned to sew, she also pieced quilts for other people. Willa Suddeth's mother regularly hosted quilting parties during which neighborhood women made quilts for poorer families while discussing everything from recipes to voter registration.[20]

In the East Bay, where store-bought blankets were affordable and readily available, women quilted for pleasure or to keep a dying tradition alive. Indeed, migrant quilters have won recognition in recent years from local collectors, museums, and filmmakers. Sewing skills, however, had lasting, practical value. Ethel Tillman, with several young children, bought "beautiful adult clothes" at Oakland's Salvation Army thrift store and "cut them down into dresses, pants, and suits" for her youngsters. Henrietta Bolden, forced onto public assistance after losing her wartime job with Southern Pacific in 1948, recalled, "[O]ne way I would make things stretch was by buying clothes from the Goodwill and altering them for my children. I always wanted them to look nice. I'll never forget the day this social worker came by when the children were going off to school and asked, 'do they dress like that everyday?' And I told her, 'yes they do.' And she said, 'it looks to me like you're living awful good on the money.' And I said, 'you mean to tell me I'm living good off the money when I'm buying clothes from Goodwill?' She shut her mouth after that."[21]

Women's knowledge of traditional folk medicine, another cultural possession that came west with migrants, also maintained its practical value in the

East Bay. In the South, particularly in rural areas, African Americans had long relied on medicinal plants, traditional healing rituals, and preventive lore to treat physical and psychological disorders. Well into the twentieth century, this knowledge continued to have practical value for communities that were routinely denied access to white medical practitioners and hospitals. Women, who learned healing arts from their mothers and grandmothers, frequently provided medical services for their families and neighbors, deriving considerable status from their work on behalf of the sick and aged. In the process, they expanded their caregiving role outside of the home and reproduced a working-class helping ethic that was rooted in reciprocity, respect for elders, and compassion for the helpless.[22]

When they arrived in the East Bay, migrants had wider access to institutional health care, particularly those who worked at Kaiser shipyards and were thus eligible for membership in the company's group medical plan. Nevertheless, many women transplanted their knowledge of medicinal plants and folk remedies and continued to practice the healing arts in their new communities. Ethel Tillman and her aunt, for example, soon acquired reputations as accomplished medical practitioners. "When we moved here, we became members of Kaiser and would go to their doctors, but we used our own remedies for common illness. For colds you make a syrup of beef tallow, mutton tallow, honey, and onions. Mullion tea is used for colds and fever. We used beechbark teas in the South for colds. People used to come from far and wide [to Berkeley] to have us cure swollen glands. You heat a fork until it's red hot and then hold it as close to the gland as you can stand it. Put a piece of fat meat on a pine stick and burn it so the pitch and fat mingle and use it to cure boils. Make a poultice and change it everyday."[23]

Some women, like Mary Lee, found a plentiful supply of wild greens and medicinal plants in the East Bay's marshlands and open fields. She used these, along with commercially available remedies like garlic, to treat her family and neighbors. "Fig leaves were for fever. You would wrap a body in a sheet with fig leaves. Fig juice was good for skin inflammation. We gave teething babies a string of garlic cloves. Garlic was also good for colds along with catnip and rose hips. Never went to a doctor." Mary, however, regarded a diet rich in greens and grains as the source of lasting health. So, too, did Lacey Gray, who stated, "[W]e could use natural remedies because we had a good diet. Today, people get sick from all the chemicals in their food."[24]

Migrant women's helping ethic extended beyond healing to routine child and elder care. Children, viewed as part of a communal trust, were only reluctantly placed in the care of strangers. Even during the war, when many women worked long hours in the shipyards, most relied on friends and relations to provide child care. Indeed, taking responsibility for others' children was consistent with women's own southern childhood. Teresa Waller, for example, recalled, "We understood that if our parents weren't home the neighbors would keep an eye on us. They had permission to spank us . . . and if anything happened, my mother would hear about it and we would get it twice." Olive Blue, echoing the same theme, remembered that "if mothers in the past left their kids, all they'd have to do is tell a neighbor and the kids would be looked after."[25]

Teresa, Olive, and countless other migrant women thus viewed collective parenting as part of their southern cultural legacy, essential to the survival of migrant communities and the reproduction of working-class values and ethics. Lacey Gray not only raised her own family but also assumed the role of neighborhood mother: "[I correct] young people who I see littering, fighting, or stealing. If they are in my neighborhood, I'll go right out and tell them . . . tell them I love them, but if they don't respect their parents they are shortening their days. My motto to youth is to patternize your life after someone who is doing good." Olive Blue, who "always feared what the Bible said, and that was to obey your parents," fostered numerous children in her neighborhood and church. She said, "[Adults] must not worry whether young people will like them; kids need advice. And I tell them to find the right way and walk in it even when things get hard and you get discouraged. . . . Shortcomings is given into each life and into each life some rain is going to fall . . . but weep not like those who have no hope, because weeping comes in the night, but joy comes in the morning."[26]

Respect for elders was a central cultural value that migrant women learned as children and wished to convey to the young. Most described deep attachments to their own parents and frequently remarked that their elders had sacrificed a great deal for them. Not surprisingly, then, women went to great lengths to bring aging relatives west, or returned to the South for extended periods to provide care. One migrant woman stressed her familial obligations above all other concerns:

> I'll tell you. You see, I am a colored woman and I am forty-two years old. I have an old mother and a crippled aunt to take care of, and I have to make as much as I can to take care of them. . . . I went down to the government office in Marshall there and they said maybe I could find a war job out here. I got my neighbors to look after my mother and aunt

and came out here on the bus. I went to work for Kaiser and saved
enough to bring my aunt and mother out here.[27]

Louise Steele demonstrated the same level of commitment to her aging grandmother whom she brought to the East Bay from their small hometown in
Louisiana soon after securing a defense job. Several years later, when her grandmother's health began to deteriorate, Louise placed her job on the line by
refusing to work overtime. "My supervisor warned me that it was either putting
my grandmother in a home or losing my job. And that said a whole heap to
me, to put this job ahead of the only woman who was Mama to me. And I just
stared at him, because my grandmama taught me that if you're going to say
the wrong thing, don't say anything."[28]

When older relatives refused to leave the South, migrant women returned
home to care for them. Marlene Lewis, for example, spent eight years commuting
between Arkansas and her East Bay home to help care for her mother and aunt.
"I was the only girl in the family who could do that, and I buried both of them."
Olive Blue returned to Louisiana for three years, sacrificing her job to nurse her
sick older brother. Still others extended care to those outside of their families.
Ethel Tillman, who joined a mutual aid association comprised of migrants from
Vicksburg, Mississippi, provided routine assistance to sick and aging members
over a forty-year period. Lovie McIntosh similarly devoted several years to the
daily supervision of an Alzheimer's stricken friend.[29]

In some cases, child care and elder care overlapped in migrant women's lives,
doubly testing their "sharing and caring" ethic. Marlene Brown, who took early
retirement from her job to care for her disabled mother and three grandchildren, modestly noted that she was simply following an established southern
tradition: "Families where I came from were close knit." Her labor, along with
that of other aging migrant women, should be recognized and rewarded as a
social resource. However, such caregiving is rendered doubly invisible because
it takes place within the "private" sphere of the home and challenges the white
public's preoccupation with the "pathology" of black culture.[30]

In practicing this helping ethic, women provided essential services to their
families and neighbors and passed the values that informed it on to the younger
generation. Cooking, gardening, healing, and caregiving, cultural belongings
that women used to strengthen their new communities, also fostered a common
bond among migrants—one that was consciously rooted in a positive identification with their southern, working-class roots. But southern identity, while
transmitted through women's labor, was also reinforced by their return visits

to the South. Death and illness drew migrants back to their birthplaces, but so too did weddings, births, annual and semiannual reunions, old friendships, and a desire to acquaint children with "home." Indeed, during return visits women brought the West to the South and the South back to the West. In this manner, southern identity was continually renewed, updated, and reevaluated in light of shifting social realities in both places.

Despite the fact that migrant women experienced the brutality and humiliation of segregation, the southern black world had provided warmth, security, and shelter. Back home, even if only in memory, people took care of their own, children were loved, elders were respected, and religious values shaped family and community life. Migrant parents, wishing to expose the younger generation to southern mores, thus sent or took their children home for extended vacations. Still others entrusted their children to southern relatives during hard times. Maya Angelou, for example, was sent back to her grandmother in Stamps, Arkansas, when her migrant parents decided to end their marriage. She later "discovered that the United States had been crossed thousands of times by frightened black children traveling to their newly affluent parents in Northern cities, or back to grandmothers in Southern towns when the urban North reneged on its economic promises." But more commonly, entire families returned for reunions to "renew old friendships and catch up on the news, to establish once again the spiritual connections of their childhoods."[31]

Women, however, returned more frequently because of their traditional role as caregivers. Caretaking involved more than nursing the old and sick. It also included maintaining the bonds of love and reciprocity that held families together over long distances. Visits were particularly important, giving women the opportunity to directly assist those in need, welcome new family members into the fold, renew childhood friendships, and strengthen existing bonds with parents, siblings, and other relatives. In exchange, women could expect material and emotional support during trying times of their own—a form of social security that benefited entire families and, by extension, East Bay migrant communities.

Lacey Gray, for example, made yearly trips to Louisiana for vacations, funerals, weddings, and one painful journey "to carry a brother back to be buried in the family cemetery." Now that her own children have left home, Lacey relies even more heavily on her southern family connections, returning for extended periods each November to "attend the church built on family land" and stay "in the old house with [her] two sisters." "That's what I like to do; I don't do anything else." She now "thinks about going back to live" on the land that her sharecropping father struggled to buy "and never wanted [and] sold, so it will just pass from one generation to the next." Like Lacey, Henrietta Bolden, from Guthrie, Oklahoma, relies more on family now that she is older. Having maintained deep attachments to her siblings, she visits twice a year, often staying for several weeks at a time to reconnect with her rich Afro–Native American cultural roots.[32]

While much of women's cultural work took place within the home, it also found expression through the black church. As a group, the migrant generation was highly "churched," steeped in a southern black religious tradition that provided spiritual and material sustenance to its members and numerous opportunities for female leadership. In the church, women enjoyed a deeply personal relationship to a just and loving God who understood their sorrows and fears and stood with them in struggle. But just as significantly, it joined women in a mutual aid association, allowing them to use their talents to benefit their communities. Indeed, southern churches served numerous functions: schools, employment and housing bureaus, and centers of social activity and political organizing. There, in their second home, congregants nursed the sick, buried the dead, cared for the poor and aged, taught the young, admonished backsliders, and ostracized chronic offenders of community norms.[33]

Being a good Christian, a central concern of this generation, required active church participation. Lacey Gray, for example, attended church events almost every day of the week under the watchful eye of her father, who was head deacon, and her mother, who baked the communion bread and washed and ironed the white cloth headbands that congregants wore when they "took the Lord's Supper." Lucille Moss, raised a Catholic, attended daily mass and recalled, "If I didn't go to church, I didn't do anything. No jump rope, no playing records. Could only sit." Louise Steele more fondly remembered that the church was the center of her social life, the only place where young people could respectably enjoy the company of their peers.[34]

Following their initiation into full church membership, usually in early adolescence, women were expected to help maintain this most important community institution. Under the tutelage of older church women, or mothers, they learned a particular style of leadership—one that placed sacrifice to others above individual achievement. Louisa Hall, for example, remembers that "women who worked behind the scenes, never calling attention to their contributions or placing themselves above others," were the most respected and admired. Similarly, Olive Blue watched her mother and other church women

quietly raise money, recruit new members, and care for sick and poor parish-
ioners while "always linking people together." Church, defined as women's
second home, thus provided a socially sanctioned and status-conferring outlet
for energetic and talented women. While it served to reinforce existing gender
roles, it also extended women's influence and transformed caregiving into a
highly visible source of community recognition and affirmation.[35]

On arrival in the East Bay, migrant women immediately replicated southern
black church ways. Some helped to establish new congregations, often following
hometown preachers out West, or urging former pastors to transplant their
ministries to underchurched East Bay boomtowns. Olive Blue, for example,
joined a newly created migrant church in Richmond and helped to establish a
second congregation two years later. After forty years, she remains dedicated to
the church that she and other migrant women built. "Don't know anything
about cards, betting, dancing. Never was a moviegoer. Church kept me busy.
Went to church six days a week: Sunday to services; Monday to Missionary
Society; Tuesday to the Usher Board; Wednesday to Sunday School; Thursday
to Choir; and Friday to the Baptist Training Union." Today she serves as church
secretary, as the president of Pastor's Aid, and as a member of the Christian Aid
Board.[36]

Still others joined existing congregations, swelling church memberships,
forcing old-time residents to adjust to new modes of worship, and demanding
positions of authority within their adopted institutions. As a consequence,
established congregations prospered. Taylor Memorial M.E. Church in Oakland
expanded from 150 members in 1940 to 1,008 in 1954 and simultaneously moved
into a larger, completely financed building. Taylor, in one of its brochures,
acknowledged the source of its good fortune: "California's total population
increased 50% between 1940 and 1950. But the Negro population galloped ahead
at the rate of 400%. . . . The greatest challenge is right here in Northern California. Oakland, for example, has a total population of nearly 400,000. 50,000
of that number are Brown Americans. In 1940 there were only 8,000 Negroes
in Oakland. The increase has been over 6 for 1."[37]

Similarly, Progressive Baptist Church in Berkeley, founded in 1935, benefited
from the migrant influx. As church leaders acknowledge, "In its early history
the church found it difficult in making arrangements for the payment of bills
because of its small membership and financial status. It encountered many
trials and tribulations, but continued to show evidence of progress, because it
was rooted in God. . . . In the nineteen forties when Christians migrated from
various states to California, this church was a shelter and place of rest for God's

people." However, it was these very migrant Christians who, during the immediate postwar years, raised money for Progressive's expansion, remodeling, a
new organ, three new pianos, and a new dining room.[38]

Women, as church membership lists reveal, created and sustained such
success stories by forming the active core of East Bay congregations. Their
labor, poignantly detailed in church funeral programs, points to a lifelong
commitment to church-based caregiving. Precious Jackson-Handy, a migrant
from Mansfield, Louisiana, was praised for "serving over the years as president
of the Young Women's Progressive Club Number One, Chairperson of Ada
Circle, member of the Deaconess Board, member and teacher of the Mixed
Bible Club, Lamanette of the Laymen League, and Secretary of the Children's
Department of Sunday School." The tribute also praised her volunteer work
on behalf of the National Council of Negro Women and the Order of Eastern
Star and concluded with one of her poems:

> I'd like to think that when this life is done
> That I had filled a needed post
> That here and there I'd paid my fare
> With more than talk and boast. . . .[39]

Ella Ward's eulogy similarly focused on the strength of her church commitments, noting her service as a "Sunday School teacher, Eastern Star member,
a chorister, a soprano soloist, and a missionary worker."[40]

Church, however, was not the only arena where women's cultural work took
a more overtly public turn. The East Bay was not the South. In their new
communities, women like Precious and Ella found access to the voting booth,
better schools, a broader range of jobs, and many modern conveniences that
had been unaffordable luxuries back home. But while most escaped Jim Crow's
innumerable dangers and humiliations, they still encountered a large measure
of racial hostility and discrimination. And like their kin who remained in the
South, East Bay migrant women joined the long, bitter struggle for equal access
to good jobs, housing, and education.

Migrants' numerical strength and unwillingness to tolerate prewar racial
boundaries expanded the influence and agendas of existing civil rights organizations, led to the creation of new, more militant coalitions, and ultimately
shifted the political configuration of East Bay communities. Women's networking
and institution-building skills, their commitment to caring and sharing, found
expression in voter registration drives, school integration efforts, union organizing campaigns, and protests against housing and employment discrimination.

As the years passed, women's helping ethic would remain a vital resource. During the 1960s, East Bay black communities were tested by poorly planned redevelopment projects that destroyed affordable housing and black businesses, promoted white and capital flight to the suburbs, continuing patterns of residential segregation and employment discrimination and, more recently, the economic dislocations created by deindustrialization and military base closures. In the absence of sustained societal commitment to providing decent jobs and housing for black communities, migrant women fought for welfare rights, community control over redevelopment and antipoverty funds, job training and employment development, and improved neighborhood services. As was the case during earlier decades, their ethic of reciprocity, desire for economic and cultural autonomy, and dedication to self-help institutions were mobilized to help their communities resist economic marginalization and its accompanying dislocations.[41]

Just as significantly, women's cultural work made sustained struggle possible by knitting migrants together and transmitting the southern self-help and caring ethic to a new generation. Their labor, in the church, home, and neighborhood, contributed to the development of stable, permanent communities and institutions, provided essential social services to members, and gave migrants a positive sense of identity in the racially hostile climate of the East Bay. While few women regarded their cultural work as a form of protest, that is exactly what it was.

Willa Suddeth, a migrant from Louisiana, minced no words: "People from the South were the ones who changed California. We had a history of pulling together as a community and southern black women were always in the forefront of change." Ruth Gracon, from Arkansas, reflected on her long history of activism in more bittersweet terms: "Lots of things in the South are just born in you, but when you come here it's like you have to create it. And I never thought I'd have to create all that."[42]

Indeed, that their communities survived is a tribute to women's helping ethic, desire for economic independence, and commitment to institution building, all pieces of a southern cultural legacy that lend support to Jacqueline Jones's assertion that "embedded in the historical record of ordinary families is a powerful refutation of the culture of poverty or culture of dependency thesis." Today, East Bay black communities face severe problems, but these are rooted in spatial isolation and chronic unemployment rather than an "ethic of dependency." This study, emphasizing the strengths rather than the "alleged pathological aspects" of African American working-class culture, challenges enduring assumptions about inner-city communities—assumptions that obscure their considerable resources and their historic struggle for self-determination.[43]

NOTES

1. Interview with Ethel Tillman, Berkeley, Calif., September 21, 1990.

2. Ibid.; Gerald Nash, *The American West Transformed: The Impact of the Second World War* (Bloomington: Indiana University Press, 1985), 26, 66, 67, 89; Marilynn S. Johnson, *The Second Gold Rush: Oakland and the East Bay in World War II* (Berkeley: University of California Press, 1993), 32, 52–53; Hubert Owen Brown, "Impact of War Worker Migration on the Public School System of Richmond, California from 1940–1945" (Ph.D. dissertation, Stanford University, 1973), 116–19, 174–77; Maya Angelou, *I Know Why the Caged Bird Sings* (New York: Bantam Books, 1969), 151–52.

3. Nash, *The American West Transformed*, 3–14, 66, 69; Brown, "Impact of War Worker Migration," 40, 117, 118; U.S. Congress, House Committee of Naval Affairs, Subcommittee of the Committee on Naval Affairs, *Investigation of Congested Areas*, 78th Cong., 1st sess., 1943, vol. 1, pt. 3, 855; Edward E. France, "Some Aspects of the Migration of the Negro to the San Francisco Bay Area since 1940" (Ph.D. dissertation, University of California, Berkeley, 1962), 24; Johnson, *Second Gold Rush*, 51–55; Charles S. Johnson, *The Negro War Worker in San Francisco* (San Francisco: YWCA, 1944), 4–6; William Sokol, "Richmond during World War II: Kaiser Comes to Town," typescript, University of California, Berkeley, 1971, copy in Richmond Collection, Richmond Public Library, 13–14; Robert Wenkert, *A Historical Digest of Negro-White Relations in Richmond, California* (Berkeley: University of California Survey Research Center, 1967), 1–20; Cy W. Record, *Characteristics of Some Unemployed Negro Shipyard Workers in Richmond, California* (Berkeley: Institute of Governmental Studies, 1947), 9.

4. Oakland Institute on Human Relations, *Seminar Report on What Tensions Exist between Groups in the Local Community* (Oakland: N.p., 1946); Johnson, *Second Gold Rush*, 143–84; Katherine Archibald, *Wartime Shipyard: A Study in Social Disunity* (Berkeley: University of California Press, 1947), 56, 69–78; *Oakland Observer*, March 1, 1944; U.S. Congress, *Investigation of Congested Areas*, 1013.

5. U.S. Congress, *Investigation of Congested Areas*, 799; Wilson Record, *Minority Group and Intergroup Relations in the San Francisco Bay Area* (Berkeley: Institute of Governmental Studies, 1966); Harvey Kerns, *Study of the Social and Economic Conditions Affecting the Local Negro Population* (Oakland: Council of Social Agencies and the Community Chest, 1945); Floyd Hunter, *Housing Discrimination in Oakland, California: A Study Prepared for the Mayor's Committee on Full Opportunity and the Council of Social Planning* (Berkeley: Floyd Hunter Company, 1963); W. Miller Barbour, *An Exploratory Study of the Socio-Economic Problems affecting the Negro White Relationship* (Richmond: United Community Defense Services and the National Urban League, 1952); Berkeley Study Committee on Equal Employment Opportunities, *Employment Opportunities for*

Members of Minority Groups (Berkeley: BSCEEO, 1958); Louis Markus, "Problems of the Negroes in Oakland" (mimeographed ms.), 145, Black Social Conditions File, Oakland History Room, Oakland Public Library; Oakland Council of Social Agencies, *Our Community: A Factual Presentation of Social Conditions* (Oakland: Community Chest, 1945); France, "Some Aspects of the Migration of the Negro," 48–53; Wenkert, *Historical Digest of Negro-White Relations*, 10–23; Brown, "Impact of War Worker Migration," 179; Fair Employment Practices Committee, *Selected Documents from the Records of the Committee on Fair Employment Practice: Region 12, Field Records* (Glen Rock, N.J.: Microfilming Corporation of America, 1971), reel 111, Richmond Prefabrication Plant file, 12-BR-108; reel 111, Richmond Shipyard #1 file, 12-BR-81; reel 110, Machinists Local 824 file; reel 108, Complaints against Boilermakers file; reel 110, Moore Shipyard File; reel 109, California Manufacturing Company File; Archibald, *Wartime Shipyard*, 79, 88–89; Richmond Shipbuilding Corporation, Shipyard No. 2, *Handbook for Workers* (Richmond: Richmond Shipbuilding Corporation, 1942), 90.

6. Harry and Marguerite Williams, *Reflections of a Longtime Black Family in Richmond* (Berkeley: University of California Regional Oral History Office, 1985), 40–41, 103–4.

7. Interview with Emmaline Benedict, Oakland, Calif., March 19, 1991.

8. Interview with Virginia Cravanas, Oakland, Calif., February 4, 1991.

9. Interview with Ethel Tillman; Interview with Carmelia Chauvin and Corneila Duvernay, Hayward, Calif., February 28, 1991; Eli Leon, *Arbie Williams Transforms the Britches Quilt* (Berkeley: Regents of the University of California and the Mary Porter Sesnon Art Gallery, University of California, Santa Cruz, 1994), 2.

10. Interview with Best Johnson, Richmond, Calif., May 21, 1991.

11. Eddie Eaton, *In Search of the American Dream: From Houston, Texas, to Richmond, California, in 1943* (Berkeley: University of California Regional Oral History Office, 1986), 52.

12. Interview with Marlene Lewis, Oakland, Calif., February 22, 1991; Interview with Estelle Peoples, Emeryville, Calif., April 30, 1991.

13. Tillman interview.

14. Interview with Theresa Waller, Oakland, Calif., March 4, 1991.

15. Tillman interview.

16. Interview with Oma June Scott, Oakland, Calif., February 6, 1991.

17. Interview with Carmelia Chauvin and Corneila Duvernay, Hayward, Calif., February 28, 1991.

18. Interview with Ruth Cherry, Oakland, Calif., March 8, 1991; Onnie Lee Logan, *Motherwit: An Alabama Midwife's Story as Told to Katherine Clark* (New York: Penguin, 1989), 6.

19. Interview with Cornelia James, Richmond, Calif., May 21, 1991; Tillman interview.

20. William Ferris, ed., *Afro-American Folk Arts and Crafts* (Boston: G. K. Hall, 1990), 86–93; Interview with Willa Suddeth, Richmond, Calif., March 6, 1991; Eli Leon, *Models in the Mind: African Prototypes in American Patchwork* (Winston-Salem: The Diggs Gallery and Winston-Salem State University, 1992).

21. Tillman interview; Interview with Henrietta Bolden, Oakland, Calif., March 14, 1991.

22. James Kirkland and Holly F. Mathews, eds., *Herbal and Magical Medicine: Traditional Healing Today* (Durham: Duke University Press, 1992), 69–78; William Pierson, *Black Legacy: America's Hidden Heritage* (Amherst: University of Massachusetts Press, 1993), 108–14.

23. Tillman interview. For a more detailed examination of folk healing practices and other cultural traditions maintained by African American migrants to the San Francisco East Bay, see Shirley Ann Wilson Moore, *To Place Our Deeds: The African American Community in Richmond, California, 1910–1963* (Berkeley: University of California Press, 2000), 127–46.

24. Interview with Mary Lee, Richmond, Calif., February 20, 1991; Interview with Lacey Gray, Richmond, Calif., May 20, 1991.

25. Waller interview; Interview with Olive Blue, Richmond, Calif., May 7, 1991.

26. Gray interview; Waller interview.

27. Records, *Characteristics of Some Unemployed Negro Shipyard Workers*, 30.

28. Interview with Louise Steele, Richmond, Calif., June 3, 1991.

29. Interview with Marlene Lewis, Oakland, Calif., February 22, 1991; Blue interview; Tillman interview; Interview with Lovie McIntosh, Richmond, Calif., March 6, 1991.

30. Interview with Marlene Brown, Oakland, Calif., March 20, 1991.

31. Angelou, *I Know Why the Caged Bird Sings*, 4; Elizabeth Rauh Bethel, *Promiseland: A Century of Life in a Negro Community* (Philadelphia: Temple University Press, 1981), 239.

32. Far West Surveys, *The Negro Consumer in the San Francisco Bay Area* (San Francisco: The Firm, 1958–60), vol. 2, 20; Gray interview; Bolden interview.

33. William E. Montgomery, *Under Their Own Vine and Fig Tree: The African American Church in the South, 1865–1900* (Baton Rouge: Louisiana State University Press, 1993), 95–96, 114–15, 139, 267–75, 291, 293–95, 320–22; Joseph W. Scott and Albert Black, "Deep Structures of African American Family Life: Female and Male Kin Networks," *Western Journal of Black Studies* 13 (Spring 1989): 22.

34. Gray interview; Interview with Lucille Moss, Oakland, Calif., April 23, 1991; Steele interview.

35. Interview with Louisa Hall, Oakland, Calif., April 26, 1991; Blue interview.

36. Blue interview; Hall interview; Johnson interview; James interview.

37. Taylor Memorial United Methodist Church, *History of the Church, Founders, and Ministers, 1921–1988*, Church File, Northern California Center for Afro-American History and Life (hereafter NCCAHL).

38. Progressive Baptist Church, *Twenty Years of Progress, 1935–1955*, Church File, NCCAHL; see also Downs Memorial Methodist Church, *A Brief History of Downs*; and Cooper AME Zion Church, *Souvenir Program 1898–1948*, in the same file.

39. Funeral Program for Precious Jackson Handy, Deaths File, Northern California Center for Afro-American History and Life.

40. Funeral Program for Elizabeth Ward, Deaths File, NCCAHL.

41. Gretchen Lemke-Santangelo, *Abiding Courage: African American Migrant Women and the East Bay Community* (Chapel Hill: University of North Carolina Press, 1996), 162–77.

42. Suddeth interview; Interview with Ruth Gracon, Oakland, Calif., March 16, 1991.

43. Jacqueline Jones, "Southern Diaspora: Origins of the Urban Underclass," in *The Underclass Debate: Views from History*, ed. Michael Katz (Princeton: Princeton University Press, 1993), 38.

CHAPTER 14

"Eight Dollars a Day and Working in the Shade"

AN ORAL HISTORY OF AFRICAN AMERICAN MIGRANT WOMEN IN THE LAS VEGAS GAMING INDUSTRY

Claytee D. White

"Come on out here, they're giving away money; eight dollars a day and working in the shade."[1] Thus Lucille Bryant persuaded many of her friends and relatives in Tallulah, Louisiana, to join her in Las Vegas. Like other African American women in Tallulah, Bryant earned either $2.50 per day chopping cotton during hot summer days or $5.00 per week cooking, taking care of children, cleaning, and ironing for white families. This job picture mirrored that of Fordyce, Arkansas, the other small southern town that produced approximately 80 percent of the World War II African American migrants to Las Vegas.[2]

When Bryant arrived in Las Vegas in 1953, the jobs available to her were still categorized as domestic work, but the intensity of the labor and the benefits from the employment differed from her previous jobs in Tallulah. Depending on the gaming establishment, ten to fourteen rooms had to be cleaned in an eight-hour shift, but the ironing, cooking, child care, and other domestic service duties in private homes were nonexistent. In addition to changed standards, the postwar emergence of the Culinary Workers Union, Local 226, provided advancement, adequate wages plus gratuities, and more leisure time.

Black women entered the gaming industry through the back doors of the hotels that provided accommodations to white casino gamblers. They worked as maids, linen room attendants, kitchen help, and casino porters.[3] These back-of-the-house workers became the trailblazers for other African American women who, beginning in the early 1970s, moved into visible jobs as cocktail waitresses and dancers and into professional positions as secretaries and midlevel managers.

The World War II migration to Las Vegas expanded as the image of the city was being established. This image was one of glamour, personified by statuesque dancers and showgirls—none of which were African American. The city beckoned visitors and gamblers through this image that became the standard of fun, sexuality, and femininity. Through an economically induced policy of racial discrimination, blacks became invisible workers in the city. Nonetheless, through community-building activities in the African American Westside community and in the Culinary Workers Union, Local 226, they gained prestige and leadership skills. This process marks the simultaneous defeminization of black women in Las Vegas and the feminization of a major local labor union.

Before this migration, a small black population was a well-established segment of the Las Vegas community. In 1940 there were 178 African Americans in Las Vegas and surrounding Clark County. By 1955 the number of blacks living exclusively on the Westside of Las Vegas had grown to 16,000.[4] This population explosion resulted almost totally from the migration of southern working-class families from Fordyce, Arkansas, and Tallulah, Louisiana. Fordyce is approximately sixty miles south of Little Rock. According to migrants who lived there, Fordyce's racial ideology and that of Little Rock were light-years apart. Though Fordyce was segregated along racial lines, there was an unspoken harmony between blacks and whites. When federally mandated integration was ordered, the process proceeded without violence, unlike the televised conflicts in Little Rock. However, jobs were scarce, and those that were available paid little money and required excessive hours of arduous physical labor.

Similar employment conditions existed in Tallulah in the late 1930s, but there were also exaggerated racial tensions. Local blacks described Tallulah, located about twenty miles west of Vicksburg, Mississippi, as the lynching capital of the South. The employment situation and racial tension as well as wartime job opportunities prompted more than five hundred thousand African Americans to leave the South between 1942 and 1945, including Fordyce and Tallulah residents who migrated to Las Vegas.[5] In the years before World War II, very few African Americans considered Nevada a migration destination, even though

President Abraham Lincoln lobbied for its statehood in 1864 to ensure passage of the antislavery amendment. World War II employment opportunities changed this situation.

Yet female migrants offered reasons besides employment and racial discrimination for leaving the South. They wanted better conditions for themselves and their families. Women wanted good schools for their children, improved physical surroundings for the family unit, and, in some cases, a sense of excitement and fun for themselves. Essie Jacobs was supposed to remain in Fordyce until after the birth of her baby before joining her husband in Las Vegas, but she could not wait: "I came on my own. I was so excited about the lights of Las Vegas. . . . One day when my husband got in from work, he was so shocked. . . . He couldn't believe I was here."[6] This additional pull of the "bright lights, big city" described a fascination with the social and entertainment attractions offered by the nightlife in cities that was lacking in rural areas.

Women participated equally in evaluating whether the family should leave the South. Hazel Gay and her husband, Jimmy, left Fordyce because they learned that there were no black embalmers in Las Vegas. "I sold my little [restaurant] business, moved in with my parents," recalled Hazel, "and [Jimmy] left immediately for Las Vegas. He sent for me in about three weeks."[7] Essie Jacobs and Hazel Gay followed the typical pattern of this migration effort: the man traveled to Las Vegas first, found work and housing, and sent for the wife and children. This usually happened after the encouragement of friends and relatives who returned from vacations or business trips and promoted the finer points of Las Vegas. Jacobs recalls her brothers boasting of Las Vegas: "They would talk about all the big money downtown. All you had to do was stick your hand in there and get a handful of it."[8] Inez Harper remembered being similarly urged to leave Fordyce with the question from her brother, "There is money to be picked up in Vegas by the tubfuls, so why are you still here picking cotton?"[9] Both families moved after repeated prodding.

Many of the earliest migrant families made the decision to leave Fordyce and Tallulah because labor agents recruited the men of the families to work at Basic Magnesium Corporation (BMI) in Henderson, Nevada.[10] BMI processed the magnesium used to build bombs during the war. Less than one month after President Franklin Roosevelt issued Executive Order 8802 forbidding discrimination on the basis of race, creed, color, or national origin in the employment of workers in defense industries or government, BMI opened and the migration ensued.

Most migrants traveled by car or bus. Unlike Fordyce, Tallulah had a bus station, but for a time blacks could not purchase one-way tickets to Las Vegas.

Lucille Bryant explained: "So many were taking the bus at one time until the people at the bus depot stopped selling blacks tickets to Las Vegas because all their help was leaving. . . . Blacks started leaving after midnight, late in the wee hours of the morning. [White] people didn't want them to leave."[11] Men who drove carloads of passengers to Las Vegas became entrepreneurial "travelcraft" experts. The successful transition necessitated an unusual combination of skills, attitudes, and outlook.[12] Fordyce's Red Mitchell and Tallulah's Willis Minor, for example, provided round-trip transportation to Las Vegas.

The drivers quickly learned when it was safe to stop and when it was necessary to continue. When Willis Minor brought Alma Whitney to Las Vegas he drove the two-and-a-half- to three-day trip without stopping to sleep.[13] Mitchell and Minor knew where to stop for the night to ensure that their passengers would be somewhat comfortable. Public accommodations were not integrated on the road to Las Vegas, so beds were made on the ground and in the car. Migrant women became travelcraft experts as well. Their system of communication prepared other women for the journey. Unlike Chicago and other big cities, Las Vegas had no African American newspaper. Information passed by word of mouth and by letter. Food had to be prepared and packed to last the entire trip. Women acquired new skills and attitudes on their arrival because of inferior, primitive accommodations.

The all-black Westside population grew more rapidly than the number of adequate dwellings, so most new arrivals were faced with substandard housing. The housing that they had left in the South, though in many cases poor, was far better than their newly acquired dwellings in Las Vegas. When Viola Johnson arrived in 1942 to join her parents, she lived in a tent on Jackson Street with six other family members:

> Seven of us lived in this one room tent; my mother, dad, stepbrother, uncle, cousin, daughter, and myself. . . . It was awful living there and it was so hot when I arrived. They said it never rained but one time it rained so hard we all got under the table, the only dry spot in the tent. . . . The men worked different shifts [at BMI] so when some were sleeping others were at work. Some of us would sleep under the trees outside. . . . We cooked on a two-burner oil stove on the inside and a huge wood stove on the outside. . . . About fifteen feet away was our neighbor in another tent.[14]

All the families used the communal wood stove located in the immediate area. Large meals were prepared outside while breakfast could be made in each individual tent. Single men sometimes cooked but usually ate at restaurants located on Jackson Street, which quickly emerged as Las Vegas's black business corridor. "Bubba" Simmons remembered eating at the Brown Derby where his sister worked as a cook. He lived in a tent with ten other men where four cots were shared in an alternate fashion depending on the shifts each man worked.[15]

Las Vegas city officials did not address the housing shortage because they thought blacks would leave when BMI's war work ended. But African Americans stayed and built homes and businesses. Beauty shops, dry cleaners, barbershops, restaurants, and nightclubs soon peppered Jackson Street. The Town Tavern, Club Louisiana, the Harlem Club, the Brown Derby, and other clubs provided an active nightlife that included gambling. Unlike other western cities such as Portland and Oakland that lost African American residents immediately after the war, blacks remained in Las Vegas because the employment picture did not dim completely when war work ended.

Jobs for women became more plentiful as hotel construction gained momentum in the late 1940s and 1950s. While employment for black men slowed, Las Vegas began to pull in additional black families as the labor market switched to a search for women. The casino building boom began in 1941 with the construction of the El Rancho Vegas and the El Cortez, followed by the Last Frontier the following year. The influx of gamblers provided Las Vegas with soaring gaming revenues. The gamblers were white, and many were southerners who had migrated to California and often traveled back and forth to Las Vegas for entertainment. The historian Eugene Moehring suggests that "these tourists increasingly expected southern Nevada to mirror the Jim Crow atmosphere of not only Dixie but the rest of the nation."[16] Las Vegas obliged them. Black entertainers were not allowed to stay in hotels where they performed. Casinos prohibited blacks from casino floors except to clean them. Most restaurants did not serve African Americans. This economically induced racism spread beyond the strip. Home loans were not extended to blacks by lending institutions. Movie theaters separated blacks from whites. And business licenses of black establishments were not renewed unless the business owner located in or relocated to the Westside. These discriminatory policies forced blacks to patronize Jackson Street businesses. The racial confinement isolated blacks and restricted their involvement in citywide revenue-producing enterprises and also prevented their participation in the city's image-building activities.

Racist practices infiltrated citywide image-building efforts as the casino building boom escalated. The showgirls that were used to sell Las Vegas to tourists were beautiful, unencumbered, and the epitome of sexuality and femininity. The Flamingo, constructed by Benjamin "Bugsy" Siegel, a known mob figure, set the pattern for glamour and customer relations for the casinos that attracted high rollers, the gamblers who spend thousands of dollars during each visit to the gaming mecca. Black artists could entertain these vacationers but not mingle among them. All-white showgirls and dancers "dressed" or "decorated" the casino as part of their employment duties. Black women would have been out of place in this capacity, therefore, they were left out of these higher-salaried glamorous positions. Even when the Flamingo hired Anna Bailey as the first black dancer in the 1960s, she was not allowed to join her fellow dancers in the entertainment of wealthy customers.[17]

Black women were spared the negative sexual connotations of some of these entertainment careers because they were not seen as feminine. Instead, they performed the backbreaking work of domestics, a job classification determined by the color of their skin. Dark skin stretched over tired bodies was not sexy, glamorous, or feminine. But they turned their work into honorable labor and gained respect for it through their labor union activism.

Within two decades nineteen major gaming properties rose in the Las Vegas desert, each demanding scores of maids.[18] The demand was so great that it was not necessary for black women to engage in lengthy job searches. Lucille Bryant told of getting a job on her first day in Las Vegas:

> I got here on the fourth of October of 1953. My cousin, Gladys, was going to the Algiers Hotel when I got here that morning to quit her job because she had found a better one. So she said, "you want to go with me?" I said, "yes." We got there and I asked the housekeeper "do you want someone to work today?" She said "yes" and took me upstairs to show me the rooms and what had to be done. When that lady left the room I got on my knees and gave God thanks, "eight dollars a day and working in the shade!"[19]

Two important facts emerge from this illustration: migrant women changed jobs whenever they found an equal position that was more attractive, and they enjoyed upward mobility. The housekeeper who hired Bryant, a migrant from Tallulah, was Owcida Brooks, a woman who had migrated from Fordyce in 1942. I call this strategy of constant movement "employment gyration." Women improved their working conditions by moving in a vertical or parallel direction within and among housekeeping departments. The entity that made this movement possible was the Culinary Workers Union, Local 226. Black women used the labor shortage in the hotels to improve their lot. They moved from hotel to hotel or gained promotion from maid to inspectress to executive housekeeper.[20]

Examples of employment gyration abound. When Bryant left the Algiers Hotel, she moved to the Silver Slipper as a ladies' room attendant for a short time, then to the Sands for a few weeks, and later to the Stardust for thirty-one years as a supervisor in the uniform room. Viola Johnson worked at the Flamingo briefly and moved to the Sands, where she worked for nine years. She ended her career as a maid after working for fourteen years at the Hilton. After retirement, she continued to work as a server for large parties, which she discovered she liked better than housekeeping work.[21] Corine Tisdale spent her entire career at the Sahara and the Mint, which had the same owner. She was the first black inspectress at the Sahara.[22] Ida Webb worked at the El Rancho, the Last Frontier, and the Flamingo. She started as a dishwasher earning $5 per shift. Her first paycheck, $100, was the largest amount of money she had ever seen. She moved into the pantry where all the sandwiches were made and became one of the fastest workers. When the chef at the Last Frontier went to the Flamingo, he took Webb with him.[23] Alma Whitney started working at the Desert Moon Motel. In 1952 she moved to the Desert Inn and was promoted to inspectress in 1966; she remained at the Desert Inn for thirty-five years.[24] Coleen Wilson worked for the Stardust for a few years, left there to become a maid when the Circus Circus Hotel opened in 1971, and was promoted to inspectress after one year.[25] These women gained confidence, attained a level of employment flexibility, and asserted control over their work environment.

One reason for their workplace power was their membership in the Culinary Workers Union, Local 226. Several migrants saw the union as much more than a vehicle for on-the-job advancement; it also provided more negotiating strength. When Hattie Canty, current union president, served as a union agent while working as a maid, she urged women to attend meetings and walk picket lines to increase the number of hotel casinos where they could seek employment.[26]

Employment mobility allowed Canty to make significant choices in her career trajectory. She migrated to Las Vegas from rural Alabama in 1961 after several years in southern California. Her husband supported their family of ten children by working in the construction industry and later in trucking. Canty worked one year at the Thunderbird Hotel, quit, and toiled as a homemaker until 1975 when her husband became ill and died. She returned to work and supported the family by again working as a maid. She worked at the Maxim Hotel and Casino, where she soon moved up to a job in the uniform room. During her twelve years there, she got involved in the Culinary Union by walking picket lines wherever protesters were needed and then by seeking elected office. In 1990 she became the first woman president of Local 226.[27]

Canty, along with Rachel Coleman, epitomized the combined process of employment gyration and participation in the Culinary Workers Union, Local 226. Coleman migrated from Vicksburg, Mississippi, in 1957 at the age of twenty. Unlike most women, Coleman did not go to work immediately but spent the first year as a stay-at-home mother for her six-month-old son. The following year she began to work as a glass washer at the Tropicana earning $5 per day. After $8 a week in Vicksburg, "I thought I was in heaven," she recalled. Soon, though, Coleman discovered that she did not like the hotel kitchen. In 1959 she found that maid's work suited her better and went to work at the Hacienda. Within four years Coleman had reached the top level in house-keeping, was bored with the work, and began to seek something different. Over the years of her hotel employment, she had gotten to know the Culinary Union representatives, Sarah Hughes and Earnestine Howard. Both of these black women had encouraged her to work for the union hall. When Coleman finally decided to give the suggestion a try, she marched into the office of Al Bramlet, secretary-treasurer of the union, and without any formalities declared, "I want to be a union representative." A few days later, Hughes called her and said, "Al said you got guts so he's going to hire you." Hughes trained her to be a repre-sentative, and she was soon assigned to work on behalf of housekeeping depart-ments in eighteen hotels. She remained as business agent from 1973 to 1981, when she was promoted to department head with duties that involved the supervision of fifteen representatives and handling the employee grievance process.[28] The career that Coleman carved out for herself took her to the highest level in housekeeping and near the top of the local union structure.

By the early 1950s the Culinary Union was well established in Las Vegas. It represented 169 job titles.[29] The union provided women with a vehicle to attain status. Although domestic jobs were stigmatized, the inferiority dissipated to some extent when the positions began to reward workers with good wages and benefits. As Rachel Coleman described maid service in Las Vegas, "When wages became substantial, white, Asian, and Mexican women entered the back-of-the-house."[30] Before this, though, the domestic segment of the industry was dominated by black women who joined the Culinary Workers Union, Local 226, with enthusiasm and with the support of the black community.

Labor union strength lay in large membership rolls that allowed effective negotiation and loud protest to secure and maintain a dynamic benefits package for workers. Blacks had been denied the opportunity to participate and share in this process. The Culinary Workers Union, Local 226, changed that experience for women in housekeeping departments in the Las Vegas gaming industry.

Blacks who migrated from Fordyce and Tallulah had little or no previous experience with organized labor, nor, for that matter, did most Las Vegans. The Culinary Workers Union leader, Al Bramlet, arrived in Las Vegas in 1946 and worked as a dishwasher. Local 226 was not chartered until 1948. Bramlet became secretary-treasurer in 1954.[31] His reputation for fairness in his dealings with members encouraged union growth until his death in 1977. Black migrants and union members described him favorably. Bryant referred to him as "the Great White Father" and Coleman stated, "You can never say enough about Al. He was fair. He always thought of the employees and he was just a fair man."[32] Contracts negotiated by the Culinary Union included adequate wages, paid holidays and vacations, sick leave, accident and life insurance, disability, medical insurance, unemployment compensation, college scholarships for members' children, and retirement income. Moreover, the union administered the Collective Bargaining Agreement that protected workers' rights by resolving on-the-job problems.[33] The union's organizational structure allowed for the professional handling of contract negotiations that determined whether local 226 would be accepted into each new hotel and be allowed to remain in existing ones.

But was there more that the union should have and could have done? Earnestine Howard, Sarah Hughes, Rachel Coleman, and Hattie Canty executed managerial responsibilities in the union but not in the gaming industry. Thus the Culinary Union recognized talent and promoted from within its ranks of talented domestic workers. Why, then, with such obvious talent, did the union neglect to send black women to apply for jobs as cocktail waitresses, slot carousel attendants, and food servers? The Culinary Union moved too slowly against the occupational guidelines imposed by the accepted, race-based standard of beauty.

As the civil rights movement exploded nightly on national television in the early 1960s, the Culinary Workers Union took a step to put an African American into a visible position in the casino industry. The president of the local National Association for the Advancement of Colored People (NAACP) branch, James McMillan, the first black dentist in Las Vegas, wrote a letter to Mayor Oran Gragson on March 11, 1960, threatening massive street protests if downtown and strip business did not end discriminatory practices by March 26. An agreement was not reached until the morning of the twenty-sixth when black and white community leaders met in the coffee shop of the Moulin Rouge Hotel Casino and decided that employment segregation would end in Las Vegas on that day at 6:00 P.M.[34]

Immediately, the Culinary Union initiated a plan to elevate black employees. But first a perfect candidate had to be located. D. D. Cotton became that person. Cotton, a dancer, migrated to Las Vegas in 1957. She danced in the line at the Carver House on the Westside and worked as a dealer, keno writer, and cocktail waitress at several Jackson Street locations. In 1966 she was hired as one of the first black cocktail waitresses for the opening of Caesar's Palace.[35] One of the most interesting periods of Cotton's career was when the Culinary Union attempted to secure positions for black women other than those in housekeeping.

Cotton joined the union and agreed to be used as a "guinea pig" to test the possibility of blacks working in a traditionally "white" job. Sarah Hughes knew Cotton and thought she would be the perfect candidate for this experiment. Cotton was sent to "every place in town" seeking employment. Finally, she was hired at the Nevada Club as a cocktail waitress in the slot machine area. Soon she grabbed the chance to work in the pit area where tips were more lucrative. She worked there until the opening of Caesar's Palace.[36]

Though the Culinary Union began to seek jobs for black women other than those in the back of the house, their progress was not rapid enough. The above action was too little, too late. The NAACP demanded an immediate fair share of nonmenial jobs for blacks. But job discrimination, one of the most debilitating effects of economic racism, continued even after the passage in March 1965 of Nevada Assembly Bill 404 outlawing discrimination on the basis of race, color, or creed in statewide public accommodations and employment. It continued after a series of meetings between black community leaders and representatives of the white power structure. It even continued after peaceful protests and violent demonstrations. Finally it ended on June 4, 1971, after a five-year battle that began in 1967 when local NAACP president, attorney Charles Kellar, filed a complaint in U.S. Federal District Court against the local Culinary Union, the Teamsters Union, and seventeen hotels that included Caesar's Palace, the Flamingo, Riviera, and the Sahara, among others.[37] Kellar initiated this action after going to the media when negotiations with the unions did not yield the fruits that he expected. He threatened "to cut the union down to size."[38] The decree spelled out what he meant by that statement:

[The unions and hotels named] shall hire and assign applicants for employment and shall promote, transfer, train, demote, and dismiss employees without regard to race and without engaging in any act or practice which has the purpose of the effect of discriminating against any individual because of his race or color in regards to his employment opportunities and shall promote and transfer employees in such a way as to provide employment opportunities to black persons which are equal to those provided to white persons.[39]

Blacks did not fit the industry's moneymaking profile. The image of black women was enmeshed in their identification with jobs in domestic work. As the historian Jacqueline Jones has shown in *Labor of Love, Labor of Sorrow*, African American women secured jobs in a "limited number of occupations clustered at the bottom of the wage scale during and after slavery. Domestic services performed for non-family members for only nominal pay became traditional black women's work."[40] Women's historians have long posed the following conundrum: is housework devalued because women do it, or are women assigned to housework because it is devalued labor? Maybe this riddle should be changed from "women" to "black women."

African American women domestics were viewed negatively from a national standpoint. Even the popular black publication *Ebony* was "not interested in mirroring traditional black women's occupational patterns in their magazine. Their purpose was to counter the image of black women as domestic drudges and to emphasize their potential for work that was better paying and more challenging and prestigious."[41] The local Culinary Union, however, challenged this middle-class bias by erasing some of the harsh stigma attached to the traditional work of black women. Consequently, the Las Vegas black community emphasized the positive aspects of unionized housekeeping by redefining the back-of-the-house as "honorable."

The generation of black women who migrated to cities for work in the pre–civil rights era could not move beyond a working-class status. By virtue of their education and job skills, they were permanently there. What does class mean when multiplied by race and then multiplied by gender? The scholar Deborah K. King has issued the caveat that race, gender, and class are not additive, having only a single, direct, and independent effect on status, but are actually three interdependent control systems. It is rather a "multiple" or a multicative relationship among them, resulting in the equation "racism *x* sexism *x* classism."[42] Thus black women in Las Vegas, even when represented by a powerful labor union, in a setting of economic racism, lacked the financial and political power necessary to defeat segregated housing, an inadequate neighborhood infrastructure that included unpaved streets and an inferior sewage system, and a segmented labor market. The Culinary Workers Union, Local 226, working alone did not have the leverage to change a system of behavior allowed to permeate the entire country. But it exerted the power that allowed freedom of movement within a limited employment space, decent wages, and a sense of rare dignity in this sphere of traditional black women's work. Las Vegas elevated black women's work to a level beyond that of other cities and eventually integrated them into other segments of the industry.

NOTES

1. Lucille Bryant, Interview by Claytee D. White, December 13, 1995, Women in Gaming and Entertainment Oral History Project, Las Vegas, Nevada.

2. Jean Norton, "Folks from Fordyce: Two Southern Towns Hold Roots for most LV Blacks," *Nevadan*, February 3, 1985, 12L. Norton was the associate producer of the PBS documentary, "Road to Las Vegas: A Black Perspective," which was funded by the Nevada Humanities Committee, Arkansas Endowment for the Humanities, and the Louisiana Committee for the Humanities.

3. A casino porter cleans the area around slot machines.

4. Eugene P. Moehring, *Resort City in the Sunbelt: Las Vegas, 1930–1970* (Las Vegas: University of Nevada Press, 1989), 175, 184.

5. Jacqueline Jones, *Labor of Love, Labor of Sorrow: Black Women, Work, and the Family from Slavery to the Present* (New York: Vintage Books, 1986), 236.

6. Essie Jacobs, Interview by Claytee D. White, February 1, 1996, Women in Gaming and Entertainment Oral History Project.

7. Hazel Gay, Interview by Claytee D. White, December 2, 1995, Women in Gaming and Entertainment Oral History Project. Jimmy Gay became the first black licensed embalmer in Nevada.

8. Jacobs interview.

9. Inez Harper, Interview by Claytee D. White, May 16, 1996, Women in Gaming and Entertainment Oral History Project.

10. Richard W. Mingus, a graduate student in the University of Nevada, Las Vegas, history department, discovered that the Congress of Industrial Organizations (CIO) recognized the need for a biracial workforce and also sent recruiters into the South. See Mingus, "Breakdown in the Broker State: The CIO in Southern Nevada During World War II" (M.A. thesis, University of Nevada at Las Vegas, 1995), 17, 42. Hazel Gay, Inez Harper, Viola Johnson, Bubba Simmons, Ida Webb, and other interviewees recalled that these agents were from the BMI facility.

11. Bryant interview.

12. The historian Douglas Henry Daniels, known for his research on nineteenth-century African American migration to San Francisco, has described the "art of travelcraft."

"Travelcraft" designates the outlook and complex of skills that facilitated long-distance travel by migrants moving to strange destinations. See Daniels, "Travelcraft and Black Pioneer Urbanites, 1850s–1870s," in *Peoples of Color in the American West*, ed. Sucheng Chan, Douglas Henry Daniels, Mario T. García, and Terry P. Wilson (Lexington, Mass.: D. C. Heath, 1994), 117–19.

13. Alma Whitney, Interview by Claytee D. White, May 28, 1996, Women in Gaming and Entertainment Oral History Project.

14. Viola Johnson, Interview by Claytee D. White, March 12, 1996, Women in Gaming and Entertainment Oral History Project.

15. Juanita and Bubba Simmons, Interview by Claytee D. White, May 21, 1996, Women in Gaming and Entertainment Oral History Project.

16. Moehring, *City in the Sunbelt*, 175.

17. Anna Bailey, Interview by Claytee D. White, March 3, 1997, Women in Gaming and Entertainment Project.

18. Eugene Moehring lists the development of casinos in Las Vegas as El Rancho Vegas and El Cortez (1941), Hotel Last Frontier (1942), Golden Nugget (1945), Flamingo (1946–47), Thunderbird (1948), Desert Inn (1950), Horseshoe (1951), Sands (1952), Sahara (1952), Showboat (1954), Dunes, Rivera, Royal Nevada, Moulin Rouge (1955), Hacienda and Fremont (1956), Tropicana (1957), Stardust (1958). From a list compiled by Eugene Moehring, Department of History, University of Nevada at Las Vegas.

19. Bryant interview.

20. The job hierarchy is maid, inspectress (this term was used by everyone interviewed), and housekeeper. "Housekeeper" and "executive housekeeper" are used interchangeably.

21. Bryant interview; Johnson interview.

22. Corinne Tisdale, Interview by Claytee D. White, May 28, 1996, Women in Gaming and Entertainment Oral History Project.

23. Ida Webb, Interview by Claytee D. White, February 6, 1996, Women in Gaming and Entertainment Oral History Project.

24. Whitney interview.

25. Coleen Wilson, Interview by Claytee D. White, June 4, 1996, Women in Gaming and Entertainment Oral History Project.

26. An agent, in this instance, is the same as a shop steward. Hattie Canty, Interview by Claytee D. White, February 27, 1998, Women in Gaming and Entertainment Oral History Project.

27. Clara Mosle, "How the Maids Fought Back," *New Yorker*, February 26 and March 4, 1996, 148–56; and Canty interview.

28. Rachel Coleman, Interview by Claytee D. White, July 24, 1996, Women in Gaming and Entertainment Oral History Project.

29. Vincent H. Eade, "Grievance and Arbitration Trends within the Culinary Workers Union, Local 226," *Labor Studies Journal* 18 (Spring 1993): 23.

30. Coleman interview.

31. Siti Zabedah Amri and April Leilani Aloiau, "Labor-Union Training Workshop," Las Vegas, unpublished ms., December 1, 1994, 3.

32. Bryant interview; Coleman interview.

33. Kim Beach, "Hotel Employees and Restaurant Employees, International Union Culinary Local 226," unpublished ms., copy in author's possession, June 30, 1993.

34. Moehring, *Resort City in the Sunbelt*, 184; and Alan Jarlson, "Color Barrier Lifted after Parley," *Las Vegas Sun*, March 26, 1960, p. A1. A group of black community activists tested this agreement that same evening. The Moulin Rouge, constructed in 1955, was the first integrated gaming establishment after the war. All hotels complied except for the Sal Sagev. Information given by a participant in the test, David Hoggard Sr. David Hoggard Sr., Interview by Claytee D. White, November 12, 1997, Women in Gaming and Entertainment Oral History Project.

35. D. D. Cotton, Interview by Claytee D. White, February 14, 1997, Women in Gaming and Entertainment Oral History Project. Two African American women were hired as cocktail waitresses for the opening of Caesar's Palace. Peggy Walker was the second one and is still employed there in that capacity.

36. Cotton interview.

37. Moehring, *City in the Sunbelt*, 199.

38. Ibid., 189.

39. *United States of America v. Nevada Resort Association* et. al., consent decree LV 1645 (1971).

40. Jones, *Labor of Love*, 74.

41. Ibid., 272.

42. Deborah K. King, "Multiple Jeopardy Consciousness: The Context of a Black Feminist Ideology" in *Words of Fire: An Anthology of African-American Feminist Thought*, ed. Beverly Guy-Sheftall (New York: New Press, 1995), 297.

The Civil Rights Era

CHAPTER 15

Lulu B. White and the Integration of the University of Texas, 1945–1950

Merline Pitre

Until the 1960s the chronicle of the American West was presented as one almost totally dominated by white males. Not only did this portrait exclude a large segment of the male population of this region of the country, but it completely ignored women. Yet new research reveals the lives and contribution of people of color and demonstrates that women figured prominently in the annals of the American West. Lulu Belle Madison White is one such woman. Civil rights activist, educator, orator, White was the first woman of the South and Southwest to become a full-time salaried executive secretary of a local chapter of the National Association for the Advancement of Colored People (NAACP). White worked all of her life to destroy the Jim Crow system of segregation and disfranchisement in Texas and throughout the United States. Unafraid of speaking her mind to powerful whites and differing black factions, Lulu White combined political radicalism with administrative skills to effect change. When these techniques did not work, she became openly defiant. To many, she was exactly what the doctor ordered for the NAACP and the civil rights movement in Texas in the 1940s and 1950s.

Lulu Madison White was born the tenth of twelve children in Elmo, Texas, in September 1900 to Easter Madison, a domestic worker, and Henry Madison, a landowning farmer. Elmo, a small, predominantly black community in

Kaufman County, is situated six miles from the nearest town of Terrell and thirty-four miles north of Dallas. It is in East Texas, a region of the state noted for its segregationist laws and customs. As Lulu White grew to maturity, East Texas was a risky place for African Americans. By all accounts, the potential for danger was never far from the minds of blacks. In the decades following the Civil War, many white East Texans stubbornly harbored antiblack attitudes that were extreme even by white supremacist standards of the rest of Texas. As such, they developed a unique form of racial intimidation called whitecapping, which, loosely defined, meant warning shots, whippings, and property destruction. When whitecapping proved ineffective, many whites resorted to lynching, giving that region of Texas the distinction of being one of the worst areas of racial violence in the nation at the turn of the century.[1]

Lulu White's parents did their best to shield their children from racism and often taught them to find ways around segregation. Henry Madison impressed on his children: "Get an education, for the man who beat[s] you thinking will always be your boss." Never taught to think or act like a second-class citizen, both as a child and a young adult, Lulu felt secure in her identity and her abilities. She could think and talk fast on her feet and was not afraid of anyone. Likewise, she was confident, made friends easily, and could put anyone at ease or cut them down to size in a flash, traits that served her well in school, in coping with Jim Crow, and in her later leadership roles.[2]

White received her elementary and secondary school training in the public schools of Elmo and Terrell, Texas. When she graduated from Old Terrell Colored High, she moved to Fort Worth, Texas, in search of a good job and a better life. Her stay in that city was short lived. Encounters with Jim Crow in the workplace soon persuaded her to accept her father's advice to acquire a sound education. In 1923 Lulu enrolled at Butler College in Tyler, Texas, and soon transferred to Prairie View College in Hempstead, Texas.[3]

On receiving her bachelor's degree in English in 1928, Lulu married Julius White, a prominent Houston businessman and long-standing member of the NAACP who been the plaintiff in several voting rights cases. Denied employment in the Houston Independent School District because of her husband's civil rights activities, White took a job in Lufkin, Texas, where she taught English and physical education.[4] After nine years, she resigned her post and became a full-time activist with the NAACP in black Texans' struggle to overturn the state statute that excluded them from the all-white Democratic primary. Since Texas was a one-party state, winning in the Democratic primary was tantamount to winning in the general election. To be excluded from the Democratic Party was, in effect, to be disenfranchised.

White's political activism began while she was a student at Prairie View, where she became involved in virtually every movement for social change on campus. The social and economic reforms she advocated mirrored those of the NAACP. "We all agree," wrote White, "that the National Association for the Advancement of Colored People is the only weapon that the Negroes have to fight for their rights as citizens in this great city, state and country."[5] Using this philosophy as her guide, White served the Texas NAACP in several capacities during its involvement in the civil rights struggle in 1940s and 1950s. In 1937 she was a field-worker and director of the Youth Council. Two years later when the national office of the NAACP investigated the Houston branch for fiscal improprieties, Lulu White became the acting president of the chapter. Elevated to the post of executive secretary in 1943, she was at the helm of the Houston chapter when one year later the U.S. Supreme Court struck down the white primary statute in *Smith v. Allwright.*

Combining her previous position as field-worker with that of executive secretary, White traveled throughout the state, garnering contributions, organizing new branches, and reactivating old ones.[6] Her aggressiveness and two-hundred-fifty-pound body commanded respect. Determined to live up to her reputation as a sharp-tongued radical, White developed an outspoken, almost deliberately provocative style. She publicly advocated the right of African American Texans to vote and to participate at all levels of government while simultaneously pushing for equal access to jobs and education. Throughout her career with the NAACP, White held fast to the philosophy that the integration of blacks into white society and its institutions was the only means by which African Americans could achieve racial parity. Her uncompromising insistence on integration set her apart from many blacks in Houston and Texas. Nowhere was this position better evidenced than in the fight White waged with Carter Wesley over the integration of the University of Texas.

Indeed, the feud between Lulu Belle White, executive secretary of the Houston NAACP, and Carter W. Wesley, editor of the *Houston Informer*, occurred in part because of their personalities and philosophies and in part because of the political context out of which each individual emerged. For example, Wesley's commitment to social justice was forged from personal experiences. Born in Houston in 1892, Wesley graduated from the public schools of the city, attended Fisk University, and became one of the first black officers in the U.S. military during World War I. On his return, he earned a doctorate in jurisprudence from Northwestern University. After four years of legal practice in Oklahoma, Wesley returned to Houston in 1927. Finding his legal practice in Texas limited because of his race, he became a businessman and bought into the newly formed publishing company that owned the *Informer*, Houston's largest black newspaper. Wesley used the paper as a weapon against racism and as a podium to become the spokesman for his people.[7]

Gaining control of the *Informer*'s parent company in 1934, Wesley publicized the battle against the white Democratic primary. The paper became Wesley's platform from which to encourage black women and men to fight for equal rights. For Wesley, any endeavor that improved the political, economic, and social conditions of black Texans was consistent with the struggle for equality. Thus Wesley, unlike White, saw no contradiction in championing the establishment of a separate black state university while pushing for the integration of the University of Texas.[8]

Desegregation of the University of Texas had been a chief objective of the Texas NAACP since its establishment in 1937. But only after successfully proving itself in campaigning against the all-white Democratic primary in 1944 did the Texas NAACP decide to launch a crusade for equal access to public colleges and universities. In June 1945 the NAACP announced it would challenge segregated public professional education in Texas. The state's immediate response to this challenge was the passage of Senate Bill 228, which changed the name of Prairie View State Normal and Industrial College to Prairie View State University. In addition, it authorized the Texas A&M Board of Directors to provide Prairie View students, on demand, with training in law, medicine, engineering, pharmacy, journalism, and any other courses taught at the University of Texas.[9] The state's action was taken to prevent racial integration at the University of Texas.

Shortly after the NAACP announced its decision to legally challenge the dual system of education in the state, Carter Wesley founded the Southern Negro Conference for the Equalization of Education. The conference denounced the segregated school system but, in stark opposition to the state NAACP, said nothing about integration. The Southern Negro Conference grew out of the Southern Regional Council, a group of African American moderates who met in Durham, North Carolina, in October 1942 to discuss World War II and its effects on race relations. This group included college presidents, school principals, publishers, businesspeople, doctors, and social workers and met to affirm loyalty to the Allies' war policies while maintaining that this loyalty

should not distract African American organizations from tackling the problems of poverty, educational inequity, and disfranchisement. Although it was
fundamentally opposed to compulsory segregation, the council believed it was
more sensible and timely to attack the problems stemming from racial discrimination. This position, shared by Wesley, would become the main area of
conflict between the *Informer*'s editor and the executive secretary of the
Houston NAACP.[10]

Whatever the tactical wisdom of establishing the Southern Negro Conference for Equalization of Education, Lulu White and the Texas NAACP sharply
rebuked Wesley's organization for its failure to confront segregation. White
challenged the "separate but equal" alternative embraced by the conference to
bring black schools up to parity with white institutions while allowing them
to remain separate. The fact that segregation was a violation of the Constitution made it awkward, in her mind, to pursue true equality in separate but
equal schools. She believed that Wesley was naive in his acceptance of some
form of equal opportunity under the current segregation law. White could see
no equality in segregation.[11]

To disarm critics who suspected that the conference supported segregation,
Wesley insisted in 1945 that the group would cooperate with the NAACP. Thurgood Marshall, legal counsel for the national NAACP, agreed to this brief organizational alliance. Wesley called for the NAACP to coordinate all court cases
involving higher education and proposed that Marshall, in return, defend the
Southern Negro Conference when necessary. In keeping with his promise to
work cooperatively with the NAACP, Wesley provided substantial publicity in
his newspaper about the anticipated lawsuit against the University of Texas.
And when the NAACP had not found a plaintiff by September 1945, Marshall
asked Wesley for advice. The two, along with A. Maceo Smith, executive secretary of the Texas State Conference of NAACP Branches, wrestled with the
problem of finding the right person for the case after dismissing five prospective plaintiffs. Then, in October, Lulu White wrote Thurgood Marshall: "I think
I have a plaintiff for the Education Case." He was Heman Marion Sweatt, a
thirty-three-year-old Houstonian with a B.S. degree from Wiley College who
was employed part time on the *Informer* staff and full time by the post office.[12]

Sweatt had already considered attending the University of Texas, but he did
not make his position known until he heard Lulu White appealing to the audience at a meeting for a volunteer to serve as plaintiff in a lawsuit against the
university. While he called it a "brash decision," Sweatt's resolution to become
a plaintiff had a great deal to do with the discrimination he had experienced

at the Houston post office as well as his family's friendship with Lulu White. Before Sweatt could have second thoughts about becoming a plaintiff, Smith and William J. Durham, resident counsel for the Texas NAACP, encouraged him to file an application for admission to the University of Texas Law School immediately. Sweatt told them that he could not do so until he had consulted with Carter Wesley, his employer. Wesley approved the idea, assuring Sweatt that a job was always waiting for him after necessary court absences.[13]

Urged on by the NAACP and accompanied by Lulu White and other supporters, Herman Sweatt attempted to register at the University of Texas on February 26, 1946. After a discussion with university president Theophilus Painter and other campus officials, Sweatt left his application at the campus and returned to Houston, hoping for a quick answer. During his stay on campus, Sweatt made no mention of his plan to file a lawsuit, but the much-publicized intention of the NAACP caused university officials to realize that one was in the making. It is not surprising that when writing Attorney General Grover Sellers for an opinion on Sweatt's application, Painter explained, "This is to be a test case on the question of admission of Negro students in higher education of the state. . . . This applicant is duly qualified for admission to the Law School, save and except for the fact that he is a Negro. {Please advise}." Sellers's ruling came on March 16, 1946. He upheld the laws of Texas that stated, "No African or persons of African descent should be admitted to the University of Texas." Adding insult to injury, Sellers concluded that Sweatt could apply for legal training at Prairie View since Senate Bill 228 had made it a university (on paper) in 1945.[14]

Attorney General Sellers's response signaled the beginning of a concerted legal campaign to end segregated education in Texas. It also exposed divisions in the state's African American leadership over racial integration. Shortly after Sellers issued his opinion, A. Maceo Smith wrote Wesley that the Sweatt case should be pursued, but "realism dictates that a special university is about all we are going to get. . . . [T]he Texas Council of Negro Organizations is the appropriate agency such as that should prepare for negotiation when the time arises." Wesley countered that "mule" caution should be taken in accepting such an alternative. "The seeming advantage," he reasoned, "that we might have in putting them on the spot might trap us."[15]

After Sweatt sued university officials on May 16, 1946, for denial of admission, Dudley K. Woodward Jr., chair of the University of Texas Board of Regents, called for the creation of a more comprehensive state-supported black university. Shortly afterward, Governor Coke Stevenson created a biracial committee to make recommendations to him that could be presented to the legislature as soon as possible. The committee arranged to meet to hear the views of African Americans in the state on the proposed institution. When Lulu White heard about the committee, she wrote to Thurgood Marshall that state officials had planned to establish a separate black university, warning, "There is a possibility that the present Houston College for Negroes will be used as the nucleus around which the Negro University will be built."[16]

Realizing that such a meeting with the governor's biracial committee might result in a fiasco unless blacks quickly reached consensus, Smith, on August 3, 1946, called together ninety-six African American leaders throughout the state to chart a uniform course of action. Eighty-three of the leaders present agreed that they should rest their case on Article 7, Section 14, of the Texas State Constitution, which stated that "the Legislature shall also, when deemed practical, establish and provide for the maintenance of a college branch university for the instruction of colored youths of the state." Blacks interpreted Section 14 to mean that such a university would share in the endowment fund of the University of Texas but would not preclude the right of blacks to enter the University of Texas. At the conclusion of this meeting, Carter Wesley and Joseph J. Rhoads, president of Bishop College, were selected to present the views of the black leadership to the biracial committee. When Wesley and Rhoads made their presentation on August 8, 1946, their demands went further than Governor Stevenson and his cohorts had expected. The two black leaders agreed to support the NAACP in the Sweatt case but also demanded that a black university be established that would share equally in an endowment fund with the University of Texas. Further, they made it clear that they had no interest in a legislative arrangement by which a makeshift university would be established.[17]

Responding to this group, University of Texas president Theophilus Painter asserted that a black university would be established. In an attempt to head off integration of other professional areas, Painter told his audience that this university should be located in Houston, not only because of the state's offer to fund Houston College for Negroes, but also because the city's two black hospitals would enable the black university to establish its own medical school. In a heated debate, Lulu White attacked Painter's statement as an insult to black people. She pointed out that the hospitals referred to were separate and unequal; one of them, Jefferson Davis, had refused to treat black patients. Painter's suggestion, she charged, was simply a ploy to prevent blacks from attending the University of Texas.[18]

Always skeptical of Wesley's Southern Negro Conference for Equalization of Education, Lulu White became incensed when on September 3, 1946, she discovered that Wesley had written a letter to the Texas Council on Negro Organizations and other black groups in the state inviting them to form a new organization to demand equality in segregation, that is, to accept Painter's position. Wesley called this group the Texas Negro Conference for Equalization of Education. White's feeling soon turned to bitterness when she discovered that the list of names Wesley used to form his new organization came from the NAACP's membership list.[19]

Writing to national NAACP executive secretary Walter White, Lulu White opposed this new group because, in her opinion, "when such an organization takes the members of the same organization that is fighting Jim Crow and [now asks them to maintain segregation], such an organization could only cloud the issue." She argued that if blacks wanted to establish a university under the present structure of segregation, they should join the Texas Council of Negro Organizations, a group already charged with pursuing that goal. She could not see how Smith had allowed himself to be used in supporting such a group. Later White speculated that this new organization was racist in nature. Writing Walter White again, she minced no words: Smith and Wesley "didn't want any white members. They said this was a Negro fight and we must have a Negro organization."[20]

The national NAACP supported Lulu White. In August 1945 Thurgood Marshall warned both Wesley and Smith against allowing the Southern Negro Conference and the NAACP to duplicate each other's efforts. One year later Wesley found himself coming under increasing attacks from Lulu White for his use of the NAACP's mailing list to establish the Texas Conference for Equalization of Education. In more forceful language than he had used previously, Marshall cautioned Wesley about the activities of this new organization, telling him "not to ask for something he found undesirable—segregation." Perturbed over Marshall's letter, Wesley answered in a scathing four-page rebuttal that he copied to all black leaders in Texas. Marshall responded in kind, and the battle was on between the two civil rights leaders, with Lulu White providing the national NAACP office with much of the ammunition.[21]

Once the educational struggle took center stage in Texas and the issue of integration versus separation became the focus of attention, neither Wesley nor White seemed interested in the other's view. This became clear in the first of a series of Wesley's *Informer* editorials that appeared on December 28, 1946. Wesley lambasted White's intransigence that made it impossible to use any other approach to eradicate inequity in education save for integration. The editor maintained that the education fight in Texas should be waged by the Texas Conference of Equalization of Education, the Texas Council of Negro Organizations, and the NAACP. He argued that the framework in which the state operated made it possible for blacks to integrate the University of Texas and gain a state-supported black university.[22]

Wesley also made unsubstantiated allegations against White that caused her to resign from the Houston branch of the NAACP. The editor claimed White was a Communist, that the NAACP wanted a monopoly on racial issues, and that White caused internal strife within the Texas leadership. Of the allegations, the last carried the most weight. In her letter of resignation, White stated, "If something could be done to prove . . . that I had not caused internal strife, I would stay on." Something was done. The Houston branch refused to accept her resignation and instead gave her a vote of confidence. White stayed on with the blessings of Thurgood Marshall, who wrote to her, "I have been accused of giving comfort to you in your stand against segregation. I think you are absolutely right." Subsequently, Carter Wesley severed all of his affiliations with the NAACP—the Houston branch, the state conference of branches, and the national organization.[23]

Meanwhile, the legal battle over the integration of the University of Texas continued. On February 28, 1947, in a maneuver to counter Heman Sweatt's lawsuit, the Board of Regents of the University of Texas established an interim black law school at 104 East 13th Street in Austin, in the basement of a building leased from a petroleum firm. At the time, only one student was enrolled at the interim law school. So, to safeguard the sanctity of segregation, on March 3, 1947, the legislature passed Senate Bill 140, providing for the "establishment of a three-million-dollar Negro University, including a law school to be located in Houston." The passage of this bill was made easier because Houston College for Negroes, then under the supervision of the University of Houston, was experiencing financial problems. When the state of Texas made an offer to purchase the institution, those in charge responded affirmatively. With the passage of House Bill 780, the fifty-three-acre site was purchased from the University of Houston and Texas State University for Negroes (TSUN; later named Texas Southern University) became a fait accompli.[24]

To ensure that TSUN would serve as a bulwark against segregation, Texas attorney general Price Daniel served as temporary chairman of the university during the organization of the nine-member Board of Regents. Among other things, he told the board that its duty was to convince black Texans that the state, through the establishment of Texas Southern, had fulfilled their desire for graduate and professional training. Sanctioning Daniel's remarks was future board chairman Craig Cullinan, who cautioned the group to be mindful of those (blacks) who were attempting to overthrow segregated education in Texas. When Lulu White learned of Cullinan's remarks, she wrote Gloster Current and told him that the "Board of Regents of the Negro University was told that their first duty was to get the subversive element [the NAACP] that divided the Negroes out of the state." She also told him "the Negro Regents took their oath of office with the understanding that they were to work for harmony among Negroes by keeping them in their place."[25]

While Carter Wesley applauded the establishment of Texas State University for Negroes, Lulu White called for a demonstration against Senate Bill 140, insisting that the state had raised the stakes in maintaining Jim Crow schools. When Wesley pointed out that he embraced the black institution because he favored taking whatever the state had to "offer in the way of improved educa-tion," both Lulu White and Thurgood Marshall interpreted his stance as meaning he was no longer willing to pursue integration in the courts. This was not the case at all. Wesley never wavered in his support of the Sweatt case, which he viewed as the litmus test for the law that excluded blacks from state tax–supported professional schools in the absence of any semblance of equal but separate facilities. But Wesley's quarrel was with the approach, not the intent of the NAACP in seeking to make blacks first-class citizens and reaping the benefits thereof. The record is replete with examples of his efforts to achieve this goal.[26]

When Sweatt's hearing convened on May 5, 1947, Wesley was there. At this hearing, the state's counsel tried to prove that since the University of Texas's basement school provided for individualized instruction for blacks, in many ways it was equal to or better than the white law school. That argument was destroyed by Thurgood Marshall before a packed courtroom. Using a quanti-tative analysis to show the inequalities in the two schools, Marshall pointed to the differences in classroom space, library size, and books. As he continued to chip away at the state's case, one observer quipped, "Attorney General Price Daniel chewed two cigars." Despite what many considered brilliant arguments made by Marshall, the judge ruled in favor of the state, to the surprise of no one. For the next three years, as the Texas state government gave scant atten-tion to TSUN, the NAACP made plans to take their case to the Supreme Court. Meanwhile, the feud between Lulu White and Carter Wesley continued.[27]

A. Maceo Smith, negotiating between White and Wesley, called on the Houston NAACP executive secretary again on August 27, 1947, to embrace Wesley's new organization, saying, "The NAACP is part of the Texas State Conference for Equalization of Education." White stubbornly refused and accused Smith of "trying to make the NAACP a puppet organization." Writing in disgust to Thurgood Marshall, White declared, "We should let Maceo go to hell with Carter. (If Maceo and Carter are so concerned about equality in education, why don't they do something about Texas State University for Negroes?) I may be called dumb, but I cannot see equality in segregation, I hope I die just that dumb."[28]

Without a doubt, Lulu White held strong and well-developed views about the inequities of segregation. Wisdom born from experience had taught her that "separate but equal" was a contradiction in terms. Thus, in responding to Wesley's argument, she took the position of the NAACP that the only thing blacks could gain from attacking the state on inequality was a rash of Jim Crow schools and any attempt to sue for equality admitted the unconstitutionality of "separate but equal." More than anything else, White wanted to destroy the legal basis on which Jim Crow rested. Despite Wesley's assertion that "we put all whites against us when we attack segregation openly and practically," White took the opposite view. In her view, the vindication of constitutional rights involved in court cases such as Sweatt's warranted prompt relief. But any relief short of integrated schools and universities implied the continued deprivation of these rights.[29]

Texas State University for Negroes became the focal point in the Texas NAACP's frontal assault on segregation. In December 1947 Lulu White encouraged W. Astor Kirk, a black professor from Tillotson College, to apply for admission to the graduate program in political science at Texas State University for Negroes in order to test the state's commitment to equality in higher education. Kirk wanted to pursue a doctoral degree, but it was not long before he discovered that the black university had neither a professor to teach the courses nor the library staff to handle the program. Kirk then applied to the University of Texas but was denied admission and encouraged to seek graduate studies out of state. When he rejected this offer, the Board of Directors at the University of Texas entered into a contractual agreement with the Board of Regents at Texas State University for Negroes. Kirk was to register at the black university but to be instructed elsewhere by the white professors. The same arrangement had been made for Henry E. Doyle when he attended the

Negro University's basement law school in 1947. But unlike Doyle, who acquiesced to the state's demand, Kirk turned to Lulu White and the NAACP for
assistance and pursued his case in the courts.[30]

White students also aided in the planned attack on Jim Crow. In 1948 two
white students tried to enroll at TSUN. It is uncertain if the NAACP was
responsible for these students' actions. What is known, however, is that when
their applications reached the campus, they went to the offices of the Registrar, the President, and the Chairman of the Board of Regents before a decision was made. When Chairman Craig Cullinan read the applications, he
wasted no time in writing TSUN president, Raphael O'Hara Lanier, voicing
his opposition based on race. These students then sought the help of Lulu
White, who gleefully wrote Gloster Current, "We are raising hell down here on
the educational front."[31]

Throughout 1948 and 1949 Lulu White and Carter Wesley held fast to their
respective philosophies and approaches to the doctrine of "separate but equal,"
thereby fostering the growing hostility between them and mirroring the divisions in the African American community. In November 1949 Lulu White
reported that the NAACP could expect very little support from the Prairie View
alumni on the issue of the integration of the University of Texas. White's statement was predicated on a conversation that she had with an alumnus of the
institution who had chided her for her position on Texas State University for
Negroes. The alumnus brashly told White, "I wish all of you who want to be
white would cross over, so we could stop all of this mess about segregation."
White replied in "good, calm and collected English, what she was, and all the
So and So's like her." This exchange revealed much more than the implicit
humor. It reflected an African American community deeply torn over the best
strategy to pursue in the campaign for equal educational opportunities in the
Lone Star state.[32]

The feud was intensified by Wesley's continued allegation that White was a
Communist, a charge that seemed credible to many Texas whites since they
refused to believe local blacks capable of initiating a sustained campaign for
integration of public education in the state. Given the racist premise that blacks
were happy and content with the status quo, the only explanation lay in some
external force; thus the NAACP must be linked to communism. Lulu White
did nothing to discourage this image, as she flirted openly with socialist sympa-
thizers. Because of the allegations of communism and the differences over the
"separate but equal" doctrine, by 1949 Wesley had become obsessed with
removing White as the executive secretary to the Houston chapter. In a series

of editorials featuring personal attacks, he finally succeeded on June 13, 1949, when Lulu White again resigned from her post in the Houston NAACP.[33]

One year later, on June 5, 1950, the United States Supreme Court announced its findings in the *Sweatt v. Painter* case. In a unanimous decision, the Court ordered Sweatt admitted to the University of Texas. Speaking for the majority, Chief Justice Fred Vinson asserted that there was no comparison between the two law schools. TSUN had twenty-three students compared to 880 at the University of Texas. The African American university had less than one-third the number of full-time instructors and the library was four times smaller than the institution at Austin. Moreover, the University of Texas had a law review journal, moot court facilities, scholarships, and many alumni. TSUN had none of these. Yet although Sweatt could now attend the University of Texas, racial segregation was still not abolished, just as Wesley had argued all along.[34]

Lulu Madison White never conceded that point or, for that matter, acknowledged the validity of the position of Carter Wesley and other moderate African Americans in the state who felt racial equality and racially separate institutions were compatible. White's belief in governmentally mandated opportunities for blacks to enter white society on an equal footing while diluting African American culture through the demised of separate institutions was nonetheless a necessary step on the road to full citizenship. Her personal attitude toward desegregation was refracted through her perception of democracy and what it entailed. To her, the benefits and responsibilities of American life were inextricably linked. With this outlook, she never doubted her correctness in the movement to integrate the University of Texas.

NOTES

1. On White's background, see *Thirteenth Census of the United States, 1910 Population: Kaufman County, Texas, Elmo Supervision District 3*, microfilm (Washington, D.C., 1910). Johnnie Jordan, Interview by Merline Pitre, February 7, 1987. Johnnie Jordan is the niece of Lulu B. White. On post-Reconstruction violence, see Alwyn Barr, *Black Texans: A History of Negroes in Texas, 1528–1995* (Norman: University of Oklahoma Press, 1995), 136–38. See also Robert Richard Butler, "A History of Kaufman County" (M.A. thesis, University of Texas, 1940); and William H. Wilson, "Growing Up Black in East Texas: Some Twentieth-Century Experiences," *East Texas Historical Journal* 22 (1994): 49–54.

2. Johnnie Jordan interview; Edwin and Billie Hardin, Interview by Merline Pitre, June 27, 1997.

3. Ibid. See J. M. McCullen to Registrar of Prairie View College, in Lulu White's Scrapbook, in the possession of Johnnie Jordan.

4. *Prairie View Standard*, June 23, 1928; Darlene Clark Hine, *Black Victory: The Rise and Fall of the White Primary in Texas* (Millwood, N.Y.: KTO Press, 1971); Lawrence D. Rice, *The Negro in Texas, 1874–1900* (Baton Rouge: Louisiana State University Press, 1971), 37–40; Johnnie Jordan interview; Ercell Pinson Hall, Interview by Merline Pitre, February 7, 1998; Barbara Johnson and Onita Cavit, Interview by Merline Pitre, February 25, 1996.

5. Minutes of the National Labor Convention of Colored Men held in Houston, 1946, in NAACP Files, Manuscript Division of the Library of Congress, Washington, D.C.

6. Lucille Black to Lulu White, October 26, 1945. Unless otherwise indicated, all letters are taken from the NAACP Files. See duties of executive secretary of the Houston NAACP Branch in Constitution and By-Laws, 5–6, NAACP Files; Michael Gillette, "Blacks Challenge the White University," *Southwestern Historical Quarterly* 86 (October 1982): 321–22; Michael Gillette, "The Rise of the NAACP in Texas," *Southwestern Historical Quarterly* 81 (April 1978): 398–416.

7. Nancy Ruth Bessent, "The Publisher: A Biography of Carter W. Wesley" (Ph.D. dissertation, University of Texas, Austin, 1981), 27. Portions of this chapter appeared in an earlier form in Pitre, "Black Houstonians and the 'Separate and Equal' Doctrine: Carter W. Wesley versus Lulu White," *Houston Review: History and Culture of the Gulf Coast* 12 (1990): 23–36.

8. Bessent, "The Publisher," 238–43.

9. Texas Legislature, *Texas General Laws of the State of Texas Passed by the Regular Session of the 49th Legislature* (Austin: State Attorney General, 1945), 506.

10. Thomas A. Krueger, *And Promises to Keep: The Southern Conference for Human Welfare, 1938–48* (Nashville: Vanderbilt University Press, 1967), 119–21; Morton Sosna, *In Search of the Silent South: Southern Liberals and the Race Issue* (New York: Columbia University Press, 1977), 114–21, 152–67; R. L. Carter to Smith, March 30, 1947.

11. Lulu White to Walter White, January 2, 1947; Lulu White to Thurgood Marshall, January 14, 1947; Lulu White to Gloster Current, January 20, 1947.

12. Carter Wesley to Thurgood Marshall, August 1, 1945; Marshall to Wesley, August 21, 1945; Marshall to Wesley, October 10, 1947; Marshall to Wesley, September 26, 1945; Lulu White to Marshall, October 10, 1945; Michael Gillette, "Heman Marion Sweatt: Civil Rights Plaintiff," in *Black Leaders: Texas for Their Times*, ed. Alwyn Barr and Robert Calvert (Austin: Texas State Historical Association, 1981), 161. Lulu White to Thurgood Marshall, October 10, 1945.

13. A. Maceo Smith to Lulu White, November 19, 1945; W. J. Durham to Marshall, January 28, 1946. See also Gillette, "Heman Marion Sweatt," 161–62.

14. The quote appears in Theophilus A. Painter to Grover Sellers, February 26, 1946. This letter was leaked to the press and later published in its entirety in the *Houston Informer*, March 2, 1946. See also Texas Attorney General Opinion Texas, #0-7126, March 16, 1946; and Texas Legislature, *General and Special Laws of the State of Texas, Passed by the Regular Session of the 49th Legislature* (Austin: State Attorney General, 1945).

15. The first quote is found in A. Maceo Smith to Carter Wesley, March 21, 1946. A small group of blacks supported Smith's position with the hope that Prairie View would be transformed from a normal school to a classic university. See also Lulu White to Thurgood Marshall, November 26, 1949. The second quote is from Wesley to Smith, March 30, 1946; Wesley to Durham, March 22, 1946. Wesley was in favor of a black "classical" university but was undecided as to whether Prairie View should be converted to such. For the time being, he wanted to have a black board of regents and a black president for Prairie View. According to oral sources, when Houston College for Negroes was first established, black families, friends, and individuals donated bricks for the construction of the first classroom building. It is this action to which Wesley refers when he speaks of reparation.

16. Dudley K. Woodward Jr. to Gibb Gilchrist, June 20, 1946, in "General—Negroes in College, 1939–1954," University of Texas Files, President's Office Record, Eugene Barker Center for American History, University of Texas at Austin (hereafter cited as UTPOR); A. Maceo Smith to R. L. Carter; Mark Magee to Coke Stevenson, December 17, 1946, General Files, UTPOR; Bi-Racial Commission Report, December 17, 1946, General Files, UTPOR. The two black members of the committee were Willette R. Baks, principal of Prairie View University, and Ernest Gavins, a dentist from Austin, Texas. See also Lulu White to Thurgood Marshall, July 30, 1946, and Gillette, "Blacks Challenge the White University," 344–84.

17. A. Maceo Smith to R. L. Carter, August 9, 1946; Houston Post, August 9, 1946. See also "Resolution of the Texas Council of Negro Organizations to the Governor's Bi-racial Commission," August 8, 1946, NAACP Files.

18. Houston Post, August 9, 1946.

19. Lulu White to Walter White, January 2, 1947; Lulu White to A. A. Lucas, December 31, 1946; A. Maceo Smith to Carter Wesley, September 3, 1946.

20. Lulu White to Walter White, January 2, 1947; Lulu White to Gloster Current, January 20, 1947; A. Maceo Smith to R. L. Carter, October 16, 1946; Lulu White to Walter White, n.d.

21. Marshall to Wesley, August 21, 1945; Wesley to Smith, March 26, 1946; Marshall to Wesley, October 25, 1946; Wesley to Marshall, December 23, 1946; Marshall to Wesley, December 27, 1946.

22. Houston Informer, December 28, 1946.

23. Lulu White to A. A. Lucas, December 31, 1946; Marshall to Lulu White, January 14, 1947; Lulu White to Lucas, December 30, 1946; Wesley to Marshall, December 27, 1946.

24. Neil G. Sapper, "The Fall of the NAACP in Texas," Houston Review 7 (November 2, 1985): 63–68; Senate Bill 140, and House Bill 780, Texas Legislature, House and Senate, General and Specific Laws Passed by the Regular Session of the 50th Legislature, 36–40.

25. Lulu White to Gloster Current, May 9, 1947.

26. A. Maceo Smith to Leslie Perry, February 21, 1947; Lulu White to Thurgood Marshall, December 11, 1946. Wesley to Smith, March 14, 1946; Houston Informer, June 7, 1947; Lulu White to A. A. Lucas, December 31, 1946.

27. Curtis McDonald, Interview by Pitre, June 5, 1996.

28. Lulu White to Marshall, August 27, 1947.

29. Lulu White to Roy Wilkins, June 14, 1948; *Houston Informer*, June 7, 1947; August 16, 1947.

30. On Kirk's efforts, see the *Daily Texan*, December 5, 1947; December 10, 1947; Lulu White to Gloster Current, December 5, 1947; Lulu White to Thurgood Marshall, September 23, 1947; T. A. Painter to D. D. Woodward, January 3, 1948, General Files, "Negroes in College 1939–1954," UTPOR; Painter to Kirk, May 4, 1949, UTPOR; Raphael O'Hara Lanier to Craig Cullinan, November 11, 1949; Lanier to Painter, June 18, 1948.

31. Craig Cullinan to Raphael O'Hara Lanier, December 17, 1948; Lanier to Harold Schachter, December 2, 1948; Lulu White to Current, December 5, 1947.

32. Lulu White to Thurgood Marshall, November 26, 1949.

33. Lulu White to L. H. Simpson, June 13, 1949; *Houston Post*, March 24, 1948; *Houston Informer*, June 11, 1949. Lulu White also supported and campaigned for Henry A. Wallace in the presidential election of 1948.

34. Sweatt v. Painter, 339 U.S. 629, 70 SC+ 848-851 (1950). After the Supreme Court found the TSUN Law School inadequate in many areas, the legislature demonstrated its commitment to TSUN in a rather ironic way. In the next session it slashed TSUN's appropriation from $1,570,000 to $958,672. See Sapper, "The Fall of the NAACP in Texas," 63–68; *Houston Informer*, June 10, 1950; *Daily Texan*, June 7, 1950; Gillette, "Herman Marion Sweatt," 178.

Ada Lois Sipuel Fisher and the U.S. Supreme Court

In 1949 the U.S. Supreme Court ordered that Ada Lois Sipuel Fisher be admitted to the University of Oklahoma.

It was a cold day, but one of crystalline purity. There I was, a preacher's daughter from Little Chickasha, Oklahoma, climbing the steps of the United States Supreme Court building. My eyes caught the words "Equal Justice under Law." Amos Hall, Thurgood Marshall, and I entered the building ahead of schedule. We walked down the wide corridor, its way marked with uniformed military personnel standing at attention at spaced intervals. Finally we came to the Court's chamber. The awesome sight seemed a fitting end of a journey two years in the making.

The chamber had plush carpet and carved, heavily padded pews for specta-tors. The Court's sergeant-at-arms sat in a high chair facing the audience. Behind him was the judge's bar, beautifully carved and long enough to accommodate nine large, overstuffed leather chairs, one for each of the nine justices. Behind the chairs was a heavy velvet curtain. The bailiff announced the imminent appearance of the justices, and everyone stood. The judges then stepped through the nine slits in the curtain.

I was thrilled. I recognized a few of them from photos that I had seen. The real thrill came from my sense that this august body was assembled that morning because of me—to recognize and affirm my rights of citizenship. . . .

As had been true at the state supreme court, the judges were free to interrupt counsel for either side at any point. This time, however, it was the state's counsel that was being interrupted. Marshall carefully presented his argument with scarcely an interruption. I believed that only one decision was plausible: my imme-diate admission to the University of Oklahoma. That seemed the only way Okla-homa could comply with the United States Constitution.

Attorneys Hansen and Merrill had a much harder and slower go of it. The state attorneys reiterated their position concerning out-of-state tuition and my failure

Source: Ada Lois Sipuel Fisher, *A Matter of Black and White: The Autobiography of Ada Lois Sipuel Fisher* (Norman: University of Oklahoma Press, 1996), 119–22.

to give the board of regents notice of my desire to study law within the state. They also spoke of the Oklahoma law prohibiting whites and blacks from attending classes together. Various justices cut in on the arguments with rather pointed questions that seemed to indicate they were leaning in my direction. At least as important as the questions' wording was their tone, a tone that ran all the way from incredulity to frustration with Oklahoma's position.

Justice William O. Douglas cut in on Merrill's and Hansen's point about the lack of prior notification to observe that I had attempted to enroll on January 14, 1946, and filed suit almost two years ago. Douglas opined that would appear to be clear notice. He said that at the rate the state was moving I would be an old lady before I would be able to practice law. Justice Robert Jackson wanted to know why, after two years, Oklahoma had made no effort to do anything about the problem. Justice Hugo Black also specifically wanted to know whether the regents had taken any action to satisfy my effort. Hansen had no direct response, saying only that the regents had no money to set up any other law school, adding that they believed I would refuse to accept a segregated law school.

Justice Felix Frankfurter systematically explored various alternatives and asked whether the state would admit me for the term beginning in a few days if the Court mandated it to do so. Hansen answered yes, if necessary, although he added that doing so would violate the laws of Oklahoma. Frankfurter then asked if a separate course of study could be arranged within the existing law school. Hansen answered that it could. Could I be admitted temporarily pending the establishment of a separate law school? Hansen said that the Oklahoma Board of Regents for Higher Education had authority to do any or all of those things.

Justice Robert Jackson interrupted to ask if counsel really believed that a school with a single student could afford an acceptable legal education. Merrill answered yes. Justice Jackson disagreed. He said such foolishness was neither reasonable nor equitable.

Dean Merrill noted that Oklahoma was one of many states with a public policy of segregation. He reminded the Court that for decades rulings had upheld that arrangement. Now, he told the Court, plaintiff is unwilling to recognize that settled policy. He was right on that.

Justice Jackson asked why I should be required to abide by a given policy more than any other person. Should I, he asked, be required to waive my constitutional rights for the benefit of the state's public policy?

They were good questions—great questions, it seemed to me. They were exactly the questions that every other court and public official had ignored. This time, this Court asked them.

Only four days after the hearing, the Court issued a terse one-page, unsigned unanimous order. With OU's second semester's enrollment to begin in exactly one week, the judgment was that I was "entitled to secure legal education afforded by a state institution." The Court ordered that Oklahoma "provide it for her in conformity with the equal protection clause of the Fourteenth Amendment and provide it as soon as it does for applicants of any other group."

CHAPTER 16

Lucinda Todd and the Invisible Petitioners of *Brown v. Board of Education of Topeka, Kansas*

Cheryl Brown Henderson

African American women in the civil rights movement were a powerfully present force whose contributions constructed the ground out of which emerged numerous advancements in social justice. The time has long since passed that their achievements be recognized. Many historians, constitutional scholars, and civil rights activists argue that the modern civil rights movement began on May 17, 1954, at 12:52 P.M. with the unanimous decision rendered by the United States Supreme Court in *Brown v. Board of Education of Topeka, Kansas*. Not only must the importance assigned to the *Brown* decision be continually examined, there must be research into the roles of little known and seldom acknowledged petitioners. More than two hundred individuals are on the roster of plaintiffs and lawyers in the cases combined by the Supreme Court and known only by the name of one of them, *Brown v. Board of Education*. These cases were part of a sweeping strategy employed by the National Association for the Advancement of Colored People (NAACP) to end the "separate but equal" era and the Jim Crow laws that kept it firmly in place. Five cases developed from Delaware, South Carolina, Virginia, the District of Columbia, and Kansas. These cases depended on petitioners willing to use the judicial system to defend their rights. Who were these petitioners? What motivated their collective action? Why are they unknown to us? Who were the women among their ranks?[1]

Women have been the linchpin in the mechanisms of progress for African American people. African American womanhood can be described as the knack of surviving, the knack of achieving, the knack of nurturing and imparting wisdom from generation to generation. Many African American women who were coming of age during the 1950s and 1960s led lives of quiet revolution. Yet most of these spiritual militants were not aware of the daily battles waged by generations before them. Perhaps these children of the civil rights movement were inspired by the realization that their education was designed to keep them ignorant of who they were. This was particularly problematic for young African American men who automatically assumed leadership roles in the parallel struggles for gender and racial equality. What were the models guiding African American grandmothers, mothers, and daughters who grappled with such conflicts? Missing from their education were accounts of women's social history that profiled the interlocking oppression of racism and sexism, affording black women little opportunity to fully control what they were or what they could become.[2]

The standard narrative of *Brown v. Board of Education*, the catalyst for the modern civil rights movement, is but one example of the patriarchal view of African American history. The irony of the male-dominated shadow cast by this landmark decision comes from two sources. First, although the legal battles waged were usually portrayed as orchestrated by a team of mainly African American male attorneys, there was one woman among their ranks, Constance Baker Motley, and one white male, Jack Greenberg. Second, the legal name carried by this case relegates all but one of the petitioners to the legal wasteland of "et al.": *Oliver L. Brown et al. v. The Board of Education of Topeka, Kansas, et al.* The question must be asked who were the "et al.," and why are they largely invisible? This legal terminology erases the participation of the African American women who were the principal petitioners in three of the five cases represented by *Brown*.[3]

Oliver Brown's gender conjures an image that has been embraced and repeated in scores of media reports and textbooks writing about this decision. The media version of the *Brown* case has eclipsed the reality. The image is that of a towering male figure valiantly fighting for the right to enroll his eldest daughter, seven-year-old Linda Carol Brown, in the third grade of Monroe Elementary School, without regard to race. The image presents plaintiff Oliver Brown and NAACP lead council Thurgood Marshall (and future Supreme

Court justice) as the men on whose shoulders rested the hope for African American children to have unrestricted access to education. The message is clear and perpetuates the belief that men were our liberators, feeding a collective amnesia over who dominated African American institutions and organizations. Yet black women, as the historian Paula Giddings reminds us, have had a long tradition of community activism.[4]

The involvement of women in all the cases resulting in the *Brown* decision guaranteed the sustained support essential for the years of legal maneuvering necessary to win. Many of the women were married and raising families while they were involved in the movement. For them, participation in the movement was a "family affair." They were all members of the NAACP. For many of these women, education was a high priority. They all recognized education as a key to self-empowerment and political and economic freedom. Given their ability to envision a better future and their determination to eliminate the barriers to the progress of their children and their communities, many of these women were natural leaders in the struggle for human rights and social justice.[5]

The case that would head the docket of school integration cases heard by the Supreme Court came from the state of Kansas. On February 28, 1951, attorneys for the Topeka, Kansas, chapter of the NAACP filed a class action lawsuit in federal district court. Their petition was filed on behalf of thirteen families against the local school board and its policies that permitted racially segregated schools. This case would be named for one of the plaintiffs, Oliver L. Brown. The resulting legal citation was *Oliver L. Brown et al. v. The Board of Education of Topeka, Kansas*. However, Brown was not among the principal initiators of this action. The first to step forward was a woman named Lucinda Todd. In spite of her courageous stand, Mrs. Todd remains largely unknown. She is not mentioned in history books. What led her to that defining movement has not been researched or examined.

At best, Todd would be a historic footnote. This chapter provides a corrective to that omission. Of the thirteen petitioners assembled as plaintiffs on behalf of their children, Oliver Brown was the sole male. He did not wear the banner of outspoken community or civil rights activist, nor was he involved in the local NAACP. Brown was a lifelong Topekan who had gone about his life like so many others in the 1940s and 1950s searching for a comfortable role for a "Negro" man with family responsibilities. When his childhood friend, local attorney Charles Scott, approached him about the impending legal action against the local Board of Education, Brown was reluctant to be recruited for such duty. But as others signed on to support the NAACP's plans, Brown finally agreed.

Why then was this case named for a figure so remote from the Kansas campaign for school integration? For years, the most plausible theory for the use of Brown's name was alphabetical placement. Yet when one examines the complete roster of petitioners in the Kansas case, the unreasonableness of this becomes evident. There was another Brown among the group, a woman named Darlene Brown. This leaves only gender as a reason for Oliver Brown's ascendance to lead plaintiff and to ultimately becoming synonymous with this momentous case. The gender politics of the 1950s insisted that men, not women, were the natural leaders.[6]

It was not in the realm of possibility for those involved in the Kansas case to have known that their action not only would be appealed to the United States Supreme Court but also would be selected to represent other school integration cases heard by the nation's highest court. After all, Supreme Court Justice Tom Clark said the *Brown* case was made first "so that the whole question would not smack of being a purely Southern one." As the historian Richard Kluger notes, it is one of the idiosyncrasies of American constitutional law that cases of profound consequence are often named for plaintiffs whose involvement in the original suit is either remote or fortuitous. Such was the case with Oliver Brown.[7]

African Americans in Kansas had always felt a certain freedom to act against racism and discrimination. Their pioneering spirit can be attributed to the fact that early settlers of their race came to Kansas because it offered the opportunity to homestead, to work on the railroad, and to be educated. Schooling was a right in Kansas, although post–Civil War legislators debated whether public schools should be integrated or segregated. Before statehood, Kansas had afforded blacks educational opportunities through a system of charity schools. These schools were funded by charitable donations, and none of the students were white. The viability of charity schools would change with the coming of statehood. In 1861, with a hard won antislavery constitution firmly in place, Kansas was admitted to the Union as the thirty-fourth state. Kansas became a "Promised Land" for blacks, particularly after the Civil War when homesteading and liberty seemed to fill the minds of the now formerly enslaved people. The state admitted free blacks in increasing numbers. The black population grew from 627 in 1860 to more than 17,000 by 1870. The resulting influx prompted the Kansas legislature to enact a law in 1879 permitting segregated elementary schools. The authority to operate such schools was granted only to cities of the "First Class," those with populations of 15,000 or more. Cities of less than this number had no legal basis to operate segregated schools under

Kansas's law. Topeka, the capital, was among several "First Class" cities in the state and could thus segregate its public schools.[8]

Nineteenth-century African American parents immediately challenged this notion of segregated schools, inspired by local leaders such as *Topeka Colored Citizen* editor William Eagleson. During the 1878 legislative debate over segregation, Eagleson argued,

> We hear of no Irish schools, no German schools, and no Swedish schools. No, not one of them. All the children in the city are at liberty to attend the school nearest them, except the poor child that God . . . chose to create with a black face instead of a white one. . . . We say to every colored man and woman in the city to come together and resolve that you will no longer submit to unjust discrimination on account of your color. This thing has gone on long enough and now if it can be stopped, let's stop it.[9]

The first challenge to school segregation in the Sunflower State was *Tinnon v. Ottawa School Board*, filed in 1881. It would be among eleven school cases to reach the Kansas supreme court between 1881 and 1949. Thus for seventy years before *Brown*, African American plaintiffs and their supporters litigated against public school segregation in the state courts. *Brown v. Board of Education of Topeka* was case number twelve in Kansas.[10]

The African American community of Topeka was rich and complex even during this era of segregation. Community life centered on the black churches and schools, which were often used as meeting places for cultural and athletic events. Women organized mothers' leagues to support their schools, and the Kansas Congress of Colored Parents and Teachers held annual state conventions. Although Topeka's only high school was said to be integrated, on closer examination, that merely meant that students attended classes together but were actively discouraged from socializing. School-sponsored extracurricular programs were strictly segregated. For example, there was a separate basketball team for African American students, complete with cheerleaders. Their team only competed against other segregated teams across the state. The same was true for football and school parties. The high school hosted dual parties on its premises with "Negro" students in the cafeteria and white students in the gymnasium. When Leola Williams (the future wife of Oliver Brown) attended Topeka High School, she was elected all-school queen by the African American student body. During the subsequent coronation and school dance, the white king and queen-elect visited the African American students in their assigned room, as Williams and her king-elect called on the white students in turn. Even school assemblies included a subtle form of discrimination. A bell would ring to alert white students to go to the auditorium. A second bell would then ring intended to alert African American students of their assembly, often in another part of the building. As the only African American inducted into the National Honor Society from her school that year, Williams was recognized in an all-school assembly. Despite this distinction, she was not encouraged to go on to college.[11]

Soon after World War II, a new vocal leadership emerged within Topeka's African American community—leadership that became increasingly intolerant of elementary school segregation. By 1949 the population of the city was 78,791; of this number, approximately 6,500 were African American. Included in the ranks of this burgeoning leadership were schoolteachers, attorneys, and other professionals who felt compelled to contest school segregation. Women comprised the majority of this new leadership group. Many of these women were part of the city's evolving African American middle class. Their status was often determined not by jobs but by their own education, employment, church affiliation, and membership in social clubs. These women encouraged serious cultural pursuits for their children. Piano lessons, church youth group participation, and club memberships were also considered activities that would groom their children to uplift the race.

These new leaders included Lucinda Todd, a former schoolteacher, Inza Brown, a legal secretary and the first African American women to work in a state civil service position, and Mamie Luella Williams, a teacher, all of whom worked in the local NAACP in pursuit of social change. The group also included Ida Norman, who became the first African American nurse in the Topeka school system. Norman, a Topeka native, had returned to the city after her husband's tour of service in the military. She later organized a Girl Scout troop that provided her daughter and other African American girls with the opportunity to participate in scouting for the first time in their community.

Much like the African American men whose experiences during World War II had taken them to foreign lands where they often witnessed more freedom than their own country afforded them, so had some African American women traveled and become incensed by U.S. policies of segregation. Such was the case of Norma Williams. A college education and a teaching job offered both the resources and a summer schedule that made travel to other countries a reality. The NAACP was a strong and viable organization that attracted those for whom Jim Crow had grown intolerable.

In 1948 the Topeka NAACP began its attack on the local school board's discriminatory policies. In *A Certain Blindness,* Paul Brady outlines the actions of the NAACP leadership. They petitioned the Board of Education to hire black teachers in the junior and senior high schools and demanded that women teachers, when qualified by training and experience, be eligible for principalships. One of the eleven previous school integration cases that reached the Kansas supreme court dealt with affording African American students an opportunity to fully attend Topeka's junior high schools. The segregated schools for African American children went through eighth grade. These students did not have the transitional period provided by attending grades seven through nine in junior high school. They also asked that Negro students be able to participate in all branches of high school athletics and other extracurricular activities and that a course in Negro history be taught in high school.[12]

Then the Topeka NAACP advanced its most controversial proposal. With a branch membership of committed women and men behind him, President McKinley Burnett appealed to the local school board to simply choose to integrate the elementary schools. Kansas's law, after all, did not require segregation in public schools but rather permitted it. When the board rejected all of the NAACP requests, the organization presented a protest petition to the school board. Paul Brady, the first African American to hold the post of Federal Administrative Law Judge, is also a nephew of the late Lucinda Todd. At the time of the *Brown* case, he was living in Topeka with his aunt. She had convinced him to move to the city and attend the local university. To those who knew her, Todd seemed to believe that any life plans that did not include education were doomed from the start. Brady recalled the monumental efforts of a relatively small group of workers in obtaining signatures:

> My Aunt Cindy was busy day and night. Since she did not drive, she traveled on foot, by bus and whenever she could hitch a ride. Often she joined with a neighbor, Mrs. Daniel Sawyer, another tireless worker who had a small truck and they rambled throughout the city in search of signatures. The petition, signed by nearly fifteen hundred people, requested that the School Board abolish racial segregation in all schools commencing with the 1950 fall term.[13]

Although NAACP branch president Burnett made the proposal for integration at virtually every school board meeting held between 1948 and 1950, the board continued to ignore all of them. Consequently, Burnett and Todd enlisted the assistance of Topeka's four black attorneys, Elisha Scott, his two sons, John and Charles, and Charles Bledsoe. The attorneys soon became a formidable legal team in the campaign against school segregation. The elder Scott had already litigated civil rights cases, including two earlier school cases in Kansas, Coffeyville in 1924 and South Park Johnson County in 1949.[14]

In summer 1950 McKinley Burnett and his wife, Lena, the Scotts, and Bledsoe met in Lucinda Todd's home to craft the legal strategy they hoped would finally abolish the dual school system in Kansas. The two-stage plan they developed was simple. First, they would assemble a group of volunteers from African American parents with elementary-aged children. The group would become the case petitioners. Their initial volunteer was Lucinda Todd; her daughter was a first grader at the segregated Buchanan Elementary School. Second, arguing that segregation violated the equal protection guarantees of the Fourteenth Amendment to the United States Constitution, they would file suit in federal rather than state court.[15]

Lucinda Todd, the guiding figure in the rapidly evolving *Brown* case, was a spiritual militant born in 1903 to the farm life of rural Kansas. Her parents, part of the post–Civil War exodus from the South into Kansas, had instilled in their children a thirst for education. Kansas for them and others was indeed a place of promise. They wanted to make certain that Lucinda and her brothers and sisters had the advantage of that promise. Fortunately, because the family lived and farmed in a small and, by population, "second-class" city, Lucinda attended integrated one-room schools. Todd also graduated from an integrated state university not far from her childhood home and began her teaching career in an integrated one-room school.

Hoping to expand her horizons, she moved to Topeka, only to face the harshest segregation of her life. Not long after she arrived in Topeka, Todd was hired to teach in the racially segregated Buchanan Elementary School, the school her daughter Nancy would eventually attend and whose segregation policies she would challenge. Because of her upbringing and educational experiences, Lucinda had little tolerance for racial discrimination and challenged it daily as she navigated the city. Richard Kluger, writing in *Simple Justice*, describes Lucinda Todd's activism:

> here was a time—1944, she places it—when Mrs. Todd bought a ticket to the Grand movie theater, the one that admitted Negroes to a section of the balcony, and when she climbed up there, the two dozen or so seats reserved for colored were filled, so she took a seat right across the aisle in the white section. A policeman came and told her that she could not

do that and would have to sit in the colored section or nowhere. They gave her money back. "They did things like that all the time," Lucinda Todd recalls. Soon she became active in the NAACP, and was elected secretary of the branch.[16]

Todd did not hesitate to become the first parent to volunteer for the ensuing NAACP litigation. Paul Brady writes of living in Topeka during the *Brown* case, noting that "one of the most difficult jobs for the NAACP was the recruitment of plaintiffs. Some, like Aunt Cindy and Lena Carper, the mother of Nancy's close friend Kathy, readily stepped forward (some of Aunt Cindy's longtime friends thereafter feared to visit her). Others agreed reluctantly, while some required great efforts to convince them the suit was in their own best interest."[17] By fall 1950 Todd and other NAACP leaders had enlisted the help of thirteen other parents, representing a total of twenty children. Topeka public schools operated eighteen elementary schools for white children and only four for African American children. The African American schools were ironically named for former U.S. Presidents Buchanan, McKinley, Monroe, and Washington. These African American families lived throughout the community, indicating that unlike most cities in the United States, housing discrimination did not reinforce school segregation. This distinction proved crucial in the plaintiff's ensuing legal argument. The Oliver Brown family, for example, resided in a predominantly white neighborhood, which also included Native American, Chicano, and African American families. Because most of the petitioners also lived in predominantly white residential areas, their children's school assignments were not based on neighborhood but on race.[18]

This group of committed and resourceful parents stood ready for the next phase of the NAACP case. Listed alphabetically, they were Darlene Brown, Oliver L. Brown, Lena Carper, Sadie Emmanuel, Marguerite Emerson, Shirla Fleming, Andrew Henderson, Shirley Hodison, Richard Lawton, Alma Lewis, Iona Richardson, Vivian Scales, and Lucinda Todd. Todd had recruited friends and fellow church members willing to participate, including some from the same families. For example, Shirley Fleming and Vivian Scales were sisters, although Darlene Brown and Oliver Brown were not related. Oliver Brown's participation came from the urging of his boyhood friendship with Charles Scott. Also, Brown's wife was expecting their third child in December, a fact that, based on 1950s standards, curtailed her activity. All of the female petitioners were married, most of them full-time homemakers with a belief in sacrificing for the next generation.[19]

Why were these women the petitioners and not their husbands? Fear of economic reprisals was an important factor, as most black men and women in Topeka held jobs that made them vulnerable to firing by angry white employers. For Oliver Brown, the sole African American male in the petitioners' ranks, employment as a welder for the Santa Fe Railroad, union membership, and part-time pastorship at the St. John AME church offered a shield from such retaliation. Moreover, many of the middle-class women who were not employed outside the home were one step removed from economic reprisals because of their husbands' financial status.[20]

These newly assembled activists were instructed by NAACP legal counsel to watch the newspaper for dates of enrollment, locate the whites-only elementary school closest to their homes, take a witness, and attempt to enroll their children in that school. So it went that in fall 1950, all across the city of Topeka, these thirteen courageous parents with children in tow sought to implement the NAACP plan. Once each was denied the right to enroll their children they returned, as instructed, to report what had taken place and exactly what had been said to them as justification for the denial. Vivian Scales recalls telling her seven-year-old daughter, Ruth Ann, that they were going on a project. She said that this project meant walking over to Parkdale Elementary School, but it did not mean she would be leaving the school she attended. When Scales arrived with Ruth Ann in tow and a family friend to act as her witness, she had the clear sense that the school principal had been alerted to the NAACP plan and was prepared to be confronted. She immediately spoke up, explaining that she was there to enroll her daughter in school. According to Scales, his reply was courteous and brief: "I'm sorry I cannot do that, you will need to enroll her in one of your own schools." She responded with a question, "So you're saying that you will not allow me to enroll my daughter here?" His last words were simply, "Yes, that's about the size of it." Once she extracted verbal clarification from him so that both she and her witness could be certain of his position, she thanked him and returned home prepared for the upcoming meeting to report on their experience. Each of the parents recounted conversations with white school officials so similar that they could have come from a script. This information provided the Topeka NAACP legal team with the evidence needed to file a class action suit against the local Board of Education.[21]

Following the various rejections, Todd wrote to NAACP executive secretary Walter White, indicating that Topeka was going to court to test the Kansas law governing segregated schools. Her letter generated immediate interest and assistance from the national office. Part of the national legal team, Robert

Carter, Thurgood Marshall, and Jack Greenberg, traveled to Topeka to meet with the local leadership. That Todd and her husband had to host the lawyers in their own home, in the absence of adequate hotels for African Americans, was yet another reminder of the discrimination African Americans faced in the Kansas capital, in addition to segregated schools. The national office assigned Robert Carter to assist the Topeka legal team with the *Brown* case.

The suit was officially filed with the federal district court on February 28, 1951. Once the legal papers were drafted and filed, the individuals who were now considered plaintiffs went back to their daily lives. Few were asked to appear in court. Among those who testified were Silas Fleming, husband of Shirla, Oliver Brown, and Lena Carper's daughter, Catherine. It has been suggested that Catherine was the only child to take the witness stand because she was the oldest among the minor children involved. Her testimony was significant because it helped to establish the absurdity of segregating African American and white children for the purpose of school attendance. In most instances, these children were neighbors who played together during summer breaks or at the end of their school day. Lena Carper testified about her conversations with white neighbors who also questioned the rationale of school assignment based solely on race. Her feelings ran deep because she lived in an expanding section of the city with streets under construction. When it rained, she would carry her daughter on her back to keep her out of the deep muddy ruts for the five blocks to the school bus stop. Young Catherine Carper then rode the bus thirty blocks to the segregated Buchanan Elementary School. Shirla Fleming testified that she avoided the long waits for the "colored" school bus by paying the fare to have her children ride the city buses twenty-one blocks to the all-black Washington Elementary School. The Flemings' neighborhood school was a mere three blocks away. Vivian Scales, Shirla Fleming's sister, said that she was willing to participate because the white school was so close she could see it from her back door, yet her daughter was assigned to Monroe Elementary School more than a mile away.[22]

As their case made its way through the federal court, Todd and other women from the NAACP spent time canvassing the African American community of Topeka to gauge support for their action. Not surprisingly, there was a split among those surveyed. Some were ambivalent and concerned about wholesale retaliation that could ultimately mean job loss. This fractured perception by the African American community was not lost on school officials. Two years into the legal maneuvering, in March 1953, the local school superintendent mailed letters to African American teachers who had been on the job for two years or less. This correspondence was an attempt to divide and conquer. The letter read in part:

> Due to the present uncertainty about enrollment next year in schools for Negro children, it is not possible at this time to offer you employment for next year. If the Court should rule that segregation in the elementary grades is unconstitutional, our Board will proceed on the assumption that the majority of people in Topeka will not want to employ Negro teachers next year for white children. It is necessary for me to notify you now that your services will not be needed for next year. This is in compliance with the continuing contract law. If it turns out that segregation is not terminated, there will be nothing to prevent us from negotiating a contract with you at some later date this spring. You will understand that I am sending letters of this kind to only those teachers of the Negro schools who have been employed during the last year or two. It is presumed that, even though segregation should be declared unconstitutional, we would have need for some schools for Negro children, and we would retain our negro teachers to teach them. I think I understand that all of you must be under considerable strain, and I sympathize with uncertainess [sic] and inconveniences which you must experience during this period of adjustment. I believe that whatever happens, will ultimately turn out to be best for everybody concerned.[23]

Topeka school officials were true to their word when, a year later, the Supreme Court found in favor of the NAACP and its plaintiffs. Those African American teachers who were subsequently fired were devastated and angry. Some of them traveled to neighboring states and found teaching jobs; others left the profession altogether. Still others left for parts unknown. Even among those whose tenure ensured continuation, misplaced anger and confusion was apparent and they were uncertain about their reception as teachers of white students and colleagues of white teachers and administrators in the now desegregated school district.

Despite school officials' threats, the NAACP focused on the task at hand, presenting evidence that would produce a winning case. The lawsuit in the Kansas capital proved the legal linchpin in the NAACP's national strategy to attack public school segregation. Only in Topeka were black and white schools basically equal with regard to facilities, teacher qualifications, salaries, and access to supplies. African American teachers actually held more advanced degrees than their white counterparts, providing a clear indication that quality education was not an issue for the plaintiffs but rather the restricted access to public schools based solely on race. Because the Topeka case presented no argument for equal buildings or equalizing other tangible factors, the issue before the Supreme Court in 1954, for the first time in more than half a century, was the constitutionality of segregation as endorsed by *Plessy v. Ferguson*. This 1896 Supreme Court decision allowed "separate but equal" public schools and transportation. It was clear that attacking *Plessy v. Ferguson* was the only course of action that would call into question whether the doctrine of segregation was constitutional. On May 17, 1954, at 12:52 P.M., the Court issued its historic decision in which it concluded that in the field of public education, separate but equal has no place. After sixty years, *Plessy v. Ferguson* was overturned.[24]

For the families in the Topeka case, the decision was bittersweet. Most of their children were now in an already integrated junior high school. With the passing of time and the years of legal maneuvering, their elementary school days had come and gone. "I vividly recall the great joy in my aunt and uncle's household," writes Paul Brady, "and my cousin Nancy Todd also remembers that 'the telephone never quit ringing.'" Although Nancy's constitutional rights were vindicated, she was never permitted to walk the few blocks to attend her neighborhood elementary school.[25] For Lena Carper, whose daughter Catherine had been the only child to take the witness stand, watching the country's response to the *Brown* decision as reported on the evening news was a sobering experience. In a 1996 interview, she recalled:

> I remember watching the television and seeing those children with armed guards trying to go to school. I remember seeing those dogs and fire hoses turned on people down south and I asked myself did we do that. Are we the cause of their suffering. It really upset me. I got involved in this case because I was thinking locally and what this meant for my daughter Kathy. I really felt bad that we may have been the cause of so much pain.[26]

Following the Supreme Court decision, the Topeka Board of Education chose to immediately integrate black and white students and retain those African American teachers with tenure (three years or more in the district). Teachers with less experience were not offered a contract. Lucinda Todd, the NAACP activist who had left teaching to marry and start a family shortly after World War II and who had worked tirelessly to desegregate the public school system, returned to teaching after the *Brown* decision. Her classroom experience soon made her one of the most sought after teachers by both white and black parents.

The district adopted a policy designed to be least offensive to white parents. School administrators, all of whom were white, were given instructions that before assigning white students to black teachers, they were to request parental permission. In essence, white parents were contacted by school principals and asked whether they would object to having their child taught by a "Negro" teacher. This policy was in place for only one year because the newly assigned African American teachers quickly become so well received that there were waiting lists to enter their classes. After all, the majority held advanced degrees, which was not the case with their white counterparts.

As the *Brown v. Board of Education* decision became more historically prominent, the participants became more obscure. When media coverage began, reporters created a story around the first named plaintiff, Oliver L. Brown, and lead NAACP attorney Thurgood Marshall, crediting the men as the primary leaders in the successful challenge to school segregation. Eventually even history textbooks adopted much of the media's version of the story. Perhaps not surprisingly, the facts and faces behind *Brown v. Board of Education* became all but completely overshadowed by the hugely popular Brown-Marshall saga.

Historians and legal scholars must look behind the media version to uncover the complex issues and varied personalities surrounding one of the most important legal cases of the twentieth century. In particular, they must acknowledge the crucial role that women such as Lucinda Todd played in overturning the doctrine of separate but equal. Each of us must remember and note the courage of Lucinda Todd, Lena Carper, Darlene Brown, Shirla Fleming, Sadie Emmanuel, Shirley Hodison, Vivian Scales, Maude Lawton, Zelma Henderson, Marguerite Emerson, Iona Richardson, and Alma Lewis of Topeka, as well as countless other African American women throughout the West. Their sacrifices are reminiscent of the historic link between past, present, and future generations of Americans. Their lives demonstrate that our history moves forward not only as a result of the actions of proclaimed leaders, but also the actions of ordinary Americans. In their everyday lives, these women worked to achieve a more just and egalitarian way of life for themselves and their children. It is the responsibility of those who record history to let the role of African American women in the landmark *Brown v. Board of Education* case be invisible no more.

On October 28, 1992, Congress passed the *Brown v. Board of Education* National Historic Site Act establishing a site in Topeka where all of the cases, people, and places behind the *Brown* case can be interpreted and remembered. The Visitors Center and exhibits will be housed in the old Monroe Elementary

School building. This site will most likely open to visitors by 2004, the fiftieth anniversary of the *Brown* decision.

NOTES

1. The four other cases were *Briggs v. Elliot* (South Carolina), *Davis v. County School Board of Prince Edward County* (Virginia), *Belton v. Gebhart* (Delaware), and *Bolling v. Sharpe* (District of Columbia). The text of the Supreme Court opinions appears in Richard Kluger, *Simple Justice: The History of Brown v. Board of Education and Black America's Struggle for Equality* (New York: Vintage Books, 1975), 779–87. See also Waldo E. Martin Jr., ed., *Brown v. Board of Education: A Brief History of Documents* (Boston: Bedford/St. Martin's, 1998), 27–32; Mark V. Tushnet, *Making Civil Rights Law: Thurgood Marshall and the Supreme Court, 1936–1961* (New York: Oxford University Press, 1994), chaps. 11–15; Teresa A. Nance, "Hearing the Missing Voice," *Journal of Black Studies* 26 (May 1996): 557–58; and Jack Greenberg, *Crusaders in the Courts: How a Dedicated Band of Lawyers Fought for the Civil Rights Revolution* (New York: Basic Books, 1994).

2. Nance, "Hearing the Missing Voice," 557.

3. Along with the Topeka women, Ethel Belton was the principal petitioner in *Belton v. Gebhart*, while Barbara Johns initiated the legal challenge in *Davis v. County School Board of Prince Edward County.* See Kluger, *Simple Justice,* 434, 466–71.

4. Paula Giddings, *When and Where I Enter: The Impact of Black Women on Race and Sex in America* (New York: William Morrow, 1984), 72; Kluger, *Simple Justice,* 408.

5. LaVerne Gyant, "Passing The Torch," *Journal of Black Studies* 26 (May 1996): 633.

6. Greenberg, *Crusaders in the Courts,* 117.

7. For the Justice Clark quote, see Kluger, *Simple Justice,* 540.

8. Quintard Taylor, *In Search of the Racial Frontier: African Americans in the American West, 1528–1990* (New York: W. W. Norton, 1998), 136–43, 215–19, 281–83.

9. *Topeka Colored Citizen,* September 20, 1878, p. 4.

10. Taylor, *In Search of the Racial Frontier,* 216–17.

11. Topeka's junior high schools were desegregated in 1941 as a consequence of *Graham v. Board of Education of Topeka.* See Kluger, *Simple Justice,* 375, 382; and Taylor, *In Search,* 281.

12. Paul Brady, *A Certain Blindness: A Black Family's Quest for the Promise of America* (Atlanta: ALP Publishing, 1990), 123.

13. Ibid., 124.

14. Kluger, *Simple Justice,* 384–93.

15. See Stephen L. Wasby, Anthony A. D'Amato, and Rosemary Metrailer, *Desegregation from Brown to Alexander: An Exploration of Supreme Court Strategies* (Carbondale: Southern Illinois University Press, 1977), 63–64. *Brown* was the fifth case brought by African American plaintiffs in Topeka since 1903. For background on the seventy-year struggle to integrate Kansas's schools, see Randall B. Woods, "Integration,

Exclusion, or Segregation? The 'Color Line' in Kansas, 1878–1900," *Western Historical Quarterly* 14 (April 1983): 181–98; and Deborah Dandridge et al., *Brown v. Board of Education: In Pursuit of Freedom and Equality: Kansas and the African American Public School Experience, 1855–1955* (Topeka: Brown Foundation for Educational Equity, Excellence and Research, 1993), 7.

16. Kluger, *Simple Justice*, 376.

17. Brady, *A Certain Blindness*, 128.

18. Kluger, *Simple Justice*, 407–8.

19. Ibid.

20. See Hugh W. Speer, *The Case of the Century: A Historical and Social Perspective on Brown v. Board of Education of Topeka with Present and Future Implications* (Kansas City: Privately printed, 1968), 31. For further background on the ability of African American women to engage in political activism, see Gyant, "Passing the Torch," 532.

21. Kluger, *Simple Justice*, 407.

22. For additional testimony, see Speer, *The Case of the Century*, 35–37.

23. Letter loaned from Veda Whiteside, Kansas Collection, University of Kansas Libraries, Lawrence.

24. See Wasby, D'Amato, and Metrailer, *Desegregation from Brown to Alexander*, 90–92; and Kluger, *Simple Justice*, 702–8. For a brief discussion of the shift in strategy from challenging school equalization to calling for full integration, see Greenberg, *Crusaders in the Courts*, 85–87, 112–15.

25. Brady, *A Certain Blindness*, 137.

26. Lena Carper, interview in *In Pursuit of Freedom and Equality: Brown vs. the Board of Education* (video produced by the Brown Foundation, 1996).

CHAPTER 17

Clara Luper and the Civil Rights Movement in Oklahoma City, 1958–1964

Linda Williams Reese

D owntown Oklahoma City was hot and humid on the evening of August 19, 1958. The department store windows proclaimed a change of season with mannequins dressed in wool coats and plaid back-to-school fashions, but the late summer heat still radiated up from the pavement in waves. Clara Luper and fourteen well-groomed children ranging in age from six to fifteen walked into Katz Drugstore, sat down, and ordered soft drinks. The waitress refused to serve them. Indeed, had Luper and the children chosen any downtown restaurant or lunch counter, they would have received the same response. They were African American, and Oklahoma, like many other states, still embraced the racial etiquette of segregation.

Luper and her youth group remained quietly in their seats for several hours as the manager fretted, white customers cursed them, police arrived, representatives of the press and television stations moved into position, and a crowd gathered. Then, as politely as they had arrived, the group left the drugstore and drove home in the cars waiting outside. Luper and more children returned the following day to sit-in for several hours. On the third day, the management of Katz Drugstore announced that service to all patrons without regard to race would now be the business policy, and the youth were served. The long season of racial discrimination in Oklahoma City was about to end, largely through the efforts of the NAACP Youth Council and its adviser, Clara Luper. Their nonviolent, direct action strategy completed the work of earlier generations of black Oklahomans to break the bondage that segregation and exclusion imposed on the freedom of all its citizens.[1]

The significance of Clara Luper's leadership of the NAACP Youth Council, the success of the sit-ins she directed two years before the famous Greensboro, North Carolina, demonstrations, and her lifelong efforts to bring about racial and social equality are little known beyond the borders of Oklahoma. Historians of the civil rights movement have concentrated on the major national organizations such as the Southern Christian Leadership Conference (SCLC), the Student Nonviolent Coordinating Committee (SNCC), the Congress of Racial Equality (CORE), and the National Association for the Advancement of Colored People (NAACP). Men invariably commanded these national organizations and gave principal direction to the marches, voter registration drives, boycotts, and demonstrations. Martin Luther King Jr. certainly served as the most prominent figure of the movement.

Recently, historians have recognized the important influence black women exerted in civil rights activities. Anne Standley has commented on the significance of black women both formally, as leaders at the highest levels of these organizations, and "informally, as spontaneous leaders and dedicated participants." When the participation of female leaders has been examined, however, the emphasis has been on women with ties to the Deep South: Ella Baker in SNCC, Septima Clark in SCLC, and Fannie Lou Hamer in the Mississippi Freedom Democratic Party. Clara Luper represents the black female leadership in the West who courageously initiated direct action that placed racial injustice before powerful white citizens for resolution, risked the brunt of violent backlash, urged black male leaders to take more aggressive positions, and laid the groundwork for future advances.[2]

Clara Shepard Luper was born in rural Okfuskee County, Oklahoma, in 1923 to Ezell and Isabell Shepard. Like most black men in Oklahoma, Ezell Shepard held various jobs to support his family including farm laborer, construction worker, and school bus driver. Shortly before his death, he explained to his daughter that every time he had to "uncle Tom" to the white man in order to keep working, he hoped that one day his children would never have to endure that kind of humiliation. Clara's mother took in laundry while raising the children. The Shepard children attended an all-black elementary school at Hoffman,

Oklahoma, whose one teacher was also the principal and the janitor. Their text-books were the worn-out discards from the white elementary school. Clara and her classmates were bused five miles to Grayson for high school classes. Books and equipment at the high school were no less inferior. Entire sections were missing from encyclopedias and dictionaries, textbooks were tattered, and there were no lenses for the microscope. These conditions resulted partly from the economic destruction of the Great Depression but mostly from an education funding system that required separate taxes to support segregated schools.[3]

Historians have characterized Oklahoma as both a western and a southern state because of its geographic location, the presence of both cotton agriculture and the cattle industry, its initial history as a territory reserved exclusively for Native Americans, and postwar migration by both African Americans and whites from the South. Oklahoma's Jim Crow laws emerged nearly twenty years after the land was opened to non-Indian settlement in 1889. Throughout the territorial period, the Republican Party controlled Congress and the presidency, encouraging a black Republican vote, especially in the twenty-seven all-black towns that flourished at that time. Edward P. McCabe, an African American politician and entrepreneur, established Langston, Oklahoma, and lobbied for the creation of an all-black state. In Okfuskee County, where Luper was born, the all-black community of Boley represented the hopes that Oklahoma African American citizens had for political, social, and economic equality, stability, and opportunity.[4]

By the time of statehood in 1907, however, the Democratic Party dominated the Constitutional Convention, controlling 90 percent of the delegates. Fearing that President Theodore Roosevelt would refuse statehood if segregation were written into the Constitution, the Democrats waited until the first legislature convened. That body's first legislative acts segregated education and transportation. The state legislature eventually passed antimiscegenation laws and extinguished black votes through a grandfather clause. With legal and political power behind them, white Oklahomans waged a war of social and economic intimidation against black citizens, especially those in all-black communities. Conditions deteriorated so badly in Okfuskee County that it became a staging area for out-migration of blacks to Canada and to Africa through a back-to-Africa repatriation scheme.[5]

Clara Luper grew up in a state where racial separation permeated every aspect of social contact. Separate hotels, restaurants, restrooms, drinking fountains, telephone booths, and even, as Luper remembered, separate picking sections of the pecan orchards—all marked the boundaries of race. "My parents spent a great deal of time telling us how to survive in our environment," Luper later wrote. Food could be bought at the back door of certain restaurants and eaten outside in the alley. Clothes and shoes could be purchased in some stores but not tried on first for fit. Her parents trained the children always to take the back seats—in the bus, on the train, in the theater. The historian David Goldfield's eloquent analysis of race relations and southern culture describes the evolution of an etiquette of segregation as a "complicated set of rules and customs" designed to fix individuals in a racial and class hierarchy, binding whites together unequally and assigning a permanent status of inferiority to blacks. "The tone of speech, the gesture, what was said and not said, where and how one stood or sat became parts of the rituals of southern personal relations" that deprived both races of genuine knowledge of each other.[6]

Segregation, however, was neither rigid nor uniform. It evolved according to the economic requirements and social demography of the region. One of the institutions that mediated the limits of racial discrimination in Oklahoma was the Colored Agriculture and Normal University at Langston. Its name was officially changed to Langston University in 1941, Clara Luper's freshman year. The school profoundly affected her consciousness as an African American woman and her belief in activism. During one of the most critical civil rights demonstrations of her life, she remembered and took strength from Reverend E. W. Perry who preached at Langston "about real freedom and real love."[7]

Langston University came into existence in 1898 through the efforts of town promoter E. P. McCabe and the residents of Langston, the largest of the all-black communities in Oklahoma Territory. McCabe and the Oklahoma Association of Negro Teachers pressured the territorial legislature to create a university for African American Oklahomans. From the beginning, black Oklahomans insisted on autonomy in the direction of their school and refused to accept the limitations of industrial education and its association with the "Negro place" in American society. The townspeople applauded the choice of Inman E. Page, a Brown University graduate and proponent of liberal arts education, as the first president. Page set to work creating a curriculum and hiring a faculty that would offer students both vocational training and a liberal arts education. Longtime Oklahoma activist and editor of the *Black Dispatch*, Roscoe Dunjee, attended Langston during these years, remembering it as the place where he "got the inspiration to do big things."[8]

Luper pursued coursework at Langston University, majoring in mathematics and minoring in history. She could not afford the $21 per month dormitory room and board fee and, like many students, roomed with local families. Luper's classmate, Ada Lois Sipuel Fisher, who would integrate the University of Oklahoma Law School in 1949, recalled that students living in the dormitories were just as strapped for funds. They heated cans of chili and soup on hot plates. Slices of bread became the medium of exchange in the student barter system.[9]

The advent of World War II diminished enrollment at Langston by 69 percent, leaving a student body composed mostly of women. Between 1941 and 1945 the Oklahoma state legislature reduced appropriations to the school by two-thirds. The students watched conditions around them deteriorate. The university had no professional accreditation. The buildings were old and run-down; the substandard library contained only eight thousand volumes and had no accurate card catalog. Rain turned the unpaved streets surrounding the buildings into muddy bogs. Langston president G. Lamar Harrison demanded a fair share of higher education funds, but the white public response usually was to counter with suggestions to close the institution. Sipuel Fisher remembered that for a time, the student body almost unanimously boycotted the cafeteria in protest against a white dining hall worker who insulted the students with impunity while boasting of her state patronage job security. Other students sneaked into President Harrison's office to telephone state officials to insist on action to upgrade the university. In 1948, long after Luper and Sipuel Fisher had finished their undergraduate degrees, Langston finally received accreditation, acquired hard-surface streets around the school, and improved the library.[10]

For all its shortcomings, Langston University provided its students not only with an understanding of the history, illegality, and nature of the racial inequality they had already experienced firsthand, but also the possibilities of coordinated, calibrated protest and action. Langston students formed a cadre of black Oklahoma activism that would claim victories in the 1950s and 1960s. Roscoe Dunjee established the *Black Dispatch* newspaper in Oklahoma City in 1915. It became the articulate, persuasive, and unifying arm of African American affairs and the journalistic voice demanding social justice in the state. Dunjee was also one of the earliest leaders of the Oklahoma NAACP, formed in 1913, gathering together influential black lawyers and clergy to protest Oklahoma's segregation laws in the courts.[11]

Clara Luper prepared for graduate school at the University of Oklahoma at the same time that her classmate, Ada Lois Sipuel Fisher, battled through the courts to gain admission to the University of Oklahoma Law School. Langston University had limited program offerings and could not provide advanced or professional degrees to African American students. To safeguard segregated education, the Oklahoma legislature appropriated money annually for grants to qualified black students to send them out of state for the programs or advanced training they needed. These grants rarely averaged more than $140 per student and failed to cover the cost of out-of-state education. Black community churches and organizations pooled funds to make up the deficit and provide their young people with training outside the state, especially in law and medicine. A Langston education, however, was the limit for most African American college students in Oklahoma.[12]

Sipuel Fisher's Supreme Court case in which she was seeking admission to the University of Oklahoma Law School would not be resolved until 1949. The Oklahoma NAACP, recognizing the cost to the state that instituting program equity at Langston would impose, supported six students who, in 1948, applied to take a variety of graduate courses at the University of Oklahoma that were unavailable at Langston. The court challenge fell to one of those students, a fifty-four-year-old Langston University teacher, George W. McLaurin. The district court ordered the university to allow McLaurin to take the courses he requested. McLaurin attended classes, but the university set up segregated areas, roping off sections in classrooms, the library, and the cafeteria. McLaurin found these exclusionary practices intolerable and appealed to the United States Supreme Court, which ruled in 1950 that the state's action violated his rights under the Fourteenth Amendment.

Shortly afterward, when Clara Luper was studying for a master's degree in secondary education and history at the University of Oklahoma, she suffered indignities similar to McLaurin's. Luper recalled that at the beginning of the year one professor told her bluntly that he "had never taught a nigger and had never wanted to." Nonetheless, she completed her master's degree in 1951. The legal challenges of Sipuel Fisher, McLaurin, and the Oklahoma NAACP in the late 1940s prepared the ground for Clara Luper's activism to take root in the 1950s and 1960s.[13]

Legally integrated universities did not resolve other areas of inequality and race discrimination in housing, employment, voting, and public accommodations. Luper found herself in accord with a growing national movement intent on engaging these issues. This movement had a dynamic leader, Martin Luther King Jr., a philosophy of nonviolence, and a strategy of direct action. In 1957 Luper's personal history converged with public history. Her experiences as an African American woman in Oklahoma, her sacrifices to acquire an education, her involvement with the Langston network, her knowledge of

American history and the Constitution, and her position at the hub of Oklahoma City civil rights activity all prepared her to assume a leadership role.

In 1957 Luper agreed to accept the position of adviser to the Oklahoma City NAACP Youth Council, a group that had fallen into inactivity some years before. As a popular history teacher at Dunjee High School and a member of the Fifth Street Baptist Church, she had ample contact with a number of bright, talented youths who became the core of the membership. They held Youth Council meetings in her home. Luper directed plays and assemblies in recognition of Black History Week every year at school, but in 1957 she wrote and produced her own play, *Brother President*, about Martin Luther King Jr. and the philosophy of nonviolent resistance that worked so well in the Montgomery, Alabama, Bus Boycott. When the students performed the play at a local church with Herbert Wright, the NAACP national youth director in attendance, he asked Luper and her students to present the performance in New York City at a recognition rally for freedom fighters. Luper and the young people raised nearly $2,000 to make the trip. It was an experience that changed their lives forever.

Most of the group had never been outside Oklahoma City. As they traveled by bus across the Midwest, they were overwhelmed by the absence of the trademarks of segregation. They delighted in their first experience with integrated food service and hotel accommodations. They met civil rights demonstrators from the South who shared their experiences with them, and they reveled in the attention their play received at performances in lower Manhattan and Harlem. These special moments gave their return trip home by a southern route all the more emphasis. They felt the injustice of eating sandwiches on the bus because restaurants refused service to African Americans. The young people resolved to challenge these practices in Oklahoma.[14]

In 1958 the Youth Council voted to initiate a campaign of civil disobedience to confront segregation in public accommodations. They received approval of their plans from the senior branch of the Oklahoma City NAACP. Senior officials directed them to avoid any situation that disturbed the peace; to select only one spokesperson; to not carry weapons, chew gum, or laugh loudly; and never to return taunts or to engage in retaliation. Luper advised them that success depended on careful planning and strict observance of a prescribed set of procedures. They set to work devising their strategy, and they pledged to take whatever action was necessary to accomplish their goal.[15]

Luper's leadership of the Youth Council illustrated her understanding of the driving forces behind the civil rights movement in the Deep South. Similar to Ella Baker's influence in SNCC, Luper encouraged participatory democracy. The three themes of this form of participation in social change—broad-based involvement in decision making, a hierarchy modest in size, and direct action on the source of discrimination—informed her direction of the youth group. Luper insisted that the young people educate themselves on the specific injustice so that they understood the facts of the situation and could distinguish between reality and emotion. She promoted the potential for leadership within the group, especially among the female members. Barbara Posey, Gwendolyn Fuller, and Betty Germany emerged as spokespersons in the initial demonstrations and remained effective leaders throughout the next six years of protest. Luper and the Youth Council were convinced that coordinated, direct action offered an effective vehicle for change. Jimmy Stewart, president of the Oklahoma City NAACP in 1958, summarized the difference of opinion between the new young leadership and the older, more cautious leaders when he wrote, "Youth believe in action and we in reaction."[16]

In accordance with her own religious and philosophical beliefs, Luper trained the Youth Council members in the spirit and the letter of nonviolence. The Oklahoma City NAACP files contain a 1957 pamphlet prepared by the Friends Peace Committee entitled "Non-Violence, a Practical Guide for Community Action in America" that served as a manual of instruction. The manual outlined the ten benchmarks of nonviolence: "Violence Renounced; Truth Seeking, Truth Speaking; Constructive Solutions; Direct Action; No Retaliation; Firm, Patient, Persistence; Willingness to Suffer; Forgiveness; Reconciliation; and Concern for Redemption." Luper cautioned her students that the victory for justice depended on their disciplined adherence to these qualities. She kept the teachings and example of Martin Luther King Jr. before them, as well as the sacrifices of the freedom fighters in other states. "Every provocation must be answered with combined good will. You must be ready for self-sacrifice that will leave no doubt as to your integrity, your dignity, and your self-respect. Suffering is a part of the non-violent approach. It is to be endured, never inflicted," she told them. When the sit-ins began, Luper often had to caution sympathetic supporters who wanted to participate but could not accept the verbal intimidation without an angry response. She frequently interposed herself between offensive individuals and members of her group, but she rarely had to remind them of their responsibilities.[17]

The Youth Council targeted five major downtown lunch counters for initial action: Katz Drugstore, Veazey's Drug, S. H. Kress Company, Green's Variety Store, and the John A. Brown department store. These highly visible establishments would focus the community's attention on the injustice of recruiting black customers to purchase merchandise but refusing to allow them to sit at the lunch counters to eat. Although there was no segregation ordinance in Oklahoma City, local practice enforced it. If intimidation failed to remove an objecting black customer, the owners resorted to trespass or loitering laws to justify a police arrest.

The Youth Council first gave the business owners and managers an opportunity to agree to equitable service. Luper and two or three young people, often accompanied by Luper's close friend, Caroline Burks, or another white person, visited the management and attempted to convince them to change their exclusionary policy. Simultaneously, they wrote letters and made visits to city officials and leading black and white church groups in Oklahoma City hoping to engender public support for integration of public accommodations. All of these groups declined to get involved for a variety of reasons. Store owners claimed they would lose customers and money, city officials argued that they could not intrude on an owner's management of his business, and church leaders cautioned against moving too fast or refused to respond at all. On August 19, 1958, the Youth Council voted to move to the final step of their plan, direct action demonstrations. Neither Luper nor the Youth Council anticipated the six-year campaign they initiated with the first sit-in in summer 1958.[18]

The first victories came relatively easy. Katz capitulated after only two days, Veazey's and Green's offered little resistance, and Kress agreed to serve the group after the embarrassed manager removed all of the stools from the counter, forcing every customer to eat standing up. The luncheonette at John A. Brown's, under the management of Frank Wade, proved much more intractable. Regardless of the rapidity of store compliance, each demonstration highlighted the tensions that swirled around Luper and the children from frustrated managers and waitresses, uneasy policemen, ambitious journalists, and angry white customers. Insults, threats, suggestive remarks, pushing and shoving, and obscene telephone calls accompanied them on all of the days they demonstrated. The protest usually began with a meeting at one of the churches where Luper and supportive ministers prepared her young people for the sit-ins. They sang hymns and prayed. Luper asked each of them if they believed that they could abide by nonviolence. Although they encountered verbal harassment, they suffered none of the violent backlash that became the theme of demonstrations in the southern states.[19]

Along with restaurant sit-ins, Youth Council members attended services at all-white churches in downtown Oklahoma City to explain their protest and enlist moral support. Seventeen churches welcomed their attendance. However, Luper's daughter, Marilyn, and a friend were asked to sit in a separate area of the Capitol Hill Baptist Church and were told, "God doesn't want the races to mix." At Kelham Avenue Baptist Church, the minister asked two girls to leave, telling them that their presence might cause trouble in his congregation. Nonetheless the young people had made their point. Christians needed to consider carefully how well segregation followed the teachings of the gospel and in which direction their future actions ought to proceed.[20]

The danger at the John A. Brown luncheonette sit-ins escalated over time. One white patron sat down in the lap of a young female demonstrator, and a twenty-three-year-old man struck one of the teenagers. The waitresses removed or rearranged tables and chairs to prevent the protesters from sitting down, and Frank Wade hired white teenagers to sit in all of the chairs, turning them over only to white customers. They were spat on, cursed at, and had coffee "accidentally" spilled on them. One man brought in a trained chimpanzee that he threatened to unleash to bite the children. The police were always present and hastily removed the troublemakers, but the environment inside the lunchroom was volatile. The children patiently read, sang, colored in coloring books, or made up stories as they sat or stood. As she waited with them, Luper wrote a series of "Letters to America," in part to capture the history of this struggle and the portrait of injustice that emerged. She also kept a journal as a reminder of the dignity and courage of those young people who sat with her and the acts of individual kindness that also became part of the demonstrations.

Luper's "Letters to America" also helped her to keep her mission in sight and not to lose hope or control of her own behavior. The entries below illustrate her commitment:

> I have just been asked, "Why did you come back here today?" We know that they don't want us here. We came today, for the same reason that we came yesterday. We have a responsibility to ourselves and our posterity to make Freedom work.

> Listen, we are waiting. Waiting for a hamburger, and in that hamburger, the whole essence of Democracy lies.

> You must understand that we are yours and "you are ours." We love you. The eyes of the world are on you. Democracy's future is in your hands.

> Some of the children are getting tired of non-violence. They want us to try just a "little violence." Sometimes I have violent thoughts. I have

violent thoughts just like you. I have evil thoughts, but history speaks to me and says, "Non-violence is the way."

If anyone is to be hurt, let it be me, not my children or my white brothers. I thought to myself, "if any blood is to be shed, let it be mine, not my children's."[21]

White segregationists terrorized Luper with hate mail, threatening telephone calls, and a bomb threat at her home. Yet some African American Oklahoma citizens also attacked Luper, claiming she endangered young people, embarrassed the African American community, put black workers at risk with their white employers, and encouraged violence. Luper wrote in her journal, "The Black people here are acting funny now. I used to be invited to Black churches to speak, but things have changed. . . . I guess they are afraid. Maybe I should be afraid, but fear is not part of my inner structure." In spite of all this, Luper reported to the press that monetary donations to the Youth Council treasury were increasing, and the demonstrations were growing daily as a result of the large number of volunteers.[22]

On September 2, 1958, the Youth Council suspended the sit-ins at John A. Brown's. Senior NAACP members applied pressure on Luper to take this action. She chose to use the beginning of the school term and her students' need to return to their classrooms as the public reason to halt the demonstrations. She also saw the wisdom in giving Vivian Reno, executive secretary of the Oklahoma City Council of Churches, time to devise a plan for cooperating with the restaurant owners to accomplish integration. Reno's plan turned out to be little more than an attempt to mobilize support for those restaurant owners who chose to desegregate. Meanwhile, NAACP leaders continued to educate the public and various religious, civic, and business interests while simultaneously calling for a city ordinance that would outlaw segregation in public accommodations. By the end of September, 114 prominent Oklahoma City residents, including members of the clergy, educators, physicians, attorneys, and other professionals, signed a formal statement urging theaters, hotels, and restaurants to extend service to all citizens without regard to race. Public opinion shifted, but official action stalled, prompting the Youth Council to resume their restaurant demonstrations in 1959.[23]

Luper often took advantage of black and white female networks to promote desegregation. One of her ablest allies was Caroline Burks, a retired white schoolteacher, who wrote to the management of the John A. Brown Company expressing her disgust at the rude treatment the luncheonette manager and waitresses gave to Luper and the Youth Council and withdrawing her patronage from the store. "Mrs. Clara Luper is one of the finest women I know. She deserves much credit for the splendid work she is doing with those young people," Burks wrote. "An insult to her and her well-trained boys and girls, is an insult to me." Luper also relied on the Mothers for Support for Non-Violent Protest, a coalition of twenty-one eastside organizations of women, most of whom had youngsters who were involved in Luper's demonstrations.[24]

Luper's gender helped the Youth Movement to achieve its most important victory, the desegregation of Brown's luncheonette. Frequently between 1957 and 1960, Luper had contacted the Brown Company requesting a meeting with Mrs. John A. Brown, director of the company since her husband's death. Luper hoped that she might be able to persuade Mrs. Brown to reconsider the policy of excluding blacks from the lunchroom. Each time she had been denied an interview. Then, in 1961, the Brown Company office telephoned Luper, requesting that she meet with Mrs. Brown. Luper and Brown met first as women and secondarily as negotiators. They discussed their families and, as Luper related, the difficulties they faced as women trying to "compete in a man's business world." They also honestly and seriously exchanged their initial opinions of each other and reports each had received about the other. Luper found out that the first time she had been arrested, Brown had called the police station to check on her safety. At the end of nearly an hour, Brown understood the appropriate action to take and assured Luper that segregation would end at the John A. Brown Company. Within the week, African Americans ate lunch for the first time in the largest department store in downtown Oklahoma City. By 1961 more than one hundred Oklahoma City restaurants had opened service regardless of race.[25]

Luper and her followers participated in sit-ins, sing-ins, pray-ins, picketing, and boycotts in segregated restaurants, theaters, swimming pools, and amusement parks all over Oklahoma between 1961 and 1964. In March 1961, however, she led a new form of protest called a "squat-in" at the Cravens Building where Anna Maude's Cafeteria was housed. This action brought her criticism from white city leaders, NAACP officials, and national NAACP legal advisers as well. Anna Maude's Cafeteria had been the location of picketing for years with no success and considerable abuse from the manager, J. W. Quillan. Luper advised the group of black and white volunteers to go as far into the Cravens Building lobby as possible, sit down on the floor, and remain silent no matter what happened. The police arrived and ordered Luper to remove the demonstrators from the premises. When she refused to respond to them, they dragged her out of the building and down the sidewalk into the waiting police car, scraping her knees badly on the pavement. Twelve other protesters received the same treatment, including Father Robert McDole, pastor of Corpus Christi Catholic Church.[26]

The method of this demonstration resulted in the police booking the thirteen "squatters" based on a complaint for blocking the entrance to the cafeteria, an injunction forbidding future demonstrations at that location, and a lawsuit against the NAACP by the Cravens Building Corporation. At the March NAACP board meeting, U. Simpson Tate, legal adviser of the NAACP in Oklahoma, lectured Luper for her failure to follow NAACP policies that expected scrupulous observance of municipal ordinances. Tate was joined in his criticism of Luper by E. Melvin Porter, a leading black attorney and NAACP activist. The leaders criticized Luper for being too independent, making unauthorized statements to the press, and other irregularities in carrying out her demonstrations. According to one newspaper report, Tate warned Luper, "[N]o one is indispensable to the NAACP." Nevertheless, NAACP attorneys, including Porter, defended Luper when her case came to trial.[27]

This publicity proved embarrassing for the more conservative NAACP leaders because Luper had been personally selected to serve on the prestigious Governor's Committee on Human Relations. A year before Luper's arrest, longtime Oklahoma City NAACP leader and *Black Dispatch* columnist, Jimmy Stewart, proposed that Governor J. Howard Edmondson create a statewide interracial committee to advise him and to work toward the goal of justice and equality in Oklahoma. Stewart outlined his views of the purpose, activities, and organization of such a group and submitted thirty names for Edmondson's consideration. He included Luper's name on the list. When Edmondson formed the group in spring 1960, Clara Luper became the vice-chairman of the Food Service, Hotel and Motel Accommodations Committee. This appointment failed to silence Luper. She continued to direct well-publicized protest activities all over the state.[28]

Six years of demonstrations by Luper and the Youth Council, lobbying by the Oklahoma City NAACP, pressure from sympathetic civic and religious organizations, the death of President John F. Kennedy, and dramatic changes in racial negotiation across the United States finally moved the Oklahoma City council toward conciliation. In spite of resistance from metropolitan business owners, the council passed a city ordinance on June 2, 1964, ending segregation in public accommodations. This law predated the national civil rights legislation pushed through by President Lyndon Johnson by one month.[29]

The few writers who have attempted to analyze the success of the Oklahoma City civil rights movement and its lack of heinous violence have pointed to many mediating factors that created a climate for effective social change. They credit city and state officials who set a tone of reason and flexibility, a police force that acted in moderation and worked to prevent violence on both sides, a press and media that in most cases emphasized cooperation rather than sensationalism, and a tradition of clearly defined objectives and strategies in the African American community.

Certainly, Clara Luper's name belongs on the list of individuals who gave this experience its integrity. An African American woman, small in stature but large in ability and heart, Luper chose the direct path to freedom for herself and the Oklahoma City community. Surely the sight of this woman, surrounded by loyal youths, who remained steadfast in her mission over six long years suggested to many the shame and dishonesty of inequality. Luper unhesitatingly placed herself at the forefront of civil rights activity, negotiating where possible, pressuring where necessary, and refusing to accept anything less than justice.[30]

NOTES

1. The most complete account of the NAACP Youth Council activities and Clara Luper's involvement is Clara Luper, *Behold the Walls* (Oklahoma City: Jim Wire, 1979); Carl R. Graves, "The Right to Be Served: Oklahoma City's Lunch Counter Sit-Ins, 1958–1964," *Chronicles of Oklahoma* 59 (1981): 152–66; Barbara Posey and Gwendolyn Fuller, "Protest Drug Counter Discrimination," *Crisis* (December 1958): 612–13; "Katz Fountain Gives Negro Group Service," *Daily Oklahoman*, August 22, 1958.

2. Anne Standley, "The Role of Black Women in the Civil Rights Movement," in *Women in the Civil Rights Movement, Trailblazers and Torchbearers, 1914-1965*, ed. Vicki L. Crawford, Jacqueline Ann Rouse, and Barbara Woods (New York: Carlson Publishing, 1990), 183–202; Harvard Sitkoff, *The Struggle for Black Equality* (New York: Hill and Wang, 1981).

3. Darlene Clark Hine, Elsa Barkely Brown, and Rosalyn Terborg-Penn, eds., *Black Women in America: An Historical Encyclopedia* (Bloomington: Indiana University Press, 1993), "Luper, Clara," by Darrell Rice, 1:735–37; Shirelle Phelps, ed., *Who's Who among African-Americans, 1996–1997*, 9th ed. (New York: Gale Research, 1996), "Luper, Clara M.," 961; Luper, *Behold the Walls*, 21, 43–45.

4. Joel Williamson, *The Crucible of Race: Black-White Relations in the American South since Emancipation* (New York: Oxford University Press, 1984), 241–43; Norman L. Crockett, *The Black Towns* (Lawrence, Kans.: Regents Press, 1979); Donald Grinde

and Quintard Taylor, "Red v Black: Conflict and Accommodation in the Post–Civil War Indian Territory, 1865–1907," *American Indian Quarterly* 8 (Summer 1984): 211–29; Arthur L. Tolson, *The Black Oklahomans: A History, 1541–1972* (New Orleans: Edwards Printing Co., 1974); Jimmie Lewis Franklin, *Journey toward Hope: A History of Blacks in Oklahoma* (Norman: University of Oklahoma Press, 1982); and Murray R. Wickett, *Contested Territory: Whites, Native Americans, and African Americans in Oklahoma, 1865–1907* (Baton Rouge: Louisiana State University Press, 2000).

5. Danney Goble, *Progressive Oklahoma: The Making of a New Kind of State* (Norman: University of Oklahoma Press, 1980); Phillip Mellinger, "Discrimination and Statehood in Oklahoma," *Chronicles of Oklahoma* 49 (Autumn 1971): 340–78; William E. Bittle and Gilbert Geis, *The Longest Way Home: Chief Alfred C. Sam's Back to Africa Movement* (Detroit: Wayne State University Press, 1964); and R. Bruce Shepard, "North to the Promised Land, Black Migration to the Canadian Plains," *Chronicles of Oklahoma* 62 (Fall 1988): 306–27.

6. Luper, *Behold the Walls*, 43–44; David R. Goldfield, *Black, White, and Southern: Race Relations and Southern Culture, 1940 to the Present* (Baton Rouge: Louisiana State University Press, 1990), 2; Danney Goble, "The Southern Influence on Oklahoma," in *"An Oklahoma I Had Never Seen Before": Alternative Views of Oklahoma History*, ed. Davis D. Joyce (Norman: University of Oklahoma Press, 1994), 280–301.

7. Goldfield, *Black, White, and Southern*, 11; Luper, *Behold the Walls*, 70.

8. Zella J. Black Patterson, *Langston University: A History* (Norman: University of Oklahoma Press, 1979), 3–18; Donald Spivey, "Crisis on a Black Campus: Langston University and Its Struggle for Survival," *Chronicles of Oklahoma* 59 (Winter 1981–82): 436.

9. Luper, *Behold the Walls*, 45; Hine, *Black Women in America*, 735; Ada Lois Sipuel Fisher, with Danney Goble, *A Matter of Black and White: The Autobiography of Ada Lois Sipuel Fisher* (Norman: University of Oklahoma Press, 1996), 69–75.

10. Patterson, *Langston*, 142–47; Spivey, "Crisis," 441–42; Sipuel Fisher, *A Matter of Black and White*, 72, 73–75.

11. Tolson, *Black Oklahomans*, 146–72; Jimmie Lewis Franklin, *The Blacks in Oklahoma*, 35–38.

12. Franklin, *The Blacks in Oklahoma*, 49.

13. Ibid., 50–53; Kaye M. Teall, *Black History in Oklahoma: A Resource Book* (Oklahoma City: Oklahoma City Public Schools, 1971), 273–78; Sipuel Fisher, *A Matter of Black and White*, 87–153; Luper, *Behold the Walls*, 45.

14. Luper, *Behold the Walls*, 1–3.

15. Ibid., 3–8; Jimmy Stewart to William Peters, September 1, 1958, Jimmy Stewart Collection, F-17, Ralph Ellison and the Downtown Branches of the Oklahoma City Library System.

16. Carol Mueller, "Ella Baker and the Origins of 'Participatory Democracy,'" in *Black Women's History, Theory and Practice*, vol. 1, ed. Darlene Clark Hine (New York: Carlson Publishing, 1990), 51–70; Darlene Clark Hine, "An Angle of Vision: Black Women and the United States Constitution, 1787–1987," in Hine, *Black Women's History*, 1-11; Jimmy Stewart to William Peters; Aldon D. Morris, *The Origins of the Civil Rights*

Movement: Black Communities Organizing for Change (New York: Freedom Press, 1984), 24–125.

17. *Non-Violence, a Practical Guide for Community Action in America* (Philadelphia: Friends Peace Committee, 1957), 4–5, 11–12, Jimmy Stewart Collection, F-16-4; Luper, *Behold the Walls*, 8.

18. Graves, "The Right to Be Served," 152–55; James G. Hochtritt Jr., "An Absence of Malice: The Oklahoma City Sit-Ins Movement, 1958–1964" (M.A. thesis, University of Oklahoma, 1994), 6–10; Saxe, "Protest and Reform," 162–67; James M. Smallwood, *Crossroads Oklahoma: The Black Experience in Oklahoma* (Stillwater: Crossroads Oklahoma Project, Oklahoma State University, 1981), 14–21.

19. "Negroes Are Served in Midwest City Café," *Black Dispatch*, August 29, 1958; "Negro Youths 'Store Sitting' in Fourth Day," *Daily Oklahoman*, August 23, 1958; "Gwendolyn Fuller Speaks," *Black Dispatch*, September 26, 1958; Luper, *Behold the Walls*, 12; Stewart Letter to Peters.

20. "Negro Youths Continue Their Store Sitting," *Daily Oklahoman*, August 24, 1958; "Negro Group Carries Plea to Churches," *Daily Oklahoman*, August 25, 1958.

21. Luper, *Behold the Walls*, 37–40.

22. Ibid., 22–26, 42; "NAACP Leaders Back 'Sitdown,'" *Daily Oklahoman*, September 1, 1958; "Oklahoma City Citizens, What Is the Answer?" *Black Dispatch*, August 29, 1958.

23. "Negroes Call Off Store 'Sitdowns,'" *Daily Oklahoman*, September 2, 1958; "NAACP Youth Suspend Campaign for Better Accommodations," *Black Dispatch*, September 5, 1958. Aldon Morris maintains that senior leaders told Luper to stop the demonstrations in *Origins of the Civil Rights Movement*, 125; "Plan Designed for Integrated Eating Places," *Daily Oklahoman*, September 10, 1958; "City Group Takes Over Youth Integration Bid," *Black Dispatch*, September 26, 1958; "114 Ask Doors Open to Negroes," *Daily Oklahoman*, September 24, 1958.

24. Letter to the Editor, *Black Dispatch*, August 29, 1958; Luper, *Behold the Walls*, 66–68; "Negro Pickets Walk at Doors of City Cafes," *Daily Oklahoman*, August 6, 1960.

25. John A. Brown's change of policy came also as a result of an economic boycott launched in August 1960. See Luper, *Behold the Walls*, 48–53. See also Saxe, "Protest and Reform," 160, 163, 168; "Negroes Vote Store Boycott in Downtown," *Daily Oklahoman*, August 20, 1960; "Pickets Gone: Negroes Push Boycott Plan," *Daily Oklahoman*, August 21, 1960; "Negroes Boycott Starts Quietly, Effect Unclear," *Daily Oklahoman*, August 23, 1960; "Negroes Insist Boycott Curbs Sales in Stores," *Daily Oklahoman*, August 24, 1960; Hochtritt, "Absence of Malice," 21; Graves, "The Right to Be Served," 156–58.

26. Luper, *Behold the Walls*, 70–72.

27. Ibid., 72–79; "Mrs. Clara Luper Called on Carpet," *Oklahoma Eagle*, March 31, 1961, clipping in Jimmy Stewart Collection, F-17-34.

28. Jimmy Stewart Letter to Governor J. Howard Edmondson, March 24, 1960, Jimmy Stewart Collection, F-25-10; Membership List and Appointments, F-25-11.

29. Hochtritt, "Absence of Malice," 27; Graves, "The Right to Be Served," 158–60.

30. Ibid., 28–35; Susan A. Gimmel, "Clara Luper, a Born Leader," *Oklahoma Woman* (January 2000): 4–5.

Elaine Brown: Black Panther

Elaine Brown assumed leadership of the Black Panther Party in Oakland, California, in August 1974.

"I have all the guns and all the money. I can withstand challenge from without and from within. Am I right, Comrade?"

Larry snapped back his answer to my rhetorical question: "Right on!" His muscular body tilted slightly as he adjusted the .45 automatic pistol under his jacket.

I was standing on the stage, with him at my side. Several of the key Brothers from the security squads were standing just in the back of us. To my left I could feel Big Bob, Huey Newton's personal bodyguard, all six feet eight inches and four hundred pounds of him. In front of me, extending all the way to the back of the auditorium, were several hundred other members of the Black Panther Party, a sea of predominately male faces. They were black men and women from the party's Central Committee and from various local leadership cadres, from the West Side of Chicago, from North Philadelphia, Harlem, New Orleans, Los Angeles, Washington, D.C., and elsewhere. They had come to Oakland this August of 1974 at my command.

I watched them carefully, noting that no one moved in response to my opening remarks. Here I was, a woman, proclaiming supreme power over the most militant organization in America. It felt natural to me. I had spent the last seven years as a dedicated member of the Black Panther Party, the last four at Huey's right hand.

"I haven't called you together to make threats, Comrades," I continued. "I've called this meeting simply to let you know the realities of our situation. The fact is, Comrade Huey is in exile. The other fact is, I'm taking his place until we make it possible for him to return."

I allowed them a moment to grasp the full meaning of my words. "I'm telling you this because it's possible some of you may balk at a woman as the leader of

Source: Elaine Brown, *A Taste of Power: A Black Woman's Story* (New York: Pantheon Books, 1992), 3–8.

the Black Panther Party. . . . If this is your attitude, you'd better get out of the Black Panther Party. Now. I am saying this also because there may be some individuals in our ranks who have private ambitions and, in Comrade Huey's absence, may imagine themselves capable of some kind of coup." I paused again. No one spoke.

Cocking my head to the side, I continued in the manner I knew was required. "If you are such an individual, you'd better run—and fast. I am, as your chairman, the leader of this party as of this moment. My leadership cannot be challenged. I will lead our party both above ground and underground. I will lead the party not only in furthering our goals but also in defending the party by any and all means. . . ."

I watched a few of the Brothers slap their palms together in common recognition. A subdued laughter of agreement rippled through the auditorium. I began to walk up and down the stage, purposely emphasizing my words with the sound of the heels of my black leather boots. I punctuated each sentence with a nod to one or another of the soldiers standing on stage with me, backing me up.

"I repeat, I have control over all the guns and all the money of this party. There will be no external or internal opposition I will not resist and put down. I will deal resolutely with anyone or anything that stands in the way. So if you don't like what we're going to do, here is your chance to leave. You'd better leave because you won't be tolerated."

They began to applaud loudly, then louder, and then suddenly they were standing. The Sisters and the Brothers were on their feet. When the ovation was over and they were seated, I released my pent-up breath and continued. "For now, Comrades, we must take the next step. We must make Oakland a base camp for revolution. This is why we can have no internal strife. We have to get moving."

"Let's get busy, then, Comrades. Return to your chapters and branches throughout this country with renewed dedication. Soon the Central Committee will be issuing orders and reports regarding the status of each chapter. . . . Let us get busy and prepare a place for the return of Comrade Huey. Let us get busy and prepare a place for the introduction of revolution!" I raised my fist in the air and shouted: "All power to the people! Panther power to the vanguard!"

They leaped to their feet, fists raised in salute: "Power to the People! Power to the People! Power to the People!"

CHAPTER 18

Black Radicalism in 1960s California

WOMEN IN THE BLACK PANTHER PARTY

Jane Rhodes

Perhaps no group of African American radicals in the second half of the twentieth century received greater notoriety or was the object of greater political repression than the Black Panther Party (BPP). Founded in Oakland, California, in 1966, the Black Panther Party was emblematic of the African American experience in the western United States during this era, representing the confluence of several circumstances—the postwar black migration to the West, the urban unrest most dramatically represented by the 1965 Watts riots, and northern black youths' estrangement from the southern civil rights movement.

Today the Black Panthers survive in the nation's historical memory through vivid images of swaggering, gun-toting black men in berets and leather jackets, clenched fists pointing skyward as they chanted, "All Power to the People." Women are generally absent from this legacy. For example, the 1995 motion picture *Panther*, written and directed by Melvin Van Peebles, failed to present black women in any active roles. During the 1960s, the public image of the Black Panther was of a highly masculine, defiant, angry youth who was willing to take up arms in defense of the black community. Huey Newton, one of the organization's founders, often appeared as a symbol of radical black nationalism. The photos of Newton draped in bullets with a rifle in hand adorned the front page of the Black Panthers' newspaper, on buttons and posters, and in national media accounts. According to the art historian Erika Doss, "[T]he Black Panther Party for Self Defense deliberately projected a visual image of black power and revolutionary martyrdom that hinged on potent black masculinity and patriarchal authority." Nevertheless, numerous women, including Kathleen Cleaver, Elaine Brown, and Angela Davis, gained national prominence through their association with the party. Equally important were the legions of women who made significant contributions to the organization outside the media limelight.[1]

In the 1960s Oakland represented the worst of the West's economic and racial crisis. Twenty years earlier the San Francisco Bay Area, particularly the naval shipyards, was a magnet for African American migrants seeking employment in the region. But postwar deindustrialization shook the region's economy, displacing black workers and throwing many into poverty. Oakland's overall population declined between 1950 and 1970, with whites fleeing the city in large numbers. During the same period, the number of blacks grew by 150 percent, making them a quarter of the total population. In the 1960s two-thirds of Oakland's nonwhite population lived in poverty, there was an acute housing shortage, and urban renewal projects were decimating black neighborhoods.[2] By the era of the Black Panther Party, the city was in full-fledged crisis. Thus, as Quintard Taylor notes, party founders Huey Newton and Bobby Seale were part of a disadvantaged generation who, "unlike their shipbuilding parents, could not secure places in the postwar Bay Area economy."[3]

Despite the increasing number of blacks, Oakland remained a largely segregated city. Poor and minority residents were confined to the flatlands, while affluent whites settled in the hills overlooking San Francisco Bay. Local businesses were notorious for refusing to hire blacks, there were only nine black officers out of six hundred on the Oakland police force, and the city's one daily newspaper, the *Oakland Tribune*, had a reputation for ignoring the concerns of minority residents. In 1963 civil rights organizations such as the Congress for Racial Equality (CORE) and the National Association for the Advancement of Colored People (NAACP) targeted Oakland, San Francisco, and neighboring Berkeley for boycotts and demonstrations to protest discrimination in housing and employment. Despite some small successes, the enthusiasm for such actions faded within a year as the area's disaffected black youth looked for other, more radical outlets.[4]

In 1966 Huey Newton and Bobby Seale, both students at Merritt Junior College in Oakland, aimed to fill the void. Newton and Seale had participated in several black nationalist groups on campus and became leaders of the Soul Students Advisory Council, which pushed for the introduction of black history courses. They also donated their time at the North Oakland Poverty Center, collaborating on strategies to organize poor and working-class blacks rather than college students. The writing of Frantz Fanon, particularly his calls for violent revolution against white oppression in *The Wretched of the Earth*, profoundly influenced the pair. Their ideology was also shaped by the work of Malcolm X and his Organization of African Unity, which stressed black cultural unity and the need for self-defense. They borrowed the name Black Panthers from a Lowndes County, Alabama, voting rights project organized by the Student Nonviolent Coordinating Committee (SNCC), and they modeled their ten-point platform after the Nation of Islam. The results were what Manning Marable has called "the most provocative challenge to white liberal politics" of the sixties, often using outrageous rhetoric, imagery, and tactics to agitate for social change. Huey Newton proclaimed that "the main function of the party is to awaken the people and teach them the strategic method of resisting a power structure which is prepared not only to combat with massive brutality the people's resistance but to annihilate totally the black population."[5]

Women were an integral part of the Black Panther Party from its inception, despite their low visibility. Prominent Black Panther Ericka Huggins noted that "women ran the party, and men thought they [the men] did." Lynn French, another former member, told a documentary filmmaker that during her years in the party from 1968 to 1773, "there were an awful lot of women who were unsung heroes in the party. . . . [T]here were a whole lot of sisters out there too, and [they were] committing heroic acts." The pattern of African American women playing an active although unrecognized role in radical social movements can be traced to nineteenth-century abolitionism and early black nationalism. Heroic figures like Sojourner Truth and Harriet Tubman were in the forefront of the fight against slavery and oppression, Ida Wells-Barnett campaigned against lynching and Jim Crow segregation, and numerous lesser-known women such as Maria Stewart, Mary Ann Shadd Cary, and Frances E. W. Harper took enormous risks as outspoken opponents of racial and gender inequality. Yet gender politics always circumscribed the extent to which black women's activism could function in largely male-dominated organizations.[6]

This was no different for black women who labored as activists in the second half of the twentieth century. In her study of women in the civil rights movement, Belinda Robnett argues that leading activists such as Fannie Lou Hamer and Jo Ann Robinson understood that gender and religious conventions prevented them from functioning as visible leaders. Rather, they performed "bridge leadership" activities by providing crucial links between formal organizations and black communities. These female bridge leaders, essential to the civil rights movement, remained generally invisible to the media and others outside of civil rights organizations.[7]

This pattern of unrecognized female leadership continued during the Black Power era, often exacerbated by gender politics that advocated an oppressive sexual division of labor and secondary status for women. Symbolizing this problem was the often-repeated story that SNCC leader Stokely Carmichael once proclaimed that "the only position of women in SNCC is prone." Numerous scholars have discussed the varying gender ideologies among black nationalists of the period. Patricia Hill Collins, for example, notes that many cultural nationalists subscribed to a theory of gender complementarity, in which men and women were expected to perform separate roles that complemented each other, as was assumed to be the case in traditional African societies.[8]

The Black Panthers were clearly influenced by these gendered discourses but at the same time sought a viable place for women in the organization. Thus the Panthers presented mixed messages about women's involvement: on one hand, women were encouraged to become black revolutionaries; on the other, they were often told that their main task was to be men's supporters. This dichotomy appeared often in the pages of the group's newspaper, the *Black Panther Intercommunal News Service*. In one early issue, a large graphic illustration entitled "A Revolutionary Sister" showed a woman wearing African garb and brandishing a rifle. On another page, an articled headlined "Sisters' Section: Black Womanhood No. 1" exhorted young women to shed their adherence to consumption and white standards of beauty and instead devote their lives to black men. Judy Hart wrote:

> In terms of survival, i.e., in 1967, the black man needs a woman as a base, an anchor, a refuge, a shelter, a haven, a place of peace, a home and institution of strength. . . . White racist America is a time bomb. And Black women reciprocate by developing a full-blown womanhood in which her man and thus his commitment becomes the essence of her life.

That this article was written by a woman underscored the manner in which black women could materially serve the organization while articulating a conservative gender ideology. In another issue of the newspaper, black women were encouraged to devote their clerical skills to the party: "Jive Sisters, don't read this. The *Black Panther* needs typists. If you can type well and want to work for black liberation, call." The implication was that this was a suitable contribution for women but not for men.[9]

Yet the rhetoric about gender did not necessarily represent the daily realities of party members. As Tracye Matthews has noted, the early self-representations of the Black Panthers were "directly linked to the regaining of Black manhood. . . . Many early statements by Newton and Seale linked Black oppression to Black male castration and focused squarely on the sexual politics of White supremacy." During the early months of the young group, Newton and Seale concentrated on recruiting young men to their fledgling organization. While men were the first to join the Panthers, the group's founders were clearly open to recruiting women. David Hilliard remembered that when Huey Newton first described the Black Panthers, the goal was to seek a membership different from existing civil rights organizations. "All of these other organizations deal with students or the churches. We're gonna get the brothers and sisters off the block like you and me," Newton told Hilliard.[10]

The fledgling party's activities concentrated on establishing armed street patrols to monitor the activities of the Oakland police in black neighborhoods and on political education—hence their original name, the Black Panther Party for Self-Defense. They opened their first storefront office in Oakland in January 1967, where they held recruitment meetings and classes on the Panthers' theories and principles. One of the first women to join the group was a local high school student who already had activist experience under her belt. J. Tarika Lewis recalled that she was encouraged to perform the same duties as her male counterparts, from learning how to use firearms to leading paramilitary drills. Ericka Huggins, who would eventually be a cofounder of the group's New Haven chapter, remembered that when she first joined the Panthers in California, "there wasn't any difference between the work women did and the work men did." Women trickled into the party's headquarters in the Bay Area on and off during the first year and were highly visible when the Panthers staged their first major public event at the state capitol in Sacramento in May 1967. On that day, a group of thirty gun-toting Panthers—men and women—marched into the capitol building to protest proposed legislation that would put an end to the Panthers' legal display of weapons. The protest, covered by the state and national news media, catapulted the Black Panther Party into the public eye. Nevertheless, the party remained a male-dominated organization in its early years.[11]

Perhaps the best known and most influential woman in the development of the Black Panther Party was Kathleen Cleaver. As communication secretary, Cleaver was the highest-ranking woman in the organization during this early period, and she had a significant impact on the policies and public image they presented. Yet she was just as often identified as the wife and helpmate of

Eldridge Cleaver, Panther minister of information and a national celebrity in his own right. Kathleen Cleaver grew up in Alabama and was involved in nonviolent resistance by the time she was in high school in the early 1960s. By 1967 she had dropped out of college to work full time for SNCC in Nashville where she was drawn to Stokely Carmichael's defiant calls for black power. That spring she met Cleaver when he spoke at a SNCC conference. Cleaver lived in San Francisco while on parole from Soledad prison, working as an editor for *Ramparts* magazine, and had become a popular lecturer on black power themes. Their relationships continued long distance until Kathleen moved to California, where they married. By this time Eldridge was involved with the Black Panther Party and Kathleen followed suit.[12]

Kathleen Cleaver arrived in the Bay Area just as the Panthers became embroiled in a controversy that shifted their focus and public identity. In October 1967 Huey Newton was at the center of an armed confrontation with the Oakland police, leaving one officer dead and another wounded. When the smoke cleared, Newton, who was also wounded, had been arrested for murder. The Panthers devoted considerable energy to his acquittal and release in what would become known as the "Free Huey" campaign. Kathleen Cleaver was a key player in this effort. In a 1971 interview, she explained that she, Eldridge Cleaver, and Panther Minister of Culture Emory Douglass were "the three functional members of the Party that began to put together a movement to liberate Huey Newton." As the first woman to have a position on the party's Central Committee, she assisted in publishing the party's newspaper, became an effective spokesperson at rallies and press conferences, and generally demonstrated the organizing skills she had honed during her years with SNCC. Cleaver told one interviewer that her administrative talents were sorely needed within the party. "I went there in the midst of a total crisis," she said. "They didn't really have any organization to speak of at that time."[13]

Life in the Black Panther Party's headquarters in Oakland exposed Kathleen Cleaver and other women to a climate of constant fear and harassment. Later, classified documents and congressional hearings revealed that the Panthers were prime targets of a FBI counterintelligence program known as COINTELPRO. Local police and federal agents routinely raided the Panthers' offices, and violence was often provoked between rival groups of black nationalists. In an article she wrote for *Ramparts*, Cleaver remembered one early morning in January 1968 when a San Francisco police squad "kicked down the door to our apartment, barged in with drawn guns, and ransacked the place." Such incidents produced a sense of dread since Cleaver was acutely aware that they could be killed or that Eldridge could be sent back to prison. Three months later, Cleaver's worst fears came true. Two days after the assassination of Martin Luther King Jr., Eldridge was pinned down in a gun battle between the Oakland police and several carloads of Black Panthers, killing Panther Minister of Finance Bobby Hutton and wounding Eldridge and several police officers. Panther Chief of Staff David Hilliard was jailed as a result of the gunfight and his parole revoked, and Eldridge was arrested and hustled off to San Quentin prison. When Kathleen was finally allowed to see her husband in a California prison medical facility, she found him bruised, bandaged, and drugged. "Eldridge looked like a captured giant, cuts and scratches on his face, the hair burned off the top of his head, his foot covered by a huge white bandage," she recalled. But she realized there was little time to mourn Bobby Hutton's death or Eldridge's capture.

Kathleen Cleaver, like many members of the organization, believed these events confirmed that the Black Panther Party was under siege by the government. Cleaver launched into a flurry of activities, giving a press conference on the steps of Sproul Hall at the University of California, Berkeley, organizing protests against police brutality at the Alameda County courthouse, and strategizing with attorneys. Said Cleaver, "The parole hold against him meant it would take more than money to win Eldridge's freedom; it would take a political campaign, and I knew that I was the one who had to get it started." Eldridge Cleaver was eventually released on bail, but his freedom was short lived.[14]

By the end of 1968, women had made themselves indispensable in the Black Panther Party. In the increasingly routine national media coverage of the group, women were seen leading demonstrations and staffing Panther headquarters. These images, disseminated around the country, helped to recruit more women to the party's ranks. Soon, women comprised as much as 60 percent of the group's membership and carried out much of the day-to-day business. Joan Kelly-Williams, a former Panther official, explained that the climate of urgency and the constant sense of being under attack meant that many party chapters dispensed with a sexual division of labor: "When there was greater police harassment, more raids, etc., women had a more equal share of responsibility for security." For example, she reminisced about working in the central distribution of the *Black Panther* newspaper, an activity necessary for raising revenue and raising consciousness: "We were hoisting bales of newsprint, driving trucks. I remember doing all kinds of very physical work." Later, Kelly-Williams would serve as an editor for the newspaper, joining a long line of women who held that position.[15]

Several scholars mark this period as a significant transition in the activities of the Black Panther Party. In September 1968 Huey Newton was sent to prison after being convicted of voluntary manslaughter. The same day that Newton was sentenced and sent to Vacaville penitentiary, the California Court of Appeals revoked Eldridge Cleaver's bail, giving him sixty days to return to prison. This sparked Eldridge's flight into exile in November, first to Cuba and then to Algeria. Kathleen Cleaver followed him to begin a life as a fugitive. Meanwhile, Bobby Seale had been arrested and placed on trial on federal charges of conspiracy to riot as part of the Chicago Eight, following the Democratic National Convention in August. David Hilliard was also arrested in December for making public threats on the life of the president. At least five Panthers were dead after violent encounters with the police. Women stepped into this vacuum; some women "assumed the rank and duties left unoccupied by the departure of their male comrades, while other women filled prominent local leadership positions from the onset."[16]

A number of women who joined the Los Angeles chapter of the Black Panther Party rose to national repute during this period. Perhaps the best known was Angela Davis. Like Kathleen Cleaver, Davis grew up in Birmingham, Alabama, and was intensely affected by the crises and changes wrought by the civil rights movement of her youth. By the time she attended Brandeis University, she was drawn to radical philosophy and seriously committed to social change. Studying in Paris in 1963, Davis learned about the bombing of the Sixteenth Street Baptist Church in Birmingham; she had known the four girls who were killed in the incident. As a philosophy student in Germany, she watched the coalescence of activism at home: the rise of Students for a Democratic Society (SDS), the cries for black power, and the urban riots. After two years abroad, she returned to the United States to continue her graduate studies at the University of California, San Diego. "I wanted to continue my academic work, but I knew I could not do it unless I was politically involved," she wrote in her autobiography.[17]

Davis arrived in southern California in fall 1967 and became deeply involved in movements for social change. As she observed the fragmentation between black nationalist groups, she found herself drawn to the arguments laid out by SNCC and by the Communist Party. In Los Angeles, Davis began attending meetings of the Che-Lumumba Club, a Communist Party offshoot. She also began building alliances with the Black Panther Party, which was working to solidify its presence in the city. "I felt it would be important for some of us to assist in the work of the Black Panther Party which, at that time, was like a magnet drawing large numbers of young Black people, all over the country, into its ranks," Davis recalled. The Panthers' political education classes helped Davis to shed the elitism she had acquired as a university student. Now she devoted much of her energy to mobilizing the residents of Los Angeles's black neighborhoods even as she continued her graduate work.[18]

Davis was also acutely aware of the gender dynamics embedded in black nationalist organizations. "I became acquainted very early with the widespread presence of an unfortunate syndrome among some Black male activists— namely, to confuse their political activity with an assertion of their maleness," she wrote. On one occasion, for example, she remembered being criticized by members of the US-Organization, another California-based black nationalist group, for doing men's work and taking on leadership activities. She was also discouraged when Panther leaders pushed her to choose between the Black Panthers and the Communist Party after fears of police infiltration prompted a purge of "suspicious" members.

In January 1969 another brutal confrontation threw the Los Angeles Panthers into disarray. For several months, the Black Panthers had been in the midst of a power and ideological struggle with the US-Organization. The latter group, founded by Maulenga Karenga, espoused an Afrocentric cultural nationalism that attracted a strong following across southern California. On January 17, a meeting between the two groups on the campus of the University of California, Los Angeles (UCLA), turned violent, and two local Panther leaders, John Huggins and Bunchy Carter, were killed. This event led to Angela Davis's decision to leave the Black Panther Party, although she remained close with many of its members. The deaths of Carter and Huggins in Los Angeles left a leadership void that was quickly filled by several women, most notably Elaine Brown, who was appointed deputy minister of information.

The incident on the UCLA campus proved far more tragic for Ericka Huggins, wife of John Huggins, mother of an infant, and active member of the Los Angeles chapter. In the ensuing months, Huggins moved to New Haven, Connecticut, to bury her husband and regroup. Local activists encouraged her to become more involved in the area's politics, and by April she was cofounder of the New Haven chapter of the Black Panther Party. This was only the beginning of Huggins's notoriety, however.[19] A month later, New Haven Black Panther Alex Rackley, suspected of being an FBI informant, was found dead. Bobby Seale and Ericka Huggins and five other women were among those arrested for the torture-murder of Rackley. They were nicknamed the New Haven 14, and the Panthers initiated a nationwide campaign for their release. Huggins joined the growing legion of imprisoned Black Panthers. Her ten-month-old baby was taken from her and prison officials employed numerous techniques that worsened her experience, such as shining bright lights in her cell at night. From prison, Huggins wrote articles about these conditions for the *Black Panther* newspaper, and she heralded their revolutionary cause. "They [the oppressors] fail, however, to realize that the masses have boundless creative power, and no matter how they kick ass, beat us, kill us, or jail us, the people, we will carry on," Huggins declared. Her impassioned critiques of racism and injustice, as well as her loyalty to the Panthers despite months of prison hardship, won her considerable admiration and status. Her plight inspired Eldridge Cleaver to write a lengthy treatise arguing, "[W]e must recognize that a woman can be just as revolutionary as a man and that she has equal stature, that, along with men, and that we cannot relegate her to an inferior position." Huggins, Seale, and other defendants were finally acquitted two years later, in May 1971.[20]

Ericka Huggins's experience had helped to open a dialogue within the party about male and female roles. In fall 1969 six unnamed Black Panther women were interviewed about sexism and women's liberation, and their comments were distributed in a four-page pamphlet, "Panther Sisters on Women's Liber-ation." One of the women noted that the visibility of Huggins's incarceration had a significant influence on the ways men and women in the party thought about gender relations. "The Brothers had to look on Ericka with the new light because she had been thru a lot of things that some Brothers hadn't even been thru. The sisters looked up to her and we all saw what we had to do. The sisters have to pick up guns just like brothers. There are a lot of things the sisters can do to change society," said one of the respondents. Another member noted that living in a state of constant crisis encouraged the Panther leadership to advo-cate for women's equality. Indeed, women had become an integral part of the group's leadership structure. "I think conditions outside the Party have forced us to realize that we have to get rid of male chauvinism. As Panthers, we cannot separate ourselves and divide ourselves. . . . There has to be unity within the Party."[21]

Exhausted and eviscerated of its most visible leaders, the Black Panthers underwent a dramatic reorganization in 1969 that placed greater emphasis on community service. Self-defense had only been one prong of the Panthers' activ-ities: in the early years, the group had worked on protests against unfair housing evictions, taught black history courses, and lobbied to install a streetlight in one of San Francisco's black neighborhoods. But now the party would invest even more energy in this direction. Programs in chapters across the nation were developed to provide free breakfasts for poor children, free health services, free neighborhood food distribution, and free transportation for families visiting loved ones in prison. These efforts attracted more women's involvement.

Among the new recruits was Assata Shakur (Joanne Chisimard), a college student in New York City who initially learned about the Panthers through national media coverage and was drawn to their community-based programs in Harlem. Shakur joined the party in 1969 and served in several capacities. Her autobiography provides a rare daily account of a typical woman's experience in the party. Shakur's first assignment was as a medical cadre, making medical and dental appointments for members, teaching basic first aid, and providing health information to poor communities. The Harlem headquarters had ambitious plans to open a free clinic and Shakur was anxious to be part of that project. She also worked for the free breakfast program, which she found especially rewarding. "The Harlem branch had breakfast programs in three different churches, and I rotated among all three. From the first day I saw those kids, my heart went out to them," Shakur wrote.[22]

During her two years as a Black Panther, Shakur found great satisfaction in her community work and built a strong network of friends and associates. At the same time, she was becoming increasingly disenchanted with the organization. "I was becoming more and more critical of what was going on in the Party, but I loved it nevertheless and wanted to see it functioning on the right track," she said. Shakur found that while political education classes for community members were often stimulating and wide ranging, those designed for party members were lacking. "The basic problem stemmed from the fact that the BPP had no systematic approach to political education," she noted. Equally problematic, according to Shakur, was that the Party failed to "teach Panthers organizing and mobilizing techniques," relying instead on whether members had natural talent in this area. Shakur also bristled at what she saw as "the macho cult that was an official body in the BPP," and she often had conflicts with domineering men. In early 1971 Shakur decided to leave the Black Panthers, dispirited by a series of expulsions from the party by Huey Newton, including some of her New York–based associates.[23]

By the time Shakur resigned from the BPP, she had become the object of intense police scrutiny. She recalled the feelings of terror as she realized that her telephone was being tapped and plainclothes officers were watching her, forcing her to flee her apartment. "Everywhere I went it seemed like I would turn around to find two detectives following behind me," she wrote. Shakur joined Angela Davis, Ericka Huggins, and dozens of other women who were incarcerated for grave crimes linked to their involvement with the Black Panthers. In 1973 she was seriously wounded in a shootout on the New Jersey Turnpike that left a state trooper and one of her closest friends dead. From 1973 to 1977 Shakur was repeatedly tried and acquitted for assorted charges, and she was finally convicted of murder and sentenced to life plus sixty-five years. During her incarceration, Shakur was impregnated and she bore the child. She escaped from prison with the help of her friends and allies in 1979 and became a fugitive, eventually gaining asylum in Cuba.[24]

Similarly, Angela Davis spent several months in hiding and more than a year in prison following a shootout in a Marin County courthouse in August 1970. Jonathan Jackson smuggled weapons in to the trial of his brother George, an organizer of the Black Panther Party in Soledad prison. But his bid to liberate his brother failed and Jonathan was killed, along with the judge and two of the other defendants. Angela Davis, a close friend of Jackson's, was miles from the courthouse, but in the aftermath of the incident, she was indicted for conspiracy and providing the weapons for the attack. Davis, who was placed on the FBI's most wanted list, fled into hiding only to be captured several months later. After a twenty-two-month trial, Davis was finally acquitted of all charges. But in the process, she had become a nationally known figure closely associated with the Panthers, although she was no longer officially a member of the party. Like Ericka Huggins, Davis became a revolutionary icon, representing women's potential as radical activists. Soon after her arrest, Huey Newton wrote, "Angela has given her energy and devotion to the people's cause without reference to her personal safety, without reference to her personal gain. She has given in a free and very pure way, in a way that sets an example for people everywhere. We must not fail Angela Davis."[25]

These stories of violence, imprisonment, and exile represented only a fraction of the experiences of women in the Black Panthers. But the threats of police harassment, arrest, and detention were ubiquitous, and there were numerous other court cases, including those of Joan Bird and Afeni Shakur of the New York 21 and lesser-known women from San Francisco to North Carolina. At the same time women were taking on leadership roles in Panther chapters across the country, including Chicago and Boston. The emphasis on community projects highlighted the talents of these women. For example, the Oakland Community School, established in 1971 by the Panthers as the Intercommunal Youth Institute, was directed by a succession of women for more than ten years, including Ericka Huggins, who returned to California after her release from prison.

Perhaps best known was Elaine Brown, who held several posts in the southern California chapter before moving to Oakland to become the highest-ranking woman in the party. Brown moved from Los Angeles to Oakland and began editing the *Black Panther* in 1970. She recalled that this was a demanding task that entailed tremendous responsibility as the newspaper was the party's primary means of communication with the public and with members across the country. "You can't imagine how hard it was," Brown said in an interview. "Editing the paper was exhausting. We sold papers on the street and that was dangerous. The police and rival groups would try to stop us. But we kept it going." Brown gradually became an integral part of the party's inner circle and helped to forge the party's entrance into local politics.

Increasingly, the Black Panthers sought a voice in local communities through electoral politics, in addition to continuing their characteristic protests and demonstrations. In the city of Oakland, the Panthers had a sufficient following to allow them to get their members on the ballot. In 1972 Elaine Brown ran as a candidate for the Oakland City Council on a ticket that included Bobby Seale. Brown lost with about 33 percent of the vote, and Seale lost a runoff election for the mayoral race. More important, they had used their political platforms to critique police, discrimination in local schools, and the economic crisis that continued to ensnare large parts of Oakland's black population.[26]

A by-product of this foray into local politics was the rapid increase in women's participation in the Panthers' national headquarters. Workers in local Black Panther chapters were ordered to report to Oakland to assist the Brown-Seale election effort, and many of them, including the campaign codirectors, were women. "This redeployment of Party members resulted in the concentration of a highly educated female cohort in Oakland," notes Angela LeBlanc-Ernest. The presence of the Panthers in the political arena paved the way for women to become involved in such groups as the Berkeley Community Development Council and the Oakland Model Cities Program.[27]

Two years later Huey Newton named Elaine Brown chairperson of the Panthers shortly before he left the country to avoid prosecution for murder and assault. Brown has been credited with advancing more women into the Panthers' leadership during this period. During her tenure from 1974 to 1977, four women served on the ten-person Central Committee, including Joan Kelly-Williams, Norma Armour, and Phyllis Jackson. Each performed crucial duties for the party; for example, Jackson and Williams oversaw much of the Panthers' financial affairs. Acutely aware of the discomfort some men felt about having women in authoritative positions, Brown recalled that once when she brought in a significant number of female officers, one male Panther muttered, "I hear we can't call them bitches no more."[28]

Brown sought elected office again in 1975, running for a seat on the Oakland City Council. She lost this second bid as well but moved into the political establishment. In 1976 former governor Jerry Brown selected her, along with Ericka Huggins, as a delegate to the Democratic National Convention. That year, Huggins was the first black woman to win a place on the Alameda County School Board as head of the Oakland Community School. The Panthers also helped in the successful election of Oakland's first black mayor in 1977, Lionel Wilson. Brown was subsequently appointed to Wilson's transition team, while Phyllis Jackson was appointed to Oakland's Civil Service Commission. The Panthers did not avoid controversy in this period, however. Elaine Brown was accused of participating in the murder of Betty Van Patter, a hired financial consultant. Though she denied the charges, Brown admits in her autobiography that violence was always an undercurrent in the group's operations. Nevertheless, Elaine Brown, Ericka Huggins, and numerous other women took the Black Panther Party into its second decade, in the process influencing California politics on the local and state levels.[29]

Huey Newton returned to California from exile in July 1977, marking the end of Brown's leadership and the rapid decline of women's involvement in the party. Although Newton praised the work of women during his absence, he reasserted his influence over the party and the climate of masculine authority returned. By the end of the year, Brown had resigned from the Black Panthers, along with many of the women who held together the national headquarters in Oakland. Only Ericka Huggins remained to run the Oakland Community School until 1981. The party membership dropped dramatically as Newton focused most of his attention and resources on his legal defense. Many of the community programs waned, and there were few new recruits as Newton's behavior became increasingly erratic. There were numerous episodes of violence and charges of mismanagement of funds by the party. The *Black Panther* newspaper, the strongest remaining vestige of the party, continued under the helm of JoNina Abron, who served as editor from 1978 to 1980, when it folded. This occurred at a time when the "black nationalist impulse had been effectively splintered, repressed, and removed from political discourse," notes Manning Marable. Indeed, frustrated with the Panthers' decline, many women left the party to join other organizations, to pursue careers in community service, or to return to school for advanced degrees. Kathleen Cleaver earned under-graduate and law degrees from Yale University, and Phyllis Jackson completed a Ph.D. in art history at Northwestern University.[30]

Women were at the heart of the Black Panther Party, and their enduring presence forced members and nonmembers alike to rethink their attitudes about gender. As former Panther Regina Jennings notes, "[T]here were women who came through the party and would immediately leave because of the vulgar male behavior. There were women in the party like me who tried to hold on because we understood the power, the significance, and the need for our organization." Today many of these women see themselves as survivors and understand that they can claim a dual legacy as agents of change both inside and outside of the party. Back in 1971, Kathleen Cleaver was acutely aware of her tenuous position in the party—a consciousness that allowed her to inte-grate feminism with black nationalism. Because of the historical denial of black men's humanity, "we see an effort towards an assertion of manhood by the black man following the European model of suppressing the woman," Cleaver observed. She called for a coalition among all women across the boundaries of race and class. "It's a struggle to totally alter and rearrange the values and organ-ization of a society that allows women to be forced into a position of submis-sion." Cleaver and her sisters in the Black Panther Party contributed mightily to this ongoing process.[31]

NOTES

1. Erika Doss, "Imaging the Panthers: Representing Black Power and Masculinity, 1960s–1990s," *Prospects: An Annual Journal of American Cultural Studies* 23 (1998): 483–516.

2. For a detailed account of Oakland during this era, see Jennifer B. Smith, *An International History of the Black Panther Party* (New York: Garland, 1999), 24–29; and Hugh Pearson, *The Shadow of the Panther: Huey Newton and the Price of Black Power in America* (Reading, Mass.: Addison-Wesley, 1994), 48–50. See also Albert Broussard, *Black San Francisco: The Struggle for Racial Equality in the West, 1900–1954* (Lawrence: University Press of Kansas, 1993).

3. Quintard Taylor, *In Search of the Racial Frontier: African Americans in the Amer-ican West, 1528–1990* (New York: W. W. Norton, 1998), 304.

4. Pearson, *The Shadow of the Panther*, 51–60; Taylor, *In Search of the Racial Fron-tier*, 289–92.

5. Manning Marable, *Race, Reform and Rebellion: The Second Reconstruction in Black America, 1945–1982* (Jackson: University Press of Mississippi, 1984), 121; Huey

Newton, *To Die for the People: The Writings of Huey P. Newton* (New York: Random House, 1972), 15.

6. Ericka Huggins and Lynn French appear in the documentary film, *Comrade Sister: Voices of Women in the Black Panther Party* (Christine L. Minor and Phyllis J. Jackson producers, 1997). On nineteenth-century women, see James Oliver Horton, "Freedom's Yoke: Gender Conventions among Antebellum Free Blacks," *Feminist Studies* 12 (Spring 1986): 51–75. There are assorted biographies of nineteenth-century black women, including Jane Rhodes, *Mary Ann Shadd Cary: The Black Press and Protest in the Nineteenth Century* (Bloomington: Indiana University Press, 1998); and Nell Irvin Painter, *Sojourner Truth: A Life, a Symbol* (New York: W. W. Norton, 1996).

7. Belinda Robnett, *How Long? How Long? African American Women in the Struggle for Civil Rights* (New York: Oxford University Press, 1997), 53–70.

8. Michelle Wallace repeats the Carmichael quote to underscore her discussion of sexism in the civil rights movement. See Michelle Wallace, *Black Macho and the Myth of the Superwoman* (London: Verso, 1990), 7. On black nationalism and gender ideologies, see Patricia Hill Collins, *Fighting Words: Black Women and the Search for Justice* (Minneapolis: University of Minnesota Press, 1998); and E. Frances White, "Africa on My Mind: Gender, Counter Discourse and African-American Nationalism," *Journal of Women's History* 2 (Spring 1990): 73–97.

9. *Black Panther*, July 20, 1967; November 23, 1967.

10. David Hilliard and Lewis Cole, *This Side of Glory: The Autobiography of David Hilliard and the Story of the Black Panther Party* (Boston: Little, Brown, 1993), 118; Tracye Matthews, "'No One Ever Asks What a Man's Place in the Revolution Is': Gender and the Politics of the Black Panther Party, 1966–1971," in *The Black Panthers (Reconsidered)*, ed. Charles E. Jones (Baltimore: Black Classic Press, 1998), 278–79.

11. Angela D. LeBlanc-Ernest, "'The Most Qualified Person to Handle the Job': Black Panther Party Women, 1966–1982," in Jones, *The Black Panthers (Reconsidered)*, 303–27, quote on p. 307. Ericka Huggins from *Comrade Sister*. On the Panthers and media exposure, see Jane Rhodes, "Fanning the Flames of Racial Discord: The National Press and the Black Panther Party," *Harvard International Journal of Press/Politics* 4 (1999): 95–118.

12. On Cleaver, see Kathleen Neal Cleaver, "Three Ways That Martin Luther King Changed My Life," *Black Renaissance/Renaissance Noir* 2 (Fall–Winter 1998): 52–62; and Kathleen Cleaver, "On Eldridge Cleaver, by Kathleen Cleaver," *Ramparts* (June 1969): 4–11.

13. Julia Herve, "*Black Scholar* Interviews Kathleen Cleaver," *Black Scholar* 2 (December 1971): 55; LeBlanc-Ernest, "'The Most Qualified Person to Handle the Job,'" 308.

14. Cleaver, "Three Ways That Martin Luther King Changed My Life," 61–62.

15. Huggins and Kelly-Williams in *Comrade Sister*.

16. See Tracye Matthews, "'No One Ever Asks What a Man's Place in the Revolution Is,'" 277; Cleaver, "On Eldridge Cleaver," 10-11; quote from LeBlanc-Ernest, "'The Most Qualified Person to Handle the Job,'" 310.

17. Angela Davis, *An Autobiography* (New York: International Publishers, 1988), 145.

18. Ibid., 145, 189–90.

19. On Ericka Huggins, see Michael J. Arlen, *An American Verdict* (New York: Anchor Books, 1974).

20. "A Letter from Sister Ericka Huggins," reprinted in G. Louis Heath, ed., *Off the Pigs! The History and Literature of the Black Panther Party* (Metuchen, N.J.: Scarecrow Press, 1976), 351; "Message to Sister Ericka Huggins of the Black Panther Party," *Black Panther*, July 5, 1969.

21. "Panther Sisters on Women's Liberation," reprinted in William Van DeBurg, ed., *Modern Black Nationalism: From Marcus Garvey to Louis Farrakhan* (New York: New York University Press, 1997), 258–68.

22. Assata Shakur, *Assata: An Autobiography* (Westport, Conn.: Lawrence Hill Books, 1987), 219.

23. Ibid., 230, 221, 223.

24. Ibid., 232.

25. See Davis, *An Autobiography*; *Black Panther*, October 17, 1970.

26. Elaine Brown, Interview by Jane Rhodes, June 3, 1998.

27. LeBlanc-Ernest, "'The Most Qualified Person to Handle the Job,'" 318.

28. Elaine Brown, *A Taste of Power: A Black Woman's Story* (New York: Pantheon Books, 1992), 363; also see pp. 363–67, 408–12.

29. Ibid., 360–71.

30. Marable, *Race, Reform and Rebellion*, 168; Brown, *A Taste of Power*, 437–50; see also Abron, "'Raising the Consciousness of the People.'"

31. Regina Jennings, "Why I Joined the Party: An Africana Womanist Reflection," in Jones, *The Black Panthers (Reconsidered)*, 263; Herve, "*Black Scholar* Interviews Kathleen Cleaver," 58–59.

Selected Bibliography

Abajian, James de T., comp. *Blacks and Their Contributions to the American West: A Bibliography and Union List of Holdings through 1970*. Boston: Hall, 1974.

Alpha Kappa Alpha Sorority, Alpha Tau Omega Chapter. *Historical Review: Sixty Years of Gems, 1930–1990*. San Antonio: Alpha Kappa Alpha, 1990.

Anderson, Karen. *Changing Woman: A History of Racial Ethnic Women in Modern America*. New York: Oxford University Press, 1996.

———. "Last Hired, First Fired: Black Women Workers during World War II." *Journal of American History* 69 (1982): 82–97.

———. "Work, Gender, and Power in the American West." *Pacific Historical Review* 61 (1992): 481–99.

Anderson, Kathie Ryckman. "Era Bell Thompson: A North Dakota Daughter." *North Dakota History* 49 (1982): 11–18.

Angelou, Maya. *I Know Why the Caged Bird Sings*. New York: Bantam, 1971.

Armitage, Susan, Theresa Banfield, and Sarah Jacobus. "Black Women and Their Communities in Colorado." *Frontiers* 2 (Summer 1977): 45–51.

Armitage, Susan, Helen Bannan, Katherine G. Morrissey, and Vicki L. Ruiz, comps. *Women in the West: A Guide to Manuscript Sources*. New York: Garland, 1991.

Armitage, Susan H., and Deborah Gallacci Wilbert. "Black Women in the Pacific Northwest: A Survey and Research Prospectus." In *Women in Pacific Northwest History: An Anthology*, ed. Karen J. Blair. Seattle: University of Washington Press, 1988.

Association of Colored Women, Wichita District. *History of Wichita District, Association of Colored Women, 1923–1941*. Wichita, Kan.: Association of Colored Women, Wichita District, 1941.

Bakken, Gordon Morris, and Brenda Farrington, eds. *The Gendered West*. New York: Garland, 2001.

Barr, Alwyn. *Black Texans: A History of African Americans in Texas, 1528–1995*. Austin: Jenkins Publishing Co., 1973; reprint Norman: University of Oklahoma Press, 1996.

Beasley, Delilah L. *The Negro Trailblazers of California*. Los Angeles, 1919; reprint New York: G. K. Hall, 1998.

Bibbs, Susheel. *Heritage of Power*. San Francisco: MEP Enterprises/Productions, 1998.

———. *Mary Ellen Pleasant, 1817 to 1904: Mother of Human Rights in California*. San Francisco: MEP Enterprises/Productions, 1996.

Billington, Monroe Lee, and Roger D. Hardaway, eds. *African Americans on the Western Frontier*. Niwot: University Press of Colorado, 1998.

"Black Women in Colorado: Two Early Portraits." *Frontiers* 7 (1984): 21.

Blackwelder, Julia Kirk. *Women of the Depression: Caste and Culture in San Antonio, 1929–1939.* College Station: Texas A&M University Press, 1984.

Bogle, Donald. *Dorothy Dandridge: A Biography.* New York: Boulevard Books, 1997.

Bogle, Kathryn Hall. "Document: Kathryn Hall Bogle's 'An American Negro Speaks of Color.'" *Oregon Historical Quarterly* 89 (1988–89): 70-81.

Bogle, Kathryn Hall, and Rick Harmon, interviewer. "Interview: Kathryn Hall Bogle on the Writing of 'An American Negro Speaks of Color.'" *Oregon Historical Quarterly* 89 (1988–89): 82–91.

———. "Oral History Interview: Kathryn Hall Bogle on the African-American Experience in Wartime Portland." *Oregon Historical Quarterly* 93 (1992–93): 394–405.

Brady, Marilyn Dell. "Kansas Federation of Colored Women's Clubs, 1900–1930." *Kansas History* 9 (1986): 19–30.

———. "Organizing Afro-American Girls' Clubs in Kansas in the 1920's." *Frontiers* 9 (1987): 69–73.

Bramlett, Sharon. *Profile and Status of African American Women in Arizona: A Background Report to the 1994 Arizona Black Town Hall.* Tempe: College of Public Programs, Arizona State University, 1994.

Brandenstein, Sherilyn Ruth. "*Sepia Record* as a Forum for Negotiating Women's Roles." In *Women and Texas History: Selected Essays,* ed. Fane Downs and Nancy Baker Jones Austin: Texas State Historical Association, 1993.

Bringhurst, Newell G. *Saints, Slaves, and Blacks: The Changing Place of Black People within Mormonism.* Westport, Conn.: Greenwood Press, 1981.

Brown, Elaine. *A Taste of Power: A Black Woman's Story.* New York: Pantheon Press, 1992.

Broussard, Albert S. *African American Odyssey: The Stewarts, 1853–1963.* Lawrence: University of Kansas Press, 1998.

———. *Black San Francisco: The Struggle for Racial Equality in the West, 1900–1954.* Lawrence: University of Kansas Press, 1993.

———. "Carlotta Stewart Lai, a Black Teacher in the Territory of Hawaii." *Hawaiian Journal of History* 24 (1990): 129–54.

Bruyn, Kathleen. *"Aunt" Clara Brown: Story of a Black Pioneer.* Boulder, Colo.: Pruett, 1970.

Bryant, Ira B. *Barbara Charline Jordan: From the Ghetto to the Capitol.* Houston: D. Armstrong, 1977.

Bunch, Lonnie, III. *Black Angelenos: The Afro-American in Los Angeles, 1850–1950.* Los Angeles: California Afro-American Museum, 1988.

Butler, Ann M. *Gendered Justice in the American West: Women Prisoners in Men's Penitentiaries.* Urbana: University of Illinois Press, 1997.

———. "'Still in Chains': Black Women in Western Prisons, 1865–1910." *Western Historical Quarterly* 20 (February 1989): 19–36.

Campbell, Randolph B. *An Empire for Slavery: The Peculiar Institution in Texas, 1821–1836.* Baton Rouge: Louisiana State University Press, 1989.

Carter, Kate. *The Story of the Negro Pioneer.* Salt Lake City: Daughters of the Utah Pioneers, 1965.

Castaneda, Antonia I. "Women of Color and the Rewriting of Western History: The Discourse, Politics, and Decolonization of History." *Pacific Historical Review* 61 (1992): 501–33.

Chaudhuri, Nupur. "'We All Seemed Like Brothers and Sisters': The African-American Community in Manhattan, Kansas, 1865–1940." *Kansas History* 14 (1991–92): 270–88.

Clayton, Sheryl H. *Black Women Role Models of Waco and Hillsboro, Texas.* East St. Louis, Ill.: Essai Seay Publications, 1986.

Coleman, Willi. "African American Women and Community Development in California, 1848–1900." In *Seeking El Dorado: African Americans in California*, ed. Lawrence B. De Graaf, Kevin Mulroy, and Quintard Taylor. Seattle: University of Washington Press, 2001.

Coray, Michael S. "Blacks in the Pacific West, 1850–1860: A View from the Census." *Nevada Historical Society Quarterly* 28 (1985): 90–121.

———. "Influences on Black Family Household Organization in the West, 1850–1860." *Nevada Historical Society Quarterly* 31 (1988): 1–31.

Cripps, Thomas. *Making Movies Black: The Hollywood Message Movie from World War II to the Civil Rights Era.* New York: Oxford University Press, 1993.

Crouch, Barry. "'The Chords of Love': Legalizing Black Marriage and Family Rights in Postwar Texas." *Journal of Negro History* (Fall 1994): 334–51.

Crouchett, Lawrence, Lonnie Bunche, and Martha Winnacker. *Visions toward Tomorrow: The History of the East Bay Afro-American Community, 1852–1977.* Oakland: Northern California Center for Afro-American History and Life, 1989.

Crouchett, Lorraine J. *Delilah Leontium Beasley: Oakland's Crusading Journalist.* El Cerrito, Calif.: Downey Place Publishing House, 1990.

Dailey, Maceo Crenshaw, Jr., and Kristine Navarro, eds. *Wheresoever My People Chance to Dwell: Oral Interviews with African American Women of El Paso.* Baltimore: Imprint Edition, 2000.

Dandridge, Dorothy, and Earl Conrad. *Everything and Nothing: The Dorothy Dandridge Tragedy.* New York: Abelard, 1970.

Daniels, Douglas Henry. *Pioneer Urbanites: A Social and Cultural History of Black San Francisco.* Berkeley: University of California Press, 1990.

Davis, Angela Yvonne. *Angela Davis: An Autobiography.* New York: Random House, 1974.

Davis, Lenwood G., comp. *Blacks in the American West: A Working Bibliography.* Monticello, Ill.: Council of Planning Librarians, 1976.

Davis, Lenwood G., and Mary Vance, comps. *Blacks in the State of Oregon, 1788-1974: A Bibliography of Published Works and of Unpublished Source Materials on the Life and Achievements of Black people in the Beaver State.* Monticello, Ill.: Council of Planning Librarians, 1974.

———. *Blacks in the Pacific Northwest, 1788–1974: A Bibliography of Published Works and of Unpublished Source Materials on the Life and Contributions of Black People in the Pacific Northwest.* Monticello, Ill.: Council of Planning Librarians, 1975.

———. *Blacks in the State of Utah: A Working Bibliography.* Monticello, Ill.: Council of Planning Librarians, 1974.

De Graaf, Lawrence B. "Race, Sex and Region: Black Women in the American West, 1850–1920." *Pacific Historical Review* 49 (May 1980): 285–313.

———. "Recognition, Racism, and Reflections on the Writing of Western Black History." *Pacific Historical Review* 44 (1975): 22–51.

Delta Sigma Theta Sorority. *A Pictorial History of Austin, Travis County, Texas' Black Community, 1839–1920: The Black Heritage Exhibit.* Austin: Delta Sigma Theta Sorority, 1970.

Dickson, Lynda Fae. "The Early Club Movement among Black Women in Denver, 1890–1925." Ph.D. dissertation, University of Colorado, 1982.

———. "The Third Shift: Black Women's Club Activities in Denver, 1900–1925." In *Women and Work: Exploring Race, Ethnicity, and Class,* ed. Elizabeth Higginbotham and Mary Romero. Thousand Oaks, Calif.: Sage, 1997.

———. "Toward a Broader Angle of Vision in Uncovering Women's History: Black Women's Clubs Revisited." *Frontiers* 9 (1987): 62–68.

Downs, Fane. "'Travels and Trubbles': Women in Early Nineteenth Century Texas." *Southwestern Historical Quarterly* 90 (1986): 35–56.

Dulaney, Marvin. *Black Presence in Dallas: A History of Black Political Activism in Dallas from 1936–1986.* Dallas: Museum of African-American Life and Culture, 1987.

Duren, Almetris Marsh, and Louise Iscoe. *Overcoming: A History of Black Integration at the University of Texas at Austin.* Austin: University of Texas Press, 1979.

Edmonds, Ruth Hill. *The Black Women Oral History Project: A Guide to the Transcripts.* Cambridge, Mass.: Radcliffe College, 1991.

Fisher, Ada Lois Sipuel. *A Matter of Black and White: The Autobiography of Ada Lois Sipuel Fisher.* Norman: University of Oklahoma Press, 1996.

Fisher, James A. "A History of the Political and Social Development of the Black Community in California, 1850-1950." Ph.D. dissertation, State University of New York at Stony Brook, 1972.

Forbes, Jack D. *Black Africans and Native Americans: Color, Race, and Caste in the Evolution of Red-Black Peoples.* New York: Basil Blackwell, 1988.

Franklin, Jimmie Lewis. *Journey toward Hope: A History of Blacks in Oklahoma.* Norman: University of Oklahoma Press, 1982.

Gatewood, Willard B., Jr. "Kate D. Chapman Reports on 'The Yankton Colored People,' 1889." *South Dakota History* 7 (1976): 28–35.

Giddings, Paula. *When and Where I Enter: The Impact of Black Women on Race and Sex in America.* New York: William Morrow, 1984.

Gill, Gerald R. "From Progressive Republican to Independent Progressive: The Political Career of Charlotta A. Bass." In *African American Women and the Vote, 1837–1965,* ed. Ann D. Gordon, Bettye Collier, John H. Bracey, Arlene Voski Avakian, and Joyce Avrech Berkman. Amherst: University of Massachusetts Press, 1997.

Govenar, Alan B. *The Life and Poems of Osceola Mays.* Racine, Wis.: Arcadian Press, 1989.

Grant, Billie Arlene. *African American Woman of the West: A Special Teacher/Special Mission. The Life Story of Carneice Brown-White.* Denver: B. A. Grant, 1991.

Haggerson, Nelson L. *Oh Yes I Can! A Biography of Arlena E. Seneca.* Tempe, Ariz.: Nornel Associates, 1994.

Hallman, Patsy Spurrier. *A Psalm of Life: The Story of a Woman Whose Life Made a Difference, Willie Lee Campbell*. Austin: Eakin Press, 1998.

Hamilton, Kenneth Marvin. *Black Towns and Profit: Promotion and Development in the Trans-Appalachian West, 1877–1915*. Urbana: University of Illinois Press, 1991.

Hardaway, Roger D. "African-American Women on the Western Frontier." *Negro History Bulletin* 60 (January–March 1997): 8–14.

———. *A Narrative Bibliography of the African-American Frontier: Blacks in the Rocky Mountain West, 1535–1912*. Lewiston, N.Y.: Mellen, 1995.

Hayden, Dolores. "Biddy Mason's Los Angeles, 1856–1891." *California History* 68 (Fall 1989): 86–99.

———. *Biddy Mason's Place: A Midwife's Homestead*. Los Angeles: Power of Place, 1988.

Hield, Melissa. "'Union-Minded': Women in the Texas ILGWU, 1933–1950." *Frontiers* 4 (1979): 59–70.

Hill, Ruth Edmonds, and Patricia Miller King, eds. *The Black Women's Oral History Project: A Guide to the Transcripts*. Cambridge, Mass.: Radcliffe College, 1989.

Hine, Darlene Clark. "Rape and the Inner Lives of Black Women in the Middle West: Preliminary Thoughts on the Culture of Dissemblance." *Signs* 14 (1989): 912–20.

Howard, Vicki. "The Courtship Letters of an African American Couple: Race, Gender, Class, and the Cult of True Womanhood." *Southwestern Historical Quarterly* 100 (1996): 64–80.

Hudson, Lynn M. "A New Look, or 'I'm Not Mammy to Everybody in California': Mary Ellen Pleasant, a Black Entrepreneur." *Journal of the West* 32 (July 1993): 35–40.

———. "'Strong Animal Passions' in the Gilded Age: Race, Sex, and a Senator on Trial." *Journal of the History of Sexuality* 9 (1999): 62–84.

Hull, Gloria T., Patricia Bell Scott, and Barbara Smith, eds. *All of the Women Are White, All the Blacks Are Men, but Some of Us Are Brave: Black Women's Studies*. Old Westbury, N.Y.: Feminist Press, 1982.

Hunt, Annie Mae, with Ruthe Winegarten. *I am Annie Mae: An Extraordinary Black Texas Woman in Her Own Words*. Austin: Rosegarden Press, 1993; reprint Austin: University of Texas Press, 1996.

Irvin, Dona L. *The Unsung Heart of Black America: A Middle-Class Church at Midcentury*. Columbia: University of Missouri Press, 1992.

Jackson, LaVonne Roberts. "'Freedom and Family': The Freedmen's Bureau and African-American Women in Texas in the Reconstruction Era, 1865–1872." Ph.D. dissertation, Howard University, 1996.

Jordan, Barbara. *Barbara C. Jordan: Selected Speeches*. Ed. Sandra Parham. Washington, D.C.: Howard University Press, 1999.

Jordan, Barbara, with Shelby Hearon. *Barbara Jordan: A Self-Portrait*. Garden City, N.Y.: Doubleday, 1979.

Jordan, Julia K. Gibson, and Charlie Mae Brown. *Beauty and the Best: Frederica Chase Dodd, the Story of a Life of Love and Dedication*. Dallas: Distributed by Dallas Alumnae Chapter of Delta Sigma Theta Sorority, 1985.

Katz, William Loren. *The Black West*. Seattle: Open Hand Publications, 1987.

Kesselman, Amy. *Fleeting Opportunities: Women Shipyard Workers in Portland and Vancouver During World War II and Reconversion*. Albany: State University of New York Press, 1990.

Klein, Ronald P. "Equal Rights Statutes." *Stanford Law Review* 10 (March 1958): 253–73.

Lapp, Rudolph M. *Blacks in Gold Rush California*. New Haven: Yale University Press, 1977.

Lark, Thomas. *History of Hope: The African American Experience in New Mexico*. Albuquerque, New Mex.: Albuquerque Museum, 1996.

LeBlanc-Ernest, Angela D. "'The Most Qualified Person to Handle the Job': Black Panther Party Women, 1966–1982." In *The Black Panther Party (Reconsidered)*, ed. Charles E. Jones. Baltimore: Black Classic Press, 1998.

Lede, Naomi W. *Precious Memories of a Black Socialite: A Narrative of the Life and Times of Constance Houston Thompson*. Houston: D. Armstrong, 1991.

Lemke-Santangelo, Gretchen. *Abiding Courage: African American Migrant Women and the East Bay Community*. Chapel Hill: University of North Carolina Press, 1996.

Leonard, Jonathan S. "The Effect of Unions on the Employment of Blacks, Hispanics, and Women." *Industrial and Labor Relations Review* 39 (1985): 115–32.

Littlefield, Daniel F. *Africans and Creeks: From the Colonial Period to the Civil War*. Westport, Conn.: Greenwood Press, 1979.

———. *Africans and Seminoles: From Removal to Emancipation*. Westport, Conn.: Greenwood Press, 1977.

———. *The Cherokee Freedmen: From Emancipation to American Citizenship*. Westport, Conn.: Greenwood Press, 1978.

———. *The Chickasaw Freedmen: A People without a Country*. Westport, Conn.: Greenwood Press, 1980.

Littlefield, Mary Ann, and Daniel F. Littlefield. "The Beams Family: Free Blacks in Indian Territory." *Journal of Negro History* 6 (1976): 16–35.

Luckingham, Bradford. *Minorities in Phoenix: A Profile of Mexican American, Chinese American, and African American Communities, 1860–1992*. Tucson: University of Arizona Press, 1994.

Luper, Clara. *Behold the Walls*. Oklahoma City: Jim Wire, 1979.

Madyun, Gail. "'In the Midst of Things': Rebecca Craft and the Women's Civic League." *Journal of San Diego History* 34 (1988): 29–37.

Malone, Ann Patton. *Women on the Texas Frontier: A CrossCultural Perspective*. El Paso: Texas Western Press, University of Texas at El Paso, 1983.

Matthews, Tracye. "'No One Ever Asks What a Man's Place in the Revolution Is': Gender and the Politics of the Black Panther Party, 1966–1971." In *The Black Panther Party (Reconsidered)*, ed. Charles E. Jones. Baltimore: Black Classic Press, 1998.

Mays, Iantha Villa. *History: California Association of Colored Women's Clubs, Inc., 1906–1955*. Oakland: The Association, 1955.

McDonald, Katrina Bell. "Black Activist Mothering: A Historical Intersection of Race, Gender, and Class." *Gender & Society* 11 (1997): 773–95.

McKnight, Mamie Lee. *African American Families and Settlements of Dallas. On the Inside Looking Out: Exhibition, Family Memoirs, Personality Profiles and Community Essays*. Dallas: Black Dallas Remembered, 1990.

————. *First African American Families of Dallas: Creative Survival.* Dallas: Black Dallas Remembered Steering Committee, 1987.

McLagan, Elizabeth. *A Peculiar Paradise: A History of Blacks in Oregon, 1788–1940.* Portland: Georgian Press, 1980.

Melcher, Mary S. "Tending Children, Chickens, and Cattle: Southern Arizona Ranch and Farm Women, 1910–1940." Ph.D. dissertation, University of Arizona, 1994.

Miles, Merle Yvonne. "Born and Bred in Texas: Three Generations of Black Females: A Critique of Social Science Perceptions of the Black Female." Ph.D. dissertation, University of Texas at Austin, 1986.

Mills, Hazel E., and Nancy Pryor, comps. *The Negro in the State of Washington, 1788–1969: A Bibliography of Published Works and of Unpublished Source Materials on the Life and Achievements of the Negro in the Evergreen State.* Olympia: Washington State Library, 1970.

Mock, Charlotte. *Bridges: New Mexican Black Women, 1900–1950.* Albuquerque: New Mexico Commission on the Study of Women, 1985.

Moore, Shirley Ann Wilson. "'Not in Somebody's Kitchen': African American Women Workers in Richmond, California and the Impact of World War II." In *Writing the Range: Race, Class, and Culture in the Women's West,* ed. Elizabeth Jameson and Susan Armitage. Norman: University of Oklahoma Press, 1997.

————. *To Place Our Deeds: The African American Community in Richmond, California, 1910–1963.* Berkeley: University of California Press, 2000.

Mumford, Esther Hall. *Calabash: A Guide to the History, Culture, and Art of African Americans in Seattle and King County, Washington.* Seattle: Ananse Press, 1993.

————. *Seattle's Black Victorians, 1852–1901.* Seattle: Ananse Press, 1980.

————, ed. *Seven Stars and Orion: Reflections of the Past.* Seattle: Ananse Press, 1986.

Nash, Sunny. *Bigmama Didn't Shop at Woolworth's.* College Station: Texas A&M University Press, 1996.

Northwood, Lawrence K. *Urban Desegregation: Negro Pioneers and Their White Neighbors.* Seattle: University of Washington Press, 1965.

Oliver, Mamie O. *Idaho Ebony: The Afro-American Presence in Idaho State History.* Boise: Idaho State Historical Society, 1990.

Painter, Nell Irvin. *Exodusters: Black Migration to Kansas after Reconstruction.* New York: Alfred A. Knopf, 1977.

Ravage, John W. *Black Pioneers: Images of the Black Experience on the North American Frontier.* Salt Lake City: University of Utah Press, 1997.

Ray, Emma. *Twice Sold, Twice Ransomed: Autobiography of Mr. and Mrs. L. O. Ray.* Chicago: N.p., 1926.

Reese, Linda Williams. *Women of Oklahoma, 1890–1920.* Norman: University of Oklahoma Press, 1997.

Rich, Doris L. *Queen Bess: Daredevil Aviator.* Washington, D.C.: Smithsonian Institution Press, 1993.

Richardson, Barbara J., comp. *Black Directory of New Mexico: Black Pioneers of New Mexico, a Documentary and Pictorial History.* Rio Rancho, New Mex.: Panorama Press, 1976.

Richardson, Barbara J., and Euola Cox. *Noteworthy Black Women of New Mexico, Past and Present*. Albuquerque: Privately published, 1977.

Riley, Carroll L. "Blacks in the Early Southwest." *Ethnohistory* 19 (1972): 247–60.

Riley, Glenda. "American Daughters: Black Women in the West." *Montana: The Magazine of Western History* 38 (Spring 1988): 14–27.

Rusco, Elmer R. *"Good Time Coming?" Black Nevadans in the Nineteenth Century*. Westport, Conn.: Greenwood Press, 1975.

Sance, Melvin M. *The Afro-American Texans*. San Antonio: University of Texas Institute of Texan Cultures at San Antonio, 1987.

Schaffer, Ruth C. "The Health and Social Functions of Black Midwives on the Texas Brazos Bottom, 1920–1985." *Rural Sociology* 56 (Spring 1991): 89–105.

Schwartz, Henry. "The Mary Walker Incident: Black Prejudice in San Diego, 1866." *Journal of San Diego History* 19 (1973): 14–20.

Shover, Michele. *Blacks in Chico, 1860–1935: Climbing the Slippery Slope*. Chico, Calif.: Association for Northern California Records and Research, 1991.

Smallwood, James M. "Black Freedwomen after Emancipation: The Texas Experience." *Prologue* 27 (1995): 302–17.

———. "Emancipation and the Black Family: A Case Study in Texas." *Social Science Quarterly* 57 (1977): 849–57.

Spickard, Paul R. "Work and Hope: African American Women in Southern California during World War II." *Journal of the West* 32 (1993): 70–79.

Spurlin, Virginia Lee. "The Connors of Waco: Black Professionals in Twentieth Century Texas." Ph.D. dissertation, Texas Tech University, 1991.

Tanner, Jo A. *Dusky Maidens: The Odyssey of the Early Black Dramatic Actress*. Westport, Conn.: Greenwood Press, 1992.

Taylor, Quintard. *The Forging of a Black Community: Seattle's Central District from 1870 through the Civil Rights Era*. Seattle: University of Washington Press, 1994.

———. "Mary Ellen Pleasant." In *By Grit and Grace: Women Who Shaped the Pioneer West*, ed. Glenda Riley and Richard Etulain. Golden, Colo.: Fulcrum, 1997.

———. *In Search of the Racial Frontier: African-Americans in the American West*. New York: W. W. Norton, 1998.

Teall, Kaye M. *Black History in Oklahoma: A Resource Book*. Oklahoma City: Oklahoma City Public Schools, 1971.

Thompson, Era Bell. *American Daughter*. Chicago: University of Chicago Press, 1946; reprint St. Paul: Minnesota Historical Society Press, 1986.

Thurman, Sue Bailey. *Pioneers of Negro Origin in California*. San Francisco: Acme, 1949; reprint San Francisco: R & E Associates, 1971.

Tolbert, Emory J. *The UNIA and Black Los Angeles*. Berkeley: University of California Press, 1980.

Toll, William. "Black Families and Migration to a Multiracial Society: Portland, Oregon, 1900–1924." *Journal of American Ethnic History* 17 (1998): 38–70.

Turner, Patricia A. *Ceramic Uncles & Celluloid Mammies: Black Images and Their Influence on Culture*. New York: Anchor Books, 1994.

Vaughn-Roberson, Courtney Ann. "Sometimes Independent but Never Equal—Women Teachers, 1900–1950: The Oklahoma Example." *Pacific Historical Review* 53 (1984): 39–58.

Whitaker, Matthew C. "In Search of Black Phoenicians: African American Culture and Community in Phoenix, Arizona, 1868–1940." Ph.D. dissertation, Arizona State University, 1997.

Winegarten, Debra L., and Ruthe Winegarten. *Strong Family Ties: The Tiny Hawkins Story.* Austin: SocialSights Press, 1998.

Winegarten, Ruthe. *Black Texas Women: 150 Years of Trial and Triumph.* Austin: University of Texas Press, 1995.

———. *Texas Women: A Pictorial History From Indians to Astronauts.* Austin: Eakin Press, 1986.

Wolfinger, Henry J. "A Test of Faith: Jane Elizabeth James and the Origins of the Utah Black Community." In *Social Accommodation in Utah,* ed. Clark Knowlton. Salt Lake City: American West Center, University of Utah, 1975.

Woll, Allen. *Black Musical Theater: From Coontown to Dreamgirls.* Baton Rouge: Louisiana State University Press, 1989.

List of Contributors

SUSAN ARMITAGE is Edward R. Meyer Distinguished Professor of History at Washington State University. An authority on women in the U.S. West, she is also the editor of *Frontiers: A Journal of Women's Studies*. Dr. Ruth Flowers was the subject of the first article she published on western women, in (fittingly) *Frontiers* in 1977.

SUSAN BRAGG is a Ph.D. candidate in the Department of History at the University of Washington. Her research interests include gender, race, and civil rights activism. She has also been published in *California History*.

RONALD G. COLEMAN is Associate Professor of History and Ethnic Studies at the University of Utah. His teaching and research areas include African American history, race and ethnic relations in the United States, and the Civil War and Reconstruction era. He has been published in the *Utah Historical Quarterly* and the *Encyclopedia of African-American Culture and History*. These publications include "The Buffalo Soldiers: Guardians of the Uninah Frontier," "Blacks in Pioneer Utah," and "Utah Slavery." He was the recipient of the Utah Governor's Award for Contributions to the Humanities in 2000.

MOYA B. HANSEN is Curator of the Decorative and Fine Arts Department of the Colorado Historical Society. Her role as curator and staff liaison with the museum's African American Advisory Council led her to research Denver's black community for an ongoing series of museum exhibits, including "It's Jazz: Black Musicians in Colorado, 1890–1950." She has published articles in the University of Colorado's *Historical Studies Journal* and the Historical Society's scholarly journal, *Colorado History*.

CHERYL BROWN HENDERSON is founder and President of the Brown Foundation for Educational Equity, Excellence and Research. Her father, the late Reverend Oliver L. Brown, is the namesake of *Brown v. Board of Education*. She has published articles in *CRM: Cultural Resource Magazine*, *Preserving Our Recent Past*, and *Land and People Magazine*. She has also produced an educational video and teachers' guide entitled *Brown v. Board of Education: In Pursuit of Freedom and Equality*. Henderson worked with Congress to pass the *Brown v. Board of Education* National Historic Site Act of 1992, which established a historic site dedicated to this history.

LYNN M. HUDSON is Assistant Professor in the Department of History at California Polytechnic State University, San Luis Obispo, where she teaches African American history, women's history, and women's studies. Her most recent publication is "'Strong Animal Passions': Race, Sex, and a Senator on Trial," published in the *Journal of the History of Sexuality*. She is writing a biography of Mary Ellen Pleasant.

GRETCHEN LEMKE-SANTANGELO is Associate Professor of History at Saint Mary's College in Moraga, California. Her book, *Abiding Courage: African American Migrant Women in the East Bay Community*, won the American Historical Association's Wesley Logan Prize in African diaspora studies. She has also contributed articles to journals and anthologies on urban poverty, black migration, and World War II era radicalism. Her current research focuses on women of the 1960s counterculture.

DEDRA S. McDONALD completed her Ph.D. degree in history at the University of New Mexico in May 2000. Her dissertation concerns domestic servants and gender in the Spanish and Mexican borderlands. She has published articles in the *American Indian Quarterly* and the *Colonial Latin American Historical Review* and compiled a guide to the Spanish and Mexican manuscripts at the Catholic Archives of Texas. She is an adjunct professor of history at Hillsdale College.

SHIRLEY ANN WILSON MOORE is Professor of History at California State University, Sacramento. Her first book, *To Place Our Deeds: The African American Community in Richmond, California, 1910–1963*, was published in 2000. Her essays and articles have appeared in a number of publications, including the *Western Historical Quarterly*, the *Encyclopedia of Social History*, and *California History Quarterly*.

MERLINE PITRE is Professor of History and Interim Dean of the College of Arts and Sciences at Texas Southern University in Houston, Texas. She is the author of *Through Many Dangers, Toils and Snares: The Black Leadership of Texas, 1868–1900*, and *In Struggle against Jim Crow: Lula White and the NAACP, 1900–1957*. Currently, she is coediting a book on black women in Texas and serves on the advisory committee of the *Magazine of History*, a publication of the Organization of American Historians.

LINDA WILLIAMS REESE is Assistant Professor of History at East Central University in Ada, Oklahoma. Her teaching and research interests focus on the intersections of race, gender, and culture in the American West. She has published an article on women in nineteenth-century all-black communities in *Kansas Quarterly*, and the University of Oklahoma Press published her book, *Women of Oklahoma, 1890-1920*, in 1997. She is currently at work on a study of freedwomen of the Five Civilized Tribes in Indian Territory after the Civil War.

JANE RHODES is Associate Professor of Ethnic Studies and Affiliated Associate Professor of Communication at the University of California, San Diego. Rhodes's research focuses on the historical relationship among race, media, and social movements. She is the author of *Mary Ann Shadd Cary: The Black Press and Protest in the Nineteenth Century* (Indiana University Press, 1998). Her book on the media and the Black Panther Party is forthcoming from New Press.

GLENDA RILEY is Alexander M. Bracken Professor of History at Ball State University. Her books include *Frontierswomen: The Iowa Experience, Women and Indians on the Frontier, The Female Frontier, A Place to Grow: Women in the American West, The Life and Legacy of Annie Oakley, Building and Breaking Families in the American West*, and *Women and Nature: Saving the "Wild" West*. Currently Riley is writing a comparative history of women settlers on the Kenya frontier and in the American West. Riley has won many awards, including a Distinguished Fulbright and membership in the Iowa Women's Hall of Fame. Recently she served as president of the Western History Association.

PEGGY RILEY teaches English and history at Las Positas College in Livermore, California. Her teaching and research interests include the literature and history of the American West. She has published a sentence-style workbook and several articles for the *Bay Area Writing Project Newsletter* and the *Center* *for the Study of Writing Quarterly*. She is currently at work on a book based on poetry written by her great-grandfather, a coal miner in Montana.

ALICIA I. RODRÍQUEZ-ESTRADA is a history instructor at Los Angeles Trade-Technical College and is also currently completing her dissertation, "Playing the Part: Gender, Race and Representation in U.S. Cinema, 1925–1965," at the Claremont Graduate University. In addition to her article in this volume, she has published in the anthology, *Writing the Range: Race, Class, and Culture in the Women's West* (1997) and contributed to the *Encyclopedia of the American West* (1996).

QUINTARD TAYLOR, Scott and Dorothy Bullitt Professor of American History at the University of Washington, is the author of *In Search of the Racial Frontier: African Americans in the American West, 1528–1990* (1998), and *The Forging of a Black Community: A History of Seattle's Central District from 1870 through the Civil Rights Era* (1994). Taylor is also the author of more than forty articles on African American western history.

BARBARA Y. WELKE is Assistant Professor of History at the University of Minnesota. Her teaching and research areas include U.S. legal and constitutional history and twentieth-century U.S. history. Welke's articles have appeared in the *University of Utah Law Review*, *Law & History Review*, and *Law & Social Inquiry*. She is also the author of *Recasting American Liberty: Gender, Race, Law, and the Railroad Revolution, 1865–1920* (Cambridge University Press, 2001). Her work has been awarded prizes in women's and legal history.

CLAYTEE D. WHITE received her master's degree in women's history at the University of Nevada at Las Vegas and is currently completing her Ph.D. at the College of William and Mary in the field of African American history. Her dissertation will focus on the black experience in Las Vegas. She is the author of "African American Women Migrants: A Las Vegas Odyssey," which appeared in the *Publication of the Nevada Women's History Project*.

Index